SBA LOANS
A Step-by-Step Guide

Second Edition

Patrick D. O'Hara, Ph.D.

John Wiley & Sons, Inc.

New York ● Chichester ● Brisbane ● Toronto ● Singapore

Library of Congress Cataloging in Publication Data:

O'Hara, Patrick D.
    SBA loans : a step-by-step guide / Patrick D. O'Hara. — 2nd ed.
        p.   cm.
    Includes bibliographic references.
    ISBN 0-471-30332-1 (alk. paper; includes disk). — ISBN 0-471-30331-3
(alk. paper : pbk.)
    1. Small business—United States—Finance. 2. Loans—United
States—Goverment policy. I. Title.
HG4027.7.O43   1994
658.15′224—dc20   93-25925

Printed in the United States of America

10 9 8 7 6 5 4 3 2

Acknowledgments

I wish to thank the San Francisco and Washington, D.C., offices of the Small Business Administration and the San Francisco SBA loan offices of the Bank of America through whose courtesies many of the forms and much of the processing information was obtained.

Also I wish to thank Mr. Mike Hamilton and Elena Paperny of John Wiley & Sons, Inc., for encouraging me to update this second edition. Their help, faith, and patience was and is greatly appreciated. And, of course, I thank the many people who gave their honest opinion regarding their experiences with the personnel of the SBA and SBA-participating institutions.

Preface

In 1981, the Small Business Administration (SBA) made 26,045 loans totaling $3 billion.

During 1985, the agency loans numbered 16,864 and amounted to $2.4 billion. In 1986, 16,767 loans were made totaling $2.5 billion; in 1987, 17,110 loans were made totaling $3 billion. Most of these loans were made by banks with Small Business Administration guarantees against default.

During 1993, the loan amount will probably exceed $6 billion.

This lending record is proof that the SBA is still very active in lending to benefit small businesses both in indirect bank participation loan guarantees and in direct lending. However, direct loans from the SBA represent a very small portion of SBA's lending activity.

Despite the fact that most people think the SBA's sole function is providing loans, it does much more. The SBA provides technical and management assistance, procurement assistance, business classes, publications, and other services to small businesses.

Besides its general lending activity, the SBA is active in promoting specific business ventures. Among these is the Pollution Control Financing Guarantee program.

If you already own or intend to start a small business, how can the SBA help you? This book was written to give you an accurate answer to that very important question. Some of the material presented may appear to reflect negatively on the SBA. That is not the intent. The intent is to give an honest view of the SBA to prepare the potential applicant to deal with the bureaucratic process.

It is my firm belief that all small business owners can benefit from the SBA program on their very own initiative even if they do not have financial or legal backgrounds. Therefore, most of the book is directed at showing you, in easy step-by-step fashion, how to prepare an SBA loan request for your new or established business.

By demonstrating clearly how to fill in all necessary forms and explaining each section in simple terms, it shows you how to prepare a write-up. It tells you exactly what information the SBA and the banks need from you as a small business owner. Numerous, easy-to-follow sample forms and examples have been included to help you understand the SBA loan process.

The purpose of this book is to provide you with sufficient know-how and insight to prepare your own SBA loan application package and obtain additional services free of charge from the SBA—an agency mandated by Congress to provide loans and assistance to encourage the establishment, growth, and success of small businesses all over the nation.

Patrick D. O'Hara

Contents

Introduction

THE SBA—WHAT'S IT ALL ABOUT?

The SBA defines small businesses as companies whose net worth is $6 million or less and whose average net (after-tax) income for the preceding two years does not exceed $2 million. Small businesses are the backbone of the U.S. economy. They create two of every three new jobs, produce 39 percent of the gross national product, and invent more than half the nation's technological innovations. Our 20 million small companies provide dynamic opportunities for all Americans.

The importance of this business sector has not been lost on the federal government. If a company is independently owned and operated, not dominant within its field, and falls within a certain size limit, the Small Business Administration (SBA) is there to help it.

Through financing guarantees, direct loans, workshops, individual counseling, publications, and videotapes, the SBA helps small business owners understand and meet the challenges of successfully operating their firms. The SBA has business development specialists stationed in more than 100 field offices nationwide. Technical assistance, training, and counseling are also offered by three partner organizations:

- More than 13,000 volunteers in the Service Corps of Retired Executives (SCORE) provide training and one-on-one counseling at no charge.
- Small business development centers (SBDCs) provide training, counseling, research, and other specialized assistance at more than 600 locations nationwide.
- Small business institutes at more than 500 universities provide free management studies, performed by advanced business students under faculty direction.

The SBA opens the doors of opportunity for small businesses by helping them secure capital; it backs eligible firms that are having trouble securing conventional financing by offering loan guarantees or loans made by private lenders. Among its many financial assistance programs are the following:

- International Trade Loan Guarantees—to finance U.S.-based facilities or equipment for producing goods or services for export.
- Export Revolving Line of Credit Guarantees—to help firms penetrate foreign markets.
- Small Loan Guarantees—to help businesses needing $50,000 or less.
- Seasonal Line of Credit Guarantees—for firms facing seasonal business increases.
- Energy Loan Guarantees—for firms that make, install, sell, or service energy equipment and technology.
- Handicapped Assistance Loans—for businesses owned by physically handicapped persons and private nonprofit organizations that employ handicapped persons and operate in their interest.
- Pollution Control Loan Guarantees—for firms involved in pollution control and reduction.
- Loans for disabled and Vietnam-era veterans—to start, operate, or expand a small business.

In addition, the Small Business Administration provides small businesses with long-term loans and venture capital by licensing, regulating, and investing in privately owned and managed small business investment companies across the country. It offers Development Company Loans, geared to create and retain jobs, and also expands access to surety bonds through guarantees on bonding for small and emerging contractors, including minority members, who otherwise could not secure bid, payment, or performance bonds.

This book has been written to assist people in the process of using SBA resources to finance and manage new businesses as well as established businesses in need of ongoing support. But before you run out and attempt to start your own business with or without the help of the SBA, you must realize there are certain basic steps to follow. Some of these are required by the SBA before they will get seriously involved in the business, and others are simply safeguards to get greater ensurance of the business's long-term success.

PERSONAL QUALIFICATIONS

Certain traits and talents are essential to the success of anyone wishing to own and operate a small business. A prospective business owner should be:

1. Experienced in the type of business being started—preferably with some management or supervisory background.
2. Farsighted—having the ability to set goals and plan ahead.
3. An organizer who can develop and establish routines and procedures for the efficient execution of plans.
4. A natural leader who can direct the activities of others and accept responsibility for the results.
5. An effective decision maker.

6. Self-disciplined—able to get things done on time.
7. Willing to work long hours.
8. A self-starter.
9. Healthy, with the stamina and energy to do everything that the business requires.
10. Able to work with customers, employees, and suppliers.
11. Willing to learn new techniques and procedures and able to adapt to change.

Once you've decided that you and/or your business team have most of the qualifications noted here, you must take the following steps to ensure your business success: deciding the type of business, selecting the type of organization, formulating a business plan, keeping accurate records, and being aware of government resources and requirements. The following paragraphs provide questions to shed more light on each of these subjects.

STEPS TO TAKE IN FORMING A BUSINESS

I. **Decide on the type of business.**
   A. What experience in this type of business do you have? Were you an employee? Manager? Owner? Apprentice?
   B. Do you understand ALL phases of the business's operation?
   C. What technical knowledge relating to the business do you possess?
   D. Does a market exist for your service or product?
   E. Can you develop the market enough to obtain the revenues needed? Your choice of business should be based upon the knowledge and experience relating to that business that you possess. If you lack either of these criteria, it would be wise to work in a similar, *already established* business. Building a profitable enterprise is difficult enough without having to learn the business from the bottom up at the same time.

II. **Select the type of organization (legal structure).**
   A. Individual proprietorship
      Also called *sole proprietorship,* this is the simplest and least expensive way to organize a business. The owner registers the business name, secures the licenses necessary for operation, applies for a tax identification number, and begins operations. He or she receives the profits, assumes the losses, and is personally responsible for the debts and obligations of the enterprise. Income and expenses are reported in the owner's personal tax returns, and profits are taxed at his or her income tax rates.
      To summarize the features of the sole proprietorship:
      1. It is the simplest of all legal forms of organization.
      2. The owner is usually the manager and does not share control of the business with anyone.
      3. Income and expenses are reported on the owner's individual income tax return, and profits are taxed at the owner's rate.

Today, more couples are starting businesses together. The number of sole proprietorships, excluding farms, that were jointly owned by a husband and wife soared 82 percent between 1980 and 1985 (the most recent year for which data are available) for a grand total of 482,993, according to the Small Business Administration. This increase far exceeded the 47 percent gain in sole proprietorships owned by women and the 31 percent increase in those owned by men. Moreover, 11 of the 50 fastest-growing new franchise chains, as ranked by *Venture* magazine in 1992, were founded by entrepreneurial couples, who have been dubbed "copreneurs."

There are many reasons for the growth of this business sector. Because of the proliferation of personal computers, new telephone services, and fax machines, more and more people are beginning to work out of their homes. Franchising is making it possible for people without much business experience to get in the act. Well-publicized success stories of entrepreneurial couples are encouraging other couples to try their hand at running a business. Women, because of job loss and the "glass ceiling," are starting businesses at twice the rate of men—and many are forming these businesses as partnerships with their husbands.

In 1990 women owned about 32 percent of the nation's sole proprietorships, a marked rise from the 26 percent share they had in 1980, according to the SBA. With women expected to form businesses 1.5 times faster than men during the 1990s, the SBA predicts they will own 40 percent of small businesses by the year 2000. According to one SBA official, entrepreneurship is, for the first time, being viewed as a career alternative by young women in their 20s.

B. Partnership

A *general partnership* is a business organization owned by two or more people who agree to form a partnership. In most cases, the partners share equally in the ownership and management responsibilities as defined in a formal (written) partnership agreement. The distribution of profits or losses, management duties, and other issues should also be defined in the written partnership agreement. The partners are also equally liable for all debts and other business obligations. A general partnership is not a taxable entity; income and expenses are reported on federal and state information returns filed by the partnership. Partners are taxed on their individual share of the partnership's profits (less expenses) and at their individual income tax rates.

A general partnership is relatively easy and inexpensive to form. Although not required by law, a written agreement is recommended, and you should consult legal counsel before entering into such an agreement.

A *limited partnership* is composed of at least one general partner and one limited partner. The general partner has the right and responsibility to manage the business and is liable for all other debts and obligations. The limited partner cannot participate in or manage the affairs of the business or be held liable for any more than his or her equity investment. The limited partner invests to experience equity (capital) growth only and will normally be held liable as a general partner if he/she participates in management. Limited partnerships must be formed in compliance with statutory requirements, including tax and securities laws. They are more expensive and complex to organize than general partnerships and should not be entered into without legal advice and representation.

These are some points to remember about partnerships:

1. In a partnership, two or more people own a business jointly.
2. You and your prospective partners should have an agreement, in writing, that sets forth the guidelines under which the firm will operate and/or dissolve. It is advisable to consult an attorney to assist in the formation of this agreement.
3. Partnerships must file a U.S. Partnership Return of Income (IRS Form 1065).
   a. This form is an information return.
   b. Partners report their share of the business's profit or loss on their individual tax return.

C. Corporation

A *corporation* is owned by one or more shareholders and is a separate legal entity from them. Corporations fall into a number of categories for tax purposes, but in all cases they must be formed in compliance with the statutory requirements of the state in which they are incorporated. The shareholders elect a board of directors, which is responsible for controlling and managing the company. Because it is a separate legal entity, the corporation, not its shareholders, is generally liable for all debts, contractual obligations, claims, and lawsuits.

The corporation's legal status also means that it is taxed separately, either under Subchapter C of the Internal Revenue Code (if it is a "C" corporation) or Subchapter S (if it is an "S" corporation). A C corporation reports its income and expenses using federal and state tax returns, and its profits are taxed before any dividends can be distributed to the shareholders. The shareholders, in turn, must report these dividends on their individual income tax returns. The result is actually "double taxation" because a C corporation's profits are taxed twice in this manner.

A company can elect to become an S corporation if it meets the respective state laws for S incorporation. In this event, the income and expenses of the business pass directly to the shareholders in proportion to their percentage of ownership in the company—very similar to a partnership. The profits, if any, are then taxed at their individual income tax rates. Usually the S corporation is a closely held business where most of the shareholders actively participate in its management. However, this is not a requirement for S status. Be sure to check with your state regarding the number of shareholders it will allow to form an S corporation and thoroughly investigate and comply with the regulatory laws that apply. Though the S corporation can offer limited liability exposure for its shareholders and has certain tax advantages over the C corporation, you should seek professional advice before deciding which form is the most appropriate.

To sum up the distinguishing characteristics of the corporation:

1. It is the most formal and complex of all legal structures.
2. It is formed under articles of incorporation, which are filed with the secretary of state and governed by laws set down in its charter (license).
3. Its business profits are taxed separately (but not always exclusively) from the earnings of owners and executives.
4. The corporation is a separate legal entity from its shareholders and has a separate, continuous life.
5. The corporation is often the last stage in a firm's evolution. Most businesses start as proprietorships or partnerships. If the business experiences continuous growth over a period of years, incorporation may become necessary (for adequate control) or advantageous. If and when you decide to incorporate, it is advisable to consult an accountant or tax consultant to review the possible tax advantages and disadvantages. Further information concerning the various types of legal structure can be obtained from SBA publication pamphlet MP 25. Do not, however, substitute the information contained in this publication for legal advice. As with partnerships, it is essential to seek competent professional advice in order to protect your interests when forming a corporation.

D. Other forms of business organization
Professional corporations, nonprofit corporations, business trusts, and cooperative associations are other forms of business organization. Because they are all regulated by state and federal laws and involve legal, financial, and accounting issues, you should not attempt to organize your business along any of these lines without legal and accounting assistance.

The organizational structure of a business can be changed under certain circumstances. For instance, it may be advantageous to change from a C corporation to an S corporation or vice versa. But this can be very troublesome. The primary guidelines are to determine the structure that will best serve the interests of all participants involved and to keep it as simple as possible.

III. **Formulate a business plan.**
A well-formulated business plan serves three important functions. First, it serves as a plan of attack—how to get started in business. Second, it serves as a guideline enabling you to steer the business into a profitable position and then keep it there. Third, in the event that

you seek to borrow money to get started, the business plan will help you answer the five basic questions that a lender will have:

1. What sort of person are you?
2. What are you going to do with the money?
3. When and how are you going to pay it back?
4. Does the amount requested make allowances for unexpected developments?
5. What is the outlook for you, your line of business, and for business in general?

Create a business plan that generally follows this outline:

A. Define carefully the business you are going to start.
B. Consider the market.
   1. What is the sales potential?
   2. How are you going to attract the customer?
   3. How are you going to sell to the customer? (For insight into items 2 and 3 above, read *The Popcorn Report* by Faith Popcorn (New York: Harper Collins, 1992).
C. Plan for buying.
   1. From whom?
   2. How? (Under what terms?)
D. Inventory control.
   1. What is on hand?
   2. What is on order?
   3. What has been sold?
E. Getting the work done (internal organization).
   1. Who is responsible for what?
   2. Are there clearly defined job descriptions so that all employees know what tasks they are required to do?
F. Determine your money needs.
   1. What are the startup costs?
   2. What are the operating expenses?
      a. Break down the expenses.
      b. Match expected sales revenues and expenses. Will sales bring in enough money to pay the bills on time?
G. Sources of additional capital (money other than your investment—for example, funds available to you from relatives or other commercial ventures).
   1. Commercial banks.
   2. Trade creditors and equipment manufacturers.
   3. Small loan companies, factors (companies that lend against accounts receivable), commercial credit companies, sales finance companies, and insurance companies.
H. Control and feedback—is the business progressing according to plan?
   1. Prepare and analyze monthly financial statements.
   2. Institute control systems that cover the following areas:
      a. Inventory.
      b. Sales.

           c. Disbursements.

           d. Break-even—at what sales level will income cover expenses without showing a profit?

    I. Will your business plan work?

        1. You are trying to predict what will happen in the future, so at this point you should review the plan to reassure yourself that you are being as realistic and accurate as possible.

        2. If someone else prepares the plan for you, make sure you go over it in detail with him or her and be sure you understand the information it contains.

    J. Put the plan into action.

    K. Keep the plan up to date. This is accomplished through your systems of control and feedback.

IV. Record keeping

    A. Determine the record-keeping requirements.

        1. Consult an independent accountant.

        2. Be sure you understand whatever record-keeping system you decide to use.

        3. Open a company bank account.

            a. Keep all business transactions separate from personal expenses. THIS IS IMPORTANT!

           b. Deposit all receipts intact and promptly.

           c. Decide on check signer(s).

           d. Pay all expenses by check.

           e. Open a tax account to keep tax collections (sales, Social Security, income) and estimates separate from sales revenues.

    B. Decide on how often you will need to see a profit and loss statement and a balance sheet.

        1. Looking at profit and loss statements on a monthly basis is a good idea.

        2. Know the industry averages for your business and see how you compare. For reference, consult Robert Morris Associates' Annual Statement Studies, Dun & Bradstreet, or the National Cash Register.

    C. If you do not know how, learn to "read" profit and loss statements and balance sheets. There is more to it than looking at the bottom line to see if you made or lost money.

        1. Records are the most important management tool you possess.

        2. If you seek management assistance from the SBA, a bank, or an outside consultant, it will be virtually impossible for them to help you if you do not have good records.

V. Governmental resources and requirements

    A. Federal

        1. The Small Business Answer Desk operated by the SBA directs small business owners to the correct source for answers to questions about government regulations as well as federal, state, and private sources of business assistance. The Small Business Answer Desk's hours are 9:00 A.M. to 5:00 P.M. (East-

ern time) Monday through Friday. Its toll-free number is (800) 827-5722.

Also available on request from the SBA is *The Small Business Resource Guide,* a 132-page book listing federal, state, and private agencies and organizations that can guide a business developer or owner.

2. The SBA also offers free counseling to people planning to start or maintain a small business through SCORE (Service Corps of Retired Executives).

B. State and local

State and local chambers of commerce are excellent guides to resources available from state and local government sources. Consult your telephone directory for the one nearest to you.

The information outlined above pertains primarily to retail businesses. It is explained in more detail (along with worksheets) in SBA publication MP 9. The SBA also publishes business plans for small service firms (MP 11), small manufacturers (MP 4), and small construction firms (MP 5). These publications are available at a nominal charge from the SBA. You may order these by using Form 115A, available upon request from your regional SBA office.

FINANCING YOUR BUSINESS

Borrowing money is something nearly all business owners do at one time or another. To be a successful loan applicant, you need to convince a lender that you are a reasonable risk. You must explain how much money you need to borrow, how you will use it, and how you will repay it.

Generally, business owners borrow to finance a start-up, an inventory build-up, accounts receivable, expansion of facilities, or the purchase of another company. But regardless of why you want to borrow, lenders always want to minimize their own risk. They will not lend you money unless you can convince them that you are able to repay the loan. Banks do not make grants; neither does the SBA's loan program. All loans made or guaranteed by the SBA must be repaid, and no loan will be approved without the borrower's showing an ability to repay.

Organizations called FACTORS will purchase accounts receivable at a discount, thus providing cash to the business. Any bad debts among these accounts receivable are charged back to the business owner; thus, he/she remains liable for the amount of the accounts receivable until paid but has the use of the full discounted value. This, in effect, is a loan against accounts receivable.

A little digging will uncover a treasure chest full of generous government programs to assist the small business owner. These programs exist on the local, state, and federal levels. A lot is made of the federal (SBA) programs, but don't overlook the offerings of your local and state governments. Remember, your tax dollars help fund these assistance programs, so make wise use of your hard-earned money.

The purpose of such programs is to provide you with assistance on two levels:

1. Financial—includes direct loans, loan guarantees, and tax relief.
2. Technical—includes management assistance and informative seminars on a broad range of topics.

By offering you, the business owner, accurate information and financial incentives, local and state governments hope to lure new businesses to the area and help resident businesses continue to grow. Their success results in economic growth, more jobs, and an increased tax base. This translates into more tax revenue available to help more businesses, encourage more growth, and collect more revenue. . . . Yes, it flows well on paper, but in real life progress often gets stuck in bureaucratic red tape.

Cutting Red Tape

Dealing with a bureaucracy is never a fun experience, as anyone who has renewed a driver's license, purchased car tags, obtained a marriage certificate, erected a sign, or added a room to a house will attest. They are likely to have experienced a system in which job security is not based on efficiency or the desire to serve the customer (that is, the public).

Instead, bureaucracies seem to thrive on customer *disservice*. Because of this reluctance to vault the many hurdles of the bureaucratic system (and the lack of accurate information on the part of the public and the bureaucracy), small business owners are reluctant to turn to the government for assistance. This is sad, because often the resources allotted to these government programs are not fully utilized. Many entrepreneurs have an exaggerated preconception of the difficulty of mixing government and business. Following these guidelines will help make the system work for you:

1. Make sure your qualifications fit the program you are pursuing. Depending on factors such as type of business, sex, race, location, government regulations, and so forth, you could possibly be eligible for several different programs. Be as sure as you can that you are pursuing the one that is best for you.
2. Seek counsel from those experienced with government assistance programs. This may include your banker, other business associates, or a professional loan packager. Your local SBA office can refer you to someone.
3. Always double-check your information. As noted before, our bureaucratic system is so large and complex that any single government employee cannot be expected to fully understand how each department interacts with the others. The result is a lot of misinformation that often causes extra work on your part. To avoid wasting time, always confirm your instructions with an additional source. You can do this with a follow-up phone call to another office employee or sometimes even another

agency. And if you are fortunate enough to find an employee who is exceptionally helpful, make a note of that name and number.

4. Be thorough with all paperwork. Don't leave any blank lines or incomplete answers. Unlike a banker who might call for the missing information, a government office is more likely to just send the application back, causing you to have to start over.

5. Prepare an in-depth and well-constructed business plan. Use realistic financial projections. Inaccurate growth projections will cast doubt on your management ability.

6. Demonstrate your good character. Use letters of recommendation from business associates, suppliers, and leaders in your community.

7. Demonstrate a strong management team. Prepare résumés for yourself, your partners, and key employees that give evidence that your company possesses a winning combination of talent and business expertise.

Local Assistance

The place to begin looking for help is at home. Contact your banker and your chamber of commerce or look in the government pages of your phone book for an industrial or economic development agency. Such agencies are plentiful and work with private development companies to assist businesses for the betterment of the community.

Remember that these programs are often offered at the city and county levels. In addition, the emphasis of each program may be continually changing to meet the most pressing needs as perceived by the community leaders. For example, newly elected officials may have a vision that differs from the previous administration and redirect focus to downtown expansions, new technology, or attracting new businesses.

State Assistance

In addition to the sources mentioned previously, you can also contact your state chamber of commerce to locate state-level programs. The assistance available will vary between different states, just as it does at the city and county levels. The following is a list of some common methods through which the state can help you with your business goals:

1. Industrial development bonds (IDBs). All states use this method to help businesses finance the building of their own facilities as well as the acquisition of property and other large assets. These bonds are sold by the state, and the interest earnings are federally tax-free.

2. Loan guarantees. A loan guarantee is not a loan but a guarantee to the lender (bank or other) to repay the loan should you default. In effect, the state becomes cosigner of the loan. (This is the primary activity of the SBA loan program.) Be sure to first determine what the state's required qualifications are for it to guarantee your loan.

3. Direct loans. Here the state is the actual lender. Normally these loans

carry excellent terms. Their purpose is to encourage the formation and continuation of particular industries or businesses that the state wants to attract. Required qualifications can run the full spectrum, sometimes even allowing unsecured, or signature, loans.

4. Venture capital funds. Today about half of the states provide some form of venture capital, possibly in the form of a loan or in exchange for equity. This money is raised from private investors by offering them such incentives as tax breaks if they participate. States are also offering incentives to lending institutions to accept more risk.

5. Business development corporations (BDCs). More than 20 states make loans through privately owned business development corporations. BDCs are chartered by the states and can be very flexible government sources. Because of this they can design financing packages that would not be available elsewhere. All types of conventional loans are available. Most can make SBA-guaranteed loans and offer purchase/leaseback programs. Some even provide venture capital.

6. Incubators. There are over 400 in 41 states, and that amount is expected to double in the next few years. The purpose of an incubator is to nurture new businesses in a somewhat controlled environment until they grow strong enough to fly on their own.

Normally located on college campuses or nearby business parks, incubators lease out space and provide management assistance and secretarial services at below-market rates to qualified tenants. With the exception of those businesses that require a retail storefront, these facilities attract entrepreneurs from almost every industry. A growing number of incubators are targeting specific industries, minorities, and women.

Incubators provide two big advantages. The first is low startup costs and overhead. In a number of cases, the amount of your rental payments is tied to your sales, starting low and growing as your sales increase. The second is the ability to make use of others' experience and ideas. This can come from the staff, fellow participants, and the facilities of the university.

The odds of a business celebrating its fifth birthday are four times greater if that business gets its start in an incubator.

You can contact the following agencies to obtain a list of incubators and business development centers near you:

Association of Small Business Development Centers
1050 Seventeenth Street, NW #810
Washington, DC 20036
(202) 887-5599

National Business Incubation Association
One President Street
Athens, Ohio 45701
(614) 593-4331

Federal Assistance

The federal government offers a multitude of financial assistance programs for the business sector. The most well-known of these is the Small Business Administration (SBA), which was established in 1953. Because it is so well-known and a bureaucracy, many myths—both good and bad—have been circulating about it. The next few pages will hopefully dispel some of these myths and give you a better understanding of what it can and can't do for you.

The most predominant myth is that the SBA is for start-ups and struggling businesses—in other words, for businesses on shaky ground. This is not the case. In practically all cases, you must demonstrate the stability and profitability of your business proposal. (The SBA specifically states it is "not actively seeking loans to businesses in existence less than one year.") The reason is that the SBA primarily issues loan guarantees to banks and other lenders. The SBA acts as a cosigner for the borrower—you. The SBA has its own requirements that must be met, and the lenders also require minimum qualifications before approving a loan, even with an SBA guarantee.

Because of this cosigner relationship, banks are growing ever fonder of the SBA guarantee. The stigma that used to be attached to SBA loans by the banks has disappeared.

Another myth regards the time required to go through the loan process. Many small business owners, for fear of red tape and perceived lengthy delays in obtaining approval, avoid the SBA. But if your proposal is properly submitted, actual processing will normally require three to six weeks, and a bank can usually release funds within a week after SBA approval.

The SBA does make direct loans but only for very specific situations. The vast majority of SBA lending assistance takes the form of loan guarantees. The SBA will guarantee 80 to 90 percent of the lender's loan amount in case you default. The two most common guarantees are the 7(A) Loan Program and the 504 Loan Program. Your local SBA office can direct you to lenders who participate in each. (See Chapter 3, "Participating Lenders.")

SBA direct loans are targeted to particular categories of individuals or circumstances. They are normally difficult to qualify for, but if you meet the criteria and don't fall into one of these denial traps, you should apply. Here are the principal reasons why the SBA will reject a loan application:

1. Funds are available elsewhere on reasonable terms.
2. Funds are to be used for speculation.
3. A portion of the business income is derived from gambling activities.
4. The loan will be used by an enterprise primarily engaged in lending or investing.
5. The loan is used to purchase real property to be held for resale or investment.
6. The loan is used to relocate your business for other than sound business purposes.

Some of the direct loans made by the SBA are issued to help businesses comply with environmental and safety laws and assist in cases of forced relocation. It also offers loans to minorities, and disadvantaged individuals. The terms of these direct loans always beat standard commercial loans, having lower interest rates and longer maturities.

Federal Venture Capital

Small business investment companies (SBICs) are licensed by the SBA to provide venture capital to expanding small businesses. These private venture capital firms receive additional funds from the SBA through the sale of SBA-guaranteed debentures of the Federal Financing Bank.

These venture firms are federally regulated and can assume more risk, thus funding more start-ups than private firms. However, they should be approached in the same manner as private firms.

There are also minority enterprise small business investment companies (MESBICs), which, as their name suggests, are specifically for minorities. To locate these firms, contact:

National Association of
Small Business Investment Companies
1156 Fifteenth Street, NW
Washington, DC 20005
(202) 833-8230

An important thing to remember is that all government programs have social, economic, and political objectives. You should not plan your business around these programs. To gain assistance, however, you should check to see if some government funds are available to help you implement your business plan.

There are many, many federal programs that offer financial assistance in addition to the SBA. To list and explain them all would double the size of this book, which would soon become outdated as these programs are continually changing. If you would like a current list of all the government assistance programs, you should order these two catalogs:

Catalog of Federal Domestic Assistance
Office Of Management And Budget
Superintendent Of Documents
U.S. Government Printing Office
Washington, DC 20402
(202) 783-3238   Cost: $46

Small Business Resource Guide
U.S. Small Business Administration
Office of Advocacy
1441 L Street, NW
Washington, DC 20416
(202) 205-6533   Cost: Free

Private Lenders

The private lender category is made up of insurance companies, pension funds, and investment trusts. These sources are interested in two types of financing transactions:

- Real estate. This covers a broad range of projects, from construction to purchase/lease back.
- Equity. Many of the pension funds allocate a portion of their portfolio to risk capital.

These sources, especially the pension funds, often prefer to deal with a financial professional rather than a principal.

Venture Capital Financing

Venture capitalists typically invest in high-growth companies with new proprietary technologies or untapped niche markets. They are known to take more risks than other institutional financing sources—hence the term *risk capital*. (Refer to my books, *The Total Business Plan* and *The Total Marketing and Sales Plan* [New York: John Wiley & Sons, Inc., 1990 and 1992, respectively], before approaching these firms.)

Their requirements are typically the following:

1. High growth—projected sales of $25 million to $100 million in five to seven years.
2. High return on investment—30 percent compounded annually.
3. Proprietary technology and/or preemptive position—they want to see some overwhelming advantage that would help a company quickly penetrate or "sweep" a market.
4. Strong management—possibly one member of the management team is a recognized expert in a certain technological area.

Investments made by venture capitalists range from $100,000 to $5,000,000. A business plan is required during the review process. Financing commitments are usually structured as equity where the venture capitalist exits in five to seven years through an initial public offering or a buyout.

Investment Banks

Investment banking covers a broad range of equity and debt funding sources.

Financing through investment banks usually involves the sale of securities to individual investors and institutions through investment vehicles such as private placements, initial public offerings, and secondary public offerings. In these instances, the investment bank is not putting up a lot of its own funds. Rather, it is investing for the account of others. The investment banker merely convinces individuals or institutions to invest in a venture project. In this way a pool of money is formed for investment in a particular project.

Very little money is directly put up by the banker. He or she merely performs an accumulation service.

Many investment banks get involved in specialty financing situations such as mergers and acquisitions, reorganizations, turnarounds, and an assortment of other complex debt and equity transactions.

Like any source of financial assistance, investment banks have certain requirements. Debt and equity securities generally must show high growth potential if the company is young. Specialty transactions are evaluated on a case-by-case basis. The reward has to adequately compensate the risk an investment bank is taking in the transaction. In risk capital situations, investment banks are looking for a 20 to 30 percent return on investment.

Areas of General Interest to Lenders

What do lenders look for from a prospective borrower? A financial institution's lending policies fall into three general areas: assessment of a borrower's personal and business history, employing a risk reduction program, and consideration of potential disqualifying factors. The SBA loan program functions in much the same way but with more latitude for special situations.

Lenders investigate the following criteria:

- Personal credit record of the borrower.
- Financial history of the business.
- Growth of the business.
- Profitability of the business.
- Physical condition of the facilities and equipment.
- Experience of the key managers.

To reduce risk, lenders require SOME of the following:

- An equity pledge by the owner to the lender.
- A personal-assets pledge by the owner to the lender.
- The cosigning on the loan by all principals or guarantors.
- A lien on all assets and personal property of the owner(s).

These are factors that MIGHT cause a loan application to be turned down:

- Prior business bankruptcy.
- A bad debt record.
- Low company earnings.
- Low value of secured collateral.
- Management inexperience.
- Unfavorable liquidity, debt, and profitability ratios.
- A criminal record.

Risk Analysis for Business Start-ups

From the perspective of a lender or investor, financing a new business always carries more risk than lending to or investing in a going enterprise. Many uncertainties vanish once the business establishes a track record.

Does the business owner have enough savings to pay personal expenses while developing the business? A good rule of thumb is that a business takes three years to generate enough ongoing income for a living wage. During those three years, personal living expenses as well as equity capital for the business must come from the owner, not a lender or investor.

Does the business owner have the managerial acumen to build a profitable, self-sustaining business? A person may have all the necessary credentials on paper and still not master the nuts-and-bolts skills to bring a new company to fruition. Technical skill could be more than enough as an employee but may not be sufficient to handle the day-to-day problem solving necessary to start and maintain a business.

Will competitive forces allow a new entrant into the market? Market research may point to a logical opening, but as soon as you start making sales calls and need orders to sustain the business, you could find the reality of the situation to be much more of a challenge. Competitors can be very protective of market share. Price cutting, advertising, and promotional gimmicks quickly restrict the new entrant's marketing program. A dramatic example of this occurred in the long-distance telephone business when AT&T decided to stop the expansion of MCI and Sprint.

Does the new product or service fill a market demand? Starting a business to make cars fireproof might sound like a great idea. Certainly people need this protection. But do they really want it? Are they willing to pay for it?

These are the types of questions financiers worry about when lending or investing in startup businesses. This also contributes to the popularity of franchise businesses. Franchises already have market acceptance, product design, and competitive position. The only remaining question is whether the franchisee has the managerial skill to succeed.

All lenders and investors are risk takers. The money game has always been a risky business and probably always will be. Of course, different levels of risk exist. And as in every other business, the higher the risk, the more money costs and the more stringent the terms.

In the hierarchy of risk taking, commercial banks continue to be by far the most conservative; venture capital firms occupy the other end of the spectrum. Finance companies, government agencies (such as the SBA), and private foundations fall between these two extremes. For comparison purposes, small investment banks can be grouped with venture capital firms.

How to Contact the SBA

To order specific publications or a list of available publications, call the Office of Public Communications at (202) 205-6743.

To get information about SBA business development programs and services, call the SBA's Small Business Answer Desk at (800) 827-5722.

To locate the SBA office nearest you, consult the U.S. Government section of your telephone directory.

The remainder of this book will expand on what has been covered in this Introduction regarding the SBA. You will not only learn about the various programs offered through the SBA and how to apply for them but will also get a feel for that agency's "personality."

1 Small Business Administration Programs

As was stated in the Introduction, there are a number of federally supported programs that regularly make loans available to existing as well as start-up businesses based on specific qualifying factors. Some of these programs have expanded, some have changed their lending policies, and a few are the result of completely new business financing methods. Many of these programs offer some excellent opportunities that were not available a few years ago. If you previously rejected the idea of borrowing money through a federally guaranteed or supported program because of the presumed red tape, you should rethink your decision. The paperwork isn't any more than one would expect in the course of securing other types of financing.

U.S. SMALL BUSINESS ADMINISTRATION

The SBA was established by Congress in 1953 to advise, assist, champion, and counsel the country's small businesses. SBA loans have helped thousands of small businesses to get started, expand, and prosper and have assisted many ambitious men and women in starting their own businesses. Besides providing loans, the SBA has guided many in properly managing their businesses and very often has provided help in procuring sales of the goods and/or services they produce.

The SBA is not permitted to provide a loan to those who can obtain financing from a bank or other private lending source. If the loan (an agreement to make funds available) is not obtainable elsewhere, the SBA will consider providing funds (actual money) on an immediate participation basis with a bank or with a guaranteed loan. The SBA will only consider providing a direct loan (in which both the agreement and the funds originate from the same agency) when these various other loans and funds are not obtainable and funds are available for direct loans.

PRODUCT OR SERVICE CLASSIFICATION GUIDELINES

When looking to borrow money to start a new business, be prepared to demonstrate to the SBA (the participating lender) that your product or service is capable of competing successfully in its marketplace. The category into which the SBA classifies your product, whether it is a new or existing item, can be crucial. Many applicants fail to understand that their application's approval or rejection could very well depend on which classification the SBA assigns to their product.

Be sure to clearly point out in your loan application the specific area or field in which your product has the ability to compete successfully. Have all the facts to support your position. For example, if the SBA, following the description of a product you intend to market as an educational game, classified it in the toy category, the chances of having your application approved would be seriously lowered. This would probably be due to the product's estimated market price as an educational game, preventing it from competing in the toy field, which generally has lower prices.

To avoid this pitfall, familiarize yourself with the SBA guidelines. *The Standard Industrial Classification Manual*, published by the Bureau of Budget, Washington, D.C., is one of the most important publications used by the SBA to assist in designating classifications for products and services. In addition to your description of the product and the *SIC Manual*, the SBA also uses information from other manufacturing firms that produce similar items.

Remember, the SBA is in business to help you. It is not the SBA's intention to make it difficult for you; thus, it is your responsibility to provide them with all the facts the SBA needs to reach a decision most favorable to you. Also, if you have a unique product, one which calls for an untried manufacturing technique or other such unique process, the SBA may require that the product undergo a feasibility study conducted by an independent organization.

There are approximately 90 SBA district offices, and they are listed for your convenience in Appendix K of this book. Visit the nearest one.

There are some other departments that provide financing and appear to be related to the SBA but are not. One of these is the Minority Business Development Agency (MBDA) in the Department of Commerce, which focuses entirely on aiding minority-owned businesses. Their chief activity, however, appears to be help in financing, and the agency carries out the programs through contracts with firms in the private sector as a system of third-party services—that is, the MBDA pays the firm to provide services to a third party.

The Department of Defense is also especially active in this field, operating its own offices responsible for protecting the interests of small and minority-owned businesses. Major defense programs have individuals assigned especially to see to it that minority firms and other small businesses are given a fair opportunity to pursue and win contracts and subcontracts.

The General Services Administration (GSA) is the federal government's housekeeper, with five subordinate divisions, including the Federal Supply Service. This agency operates 13 business service centers in major cities, whose major function is to help orient you in pursuing government contracts.

SBA PROGRAMS

The Small Business Administration is the largest source of long-term small business financing in the nation. In fiscal year 1990, the San Francisco District by itself made 1,119 loans for over $349.2 million, the highest volume done by an SBA district in the nation.

In fact, businesses that received a 7(a) loan (the largest guaranteed loan program) registered an average sales growth of 123 percent from 1985 to 1989 (the latest figures available), compared to 101 percent cited by a comparison group. And employment grew an average of 101 percent, compared to only 36 percent.

Recipients of 7(a) loans also tend to have a greater survival rate. Approximately three-fourths of the 1,430 SBA-backed firms were still in business after the four-year study, compared to only 64 percent of those in the comparison group. Businesses that have the money they need to continue growing have a greater chance of survival, according to Mr. Stamler.

The vast majority of new and existing small businesses are eligible for SBA financial assistance if they do not dominate their field, are independently owned, and can prove they have been unable to obtain a bank loan or other private financing without the SBA's assistance. In fact, the SBA's definition of a small business includes 80 to 90 percent of all businesses in the United States. So you can presume you have met that requirement already.

To determine whether you qualify for an SBA business loan or if one best suits your financing needs, *please read this material carefully.* If you have further questions, please contact your own banker, one of the active SBA guaranteed lenders listed in Chapter 3, or an SBA loan officer.

Although the SBA does make a limited number of direct loans, it normally provides a guarantee to a private lender, who in turn makes the loan directly to the borrower. With the exception of a few joint programs with state agencies, the maximum amount the SBA can loan to any one business is currently $750,000. This includes working capital funds and long-term loans. The SBA can guarantee up to 90 percent of a loan, depending on the loan amount. Maturity may be up to 25 years. The average size of a guaranteed business loan is $175,000, with an average maturity of about 8 years.

The SBA offers assistance under several programs, some designated by the numbered section of the Small Business Act to which they apply:

- 7(a) Loans
- 502 Program
- 504 Program
- Handicapped Assistance Loans (HAL-1 and HAL-2)
- Energy Loans
- Disaster Assistance Loans

- Pollution Control Financing
- 8(a) Minority-owned Business Loans

7(a) Loan Program

This, the largest program, is specifically designed to help small businesses with credit problems.

Guarantees require a commercial bank to actually supply the funds. The bank must participate 10 percent for loans up to $155,000 and 15 percent for loans between $155,000 and $750,000. Interest rates cannot be more than 2.25 to 2.75 percent over prime. The material to be purchased may serve as collateral, although personal guarantees might be required.

The SBA's basic program includes the following:

  I. Regular business loans

  II. Special loan programs that offer:
    A. Small general contractor loans.
    B. Seasonal line of credit guarantees.
    C. Energy loans.
    D. Handicapped assistance loans.
    E. Export revolving lines of credit.
    F. International trade loans.
    G. Disaster assistance.
      1. Physical disaster loans.
      2. Economic injury disaster loans.
    H. Pollution control financing.
    I. Assistance to veterans.
    J. Assistance to women and minorities.
    K. Business development programs.
    L. Small Business Innovation Research programs (SBIR).

  III. Certified Lenders Program

  IV. Development Company Loans

  V. Surety Bonds

  VI. Small business investment companies (SBICs)

  VII. Minority enterprise small business investment companies (MESBICs), also known as special small business investment companies (SSBICs)

As you can see, there are quite a number of SBA programs and services available under the 7(a) loan program. They will be briefly explained in the following paragraphs. You can also request a free directory of business development publications by contacting your local SBA office or calling the Small Business Answer Desk at (800) 827-5722 (in Washington, D.C., call 653-7561). Their directory has over 100 business publications available for a nominal fee (a few are listed in Appendix J). These materials are designed to answer your questions about how to start, operate, and manage a business and where to get SBA financing and assistance.

SBA Basic Eligibility Requirements

Depending on the type of business seeking SBA financing, certain standards will determine eligibility as follows:

- **Manufacturing.** The total number of employees may range up to 1,500, but the actual number is based on the industry in which the business is engaged.
- **Wholesale.** Up to 100 employees are permitted.
- **Service Companies.** Maximum annual sales can range from $3.5 to $14.5 million, depending on the industry.
- **Retail Companies.** Maximum annual sales can range from $3.5 million to $13.5 million, depending on the industry.
- **General Construction.** Maximum annual sales can range from $9.5 to $17 million, depending on the industry.
- **Special Trade Construction.** Average annual receipts cannot exceed $7 million.
- **Agriculture.** Annual sales receipts cannot exceed $500,000 to $3.5 million, depending on the industry.

Recently the SBA issued an "alternate standard" ruling regarding the 7(a) loan program under which a company can qualify as a small business if its net worth is up to $6 million and it had an annual after-tax net income of up to $2 million in each of the past two years. This alternate standard ruling opens the program to a much wider group of businesses while making no mention of providing additional funds to compensate for the influx of these larger small businesses.

Ineligible Businesses

The Small Business Act does exclude some forms of businesses from receiving loans. These include the following:

- Not-for-profit organizations, except sheltered workshops.
- Newspapers.
- Magazines.
- Movie theaters.
- Radio and television stations.
- Theatrical productions.
- Dinner theaters.
- Book publishers.

- Film, record, or tape distributors.

- Businesses involved in the creation, origination, expression, or distribution of ideas, values, thoughts, or opinions.

- Manufacturers, importers, exporters, retailers, or distributors of communications such as greeting cards, books, sheet music, pictures, posters, films, tapes, broadcasters, or other performances and recordings of musical programs.

Those firms engaged as commercial printers; those producing advertising and promotional materials for others or providing motion pictures, videotapes, sound recording facilities, or technical services *without* editorial or artistic contribution; and general merchandisers that sell magazines, books, and so on, ARE ELIGIBLE.

Other excluded businesses include those engaged in floor planning, gambling, speculation of any kind, and illegal activities. Applications from incarcerated persons or persons on probation or parole for serious offenses will not be accepted.

To determine if your business or proposed enterprise is eligible, contact the nearest SBA office or your bank.

Other SBA Loan Requirements

Before the SBA will guarantee a loan through a lender, the applicant must demonstrate that these conditions apply:

- The business will be able to repay its current debts in addition to the new loan requested.

- There is a reasonable amount of equity invested in the business or collateral that the borrower can pledge for the loan. Generally, a new business applicant should have between 20 and 30 percent of the required equity investment to start a new business. The actual percentage is determined by the lender and the SBA. For existing businesses, the SBA considers a number of credit factors and the company's history before reaching a decision, which is essentially the same policy as any other lender.

- The company's past track record has been good and/or its financial projections are realistic and supportable.

- The company's management has the expertise to adequately conduct the operations of the business.

The fastest way to determine whether or not an SBA-guaranteed loan is a viable option for your financing needs is to call your banker for an appointment. After all, you have to be turned down by at least one bank before you can qualify for SBA assistance anyway. Maybe your bank won't give you a loan directly, but if it says no, ask if it would be interested in participating in an SBA-guaranteed loan. If the answer is yes, give the bank all of the information it requests. It will help you complete the loan application and forward it to the SBA for approval. The entire process can take just a few weeks or several, depending on how well your business plan and the application have been prepared.

Guaranteed Loans

Guaranteed loans are made by private lenders; a percentage of the loan amount up to $750,000 is guaranteed by the SBA.

A loan application is submitted to a lender that participates in the SBA loan guarantee program. The application must meet the SBA's eligibility and credit requirements as well as all requirements of the lender. If the application is approved by the lender, it is then submitted to the SBA for approval. The SBA usually makes a credit decision on loans within ten working days.

Basic Terms and Conditions of SBA-Guaranteed Loans

Loan Limits.   There is no maximum loan limit that can be obtained through the guarantee program. The maximum amount that the SBA can guarantee is $750,000. The SBA guarantees a percentage of the loan amount to the lender. There is a 2 percent fee on the guaranteed amount. The average loan made under the guarantee program is approximately $210,000. Although the SBA does not set minimum loan amounts, many lenders will not make loans below $50,000; very few lenders will consider loans below $25,000. (For these amounts see the Microloan program mentioned later.)

Use of Proceeds.   The loan proceeds may be used for a variety of business purposes including working capital, inventory, machinery and equipment, leasehold improvements, and the acquisition or construction of commercial business property.

Loan Term.   The maturity of the loan is dependent on the use of the loan proceeds and may vary from 5 to 7 years for working capital, 10 years for fixed assets, or 25 years for real estate acquisitions.

How to Apply for a Loan

Applications may be obtained from participating lenders. Generally, the documentation required is as follows:

- A current profit and loss statement and balance sheet for existing businesses or a proforma statement for new businesses; you should provide a realistic projected cash flow and profit and loss statement for one year (monthly breakdown).
- A current personal financial statement of the owner/manager or each partner or stockholder owning 20 percent or more of the corporate stock.
- Itemized use of loan proceeds.
- Collateral, with an estimate of current market value and liens against the collateral.
- A business plan, including résumés of the principals.

- A schedule of business debt, aging of accounts receivable, and accounts payable.
- Personal and business tax returns for the past three years.
- Copy of lease (if property is to be leased).
- Any contracts or agreements pertinent to the applicant.

Summary of SBA-Guaranteed Loans

The following general information is provided so that you will have a better understanding of the SBA-7(a) guaranteed loan program. The information is general; each loan application is reviewed individually by an SBA lender and an SBA loan officer to determine eligibility.

I. **The SBA generally *does not* make loans;** the SBA *guarantees* loans submitted and made by financial institutions, generally banks. The SBA *does not* have a "grant" program for starting small businesses (see the SBIR program mentioned later).

  A. The SBA guarantees loans up to $750,000. There is no theoretical minimum; however, most lenders are reluctant to process commercial loans of less than $25,000.

  B. The prospective borrower *will be required* to provide a capital contribution. This contribution will normally be 30 to 50 percent of the total capitalization of the business. Often real estate acquisitions can be financed for up to 90 percent with only the support of the first deed of trust and the owner's personal guarantee.

  C. An existing business will be required to provide financial statements showing the business is a profit-making concern, does not have delinquent tax, and will have a debt-to-net worth ratio of approximately 3:1 after the loan is made.

  D. Many borrowers confuse collateral and equity. *Equity* is the owner's investment or net worth in the business. *Collateral* is anything of value, business or personal, that may be pledged to secure the loan.

  E. The SBA charges the lender a 2 percent guarantee fee on the guaranteed portion of the loan. SBA policy allows the lender to charge this fee to the borrower.

II. **The SBA-guaranteed loan program's "interest rates"** are based on the prime rate as advertised in the *Wall Street Journal* according to the following schedule:

  A. Loans of less than seven years: prime rate plus 2.25 percent.

  B. Loans of seven years or more: prime rate plus 2.75 percent.

III. **The SBA-guaranteed loan maturity** (length of loan) is based upon the following schedule:

  A. Working capital loans: 5 to 7 years.

  B. Fixed asset loans: 7 to 10 years.

  C. Real estate and building: up to 25 years.

      These loans are not subject to prepayment penalty.

IV. **The average size standards** for SBA-guaranteed business loans are based on the average number of employees for the preceding 12 months or on the sales volume averaged over a three-year period according to the following schedule:
   A. **Manufacturing.** Maximum number of employees may range from 500 to 1,500, depending on the type of product manufactured.
   B. **Wholesaling.** Maximum number of employees may not exceed 100.
   C. **Services.** Annual receipts may not exceed $3.5 million to $14.5 million, depending on the industry.
   D. **Retailing.** Annual receipts may not exceed $3.5 million to $13.5 million, depending on the industry.
   E. **Construction.** General construction annual receipts may not exceed $9.5 million to $17 million, depending on the industry.
   F. **Special Trade Construction.** Annual receipts may not exceed $7 million.
   G. **Agriculture.** Annual receipts may not exceed $0.5 million to $3.5 million, depending on the industry.

V. **Most importantly,** during your discussion with the lender, be prepared with data to answer the lender's questions. A business plan that includes these items will help you in presenting your proposal:
   A. Projected profit and loss statement.
   B. Cash flow projections.
   C. Market analysis.
   D. Marketing strategy.
   E. Description of the business.
   F. Product's or service's advantage.
   G. Management ability—résumés of the key staff should be included.
   H. Financial information (personal and business).
   I. Cash requirements.

VI. **Business proposals** that are ineligible for the SBA-guaranteed loan program are as follows:
   A. Partial purchase of a business.
   B. Lending institutions.
   C. Real estate held for speculation, investment, or rental.
   D. Opinion molders—magazines, newspapers, trade journals, radio, television, live entertainment, schools, and so on.
   E. Religious organizations and their affiliates.

Please note that the SBA has issued the statement that they are not encouraging applications from businesses that are less than one year old.

SPECIAL SBA 7(a) GUARANTEED LOAN PROGRAMS

In the general area of financial assistance, SBA also offers several special loan programs.

Small General Contractor Loans

These are designed to assist small construction firms with short-term financing. Loan proceeds can be used to finance residential or commercial construction or rehabilitation of property for sale. Proceeds cannot be used for owning or operating real estate for investment purposes.

Seasonal Line of Credit Guarantee

These loans are designed to provide short-term financing for small firms having a seasonal loan requirement due to a seasonal increase in business activity.

Energy Loans

These are available to firms engaged in manufacturing, selling, installing, servicing, or developing specific energy-saving measures.

Handicapped Assistance Loans

This loan program is earmarked for physically handicapped small business owners and private nonprofit organizations that employ handicapped persons and operate in their interest—for example, sheltered workshops.

Export Revolving Lines of Credit (ERLC)

This program offers guarantees to provide short-term financing for exporting firms having been in existence for one year or more and for the purpose of developing or penetrating foreign markets.

International Trade Loans

One of the SBA's most important missions is to encourage small businesses to export their products or services overseas. It has several programs to achieve this goal, including guaranteed loans to exporters of up to $1.25 million ($250,000 for working capital; $1 million for facilities or equipment to be used in the United States in the production of goods and services involved in international trade) and the ERLC. Through the ERLC, the SBA can guarantee up to 90 percent of a credit line extended by a bank to an exporter. The SBA also offers referrals to other agencies involved in exporting, sponsors regular export seminars and workshops, and has free counseling available through SCORE.

Disaster Assistance

When the president of the United States or the administrator of the SBA declares a specific area to be a disaster area, two types of loans are offered:

- Physical Disaster Loans are made available to homeowners, renters, businesses (large and small), and nonprofit organizations within the disaster area. Loan proceeds can be used to repair or replace damaged or destroyed homes, personal property, and businesses.

- Economic Injury Disaster Loans are made available to small businesses that suffer substantial economic injury because of the disaster. Loan proceeds may be used for working capital and to pay financial obligations that the small business could have met had the disaster not occurred.

  When a disaster is declared, the SBA establishes on-site offices with experienced personnel to help with loan information, processing, and disbursement.

Pollution Control Financing

The SBA assists those small businesses needing long-term financing for planning, design, and installation of pollution control facilities or equipment. This financing is available through the loan guarantee program, which offers a maximum of $1 million per small business with a guarantee of up to 100 percent by the SBA.

Public Law 94-305, passed by Congress in 1976, authorizes the SBA to guarantee 100 percent of the payments due under qualified contracts for the planning, design, financing, and installation of pollution control facilities or equipment by eligible small businesses. Loans are made through lenders participating in the SBA's guaranteed loan program and are therefore guaranteed by the SBA.

Also, the SBA guarantee pledges the full faith and credit of the federal government to the payment of the principal and interest for the full term of those contracts (loans, leases, and so on) financed from the proceeds of taxable or tax-exempt bonds issued by a state or municipal authority for pollution control facilities or equipment for small businesses.

To deliver this program, the SBA cooperates with various groups with a potential interest in it:

- State and local regulatory agencies.
- Financial institutions.
- Commercial and investment banks.
- Other parties interested in identifying eligible small businesses needing pollution control financing.

SBA officials also provide technical assistance to applicants as well as to lending institutions with respect to the packaging and processing of the financial assistance.

Who Benefits from the Program?

- Small businesses—those needing long-term, low-interest financing for their pollution control facilities, thereby minimizing the adverse effects upon their working capital and cash flow.
- Commercial banks—by having another financing mechanism available to help their small business customers.
- Localities, states, and the nation as a whole—by helping to create a cleaner environment and a stronger economy by ensuring the continued health and growth of small businesses.
- Investors—through increased security for their invested dollars.

Eligibility

There are no special eligibility requirements. Applicants must meet the eligibility criteria applicable to loans made under the SBA's 7(a) loan program. Any small business that is now or is likely to be at an operational or financial disadvantage with respect to similar business concerns by virtue of government-mandated planning, design, or installation of pollution control facilities or is otherwise at a disadvantage in obtaining financing for such facilities is encouraged to apply.

The following is a summary of the basic guidelines used in considering individual applications for assistance under this program:

1. The applicant must meet the broad size standards. Although different industries have different standards, only sheltered workshops under the Handicapped Assistance Loan program are exempt from them.
2. The applicant must be or be likely to be at an operational or financial disadvantage relative to other businesses.
3. The pollution control facilities to be financed help prevent, reduce, abate, or control pollution or contamination.
4. The applicant must have been in business for at least five years and been profitable for three of the last five years. The businesses must be operated for profit.
5. The business must be able to generate cash flow sufficient to pay all debt service requirements on the proposed financing.

Use of Proceeds

As mentioned previously, a Pollution Control Loan can be used only to finance the planning, design, or installation of a "pollution control facility," which is defined as follows:

1. Real or personal property that is likely to help prevent, reduce, abate, or control noise, air, or water pollution or contamination by removing, altering, disposing, or storing pollutants, contaminants, wastes, or heat.
2. Real or personal property that will be used for the collection, storage, treatment, utilization, processing, or final disposal of solid or liquid waste.

3. Any related recycling property when a local, state, or federal environmental regulatory agency says it will be useful for pollution control.

What Is the Application Procedure?

According to rules set down by the SBA in April 1990, the small business concern should review the contemplated financing with its participating commercial bank (the "qualified sponsor") and a knowledgeable financing underwriter (accountant) before starting the application process.

It is suggested that the sponsor contact SBA Pollution Control officials in Washington, D.C., and the Pollution Control Program Specialist of the regional SBA office prior to filling out an application. This will provide an opportunity to discuss and clarify the requirements of the program prior to actual filing. After all required information has been gathered, the application package should be submitted to the Washington, D.C., office for processing.

Application Requirements

Along with the normal application requirements, applicants must provide plans and/or specifications, as appropriate, for the pollution control facility, along with written, realistic cost estimates. They must also provide copies of any local, state, or federal environmental regulations that relate to the proposed facility.

What Are the SBA Guarantee Limits?

There are no statutory limits on the amount the SBA may guarantee for any one small business concern under this program. However, the SBA recognizes that there is substantial risk involved in guaranteeing 100 percent of these payments on long-term financing. For this and other reasons, a limit of $1 million per company has been established. This will be reduced by the amount owed by the borrower on any other loan made under the basic SBA 7(a) guaranteed lending program.

Financing of amounts above $200,000 has, thus far, proved to be most economical to small businesses.

What Does the SBA Guarantee Cost?

The guarantee fee is 3.5 percent of the aggregate amount guaranteed and is payable to SBA upon issuance of the guarantee. It is computed in the following manner:

Aggregate amount guaranteed (total of principal and interest
at maturity) − escrow (three month's payments) × 3.5%

Additionally, a processing and administrative fee is charged as follows:

$550 + ($30 × number of years of the guarantee)

Each application submitted to the SBA must be accompanied by $250 of the processing and administrative fee, which is not refundable. The remainder of the fees are payable upon the SBA's issuance of its guarantee.

Tax-exempt bond financing by nature necessitates substantial, additional up-front soft costs such as bond counsel fees, printing costs for the official statement and the bond, other attorney's fees, and application fees for both the SBA and the state's issuing authority. These costs add 0.5 percent to 1 percent to the total small business financing costs.

Interest Rates

Interest rate limits are the same as for the SBA's regular 7(a) loan program. Participating lenders may charge as much as 2.75 percentage points over the New York prime lending rate.

Additional Information

For additional information and details, contact:

> U.S. Small Business Administration
> Pollution Control Financing Staff
> 1441 L Street, N.W., Room 808
> Washington, DC 20416
> (202) 653-2548 and/or (202) 205-6600

The SBA Answer Desk at (800) 827-5722 can give you the location and telephone number of your regional SBA office.

Assistance to Veterans

The SBA makes special efforts to help veterans get into business and expand existing veteran-owned small firms. Acting on its own or with the help of veterans' organizations, it sponsors special business training workshops for veterans. In some areas of the country, the SBA sponsors special computer-based training and long-term entrepreneurial programs for veterans. Each SBA office has a veterans' affairs specialist, or veterans' advocate, to provide veterans with special consideration for loans, training, and/or procurement.

Assistance to Women and Minorities—8(a)

The 8(a) Business Development Program helps disadvantaged small businesses obtain federal government contracts. Under the program, the SBA acts as a prime contractor and enters into all types of federal government contracts (including but not limited to supplies, services, construction, and research and development) with other government departments and agencies. The SBA then subcontracts the performance of that contract to small businesses participating in the 8(a) program.

To be eligible for the 8(a) program, firms must demonstrate that they are at least 51 percent owned and managed by one or more individuals who are U.S. citizens and who are determined to be socially and economically disadvantaged. The firm must also have been in business for at least two full years. Please note that 8(a) is not a certification program; it's a business development program.

Since 1977 SBA has had an ongoing women's business ownership program. In 1983, under the 8(a) program, the SBA began organizing an additional series of business training seminars and workshops for women already running a firm as well as those wanting to do so that focuses on business planning and development. A woman-owned business is defined by the SBA as a "business that is at least 51 percent owned by a woman, or women, who also control and operate it."

Business Development Programs

These programs are extensive and diversified. They include individual counseling, courses, conferences, and workshops and offer a wide range of publications. Counseling and training are limited to small businesses encountering difficulties, people considering starting a business, and managers of successful firms who wish to review their objectives and long-range plans for expansion.

Counseling is provided through the Service Corps of Retired Executives (SCORE), small business institutes (SBIs), small business development centers (SBDCs), and numerous professional associations. Realizing the importance of counseling, the SBA strives to match the needs of each business with the expertise available.

SCORE is a 13,000-person volunteer program with over 750 locations that helps small businesses solve their operating problems through one-on-one counseling and a well-developed system of workshops and training sessions. Retired executives volunteer their time to counsel small business owners and managers on pertinent issues ranging from writing a business plan to developing export markets. SCORE counseling is available at no charge. Another arm of SCORE is the Active Corps of Executives (ACE), which is staffed by actively employed businesspeople. To locate the SCORE/ACE chapter in your area, check your telephone directory or call the nearest SBA office.

SCORE also sponsors or cosponsors many training events including conferences on finance, exporting, and issues relevant to women and minorities in business.

SCORE puts on monthly prebusiness workshops that are designed to cover issues basic to starting a small business, including business plans, financing, marketing and advertising, cash management, and business insurance and law. It is recommended that prospective entrepreneurs attend one of these before making a counseling appointment.

Small Business Innovation Research Program (SBIR)

This program came into existence with the enactment of the Small Business Innovation Development Act of 1982. Under SBIR, agencies of the federal government with the largest research and development budgets are mandated to set aside funds each year for the competitive award (grant) of SBIR monies to qualified high-technology small businesses.

The SBA was designated by this legislation as the federal agency having unilateral authority and responsibility for coordinating and monitoring the government-wide activities of the SBIR program, and it reports on its actions annually to Congress. In line with this responsibility, it also publishes the *SBIR Pre-Solicitation Announcement (PSA)* quarterly, which contains pertinent information about the program and specific data on upcoming SBIR solicitations.

These grants are available, but they are not easy to obtain. If you plan to be the one out of ten whose proposal is accepted, you will have to demonstrate a level of planning, preparation, and presentation that surpasses your competition. The best way to do that is to hire a grant consultant, someone who already knows the right answers to the questions.

The most-qualified prospects for government grants are those who can build a case for researching the potential for new products, new technologies, new processes, and so on. Such high-risk research and development projects find private sector funding difficult, if not impossible, to obtain due to the expense, the typically long-term payoff, and the uncertainty of success. Because of American businesses' reluctance to commit to long-term R&D, this program plays a major role in helping the United States maintain a technological advantage over other countries.

The Small Business Innovation Research program is divided into three phases. Phase I consists entirely of individual grants up to $50,000 to study the feasibility of or to perform theoretical research and development of product design and modeling for projects with significant interest to the U.S. government. These studies may last up to six months. After completing the feasibility study, the applicant may submit a bid for funding under Phase II, designed to assist companies in developing product prototypes to production status. Most companies engaging in Phase II need to acquire small quantities of production and testing equipment. Funding in the form of grants, awards, and low-cost loans during this period can be used for the acquisition of this equipment as well as to supply working capital needs.

Both Phase I and Phase II require competitive bidding. Funding may take the form of outright grants, or it may involve actual contracts to develop a specific product. Small businesses applying for this assistance must be over 50 percent U.S. owned and operated. Furthermore, the project must provide the primary employment for the individual making application. (Primary employment is defined as over 50 percent of a person's time and income.)

Phase II provides financing of up to $500,000 for the further development of the most promising projects from Phase I. Successful completion of Phase II leads to the opportunity to enter Phase III.

Phase III covers the commercialization of the product. This may involve the acquisition of a production facility and equipment, implementing a marketing organization, and advertising or sales promotion programs. Phase III does not provide direct funding from the government. However, once a company achieves success through Phases I and II, the appropriate governmental agency stands ready to lend a hand in sourcing private capital for production uses from a bank or some other financial institution. Such backing goes a long way toward assuring immediate and serious attention to a company's loan application. Quite often, knowing that a government agency is backing an applicant causes financial institutions to offer lower interest rates, demand less outside collateral, and grant longer payment terms than if the small business had applied by itself.

There is no obligation to sell the finished products financed by Phase III to the government. They can be—and most are—sold in the private sector. Identification of the ultimate customer of production-run products has no bearing on getting assistance from the government for equipment financing.

The SBIR program is a set-aside allocation of funds by 11 federal departments. These allocations are to be used for grants and initial contracts with entrepreneurs to develop new products and services and then bring these innovations to market. The application process involves the submission of competitive bids to one or more of these 11 departments and agencies, each of which publishes annual listings of proposed topics. These topics cover very real needs of the department or agency and reflect requirements for products or services that cannot be developed internally.

A great deal of departmental independence exists in determining which topics to solicit. Congress allocates R&D funds to each of the departments and agencies, and the appropriate officials then decide how to spend these funds and when to grant the awards. It doesn't take long to determine that some agencies are easier to work with than others. The applicant has the right to choose the department or agency to which the bid is to be submitted. Several may list the same topic, in which case simultaneous bids may be submitted.

The SBA can tell you which SBIR projects will be included in forthcoming bid lists. They are published in "pre-solicitation" lists, available on request from:

Office of Innovation Research and Technology
U.S. Small Business Administration
1441 L Street, NW, Rm 500
Washington, DC 20416
(202)205-6600

After choosing the topic (or topics), contact the appropriate department or agency directly to receive solicitations as soon as they are released.

The content of bid packages (limited to no more than 30 pages) follows the same format as financing plans used for private financial institutions, with slight modifications. One exception requires applicants to provide a narrative describing the importance of the product being developed. Be sure to include persuasive material explaining why and how the product's application frequently provides the edge in competitive evaluation.

Successfully meeting all the terms and conditions of the development contract enables the developer to retain ownership of the technology. A product with commercial value may be marketed in the private sector rather than to the government. There is no obligation to enter into extended government contracts.

As with raising capital from any source, relationships are important. Because many companies are submitting bid proposals, yours can easily be overlooked. Two relationships prevent this from happening. First, get the support of your congressional representative or senator. Others use this method; you might as well, too. Second, employ a professional advisor to help with the preparation of the bid package. Be sure the advisor is well known in the specific department or agency to which you apply. To be of real assistance, the advisor must have concrete experience submitting SBIR bids.

Employees of state organizations that work with the SBIR provide excellent advisory assistance. They can help you select the most favorable departments and agencies as well as the most desirable topics. Their contacts in the Washington bureaucracy provide a means for arranging confidential evaluations of your project before submitting the bid. They can also point the way toward professors in local universities whose stamp of approval on your bid will give it an air of legitimacy.

In addition to providing assistance in the preparation of bid packages, many states and some cities provide direct financial assistance for small business research and development projects. These local agencies do not compete with the SBIR but are complementary to the program; they finance companies not otherwise qualified to receive federal funds. Your state small business development agency can identify what is available in your locale. If you can't locate the phone number, ask your local chamber of commerce for it.

SBIR funding is not available to every company. To gain entrance to the program, companies must submit bids to government agencies for products that have been listed by those agencies as needed. There is no assurance of winning the bidding competition. To participate in Phase II funding, a company must first enter—and win—the competition for an award under Phase I. A second roadblock is that the products resulting from research efforts must have a practical and needed use in the specific government department or agency sponsoring them. This eliminates a great many products developed every year with commercial value.

Continued annual funding by Congress ensures that money is available to successful bidders. Clearly, if a company is developing prototypes for a product and if it fits government applications, SBIR money can be a cheap, effective way to acquire first-stage financing for at least some production and testing equipment.

For complete information on this program, refer to my book *Funding Research & Development* (Chicago: Probus Publishing Co., 1990). You may also contact:

Office of Innovation Research and Technology
U.S. Small Business Administration
1441 L Street, NW
Washington, DC 20416
(202) 205-6600

Or you may contact these agencies directly. They all participate and have SBIR grants to award. (Note: The phone numbers for these agencies change frequently. Call directory assistance if the number given does not respond properly.):

Department of Agriculture	(202) 720-2791
Department of Commerce	(202) 482-2000
Department of Defense	(703) 545-6700
Department of Education	(202) 708-5366
Department of Energy	(301) 903-5867
Department of Health and Human Services	(301) 496-1968
Department of Transportation	(617) 494-2051
Environmental Protection Agency	(919) 541-3113
National Aeronautics and Space Administration	(202) 358-0000
National Science Foundation	(202) 357-9859
Nuclear Regulatory Commission	(301) 492-4297

Certified Lenders Program

An increasing number of lenders throughout the country serve the SBA's Certified Lenders Program. Acting under SBA supervision, they review a client's financial information and process much of the necessary paperwork. This speeds up the loan process and frees SBA personnel for other small business assistance programs.

A very select group of lenders participates in the Preferred Lenders Program. They handle all of the paperwork, processing, and servicing and are authorized by SBA to act in its behalf in the loan approval process. Although any lender can work with the SBA, you may wish to contact a Certified or Preferred institution directly. All of them understand small business problems, offer a variety of excellent banking services, and do make loans without SBA participation.

SBA Certified Development Companies (502 Program)

Development loans are made to organizations approved by the SBA for the purpose of encouraging economic growth through job creation and retention. Loan proceeds are used by the development companies to assist small business enterprises with plant acquisitions, construction, conversion, or expansion, including the purchase of machinery and equipment.

The 502 Loan Program provides guarantees on loans up to $750,000 and terms up to 25 years. These loans carry a maximum SBA guarantee of 90 percent (depending on the actual loan amount) to participating lending institutions.

The 502 program is specifically designed to help small businesses acquire hard assets, equipment, and facilities. Financing through this program requires the cooperation of the SBA, a commercial bond, and a local development company (LDC). Local development companies are business development organizations formed by municipal governments and private businesses to improve the local economy in a specific area.

The LDC actually borrows the funds from a local bank under a guarantee from the SBA. A small business doesn't take title to the item(s) it acquires under this program; rather, the LDC lays out the funds and then leases the item(s) to the small business under a lease-purchase plan. The SBA guarantees 90 percent of loans up to a maximum of $750,000. The loan period extends to 25 years, with the standard SBA interest caps—2.25 to 2.75 percentage points over prime. Because a bank must participate, the borrower must locate one that is willing to amortize its share of the loan over the same period.

Contact the nearest LDC that serves your county or community for complete information about its business services and loan programs.

Section 504 Certified Development Company (CDC) Program

The 504 Loan Program links the SBA, a certified development company, and a private lender in a 10- to 20-year financial package. The 504 program was updated and finalized in 1989. Although similar to the 502 program, the 504 program provides assistance for projects costing well above $1 million, most of which involve the acquisition of land, buildings, machinery, and equipment or construction, modernizing, renovating, or restoring existing facilities.

A 504 certified development company is a private, public sector nonprofit corporation that is set up to contribute to the economic development of its community or region. It must:

1. Operate in a defined area.
2. Be composed of 25 or more members who are geographically representative of the CDC's area of operation and include representatives from government agencies in the area of operation, private sector lending institutions, businesses, and community organizations.
3. Provide a full-time professional staff who can market the program and process, close, and service its loan portfolio.
4. Have the ability to sustain its operations on a continuous basis from reliable sources of funds.
5. Have five or more directors who meet quarterly, at least one of whom must have commercial lending experience.
6. Have incorporated within its bylaws and articles that its chief purpose is to "promote and assist the growth and development of business concerns in its operation area."

A CDC is responsible for assisting at least two small businesses a year, injecting 10 percent of the funds necessary to complete each project, and ensuring that the debentures are correctly closed and secured. (Debentures, pooled through a certificate mechanism, are sold publicly to investors [e.g., pension funds, insurance companies, or private individuals]). It must maintain a place of business that is open to the public during business hours and listed under a separate phone number. The CDC is also responsible for submitting an annual report containing financial statements, management information, a full activity report, and an analysis of its assistance to small businesses.

How does a CDC work? CDCs can sell completely SBA-guaranteed debentures to private investors in amounts up to 40 percent of a project or $750,000, whichever is less (in some cases, the maximum SBA portion may be $1 million). In addition, a CDC's portfolio must create or retain one job for every $35,000 worth of debenture financing.

Debenture proceeds must be used for permanent financing. Interim financing may be required to bridge the gap between the loan approval date and receipt of funding from the debentures.

A typical finance structure for a CDC project would include a first mortgage from a private sector lender covering 50 percent of the cost, a second mortgage from the CDC (a 100 percent SBA-guaranteed debenture) covering 40 percent, and a contribution of at least 10 percent by either the CDC or the small business being helped.

The CDC program assists in the development and expansion of small firms and the creation of jobs. This program is designed to provide fixed-asset financing to small businesses for the construction or rehabilitation of owner-occupied or leased premises.

Loan proceeds may be used for plant acquisition, construction, conversion, or expansion; for the rehabilitation of commercial structures; and for the purchase and installation of machinery and equipment with a useful life of ten years or more. In addition, certain soft costs can be paid with loan proceeds, including interim interest costs and professional fees for items such as appraisals, surveying, accounting, engineering, and architectural services.

Although the total size of projects using CDC financing is unlimited, the maximum amount of CDC participation in any individual project is $750,000 (or $1 million for some projects). Typical projects range in size from $500,000 to $2 million; the average is about $1 million. The minimum amount of CDC participation is $50,000, although a $25,000 debenture may be approved in special cases. Proceeds may be used to purchase existing buildings or to purchase land and land improvements such as:

- Grading, street improvements, utilities, parking lots, and landscaping.
- Construction.
- Modernizing, renovating, or converting existing facilities.
- Purchasing machinery and equipment.
- Financing a construction contingency fund; this cannot exceed 10 percent of total construction costs.
- Paying interest on interim financing.
- Paying professional fees directly attributable to the project, such as surveying, engineering, architectural, appraisal, legal, and accounting fees.

Interest rates are based on the current market rate for 5- and 10-year

U.S. Treasury issues plus an increment above the Treasury rate based on market conditions. Machinery and equipment terms are 10 years, and real estate terms are 20 years. Repayment is made in monthly, level-debt installments.

Collateral may include a mortgage on the land and the building being financed; liens on machinery, equipment, and fixtures; and lease assignments. Private sector lenders are secured by a first lien on the project. The SBA is secured by a second lien.

The SBA also requires personal guarantees from all persons who own 20 percent or more of a company that is financed by a CDC.

SBA regulations specify limits on fees that must be paid in connection with SBA funding. The development company fee cannot exceed the 1.5 percent processing fee on the SBA's debenture and a monthly service fee of not less than 0.5 percent or more than 2 percent per annum on the unpaid debenture balance. Development company legal fees related to loan closing cannot exceed $2,500 without prior approval by the SBA.

A funding fee of 0.25 percent to cover the cost of public issuance of securities and a reserve deposit of 0.5 percent are required, as is an underwriting fee of 0.625 percent of the total debenture amount.

Eligibility for a CDC loan requires that a business be a for-profit organization, partnership, or proprietorship with a net worth not to exceed $6 million and net profits (after taxes) averaging less than $2 million during the previous two years. Ineligible applicants are the same as described for a regular SBA loan. Due to the number of lenders involved and other requirements, the average size of any project is usually above $250,000 and would not normally exceed $1.25 million.

CDC investment funds cannot be used for working capital or inventory, consolidating or repaying debt, refinancing, or financing a plant not located in the U.S. or its possessions.

With radical changes currently transpiring in the banking industry and the continuing emphasis on bank liquidity, locating a bank willing to participate in SBA-guaranteed funding can be a chore. If one can be found, however, SBA-guaranteed long-term debt is an excellent way to keep debt service payments to a minimum.

The SBA portion of the financing consists of a debenture—a type of bond. Each debenture is issued in connection with the making of a loan or leasing of assets by a CDC to an SBC (small business concern). Each loan must be approved by the SBA with a "full faith and credit guaranty" issued by the U.S. Treasury. If an SBC defaults, the SBA is responsible for timely payment of the debenture to the investors.

All debentures guaranteed under the 504 program must be secured to ensure repayment. Collateral may include a mortgage on the land and the building being financed; liens on machinery, equipment, and fixtures; lease assignments; and personal guarantees from individuals with at least 20 percent ownership in the company. The third-party financier has the security of a first lien on the land and the building being financed, as well as other collateral involved. The SBA is secured by a second lien. The CDC (or SBC) holds the most junior position in the project. This explains why mortgage banks like to participate in 504 programs—even though they only lend 50 percent of the project cost, they get the senior position on all the collateral. The SBA settles for a second.

Loan repayment begins on the first day of the month following funding. Only a completed project can ensure the SBC of the operation capacity needed to make payments, so interim financing is needed for all projects. The interim financier (frequently the first mortgage lender) provides the needed capital ("bridge" financing) at the project's start and is repaid from debenture proceeds.

If financing is not available from nonfederal sources on reasonable terms, an SBC must meet the following criteria to qualify for 504 assistance:

1. It must be small. A business is considered small if it has 500 or fewer employees; for purposes of 504 financing, certain manufacturing companies may have more than 500 employees based on SBA size standard regulations contained in the Federal Code of Regulations, Business Credit and Assistance Section.
2. Its net worth must not exceed $6 million, and its average net income after taxes for the preceding two years must not exceed $2 million.
3. It must be a for-profit corporation, partnership, or proprietorship.
4. It must have a sound business purpose.
5. Its project must demonstrate a significant economic impact on the community in which it is located, primarily through job creation or retention.

The following types of businesses are ineligible for 504 financing: nonprofit organizations; investment companies; gambling facilities; lending institutions such as banks or financing companies; and media such as newspapers, magazines, book publishers, radio, and television systems.

Small business concerns should make appointments with loan officers from a bank and a CDC. The following documents should be prepared for any initial meeting:

1. A description of the project.
2. An estimate of the total project costs, including estimates on new construction, renovation, machinery, or equipment.
3. A purchase agreement or an offer to purchase for any real estate involved in the project.
4. Product description and product literature. An SBC should be prepared to discuss its competition, the strengths and weaknesses of the product, its method of distribution, the type of marketing it uses, future plans, and management.
5. Financial statements of the company for the past three years and an interim statement (profit and loss statement) that is less than 90 days old.
6. Personal financial statements of all officers and stockholders with 20 percent or more ownership in the company.

Because of the high level of funding, this program is especially helpful for financing new facilities, although it can also be used for major equipment purchases. As you've already seen, several features make 504 funding significantly different from other SBA assistance. Here is a summary of the 504 program's features and requirements:

1. The borrower must contribute 10 percent of the cost of the project, a private sector lender (nonfederal) must contribute 50 percent, and an SBA-guaranteed CDC loans the remaining 40 percent.

    The SBA may guarantee up to 40 percent or $50,000 to $750,000 in the form of a debenture to any approved project (special circumstances may allow a $25,000 debenture). The SBA debenture combined with any other federal funds may not exceed 50 percent of the total financing for the project.

    A CDC or the small business concern (SBC) receiving the financial assistance is required to inject at least 10 percent of the total funds for any project. A CDC is an economic development entity created under the auspices of SBA to foster development in both urban and rural areas. Only CDCs may administer the 504 program.

    Third-party financiers (a bank or savings and loan institution, for example) must provide the remaining 50 percent of the 504 financial package.

2. To qualify for 504 assistance, the project must demonstrate a positive impact on the local economy. The normal standard necessary to meet this criterion is the creation of at least one new job for each $15,000 worth of debt secured by the SBA guarantee. The higher the job ratio, the greater the likelihood of getting the funding.

3. A Certified Development Company (CDC) must act as the agent for the loan. Many municipalities already have CDCs in existence. For those that don't, state CDCs will suffice. Local SBA offices know what the choices are in your area.

4. No 504 program funding may be used for working capital.

5. In order to enlist commercial banks, mortgage banks, and other private lenders, the program carries two separate interest rates. One rate applies to the loan from a private lender and is set at the lender's discretion. A second rate applies to the SBA-guaranteed portion; this rate fluctuates between 0.25 and 0.75 percent above U.S. Treasury bond rates of similar maturity.

6. The company's ability to generate cash flow to service the debt determines the primary criterion in placing this financing. Collateral consists of the building or other assets being acquired. In addition, personal guarantees and an insurance policy on the owner's life payable to the lending institutions are usually required. On the other hand, owners do not have to pledge all or even a major portion of their net worth if the project will have significant economic impact on the community.

Normally the CDC will guide the small business concerns through the process from start to finish. To locate the nearest CDC, contact your SBA field office.

SBA Surety Bonds

Through its Surety Bond Guarantee Program, the SBA can help to make the bonding process accessible to small and emerging contractors who find bonding unavailable to them. It is authorized to guarantee to a qualified surety company up to 90 percent of the losses incurred under a prospective bid as well as payment of performance bonds issued to contractors on contracts valued up to $1.25 million. The contracts may be for construction, supplies, manufacturing, or services provided by either a prime or subcontractor for government or nongovernment work. This program is administered through the ten regional offices of the SBA in conjunction with the participating surety companies and their agents throughout the United States.

Small Business Investment Companies (SBICs and MESBICs)

Money for venture or risk investments is difficult for small businesses to obtain, but the SBA also licenses, regulates, and provides financial assistance to privately owned and operated small business investment companies (SBICs). Their main function is to make venture and risk investments by supplying equity capital and providing unsecured loans and loans not fully collateralized to small enterprises that meet their individual investment criteria. SBICs are privately owned but obtain their financial leverage from the SBA. They are intended to be profit-making corporations, so many SBICs will not make loans or investments under $100,000.

SBICs finance small firms in two general ways: either by straight loans or by equity-type investments, which give the SBIC actual or potential ownership of a portion of a small business's equity securities (shares of stock). Many SBICs provide management assistance to the companies they finance. The SBA also licenses a specialized type of SBIC solely to help small businesses owned and operated by socially or economically disadvantaged persons: the Section 310(d) SBIC, formerly referred to as a MESBIC, or minority enterprise small business investment company (also known as a special small business investment company, or SSBIC). As a general rule, companies are eligible if they have a net worth under $6 million and after-tax earnings of less than $2 million annually during the past two years.

When preparing a report on a new or existing business, be sure to include complete information about its operations, financial condition, key personnel, products, proposed new products or services, patent positions, market data, competitive position, distribution and sales methods, and financial projections.

Ideally, a complete business plan can speed up the process. There are no specific guidelines regarding the length of time it takes an SBIC/MESBIC to investigate and close a transaction. Usually, an initial response, either positive or negative, is made quickly. On the other hand, the thorough study that is required before making a final decision can take several weeks.

Generally speaking, SBICs are interested in generating capital gains, so they may want to purchase stock in a company or advance funds through a note or debenture with conversion privileges or rights to buy stock at a predetermined later date. Furthermore, SBICs often work together in making loans or investments in amounts larger than any of them could make separately. No SBIC should be ruled out as a possible source of financing whether you are searching for a loan or equity investment to begin or expand a business.

State and Community Loan Programs

In addition to the SBA's certified development companies or 504 Loan Programs described earlier, many states and communities offer loan and business services of which entrepreneurs and small business owners are not aware. The names of these programs vary from state to state, but they frequently include the word *development* to describe their services—for example, Small Business Development, Community Development, Economical Development, Rural Development, Research Development, and Capital Development. To help small businesses with finance, production, marketing, distribution, and technical problems, many offer loans and/or professional services that are often free or available at modest cost.

MICROLOAN PROGRAM

In 1992, the SBA unveiled a "microloan" program designed to assist very small businesses, especially those run by women, minorities, and low-income entrepreneurs who often have serious trouble raising capital. In some cases, a good reputation in the community is the only collateral required.

The Bush administration started this one-year pilot program to help people such as single mothers and public housing tenants toward self-employment. It was the first SBA program specifically designed to help the poor become business owners. Under this program, loans range from less than $100 to a maximum of $25,000, averaging about $10,000, and it also offers clients technical help and counseling.

The SBA has made funds available to nonprofit organizations for the purpose of lending to small businesses like yours. For example, a Los Angeles nonprofit agency, the Coalition for Women's Economic Development, received a $750,000 SBA loan from which it makes microloans. These organizations can also provide you with management and technical assistance.

Loans under this pilot program started flowing in July 1992. Then SBA Administrator Patricia Saiki said at the time, "I hope this program will give an opportunity to the small cottage industry . . . [to] people who haven't had a chance before. Home-based sole proprietorships, including 'homemakers who want to start something in the basement,' are a target of the microloan program."

The microloan idea is now one of several domestic initiatives aimed at empowering the poor. The SBA experiment is modeled after several seed-loan programs run by nonprofit groups in recent years that have helped start businesses or fund ongoing "mom-and-pop" operations.

Microloans are offered as part of the SBA's direct-loan program, which offers direct loans at slightly below-market rates to military veterans, disabled business owners, and those who want to start companies in economically depressed areas. Funds for such programs currently total $17 million annually and may be increased.

The program was introduced in a limited number of cities in the Northeast to test its feasibility. News of the plan came as a surprise to some of those involved with existing non-SBA programs, such as Women's Economic Development Corp. (Wedco) of St. Paul, Minnesota. This micro-enterprise loan organization, founded by Ms. Kathryn Keeley, has offered self-employment loans for eight years, helped start over 900 businesses (of which 87 percent are still in operation), and served as one of the SBA's program models.

Another such program is operating in North Carolina. Scot Sanderson of Marshall built his ABC Recycling Service, Inc., into a $180,000-a-year company after starting with a $2,500 micro-enterprise loan from the North Carolina Rural Economic Development Center, which is administered by Mr. Chris Just. In business for about two years, the concern has doubled in size every six months and at last report had four employees and is handling 30 different classes of materials.

Although the money attracts people to the program—most banks don't consider very small loans worth the paperwork—the biggest gain is reported to be the exchange of ideas with other business owners in the peer group established as part of the program. This group becomes a brain trust and a sounding board that multiplies members' capabilities four or five times. Everybody knows the statistics for small-business failure, but participants in this program are certain that if programs like it were to be established on a larger scale, the statistics would be reversed: Most would succeed rather than fail.

Some other veterans of enterprise programs for low-income people express caution. They warn that without substantial counseling and guidance, this SBA direct-loan program will not succeed.

This SBA program includes a demanding training and counseling process for applicants before they get a loan. Directors of the microloan programs that have served as models for the SBA effort claim their programs are both tough and successful.

The North Carolina program began in the fall of 1989 and has made 57 loans. It has a 90 percent repayment rate so far. Modeled in part after a peer-group lending program used by the Grameen Bank of Bangladesh, the program forms teams of five people with a shared interest in starting or developing their own businesses. The group chooses two of its members to receive the first loans, and no one else in that particular group can get a loan until the original recipients have made four consecutive payments. The loan amounts range from about $500 to $8,000 at market interest rates but are made without collateral. Peer pressure and support from other members of the group are supposed to keep the payments coming. The program operates statewide, using local community organizations to provide business counseling services and a nonprofit credit union to handle the paperwork on the loans. This program was started to reach small rural businesses that couldn't even qualify for credit union financing.

The $17 million SBA microloan program operates in 35 cities and towns. (The SBA and Congress have established this as a size limit for the program; see the list on page 47.) In each of these cities and towns, a nonprofit agency, chosen because of its familiarity with the local business scene, decides who qualifies for the SBA money and sets the terms of the loans. The maximum loan is $25,000, and the maximum term is six years. The negotiated interest rate can't exceed four percentage points over the prime lending rate charged by commercial banks. Asset collateral is required for larger loans. But for a loan in the $600-to-$700 range, the lending requirement could be a character reference.

The 35 nonprofit agencies from urban and rural areas use their own judgment about who gets the loan funds and for what purposes, although Congress requires that half the loans be made to small businesses in rural areas. The SBA stresses that the funds are not grants. The nonprofit agencies are expected to eventually repay these funds to the federal treasury, with interest.

The microloan program is a risk venture to which the SBA has committed itself. The end result cannot be predicted, because the nonprofit agencies are the ones who will make it work or not.

Politics appeared to play a part in how the funds were distributed during the feasibility test period. A total of $3 million of the loan fund was earmarked for agencies in the four states represented by the chair and ranking minority members of the House and Senate Small Business Committees.

The Arkansas Enterprise Group in Arkadelphia received the maximum $750,000 to relend. Senator Dale Bumpers (D=Ark.) heads the Senate's small business panel.

Eligibility Requirements

Practically all types of businesses are eligible for a microloan. To be eligible, your business must be operated for profit and fall within six standards set by the SBA (most businesses are well within the standards).

Use of Funds

Money borrowed under this program can be used for the purchase of machinery and equipment, furniture and fixtures, inventory, supplies, and working capital. You may not use it to pay existing debts.

Terms of Loan

A microloan must be paid on the shortest term possible—no longer than six years—depending on the earnings of the business. The interest rate on these loans cannot be higher than 4 percent over the New York prime rate.

Credit Requirements

As a loan applicant, you must demonstrate good character and management expertise and commitment sufficient for a successful operation.

Collateral Requirements

Each nonprofit lending organization will have its own requirements about collateral. However, the organization must at least take as collateral any assets that are bought with the microloan. In most cases, the personal guarantees of the business owner(s) will also be required.

Applying for a Microloan

The first step in applying for a microloan is to call or visit the local SBA office and find out if your company meets the qualifications. The people there will explain what information you must supply and how to apply.

Remember that this program is primarily designed to assist women, low-income, and minority entrepreneurs, business owners, and others who show they can operate small businesses successfully. Most likely to benefit are new and existing part-time and home-based sole proprietorships.

The SBA provides the funds to the 35 preselected nonprofit agencies because of their familiarity with the local business communities. These agencies decide who receives microloans and set the loan terms. The agencies are expected to repay the SBA for the funds with interest within 10 years. The following is a list of the nonprofit agencies and the total amounts of funds available from them:

Albuquerque, New Mexico: Women's Economic Self-Sufficiency Team, $80,000.

Anchorage, Alaska: Community Enterprise Development of Alaska, $200,000.

Arcata, California: Arcata Economic Development Corp., $200,000.

Arkadelphia, Arkansas: The Arkansas Enterprise Group, $750,000.

Athens, Ohio: Athens Small Business Center, Inc., $250,000.

Baltimore, Maryland: Council for Equal Business Opportunity, $345,000.

Bozeman, Montana: Capital Opportunities, $60,000.

Charleston, South Carolina: The Charleston Citywide Local Development Corp., $300,000.

Chicago, Illinois: The Neighborhood Institute & Women's Self-Employment Project, $750,000.

Dallas, Texas: Southern Dallas Development Corp., $750,000.

Denver, Colorado: Greater Denver Local Development Corp., $250,000.

Durham, North Carolina: Self-Help Ventures Fund, $500,000.

Fond du Lac, Wisconsin: Advocap, Inc., $100,000.

Greenfield, Massachusetts: The Western Massachusetts Enterprise Fund, $125,000.

Greenville, Mississippi: Delta Foundation, $500,000.

Hayden, Idaho: Panhandle Area Council, $200,000.

Indianapolis, Indiana: Eastside Community Investments, Inc., $175,000.

London, Kentucky: Kentucky Highlands Investment Corp., $750,000.

Los Angeles, California: Coalition for Women's Economic Development, $750,000.

Manchester, New Hampshire: Institute for Cooperative Community Development, Inc., $500,000.

Milwaukee, Wisconsin: Women's Business Initiative Corp., $750,000.

Pensacola, Florida: Community Equity Investments, Inc., $500,000.

Phoenix, Arizona: Chicanos Por La Causa, Inc., $300,000.

Providence, Rhode Island: Elmwood Neighborhood Housing Services, $150,000.

Rochester, New York: Rural Opportunities Inc., $400,000.

Saranac Lake, New York: Adirondack Economic Development Corp., $500,000.

Savannah, Georgia: Small Business Assistance Corp., $175,000.

Sioux City, Iowa: Siouxland Economic Development Corp., $200,000.

Sisseton, South Dakota: Northeast South Dakota Energy Conservation Corp., $120,000.

St. Johnsbury, Vermont: Northern Community Investment Corp., $375,000.

St. Paul, Minnesota: Women Venture, $500,000.

Sterling, Illinois: Greater Sterling Development Corp., $150,000.

Virginia, Minnesota: Northeast Entrepreneur Fund, Inc., $200,000.

Walthill, Nebraska: Rural Enterprise Assistance Project, $80,000.

Wiscasset, Maine: Coastal Enterprises, Inc., $750,000.

Contact your nearest SBA office for a current list of participating agencies.

VETERANS FRANCHISE PROGRAM (VETFRAN)

The SBA and International Franchise Association are cosponsoring a program to reduce the capital that veterans need to buy a franchise. The Veterans' Transition Franchise Initiative, or VETFRAN, was officially launched on November 7, 1991, after three months of preliminary organization at a press conference at the National Press Club in Washington, D.C.

One of the first franchises under the program was awarded to Mr. Rooter Corp., which operates about 100 plumbing-service franchises in 27 states.

The franchisee, an Army veteran, put down only $5,000, instead of the usual $17,500, to purchase his first franchise.

Under the program, about 100 franchisers, including Beech Holdings Corporation's Budget Rent-a-Car Corporation; Barbizon International, Inc.; and Maids International, Inc., have agreed either to reduce the franchise fee they ask of potential franchisees or to finance as much as 50 percent of it. Aside from the public-relations value of VETFRAN, participants hope it will help them recruit franchisees.

The SBA has pledged to accelerate loan guarantee approvals to help VETFRAN applicants pay for the remainder of the franchise fee and equipment costs.

Publicity for the program put the franchise industry in the media spotlight across the country. Articles concerning VETFRAN have been featured in the *Wall Street Journal, Success* magazine, *USA Today, U.S. News & World Report, New York Times, Nation's Business, Good Housekeeping, American Legion, D.A.V. Magazine,* all the military periodicals, national television programs, and more than three dozen newspapers in 22 major cities across the nation.

This multimillion-dollar publicity campaign, spearheaded by the Hayes Group of Pennsylvania, has generated more than 1,000 veteran inquiries per month. A large number of these inquiries have been from enlisted personnel stationed at military bases that have been targeted for downsizing. Many of these people have received lump-sum financial compensation from the government and are looking to invest in second career opportunities. Dozens of inquiries have been received from professional people (doctors, dentists, and so on) who are veterans of earlier conflicts and want to leave their liability-intensive careers.

Since VETFRAN has become a reality, some of the banks and franchisors that had initially withheld their support are now joining the program. There are more than 125 franchisors and over 200 lending institutions participating in the program. Participating franchisors contribute $1,000 per year to help defray the $10,000 per month cost of administering VETFRAN's national network of 1,000 veterans' hotlines, its national publicity campaign, and its more than 3,000 newsletters.

VETFRAN is a cooperative effort of the public and private sectors: the International Franchise Association (IFA), a cosponsor of the program; the participating franchisors; and Worldwide Franchise Consultants, which is administering the program for Don Dwyer, founder and underwriter of the program.

Veterans are made aware of the program through the *VETFRAN Newsletter,* IFA franchise shows, veterans' organizations, job fairs, or the national media. Veterans must be able to meet all usual and customary qualifications of their selected franchisor prior to being accepted as a franchisee. An individual must show proof of veteran's status (for example, DD 214) and must have been discharged other than dishonorably.

Veterans can obtain the *VETFRAN Newsletter,* which includes a fact sheet and an updated list of participating franchisors, their telephone numbers, and the contact people, by sending a stamped, self-addressed business envelope and one dollar to:

VETFRAN
P.O. Box 3146
Waco, TX 76707

The primary contacts for developments in the program are:

Baxter Coffee and Patti Fornelius
VETFRAN
Administrators
P.O. Box 3146
Waco, TX 76707
(817) 753-4555

The purpose of the VETFRAN program is to introduce veterans to business opportunities in the franchise industry. The International Franchise Association (IFA) was motivated by President Bush's appeal to the American business community to provide more and better business opportunities for America's veterans. Don Dwyer, VETFRAN creator and founder, petitioned William Cherkasky, president of the International Franchise Association, for national support from the franchise community.

Franchisors across the nation rallied behind the program, and on August 14, 1991, after seven months of organization, the Veterans Transition Franchise Initiative was made a reality.

The IFA has asked participating franchisors to create a program of tangible benefits for veterans in the form of discounted franchise fees and/or by agreeing to finance a percentage of the franchise fee. Veterans must be able to meet all usual and customary qualifications of their selected franchisor prior to being accepted as a franchisee. These became the primary benefits of the VETFRAN program.

The Application Procedure

The VETFRAN program includes a wide range of franchise opportunities to choose from, and the list of "Participating Franchisors" should greatly increase in the future. The steps to take to participate in the program are as follows:

1. The veteran sends a self-addressed, stamped envelope and one dollar to VETFRAN, P.O. Box 3146, Waco, TX 76707.
2. The veteran contacts the franchisor of his or her choice; the franchisor mails the veteran an information packet about its particular franchise opportunity.
3. If the veteran wishes to pursue the franchise opportunity, the veteran will then be prequalified by the franchisor according to ability, credit history, personal financial statement, and so on.
4. The franchisor will counsel the veteran regarding the franchise industry as well as discuss the most appropriate vehicle to finance the franchise purchase—personal assets, friends or relatives, a conventional loan, or an SBA-guaranteed loan.
5. If a conventional bank loan or bank loan guaranteed by the SBA is re-

quired, the franchisor may direct the veteran to a lending institution or in some cases provide in-house financing. The lender may direct the veteran to a CPA or "loan packager" to assist him or her in completing the loan application, business plan, and other additional forms. Loan packagers charge from $250 to $1,500 to provide these services. Some franchisors have in-house loan packagers that can provide assistance.

6. If the loan requires an SBA guarantee, there will be an additional loan packet from the SBA that the lender will also give the veteran to fill out. The SBA and its associated resources (SCORE and SBDC) also can assist veterans in developing a business plan and loan application; however, neither the SBA, SCORE, nor the SBDCs can fill out SBA loan application forms for the veteran.

7. When the loan package is complete, the veteran takes the package to the bank. If the lender approves, the loan package goes to the SBA for approval; if they agree to guarantee it, the bank, not the SBA, will issue the check to the veteran. If the applicant is a Vietnam-era veteran or has a 30 percent or more compensable disability and if the veteran has been turned down by a bank for a commercial loan and the SBA for a guaranteed loan (for other than credit reasons), the veteran may take the loan application and the bank's written rejection (two written lender rejections are required in cities with populations over 200,000) to the SBA for a possible direct loan from the SBA. The SBA Direct Loan Progam is available to make direct loans (with ceilings of $150,000) to these two groups. Veterans with poor credit histories and little or no collateral will generally not be considered for loans by either the banks or the SBA under its guaranteed loan program.

8. The veteran can now complete negotiations with the franchisor and, if all pertinent items are in order, commence the venture.

As soon as you receive your package from VETFRAN, you may begin contacting the franchise of your choice. If there is a specific franchise you are interested in that does not appear on the list of participating franchisors, call VETFRAN at (817) 753-4555, and they will immediately contact the franchisor and make them aware of the program. If you belong to a veterans' group or organization, please feel free to have the group's officials contact VETFRAN so that they can be included on the VETFRAN mailing list.

All veterans are encouraged to seek out those franchisors who are displaying the VETFRAN logo in their promotional materials. As you attend job fairs and joint National Campground Owners' Association (NCOA)/ International Franchise Association exposition seminars, be sure to look for the VETFRAN logo being displayed in the participating franchisors' trade booths; this logo means that they support VETFRAN and are offering special discounts and/or financing arrangements for veterans.

PROCUREMENT ASSISTANCE PROGRAMS

The SBA helps small businesses obtain a fair share of federal government contracts through several programs, which include the following:

- **Procurement Automated Source System (PASS)** provides a nationwide computerized listing of small firms interested in federal contracts and subcontracting opportunities. PASS listings are available to purchasing officials at more than 300 government and industry locations.

- **Prime Contracts.** The SBA works closely with federal agencies to increase the dollars and percentage of total federal procurement awards to small business firms by identifying items that small firms could supply. (See the section on Public Law 95-507, page 53.)

- **Subcontracts.** SBA monitors prime contractors to ensure that small businesses receive a fair share of subcontracting opportunities.

- **Certificates of Competency.** To help small firms qualify for government contracts they might not otherwise receive, SBA may provide them with a certificate of competency, assuring the contracting agency of the firm's performance for a specific contract.

- **Natural Resources Sales Assistance.** This program helps small firms obtain property sales/leases for timber, royalty oil, minerals, and real and personal property.

Procurement Automated Source System (PASS)

PASS was designed to establish a centralized, computer-based inventory and referral system of small businesses interested in becoming prime or subcontractors for federal requirements. Using computers and remote video terminals, PASS furnishes sources by matching keywords that small firms have used to describe their capabilities. Listings for firms are also made available by using Standard Industrial Classification (SIC) Codes, Federal Supply Codes, or DUNS numbers. Sources may also be retrieved by geographic region. When procurement agencies or prime contractors request small business sources, the SBA can furnish the names and capabilities of those firms meeting the buyers' specifications. Also, a profile of the firm can be made available giving information as to minority status, quality assurance programs, and other useful information.

Since 1978, the system has grown to become an inventory of over 230,000 firms and is growing every day. The SBA is also expanding the number of terminals through which federal agencies and the private sector can obtain small business sources. If your firm provides goods or services purchased by the federal government and has not registered in PASS, you can obtain the simple one-page registration form from your nearest SBA office. It can be completed in a few minutes, and your firm will be profiled in the system within a few weeks from the day the completed form is received. PASS registration is not intended to guarantee contracting opportunities, but small firms registered with the system will have their capabilities available if requests are made by the federal procuring offices or purchasing agents of prime contractors. Small firms should never rely on PASS registration to replace their regular marketing and sales efforts but merely to augment them. Although increasing numbers of governmental agencies and commercial contractors use PASS, it is not a universal federal source list, and new business cannot be guaranteed.

Public Law 95-507

Many laws that apply to federal procurement have some special provisions about small business and disadvantaged or minority small business contracting. However, no law has had a more profound effect than Public Law 95-507. This law (enacted in October 1978) made major revisions to the Small Business Act. In summary, the law requires the following:

1. A strong and specific commitment to subcontracting with small and small disadvantaged businesses by large business prime contractors.
2. Detailed subcontracting plans for larger contracts. These plans may be accepted or rejected by the government contracting officer in a negotiated procurement and must be carried out forcefully in either a negotiated or sealed-bid procurement by the successful large business.
3. Monitoring of performance against the plan by the SBA and by the procuring activity's contracting officer.
4. Federal buying agencies are to establish an Office of Small and Disadvantaged Business Utilization to assist small businesses by expanding their contracting opportunities and by helping solve problems.
5. Annual goals for contracting with small and small disadvantaged businesses are to be set by federal agencies.

Certificate of Competency

The SBA's procurement assistance effort is greatly strengthened by the Certificate of Competency (COC) program. The SBA is authorized by Congress to certify as to a small company's "capability, competency, credit, integrity, perseverance and tenacity" to perform a specific government contract. If a contracting officer proposes to reject the offer of a small business firm that is a low offerer because he or she questions the firm's ability to perform the contract on any of the previously mentioned grounds, the case is referred to the SBA. SBA personnel then contact the company concerned to inform it of the impending decision and to offer an opportunity to apply to the SBA for a Certificate of Competency, which, if granted, would require awarding the contract to the firm in accordance with the Small Business Act. The SBA may also, at its discretion, issue a Certificate of Competency in connection with the sale of federal property if the responsibility (that is, the capability, competency, credit, integrity, perseverance, and tenacity) of the purchaser is questioned and for firms found ineligible by a contracting officer due to a provision of the Walsh-Healey Public Contracts Act that requires that a government contractor be either a manufacturer or a regular dealer.

The COC program is carried out by a specialized SBA field staff of individuals with technical, engineering, and government procurement backgrounds in cooperation with financial specialists who are also of the SBA field staff. On receipt of a COC application, the contracting officer of the purchasing agency is notified that the prospective contractor has applied, and a team of financial and technical personnel is sent to the firm to survey its potential. Although the SBA has access to the purchasing agency's pre-award survey, which served as the basis of the contracting officer's decision, the SBA conducts a completely new survey, which evaluates the characteristics of the applicant in terms of the needs of the specific acquisition in question. Credit ratings, past performance, management capabilities, management schedules, and the prospects for obtaining needed financial help or equipment are considered.

The team's findings are presented to a COC Review Committee composed of legal, technical, and financial representatives, which makes a detailed review of the case and recommends approval or disapproval. If the decision is negative, the firm and the purchasing agency are so informed; if affirmative, a letter certifying the responsibility of the firm to perform the contract (the Certificate of Competency) is sent to the purchasing agency. By terms of the Small Business Act, the COC is conclusive on questions of responsibility, and the contract must be awarded.

A COC is valid only for the specific contract for which it is issued. A business concern that is capable of handling one contract may not be qualified to handle another. Each case is considered separately, and each case is considered only if and after the contracting officer has made a negative determination of responsibility or eligibility. Firms may not apply for a COC until a contracting officer makes a non-responsibility determination and refers the matter to the SBA.

How to Get on Solicitation Mailing Lists

After determining which agencies procure the items or services a small firm can supply, the small business owner or manager should ask the appropriate agencies for the necessary forms to place the company's name on their solicitation mailing lists for specific items or services.

All published government specifications and standards for items or services purchased by military and civilian departments and agencies may be obtained from the following locations:

Federal specifications and standards and commercial item descriptions
Nearest Business Service Center of the General Services Administration
    or the Federal Specifications Distribution Center
Federal Supply Service, GSA
7th & D Streets, SW
Washington, DC 20407

Military Specifications
Commanding Officer
Naval Publications and Forms Center
5801 Tabor Avenue
Philadelphia, PA 19120

Copies of specifications and standards needed by business concerns for government bidding and contracting purposes are available without charge. However, there will be a charge for large quantities, complete libraries, and copies wanted by individuals or organizations not directly involved in government bidding or contracting.

Business concerns that are not certain what specification or standard is needed should contact the specific government agency contracting office that is requesting offers or that awarded the contract referencing the documents.

After the specifications have been studied and the firm believes it is capable of producing the item(s), it should request the buying agency to place its name on the appropriate list.

In answer to the firm's request, the purchasing office should send a Solicitation Mailing List Application, Form 128, to the requested firm. If the purchasing activity does not include a buying list or if the buying list does not include the exact products or services the firm can supply, a separate sheet should be attached to the completed form showing the following:

- The specific name of each product or service the firm offers.
- Additional items or services that the firm could provide the purchasing agency other than those already listed.
- Any item or service the firm has supplied in the past under government contracts.

Each product or service listed in the attached sheet should be fully described, and, if possible, should indicate the government specification number for each item.

When returning the completed form to the purchasing activity, a small firm should continue to seek other opportunities. The U.S. Government Purchasing and Sales Directory and the Commerce Business Daily are both useful in this regard.

Firms that receive invitations to bid or requests for proposals from a purchasing agency should either submit offers or notify the purchasing office that they are unable to offer on the particular item or service but wish to remain on the active list for future purchases of the specific product. Otherwise, they may be dropped from the list.

Natural Resources Sales Assistance Program

The federal government sells large quantities of many kinds of real and personal property, property surplus to federal needs (for example, military or NASA surplus), and resources authorized for sale in accordance with public law. The SBA cooperates with other federal agencies to channel a fair share of these properties and resources to small businesses. However, the SBA does not itself sell real or personal property, except property held as collateral for SBA loans foreclosed because of default.

The SBA's Natural Resources Sales Assistance Program is intended to ensure that small business concerns obtain a fair share of government property sales/leases to include, where necessary, small business set-aside and to provide aid, counsel, and other available assistance to small business concerns on all matters pertaining to government sales/leases.

The program is directed by SBA's central office staff and carried out by industrial specialists at key geographic locations throughout the United States.

Five categories of federal resources are covered by the program:

1. **Timber and related forest products.** Timber is regularly sold from the federal forests managed by the Forest Service, U.S. Department of Agriculture, and the Bureau of Land Management, U.S. Department of the Interior. On occasion, timber is sold from federal forests that are under the supervision of the Department of Defense, the Department of Energy, the Fish and Wildlife Service, and the Tennessee Valley Authority.

    The SBA and these agencies work together to ensure opportunities for small business concerns to bid on federal timber sales. In addition, the SBA and the sales agencies jointly set aside timber sales for bidding by small concerns when it appears that small businesses would not obtain their fair share under open sales.

2. **Strategic materials from the National Stockpile.** The General Services Administration regulates the procurement and disposal of strategic materials in accordance with statutory requirements. Whenever a stockpile requirement is lowered, any oversupply of the material may be sold.

    In those instances where small businesses may find it difficult to purchase their fair share because of the large quantities, the agencies may agree to divide materials into small parcels and/or set aside a reasonable amount for exclusive bidding by small businesses.

3. **Royalty Oil.** Royalties due the government under leases of federal oil rights for the exploration of oil may be accepted by the secretary of the interior in the form of oil or money. If the secretary elects to accept oil in lieu of money, the oil is identified as *royalty oil.*

    When the secretary of the interior determines that sufficient supplies of crude oil are not available in the open market to small business refineries, preference will be granted to these refineries for processing royalty oil.

    The SBA refers qualified small business refineries to the Minerals Management Service, U.S. Department of the Interior, to assist them in obtaining royalty oil.

4. **Leases involving rights to minerals, coal, oil, and gas.** The federal government is an extensive owner of mineral, oil, coal, and gas rights. Usually leases to recover these natural resources are competitively sold.

    The SBA and the sales agency may jointly set aside a reasonable amount of leases for bidding by small businesses when it appears that under open bidding they would not obtain their fair share.

5. **Surplus real and personal property.** The federal government disposes of property for which it has no foreseeable need. Such property is first made available for donation to recipients authorized by law, such as educational and public health facilities, state and local governments, and so on. The remainder is sold.

The two agencies of the government principally concerned with surplus personal property sales are the Department of Defense and the General

Services Administration. Scheduled sales are widely publicized and are normally competitive bid sales. The Department of Defense has a single contact point for any concern interested in purchasing its surplus personal property in the United States—the Defense Reutilization and Marketing Service, Federal Center, Battle Creek, MI 49017. GSA surplus personal property and federal real property sales are conducted through the GSA's regional headquarters.

How the Government Buys

Military and civilian purchasing activities, installations, or offices scattered throughout the country buy through two methods: sealed bidding and negotiation.

When soliciting for bids, a purchasing office normally sends bid invitations to firms listed on their solicitation mailing lists—or, if a given list is unduly long, the purchasing office may solicit segments of the total list. The solicitation mailing list is composed of business firms that have advised the buying office that they want to offer on particular solicitations and have supplied data showing their ability to fulfill contracts for the item, service, or project.

In some cases, the purchasing installation or office will want offers from additional firms not listed on its solicitation mailing list. These firms are usually located through public advertisements in the *Commerce Business Daily* (CBD), trade papers, notices in post offices, and by Small Business Administration representatives.

Invitations for Bids (IFBs) usually include a copy of the specifications for the particular proposed purchase; instructions for preparation of bids; and the conditions of purchase, delivery, and payment. The IFB also designates the date and time of bid opening. Each sealed bid is opened in public at the purchasing office at the time designated in the invitation. Facts about each bid are read aloud and recorded. A contract is then awarded to the low bidder whose bid conforms with all requirements of the invitation and will be advantageous to the government in terms of price and price-related factors included in the invitation.

When buying by negotiation, the government uses procedures that differ from sealed bidding. Buying by negotiation is authorized in certain circumstances by law under applicable federal acquisition regulations, or FAR. Often, negotiated contracts cover advanced technology not widely supplied by small businesses and may include very complex areas of research and development, projects connected with highly sophisticated systems, missile programs, aircraft, and weapons systems. However, negotiation procedures also may be applied to more or less standard items when negotiation authority has been properly documented by the contracting office. For example, items or services may be purchased by negotiation when it is impossible to draft adequate specifications or to describe fully the specific item, service, or project.

When purchasing by negotiation, the purchasing office also makes use of its solicitation mailing list for the particular item or service. It may also ask for detailed statements of estimated costs or other evidence of reasonable price. These Requests for Proposals (RFPs) are sent to a number of offerors so that the purchase may be made on a competitive basis.

Requests for Quotations (RFQs) may be used in negotiated procurements to communicate government requirements to prospective contractors. A quotation received in response to an RFQ is not an offer and cannot be accepted by the government to create a binding contract. An RFQ may be used when the government does not intend to award a contract on the basis of the solicitation but wishes to obtain price, terms of delivery, or other information for planning purposes.

After reviewing the various quotations received on the proposed purchase, the contracting officer may negotiate further with the firms that have submitted acceptable proposals to assure the contract most advantageous to the government.

ORGANIZATION OF SMALL BUSINESS INVESTMENT COMPANIES (SBICs)

Thirty-five years ago an entrepreneur looking for the capital to launch a small business had very few sources to which to turn. There was no institutional resource to back up promising but untried ideas. Again and again, businesses with great potential for innovation failed—or never got off the ground.

To help solve this problem, Congress created the Small Business Investment Company (SBIC) program in 1958. SBICs, licensed by the Small Business Administration, are privately organized and managed investment firms. They are participants in a vital partnership between government and the private sector economy. With their own capital and with funds borrowed at favorable rates through the federal government, SBICs provide venture capital to small independent businesses, both new and already established.

Virtually all SBICs are profit-motivated businesses. They provide equity capital, long-term loans, debt-equity investments, and management assistance to qualifying small businesses. Their incentive is the chance to share in the success of the small business as it grows and prospers.

Today there are two types of SBICs—the original, or "regular," SBICs and SSBICs—Specialized Small Business Investment Companies. SSBICs are specifically targeted toward the needs of entrepreneurs who have been denied the opportunity to own and operate a business because of social or economic disadvantage.

The name SSBIC is used to describe this type of SBIC; therefore, it is used in this book. However, this name is unofficial. The official name for such SBICs is Section 301(d) SBICs because they are organized under Section 301(d) of the Small Business Investment Act.

With few exceptions, the same rules and regulations apply to both regular SBICs and SSBICs. Therefore, the SBIC name is generally used to refer to both SSBICs and regular SBICs simultaneously.

The program makes funding available to all types of manufacturing and service industries. Many investment companies seek out small businesses with new products or services because of the strong growth potential of such firms. Some SBICs specialize in the field in which their management has special knowledge or competency. Most, however, consider a wide variety of investment opportunities.

Who Benefits from the SBIC Program?

Small businesses qualifying for assistance from the SBIC program are able to receive equity capital, long-term loans, and expert management assistance. Venture capitalists participating in the SBIC program can supplement their own private investment capital with funds borrowed at favorable rates through the federal government.

Most important, the U. S. taxpayer benefits. Tax revenue generated each year from successful SBIC investments more than covers the cost of the program.

The SBIC program also provides the taxpayer with more job opportunities. SBIC-financed small businesses are proven job creators.

The Program's Principal Advantages to the SBIC

An SBIC begins with people who have venture capital expertise and capital and who want to form a venture capital investment company. By law, an SBIC can be organized in any state as either a corporation or a limited partnership. Most SBICs are owned by relatively small groups of local investors. Many, however, are owned by commercial banks. Some SBICs are corporations with publicly traded stock, and some are subsidiaries of corporations. The SBA requires a minimum private capital investment of $2.5 million for an SBIC and $1.5 million for an SSBIC.

An SBIC or SSBIC in good standing, with a demonstrated need for funds, may receive leverage equal to 300 percent of its private capital. In addition, an SBIC with at least 65 percent (30 percent for SSBICs) of its total funds available for investment invested or committed in venture capital may receive an additional tier of leverage per dollar of private capital for total leverage of 400 percent of private capital. However, in no event may any SBIC or SSBIC draw down leverage in excess of $35 million.

To obtain leverage, regular SBICs issue their debentures, which are guaranteed by the SBA. Pools of these SBA-guaranteed debentures are formed, and SBA-guaranteed participation certificates, representing an undivided interest in the pools, are sold to investors through a public offering. Under current procedures, the debentures have a term of three or ten years and provide for semiannual interest payments and a lump-sum principal payment at maturity. The three-year debenture does not allow prepayment, and the ten-year debenture does not allow prepayment during the first five years. Thereafter, the debenture may be prepaid with a penalty. In either case, the rate of interest on the debenture is determined by market conditions at the time of the sale.

Like the SBICs, SSBICs may receive leverage equal to 400 percent of private capital, not to exceed $35 million. Unlike an SBIC, however, an

SSBIC qualifies for leverage equal to 100 percent of its private capital through the sale of its 4 percent, cumulative, preferred stock to SBA. The preferred stock provides for its mandatory redemption within 15 years. SSBICs may also sell a second tier of preferred stock to SBA if they have committed or invested a like amount of funds in qualified securities of small business concerns such as equity securities or unsecured, subordinated debt instruments.

SSBICs may also issue their debentures for inclusion in the aforementioned guaranteed debenture pools and public offerings of guaranteed participation certificates together with the regular SBICs. SSBIC debentures have a term of ten years and provide for semiannual interest payments and a lump-sum principal payment at maturity. There can be no prepayment during the first five years; prepayment thereafter would incur a penalty.

Although the rate of interest is determined by market conditions at the time of the sale, SSBICs receive an interest rate subsidy of three percentage points for the first five years of the ten-year term. To effect the subsidy, an SSBIC's reduced interest payments during the subsidy period are supplemented by interest payments made by SBA on behalf of the SSBIC.

Besides the opportunities for government leverage, all SBICs can benefit from a number of tax advantages. Tax counsel should be consulted regarding tax laws and regulations.

Advantage to Banks

Bank ownership in an SBIC subsidiary permits banks to invest in small businesses in which they could not have otherwise invested because of banking laws and regulations. A bank may invest up to 5 percent of its capital and surplus in a partially or wholly owned SBIC.

SBICs can obtain financing through a number of means: acquiring private equity capital, publicly selling stock, taking advantage of government leverage, issuing debt securities, and obtaining loans. In turn, it is the function of the SBIC to act as a financier for small business concerns. Such financing is specifically tailored to the needs of each small business concern. As financier, the SBIC has a variety of options.

SBICs can make long-term loans to small business concerns in order to provide them with funds needed for their sound financing, growth, modernization, and expansion.

An SBIC may provide loans independently or in cooperation with other public or private lenders. SBIC loans to small business concerns may be secured and should be of reasonably sound value. Such loans may have a maturity of no more than 20 years, although under certain conditions the SBIC may renew or extend a loan's maturity for up to 10 years.

An SBIC may elect to loan money to a small business concern in the form of debt securities—loans for which the small business concern issues a security, which may be convertible into or have rights to purchase equity in the small business concern. These securities may also have special amortization and subordination terms. By law, the SBIC must provide equity capital to small business concerns and may do so by purchasing the small business concern's equity securities. The SBIC may not, however, become a general partner in any unincorporated small business concern or otherwise become liable for the general obligations of an unincorporated concern.

Licensing Requirements

A corporation or limited partnership may apply to the Small Business Administration for a license to operate as a federal licensee under the Small Business Investment Act of 1958 as amended and the rules and regulations issued thereunder.

With only a few exceptions, there are no restrictions on the ownership of SBICs. Almost any person or organization with a minimum initial private capitalization of $2.5 million ($1.5 million for SSBICs) and an SBA-approved full-time manager who will be in charge of the licensee's operations and who will be able to serve the licensee's small business concerns may be approved for ownership.

For example, SBICs may be:

- Owned and operated by U.S. or foreign operating companies, banks, insurance companies, finance companies, or savings institutions.
- Publicly or privately held.
- Managed under contract by asset management companies or fiduciaries.
- Owned as subsidiaries of other venture capital organizations that want to realize the advantages of the SBIC form of organization while retaining the parent company's autonomy.

Once licensed, each SBIC is subject to annual financial reporting and biennial on-site compliance examinations by the SBA and is required to meet certain statutory and regulatory restrictions regarding approved investments and operating rules.

The SBA, in the regulatory process, seeks to minimize its oversight of SBICs. The regulations that follow exist to protect the interests of small business concerns and the integrity of the program and to ensure its overall effectiveness.

SBICs may invest only in qualifying small business concerns or, if the SBIC has temporary idle funds, certain short-term instruments (federal government securities, insured S&L deposits, CDs, and demand deposits). SBICs may not invest in the following: other SBICs, finance and investment companies or finance-type leasing companies, unimproved real estate, companies with less than one-half of their assets and operations in the United States, passive or casual businesses (those not engaged in a regular and continuous business operation), or companies that will use the proceeds to acquire farmland.

An SBIC may not engage in ''self-dealing'' to the advantage of or with favoritism to its associates. The SBA defines associates broadly to include:

- Certain of its shareholders, officers, directors, and employees.
- In an unincorporated SBIC, its members, control persons, and employees.

The SBIC may not directly or indirectly provide financing to any of its associates. It may borrow money neither from a small business concern it has financed nor from the small concern's owner or officers.

An SBIC is not permitted to control, either directly or indirectly, any small business on a permanent basis. Nor may it control a small business in participation with another SBIC or its associates. In cases of inordinately high risk, the SBA may allow an SBIC to assume temporary control in order to protect its investment. But in those cases the SBIC and the small concern must have an SBA-approved plan of divestiture in effect.

Without written SBA approval an SBIC may invest no more than 20 percent of its private capital in securities, commitments, and guarantees for any one small business concern. For SSBICs the limit is 30 percent.

The cost of money on SBIC loans and debt securities issued by small concerns is regulated by the SBA in the interest of the small business concerns and is limited to the applicable state regulations governing such loans and debt securities or by SBA regulations, whichever is lower.

Prohibited Real Estate Investments

An SBIC may not invest in farmland, unimproved land, cemetery subdividers or developers, or any small business concerns classified under Major Group 65 (Real Estate) of the SIC Manual, with the exception of subdividers and developers, title abstract companies, real estate agents, brokers, and managers.

Investment in real estate–related businesses is limited to one-third of the SBIC's portfolio, and combined investment in real estate–related activities (building contractors, hotels, and lodging places, and so on) is limited to two-thirds of an SBIC's portfolio investments.

SBICs may not provide funds for a small concern whose primary business activity involves directly or indirectly providing funds to others, purchasing debt obligations, factoring, or leasing equipment on a long-term basis with no provision for maintenance or repair.

However, SBICs and SSBICs may finance disadvantaged concerns engaged in relending or reinvesting activities (except agricultural credit companies and those banking and savings and loan institutions not insured by agencies of the federal government).

In general, investment funds used to purchase securities must go directly to the small business concern issuing the securities. They should not be used to purchase already outstanding securities such as those on a stock exchange unless such a purchase is necessary to ensure the sound financing of a small concern or when the securities will be used to finance a change of ownership. The purchase of publicly offered small business securities through an underwriter is permitted as long as the proceeds of the purchase will go to the issuing company.

Minimum Period of Financing

Loans made to and debt securities purchased from small business concerns should have minimum terms of five years. Under certain circumstances, loans to disadvantaged concerns may be for minimum terms of four years. The small concern should have the right to prepay a loan or debt security with a reasonable penalty where appropriate.

Loans and debt securities with terms less than five years are acceptable only when they are necessary to protect existing financings, are made in contemplation of long-term financing, or are made to finance a change of ownership.

Miscellaneous Regulations

In addition to the specific regulations listed here, SBICs are subject to certain other regulations regarding activities, operations, and reporting that must be followed to ensure the continuation of the SBIC license and its related advantages.

The Basics of Setting Up an SBIC

1. Commit the necessary capital. To qualify, you must have a minimum of $2.5 million ($1.5 million for SSBICs) in private capitalization. The SBA may require additional capital in certain market areas.
2. Prepare a well-structured business plan to be included in the license application, detailing the SBIC's plans for investing in small business concerns. Include information on the proposed types of investments, the types of industries in which the SBIC plans to invest, the developmental stages of these businesses, their geographic locations, and other factors relevant to the investment activities of the proposed SBIC.
3. Make sure you have qualified management on your staff. To be licensed, your company must be managed by individuals with a real interest in serving small business concerns and the necessary expertise to do so. A well-qualified manager would have at least five years of successful experience in a responsible position in a business involved with investing in business concerns—for example, a venture capital firm or an investment banking firm. Individuals with comparable experience and educational backgrounds may also be acceptable. A degree in a business-related field may be substituted for up to two years of practical experience.
4. Obtain an SBIC "licensing kit" from the SBA's central office in Washington, D.C. Be sure to review the application and instructions as well as the SBA's Regulations and Small Business Investment Act of 1958, as amended. The SBA is vitally interested in encouraging responsible individuals and organizations to establish SBICs.

    Although you are welcome to contact the SBA yourself with any questions about preparation of required documents, legal counsel is usually advisable because of the complexities of organizing an SBIC.

5. Submit a license application along with all pertinent exhibits and required forms to the Investment Division of the Small Business Administration in Washington, D.C. Enclose a check for the nonrefundable filing fee of $5,000. The application will not be processed until the filing fee is received.

Expect that the time required to process your application may be as long as four months. A significant portion of that time is needed for background checks of the individuals who will be involved in the ownership and management of your prospective SBIC. During the application process, the SBA may find that additional information is necessary and, if so, will notify you in writing. The quicker you reply, the quicker the SBA can process your application.

The SBA encourages responsible individuals and organizations to establish SBICs. For more detailed information, write:

Associate Administrator for Investment
U.S. Small Business Administration
409 Third Street, SW
Washington, DC 20416

The previous statements contain, in many cases, simplified summaries of complex regulatory and statutory provisions. Before any business decision is made, relevant and current regulations and statutes should be consulted and, if necessary, legal counsel should also be consulted.

The Program

Like venture capitalists, small business investment companies typically invest in high-growth companies with new proprietary technologies or untapped niche markets.

The SBIC's requirements of companies to be financed are:

- High growth—projected sales of $25 million to $100 million in five to seven years.
- High return on investment—30 percent average compounded annually.
- Proprietary technology and/or preemptive position—they want to see some overwhelming advantage that would help a company quickly penetrate or sweep a market.
- Strong management—possibly one member of the management is a recognized expert in a certain technological area.

Investment Structure

Investments range from $100,000 to $5,000,000. A business plan is required during the review process. Financing commitments are usually structured as equity where the SBIC exits in five to seven years through an initial public offering or a buyout. SBICs can also leverage their investments with SBA loans.

Only firms defined by the SBA as small are eligible for SBIC financing.

For businesses in those industries for which the above standards are too low, alternative size standards are available. In determining whether or not a business qualifies, its parent, subsidiaries, and affiliates must also be considered.

If you own or operate a small business and would like to obtain SBIC financing, you should first identify and investigate existing SBICs that may be interested in financing your company. You should also consider whether or not the SBIC can offer you management services appropriate to your needs.

The SBA publishes a regularly updated directory listing all current SBIC licensees. The amount of each SBIC's private capital and the amount of government leverage it has received are listed as well as information on each SBIC's type of ownership and investment policy.

You should research SBICs and determine your company's needs well in advance—long before you will actually need the money. Your research will take time.

When you've identified the SBICs you think are best suited for financing for your company, you'll need to prepare for a presentation. Your initial presentation will play a major role in your success in obtaining financing. It's up to you to demonstrate that an investment in your firm is worthwhile. The best way to achieve this is to present a detailed and comprehensive business plan, or prospectus. You should include at a minimum the following information about your business:

I. Identification
    A. Name of the business as it appears on the official record of the state or community in which it operates.
    B. City, county, and state of the principal location and any branch offices or facilities.
    C. Business organization; if a corporation, date and state of incorporation.

II. Product or Service
    A. Description of the business performed, including the principal products sold or services rendered.
    B. History of the development of the products and/or service during the past five years or since inception.
    C. Relative importance of each product or service to the volume of the business and to its profits.

III. Marketing
    A. Detailed information about your business's customer base, including potential customers. Indicate the percentage of gross revenue accounted for by your five largest customers.
    B. Marketing survey and/or economic feasibility study.
    C. Distribution system by which products or services are provided to customers.

IV. Competition
    A. Competitive conditions in the industry in which your business is engaged, including your company's position relative to its largest and smallest competitors.

    B. Full explanation and summary of your business's pricing policies.

V. **Management**
    A. Brief résumés of management and principal owners, including their ages, education, and business experience.
    B. Banking, business, and personal references for each member of management and for the principal owners.

VI. **Financial Statements**
    A. Balance sheets and profit and loss statements for the last three fiscal years or from your business's inception.
    B. Detailed projections of revenues, expenses, and net earnings for the coming year.
    C. Amount of funding you are requesting and the time requirement for the funds.
    D. Reasons for your request for funds and a description of the proposed uses.
    E. Benefits you expect your business to gain from the financing—improvement of financial position, increases in revenues, expense reduction, increase in efficiency.

VII. **Production Facilities and Property**
    A. Description of real and physical property and adaptability to new or existing business ventures.
    B. Description of technical attributes of production facilities.

You may obtain an up-to-date Directory of Operating Small Business Investment Companies by visiting the SBA regional or district office nearest you or by writing to:

Associate Administrator for Investment
U.S. Small Business Administration
409 Third Street, SW
Washington, DC 20416

A Short History of the SBIC Program

The investment company program has been the target of both praise and condemnation over the years. Some of the companies backed by the program—including Apple Computer and Federal Express—have been outstandingly successful. But critics have also dubbed it "food stamps for the rich" and an "evergreen money tree" because some of its dollars ended up backing pornographic theaters and rock-concert promoters in the early 1980s.

To be licensed as an SBIC, investors need $1 million in private capital. They can then borrow as much as four times that amount from the agency. They can also renew their debentures or loan commitments. The result, says one official, can be continuous, rolling loans that last until a company's investments run into trouble.

But don't be fooled into thinking that the SBA closely monitors and regulates the organizations that it has licensed to issue equity investments, even though the SBA itself provides a portion of the invested monies. Here are some cases in point.

Mr. John Pointer was happy when Tennessee Equity Capital Corp., an investment company licensed by the Small Business Administration, decided to assist him. Tennessee Equity Capital Corp. promised to invest in his fuel brokerage company, Porter Oil Co., and proceeded to apply for additional funds from the SBA.

To Mr. Pointer's surprise, the investment company—specifically, Mr. Walter Cohen, Tennessee Equity's owner—took an immediate, active management role in Porter Oil Co. But Mr. Pointer felt no reason to worry— the SBA's backing was full assurance that the arrangement was correct and proper, regulated and monitored by the SBA.

Mr. Pointer knows better today. In violation of federal law, Mr. Cohen took control of Pointer Oil Co.'s finances, helping himself to the money. As a result, Mr. Pointer lost control of his company to Mr. Cohen, who early in 1992 was indicted for fraud. Mr. Pointer's company is, of course, bankrupt. Mr. Pointer never received any of the money, and most aspects of his business, other than winning contracts to purchase oil, were controlled by Tennessee Equity officers.

The unquestioning belief that Tennessee Equity was regulated by the SBA destroyed Mr. Pointer's business. However, he is not the only victim. Nor is the SBA the only agency of the government guilty of such oversights. Each year, tens of thousands of entrepreneurs take part in government-backed private sector programs, from SBA lending to lotteries by other agencies for winning federal cable licenses and oil leases. Often they simply assume that federal involvement safeguards them against fraud. Although it is true that federal agencies are expected to oversee the programs, it is also true that they can't be held accountable for everything that goes wrong.

Mr. Pointer alerted the SBA to evidence that resulted in the federal indictment against Mr. Cohen. The indictment, delivered by the U.S. District Court in Nashville, accuses Mr. Cohen and two of his associates of defrauding the government by misusing federal funds and taking direct control of companies that were supposed to receive the funds, in violation of federal law. According to the federal indictment, Tennessee Equity used its investment in Pointer Oil Co. as a means to secure $250,000 in SBA financing. The indictment accuses Mr. Cohen of submitting fraudulent documents to get the SBA to approve Tennessee Equity's applications for financial assistance and lists nine small Tennessee concerns that allegedly were improperly financed and managed by Tennessee Equity beginning as far back as 1985.

While expressing sympathy for Mr. Pointer and acknowledging it should have been more diligent in its oversight, the SBA says it owes him no special considerations to help him recover some of his assets and get back into business.

Investment companies such as Mr. Cohen's might be licensed by the SBA, but the SBA can't guarantee to the world at large that these companies follow all SBA rules. When the SBA finds that they don't, it brings them back into compliance or does its best to get them out of the program.

The SBA's inspector general started looking into the case when Mr.

Pointer took his complaints to the agency in 1989. But because the inspector general's office is independent and doesn't share details of its work with other SBA officials, no administrative action was taken against Tennessee Equity until after the indictment in February 1992. Then the SBA took control of the investment company, and officials are still trying to unravel two years' worth of legal actions brought by and against the company.

By all appearances the agency probably wouldn't have won control of Tennessee Equity if Pointer and Grady Ring, another business owner financed by Tennessee Equity, hadn't voluntarily testified during the federal court proceeding.

Recent studies, including one in 1991 commissioned by the Senate Small Business Committee, concluded that the SBA's oversight and regulation of the SBIC program during the 1980s had been inadequate. In the wake of several SBIC failures, the SBA adopted new rules in 1991 to govern the program and beefed up the staff charged with their oversight. The failed companies still owe the SBA about $525 million.

Another example of the SBA's deficiencies in monitoring its SBIC program is the Conquistador ski resort, located in Westcliffe, Colorado, and owned by Royal Business Funds Corp. of New York. After the company defaulted on its loans in 1982—owing the SBA $23 million, including interest—the SBA was faced with the task of liquidating the company's assets. In addition to the ski resort, these included undeveloped land in Florida and an apartment complex in Ithaca, New York.

In this case, the SBA took the unusual step of deciding to operate the failed business because it couldn't find any buyers and was already overwhelmed with the task of liquidating so many other companies. But the SBA's inspector general took the position, in a recent audit, that the agency violated federal rules when it tried to run the business itself. The report also cited agency officials for possible conflicts of interest and poor record keeping.

The officials criticized by the auditors blame their problems in managing the liquidation on a lack of staff. At the time there were 6 professional staffers handling SBIC liquidations and an additional 12 who worked at times under contract. Those people were aided by several more SBA lawyers.

The SBA set up a separate company, EWE Properties Ltd., to liquidate the Royal Business assets. When EWE was unable to sell the ski resort, it spent about $10 million to operate and improve it. SBA officials say the idea was to maintain the property's value until a buyer could be found. But the inspector general's report said federal rules prohibit a corporation from acting for a government agency. The auditors also said SBA officials should have sold the various properties "as is." No criminal activity has been alleged, but a management task force was appointed to review the case and to find the reason for the growing number of SBIC failures.

On last report the resort, which was closed in 1988, still hasn't been sold. The auditors say the SBA eventually may lose between $11 million and $15 million on the Royal Business failure. The audit also showed that records for some major transactions are missing or incomplete, although no funds were missing. The auditors also questioned EWE's hiring of several consultants, one of whom was an acquaintance of an SBA employee involved in EWE.

The SBA officials involved have reacted angrily to the auditors' report, arguing that the head of the SBA has broad authority to take such action and that they were working to settle the matter to the agency's advantage.

A total of 170 SBICs, or more than a quarter of all such companies, are now in liquidation proceedings. They owe the SBA at least $369 million. Although such businesses are risky by nature, the number of failures surged from about 16 companies a year in the early 1980s to 26 in 1986, 38 in 1987, and 26 in 1988. In addition to the ski resort, some of the companies' failed investments include office buildings, shopping malls, and a cable television station.

As you can see by this short history of this program, it has had its problems. But it is still most effective in helping new ventures get off the ground. This history was not presented to discourage the use of this program but instead to alert you to the caution you must exercise when seeking help from any source, private or governmental. Don't be lulled into a false sense of security because your capital needs appear to be serviced smoothly. Remember, you are still the one ultimately responsible and the one who can lose everything for which you've worked extremely hard. In fact, you'll read more regarding the SBA's action or inaction in Chapter 2, "What Makes the SBA Run?," on page 74.

EXPORT REVOLVING LINE OF CREDIT (ERLC) PROGRAM

Export revolving line of credit loans are available only under SBA's guarantee program to provide financial assistance to small business exporters. This program assists exporters in financing the manufacture or purchase of goods and services for export or for the development of a foreign market. This program has a revolving feature, whereby the borrower can make any number of withdrawals and repayments within the dollar limit and stated maturity period of the loan.

Eligible businesses are those that have been in operation for at least 12 months prior to filing an application (unless waived by a regional office) and that meet SBA's other size and policy requirements. This program can be used by manufacturers, wholesalers, and export management companies. Applicants must be current on all payroll taxes and have in operation a depository plan for the payment of future withholding taxes.

Loan proceeds can be used to finance the labor and materials needed to manufacture or purchase goods and services for sale overseas or to develop a foreign market, including such things as professional advice or assistance, foreign business travel, and participation in trade shows. Proceeds may also be used to provide a manufacturer with the working capital necessary to perform on an export sales contract already secured. Funds may not be used to pay existing obligations or to purchase fixed assets.

The maturity of an ERLC is based on an applicant's business cycle, but cannot exceed 18 months. Collateral requirements may include an assignment of contract proceeds, accounts receivable, bank letters of credit, other business assets, and personal guarantees. Only collateral located in the United States is acceptable.

SBA's regular guarantee fees apply to ERLC loans except for those with maturities of 12 months or less, in which case the guaranty fee is 0.25 percent of the guaranteed portion of the loan. The lender may also charge the borrower a commitment fee of 0.25 percent of the loan (or a minimum of $200) after SBA approves the ERLC.

SBA ONLINE

The Small Business Administration recently launched a free on-line service that gives any entrepreneur with a computer and a modem 24-hour access to an information-packed bulletin board. Sponsored by Sprint, Apple Computers, Dun & Bradstreet, Microsoft, and other corporations, SBA Online offers information on the agency's loan programs, specialty publications, workshops, and other services.

You are limited to 120 minutes (2 hours) per call. The service is very user-friendly.

The service has had 151,083 calls registered to it as of March 17, 1993, with a total user base of 48,906 and an average call rate per day of 1,238:

SBA Online offers:

- SBA information and services
- SBA publications
- Files relating to business
- Mailboxes for business-related topics

When calling in the first time, you will create a password for future use. Then the main menu will appear. This gives you the following selections:

1. General Information
2. Services Available
3. Local Information
4. Outside Resources
5. Quick Search Menu

Going to the General Information menu gives you the following choices:

1. Overview of SBA
2. Thirty Most Asked Questions
3. SBA Employment Information
4. Other Federal Employment Info

The SBA Services menu provides the following information categories:

1. Overview of SBA Programs
2. Business Development
3. Financing Services
4. Government Contracting Opportunities
5. Legislation and Regulations

6. Small Business Facts
7. Small Business Minority Program

The Local Information menu lists the following information categories:

1. Local SBA Offices
2. Calendar of Events
3. Counseling (SCORE)
4. Small Business Development Centers
5. SBA Disaster Area Offices
6. Preferred/Certified Lenders
7. Business Information Centers

The Outside Resources menu lists the following information categories:

1. Gateways to Other Online Services (not available as of July 19, 1993)

The Quick Search menu provides direct access by keyword or topic and lists the following:

1. 7(j) Minority Counseling
2. 8(a) Contracting Opportunities
3. Advocacy
4. American Indians
5. Asian
6. Banks and Other Lenders
7. Black-owned Businesses
8. Business Development
9. Business Plan
0. Counseling
A. Development Companies
B. Disaster Assistance
C. Exporting
D. Financial Assistance
E. Government Contracting Opportunities
I. Hispanic
J. International Trade
K. Investment
L. Legislation
N. Lenders
O. Loans
Q. Marketing
R. Microloans
S. Minorities
U. Physically Challenged
V. Procurement Assistance
W. Service Corps of Retired Execs
X. Small Business Institutes
Y. Small Business Investment Companies

Z. Small Bus. Development Centers
\#   Starting Out
*   Surety Guarantee
\$ Training
—   Veterans
+   Women's Business Ownership

The mail box section contains a SYSOP (system operator) mailbox, which is for suggestions and technical questions only; a GENERAL mailbox for leaving messages to the general public; and SPECIAL INTEREST mailboxes, which let you communicate with others who have similar interests.

The mail box user guidelines are:

1. The mail boxes are not to be used for personal mail that does not pertain to operating a small business. Such mail will be removed.
2. The mail boxes are not to be used for public advertising or carrying out business activities such as providing lists of products, prices, taking orders, and so on. Such mail will be removed.
3. Callers who misuse the mail boxes will be deleted.
4. The SYSOP (system operator) has access to both private and public mail and may read and remove any message that is not within SBA's guidelines.
5. Messages not intended for ALL to read should be made private.
6. Profanity will result in immediate removal of mail privileges.
7. Mail over 14 days old will be deleted in all boxes except GENERAL, which will be deleted every 7 days.

The mail box subjects available are:

1. General
2. Messages to the SYSOP
3. Cubbyhole
4. Answers from the SYSOP
A. Starting Up
B. Management
C. Financing
D. Marketing
E. Advertising
I. Agriculture
J. Aviation
K. Communication
L. Computer/Technology
M. Construction
N. Educational Services
O. Engineering/Technology
Q. Entertainment
R. Financial Services
S. Government
U. Health Professions

V. Home Business
W. Hospitality Services
X. Insurance Services
Y. International Business
Z. Journalism
!   Legal Services
@   Mail Order
#   Manufacturing
+   DTPublishing
%   Real Estate
$ Retail
&   Transportation
/   QSO Offline Mail Reader (new feature)

As you can see, there is a lot of information available on this service; it is highly recommended you make it available to yourself. To contact SBA Online, set your communications parameters for:

No parity (N)

Eight data bits

One stop bit

Call in at (800)859-4636 for 2,400 bps or (800)697-4636 for 9,600 bps.

This completes the section on programs offered by the SBA. As you can see, it's quite exhaustive. A business entrepreneur could quite literally get the financial support necessary to see a business enterprise through from product feasibility studies (SBIR) to the final manufacturing and distribution [7(a) and SBICs]. But keep in mind that these programs are not static—they are constantly changing, and not all programs are offered by all SBA regional offices. So, if you determine that one of these programs fits your needs, contact the regional office that services your area and make sure it's recognized by that office and that it's still an active program.

The next chapter was written to help you deal with the SBA and explains why doing so requires perseverance and patience. It will give you an insight into the "personality" of the SBA and why that personality exists.

2 What Makes the SBA Run?

The U.S. Small Business Administration was created by Congress in 1953 to encourage the formation of new enterprises and to nurture their growth. It exists to serve small businesses by providing information and financial backing and speaks on their behalf in the corridors of Capitol Hill. In doing this, the SBA performs the critical task of informing Congress of the state of, and needs of, small businesses.

But the SBA's mandate is broad, and like many agencies its resources are limited. Its definition of small business—service businesses and retailers with annual revenues of $3.5 million or less, manufacturers with fewer than 500 employees, and wholesalers employing fewer than 100 workers—covers more than 95 percent of the companies in the United States. The SBA's staff numbers just 4,000 nationwide, organized in 110 offices. So taking advantage of the SBA requires learning what it's equipped to offer and then how to tap into its abundant resources.

Many self-employed people perceive the SBA as having been designed to help "big" small businesses, and they don't even bother to approach it for help. This segment of business is composed of firms with up to five or so employees, and by government standards they are very small businesses. This causes a certain distrust of the SBA because it is a government agency and contact is thus limited.

But if you know where to look and are fortunate enough to make contact with the people that care, the SBA has much to offer even the smallest of companies.

The SBA has been described as a cautiously optimistic group of people who'll tell you that other people have started businesses and succeeded and that you can, too. That provides sufficient encouragement and enthusiasm to push some people into proceeding with their dream. This is considered, by some people, one of the best things the SBA has to offer.

Small businesses with up to five employees can contact a Small Business Development Center (SBDC) for help reviewing the proposal to be sent out to federal agencies; take their course in government contracting. Also have the SBDC review your business plan. You'll certainly get your money's worth out of the SBA in this way, as the agency's services are free.

Thousands of small businesses have benefited and are benefiting from the SBA's free advice, publications, business counseling, and direct loans and loan guarantees. However, many businesspeople walk away empty-handed and disappointed because the SBA is so big, caters to such a diverse group of businesses, and has a relatively small budget that it cannot possibly give everyone what they want.

There seems to be a big gap between the number of people who apply and the number of people who wind up with results from the SBA. It's clear that people who have received help from the SBA applaud it, and those who haven't think it's a bureaucratic smoke screen. But part of figuring it out is knowing what the SBA has to offer and deciding whether you're the type of person it can benefit.

SEEKING A LOAN FROM THE SMALL BUSINESS ADMINISTRATION

In one case, a marketing specialist in California saw the need for a company that could package other companies' food products. In 1987, he started his contract packaging company, financing the startup costs himself.

When the facility's capacity could not meet demand, he decided to expand. He applied for and obtained loan assistance through the SBA. He used one SBA-backed loan, for about $200,000, to improve the company's leased facility. He secured another, for $275,000, for equipment purchases.

He saw the potential and went from 10,000 square feet to 80,000 square feet in one jump, going from 5 production lines to 20.

It is his contention that the loan program is well suited to entrepreneurs who don't fit a bank's ideal borrowing profile. When the SBA guarantees loans to these entrepreneurs, banks receive the "comfort level" necessary to extend financing.

When lenders tighten requirements, prospective or fledgling small business owners turn increasingly to the government for financing assistance. The SBA was once considered a last resort source of funding for high-risk borrowers. Of that funding, the SBA's $3.8 billion loan guarantee program is probably the best known.

Between October 1990 and June 1991, the SBA guaranteed more than 14,000 loans. During 1992, the agency expected to back more than 17,000 loans. It is now estimated that between 30 and 40 percent of all small business loans have SBA backing.

The following are examples of SBA activity. Through the first seven months of the government's 1992–93 fiscal year, the SBA guaranteed 956 loans worth $156.7 million in the New York region. Denver had 1,112 loans at $168 million. Chicago accounted for 1,347 loans worth $279.9 million. And the San Francisco office produced 2,154 loans totaling $581.2 million. Only districts with headquarters in Boston, Seattle, and Philadelphia had smaller totals than the New York area.

The typical guaranteed loan is for $175,000 to be repaid in eight years, but wide variations exist. In Idaho, for example, a Pocatello manufacturing concern received $883,000, the largest loan backing of 1992. The smallest guarantee—for $11,000—was lent to a Boise clinic.

However, even as more small business owners seek SBA assistance, the agency isn't reporting an increase in the number of defaults. Nationally, 93 percent of all SBA-guaranteed loans are current and performing.

Again, as financing becomes less available, more entrepreneurs are expected to seek that financing through the government. But the government's requirements aren't lenient. Entrepreneurs must determine which programs are most appropriate to their businesses and follow the current requirements on how to apply.

WHAT'S AVAILABLE

Start by reading the *Catalog of Federal Domestic Assistance*, published by the U.S. Government Printing Office, to begin to determine what's available for you. It describes the types of loans offered to small businesses by various agencies. For example, the Department of Agriculture provides funding for businesses in communities of less than 50,000 people. The Department of Housing and Urban Development has millions of dollars available for real estate ventures. Found in most public libraries, the catalog includes the requirements for each type of loan as well as the amount of financing typically provided.

The 59.000 series of catalog listings of these programs and their originating agencies includes the SBA loan programs, including the two primary vehicles—guaranteed loans and direct loans.

DEVELOPMENT COMPANIES

Another way to seek SBA backing is through economic development companies formed to foster growth in specific rural or urban areas. Small businesses that qualify can obtain financing to acquire, build, or expand their facilities or to buy machinery and equipment.

Under the 504 loan program, the SBA joins forces with an approved development company and private lenders in 10- or 20-year financial packages. The SBA can provide up to $750,000 toward a total loan package by issuing completely guaranteed bonds that are sold in the capital market.

INFORMATION SOURCES

When television came along in the early 1950s, furniture dealers, department stores, and others quickly added TV receivers to the lines of merchandise they sold. But more than a few people who had not been in business rushed to open TV stores, retail establishments that sold nothing but TV receivers. Most failed in a short time because the sale of TV sets alone was not enough to support a full-time business. The people who leaped into that kind of venture simply had not thought things out. They had acted on a notion. Had they done some research into how much profit they could expect to make on TV sales, what their costs would be, and how much business they could expect to do (a good formula for this is to make a conservative estimate of sales and then cut that figure in half), they would have been less eager to leap into this new business with nothing else to support their venture.

Such information is not easy, though not impossible, to come by. There are many places to get help. Federal, state, and local government agencies can help you gather information and develop market estimates. Many of these agencies will furnish brochures, pamphlets, and even complete manuals. The U.S. Small Business Administration is such an agency. But the government is not the only source of information and help. Check your local library. Most libraries have reference works that contain useful market information. Check also with local services such as your chamber of commerce, business association (Rotary or Lions Clubs), trade association, and others. (Check your telephone book under the heading "Associations.")

DISPELLING THE MYTHS

A common misperception among entrepreneurs is that SBA loans and guarantees are ideally suited to struggling start-ups. This is not so. If your business isn't basically stable and you don't have a track record, the SBA probably isn't going to lend you money or guarantee your loan.

However, SBA officials say each case is decided on its own merits. The SBA does provide loan guarantees to start-ups, but the equity has to be stronger than for a firm with a track record. And the SBA does directly state in its current loan packages that it is not actively seeking loans from businesses that have been in existence for less than one year.

It is advised that owners be in business for at least a year or two before seeking SBA backing. Franchisees also qualify; they account for about five percent of the agency's guarantees.

HOW TO SEEK FINANCING

When applying for SBA guarantees, you'll normally work directly with a lender, not the SBA. For this reason, select a bank with which you're comfortable that has sufficient experience with SBA programs.

The SBA divides banks into three categories. The first level includes "regular" banks, which help applicants prepare SBA loan applications and then submit them to regional offices for approval. The second level, made up of "certified" lenders, includes banks that conduct the financial analysis necessary to expedite SBA loans. The third level consists of "preferred" lenders, which have sufficient experience with SBA requirements to commit to SBA loans (the SBA lets them act in its stead).

Being turned down for a regular business loan is the first step in qualifying for SBA financing. If you lack sufficient equity or experience yet your idea and approach are sound, you may be advised to apply for an SBA loan guarantee. Most banks will do so for you once you provide sufficient details in an application.

The SBA's collateral requirements are strict. Applicants are asked to pledge one-third to one-half of the assets needed to launch a new business. In addition, principals may be asked to make personal guarantees. Understand that SBA loans are totally and completely secured. If you're a small, struggling company and have no collateral, you stand very little chance of getting a loan.

You'll also be asked to submit a business plan describing the company's market, products or services, marketing plan, and long-term goals and objectives as well as a balance sheet listing assets, liabilities, and net worth. Income (profit and loss) statements should be submitted for the current period and, if available, the previous three years. Also include monthly cash-flow statements.

New business applicants should prepare an estimated (pro forma) balance sheet, including personal startup funds, as of the day the business was, or is to be, started. Detailed (pro forma) projections of earnings and expenses for at least the first year of operation and estimated (pro forma) monthly cash-flow statements also should be included. In short, you want to end up with a short, detailed package on why you need the money. Tell who you are and what you sell and include a good financial profile and projections.

Finally, prepare a personal financial statement for each owner. List collateral being offered as security for the loan, including estimates of the present market value of each item. State the size of the loan you're requesting and what it's for. If you're uncertain how to prepare these documents, seek assistance from a financial professional.

SBA approval takes up to four months, with the average usually half that.

FINANCING BASICS AND COMMERCIAL BANKING

Let's take a step back for a moment before getting into specific sources of capital and how they work to look at some of the principles of financing. The SBA recognizes and operates by these principles just as banks do, but the SBA has more latitude in their application.

Risk versus Reward

All investors and lenders will desire a reward equal to or greater than the level of risk that they perceive in capitalizing an expansion or new venture. The higher the risk, the higher the rent on the money (interest rate). Take note that this risk factor, derived from careful evaluation of industry variables and the many resources you will provide, is calculated according to the perceptions of the lender. So, if the lender's perceived level of risk is what determines your cost, it is in your best interests financially to do everything possible to reduce that risk factor in the mind of the lender. To do this effectively, you must be able to mentally cross over and "see how the other half lives." Consequently, in preparing and presenting a loan proposal, it is vital that you step into the lender's shoes and scrutinize your plan not only with objectivity but also with the lender's subjective standpoint in mind.

There are many variables that make up the whole risk equation, but the single largest factor weighing on the lender's mind is the amount of owner's commitment (or collateral). Ask yourself: How much of your personal wealth is at risk? Or how much motivation is there for you to make certain the loan is repaid? The more personal assets that you commit, the lower the risk as far as lenders are concerned. This commitment, or security, can be a lien on a property; it can be a debenture placed against all assets and ranking after specific charges; or in some cases it could even be your signature backed by an A-rated credit record. A person's desire to maintain a good credit rating is considered strong motivation, and an intangible credit file can often be equal to real property in security value.

The value of your security will directly affect both risk (which determines your cost) and your chances of getting approval. And, of course, the value of security is also subject to the lender's perception. Its value will be adjusted according to its liquidity, the ease with which a lender could convert the asset(s) into cash. For example, accounts receivable are considered very liquid. But a large piece of equipment designed for highly specialized applications, although acquired by you at great expense, may be of little security value to a lender who sees difficulty in finding a buyer should you default.

Luckily, lenders are still human and as such will assess things differently from one another. Just because one lender or investor turned you down doesn't mean they all will or even that the next one will. Individual judgment, loan availability, and tightening government regulations that limit the percentage of loans a bank can make in certain areas will all weigh in the decision process.

As a general rule you should approach money sources that are familiar with your industry. Self-preservation is the dominant instinct in all humans, especially financiers. When we are in doubt, our first instinct is to avoid unnecessary risk and play it safe. Because of this desire to stay in familiar territory, you will usually find quicker and more favorable results (and better terms) by approaching those who are already financing your competition. They are better able to assess risk and can quickly make a decision.

Debt versus Equity

There are two basic types of financing: *debt*, which is a promise to repay a loan (secured or unsecured), and *equity*, in which you sell a portion of ownership for the needed capital or resources. Most business owners desire to remain in total control; that's why they are self-employed in the first place. As a result of this pride and an abundant lack of knowledge, many business owners will exhaust all avenues of debt financing and never give serious consideration to equity funding, sometimes resulting in the death of their livelihood.

It's true that equity financing will cost you a portion of ownership, but you may also gain valuable experience from an investor/firm with a working knowledge of your industry. If you gave up 20 percent equity in exchange for working capital and added experience that resulted in a 30 percent increase in sales, did you make a bad deal? If you gave up 45 percent equity but received new life in a company that was headed for bankruptcy, did you make a good deal? Sometimes the only way to win is to lose—a little.

General Guidelines

1. One of the best but least used strategies is to forge relationships with bankers and other sources long before capital is needed. A little extra time and effort spent in this direction now will result in a much warmer reception during cold spells, when you really need one.
2. Use professionals that you know to lead you to potential money sources. A third-party referral is a far better start than a cold call, but don't let the third-party become your negotiator. It's your business; you need to sell yourself.
3. Go to the right source for the right financing. Don't waste time trying to get startup capital out of a bank if you don't have collateral. Don't go looking for an investor if you just need short-term operating capital. Make sure the amount that you need is not below the minimum financed by that source.
4. Be willing to negotiate. Talk in terms of making deals and win-win situations. "How can we make this work?" A little humility will go a long way.
5. In determining your company's ability to repay a loan, lenders will seek a complete business plan including cash-flow projections, a profit and loss statement, a balance sheet, and a detailed explanation of how the funds will be used. Make sure these documents are complete and demonstrate that you are on top of your business.
6. Investigate the investigator. Just as your potential sources will check you out to confirm the accuracy of your information and character, you should do some checking of your own.

   Is the institution with which you are investing your time to build a relationship for the future going to be around in the future? Is it financially sound? Ask for a balance sheet and profit and loss statement.

   Is the equity investor with whom you are about to walk down the aisle a person to whom you want to be financially married? Instead of asking for a few references, which will always be good ones, ask for a larger list of their investors or loan recipients. Randomly select names and ask these individuals about the nature of your potential source. Did they jump ship in hard times, or did they offer additional support?

   Checking out your sources will not create ill will or discourage them from doing business with you. Quite the contrary—it will gain you respect and help demonstrate your confidence and business savvy. They may be convinced that you investigate everything as closely, including your other business decisions.

COMMERCIAL BANKING

On the surface, it would appear that there could be no working relationship more difficult than that of an entrepreneur and a banker. Entrepreneurs are gamblers; they are comfortable taking risks with other people's money.

Bankers are taught to be conservative and calculating. They are entrusted to watch over others' fortunes. As a result, many business owners are convinced that bankers don't like doing business with them.

Of course, this is not true. But these business owners will continue to feel shunned until they gain the banker's perspective. Bankers are not anti-business. In fact, major losses in overseas loans have refocused the industry's attention toward servicing the small-to-medium business owner with a broader selection of financial amenities than ever before. The delays in funding experienced by most business owners occur not because they own businesses but because of the way in which they go about asking banks for money. An entrepreneur can't understand why a banker doesn't share the same enthusiasm for his or her new project. But bankers want to see numbers, facts, and accurate projections. Once you understand the perspective of your banker, you can alter your plan of attack to accommodate the system.

This does not mean, however, that bankers are void of emotions, with ice coursing through their veins. There is a place for emotion. Tell (sell) your banker why your product or service is the best in the industry. What is unique about it? A loan officer who becomes enthusiastic about your company is much more likely to make a good presentation to the loan committee. Use subtle appeals to emotion to dress your completed loan package with a big red bow. But remember, they won't buy just sizzle. Sizzle is good, but you must also deliver the steak.

THE LOAN PACKAGE

Completing the checklist below will ensure that you are fully prepared to deliver that steak. At maximum, your loan presentation should include the following:

    I. **A one-page summary disclosing:**
        A. The loan amount requested.
        B. How it will be used (refinance existing debt, expansion, new product, long- or short-term working capital, and so on).
        C. Method of repayment and the desired length of term.
        D. A secondary repayment source/collateral.

   II. **A complete business plan that includes:**
        A. A mission statement (your company's purpose).
        B. A historical summary of your company.
        C. Resumes for yourself, any partners, and key personnel.
        D. Product or service information.
            1. Description and application.
            2. Exclusivity information such as patents, licenses, copyrights, trademarks, and so on.
        E. Market.
            1. Historical summary with industry and personal growth figures.
            2. Competition/pricing.
            3. Customer demographics.

    F. Production.
1. Facilities (type, size, and location).
2. Capacity (used and potential).
3. Number of employees.
4. Overhead.
5. Supplies and cost.
6. Gross margins.
7. Any industry regulations such as shipping regulations or tariffs.

    G. Current financial data.
1. Detailed company financial returns.
2. Balance sheet (present and last three years).
3. Income statements (present and last three years, audited or substantiated by tax returns).
   (NOTE: Tax returns are prepared in a manner that legally minimizes taxable income. The result is a distorted picture of your company's true ability to service the debt. Discuss this with your banker.)
4. Credit references.
5. Bank and name of manager.

    H. Income projections (three years).
1. Summary.
2. Detailed by month for first year.
3. Detailed by quarter for second and third years.
   [Three projections are preferred: high, medium (expected), and low (break-even). Show gross sales, cost of sales, gross profit, and net profit before tax.]

    I. Cash flow projections (3-year).
1. Detailed by month for first year.
2. Detailed by quarter for second and third year.

    J. Appendixes can include:
1. Any promotional literature or brochures.
2. Complete list of assets.
3. Contracts.
4. Any legal documents of relevance.
5. Any supporting documents that you feel will enhance your plan.
6. It would be good to pull a current credit report so that the lender does not have to during its preliminary review. The more inquiries that you can keep off your credit report, the better.

In addition:

Don't forget to fully explain your business cycles and any major assumptions that you've made. Also, deal with all of the negatives. Everyone knows there will be downside risks in any business. To ignore them in your plan is to say you are not prepared to deal with them. Make mention of them and overcome them in a positive manner.

OTHER CONSIDERATIONS

Banks are an excellent source for short-term loans as well as one- to five-year terms, leasing, and mortgage financing.

There is little mystery why banks approve or deny a loan. There are five areas they will look at:

1. **Security.** They love liquidity such as bonds, accounts receivable, and some types of inventory. You may borrow up to 80 percent of your accounts receivable that are not more than 90 days old. Lower your expectations when borrowing against inventory. It's not as liquid as receivables and will peak around 50 percent.

    In addition to security, banks will often require collateral security such as properties or houses and the personal guarantees of all principals.

2. **Your ability to service the debt.** Banks will want to see net cash-flow projections of two to three times that necessary to pay interest and principal.

3. **Competent management.** Few things will relax a bank manager more than to sense that you know your business. The very best way to demonstrate that you're on top of things is to produce ready, accurate facts and figures (preferably audited statements, records, and projections).

4. **Company stability and owner commitment.** This involves looking at past performance as well as the current balance statement. Have you accumulated equity (paid-in capital)? Do your retained earnings look impressive? If not, you must be drawing everything out by means of salary, bonuses, and dividends. This won't sit well with the bank and will leave you with the only other possible option, which is to tie up all kinds of collateral.

5. **Your company as compared to industry standards.** Does your business appear liquid when placed next to your competitors? Each industry has its own average. The fastest way to figure your liquidity ratio is to add your accounts receivable, cash on hand, and marketable securities. Then divide that total by the sum of your accounts payable, salaries, and outstanding loans.

If your business is a corporation, the banker will need to know if shareholders will cover any losses. If it's a partnership, most banks will require all principals to back the loan by signing a personal guarantee (a recourse loan).

To summarize this short explanation of commercial banking, it is worth reiterating that there is no magic to getting money out of a bank. The formula for success is a three-year track record, well-prepared documents, and good communication between you and your loan officer.

There is a very helpful publication that is jointly published by the American Banker's Association and the National Federation of Independent Business. To receive a copy, send $2.50 to:

Small Business Financing
NFIB Foundation
Box 7575
San Mateo, CA 94403

INTERNATIONAL (SCHEDULE B) BANKS

International banks can be of great help to an import/export business, especially if you locate a bank with roots in the country with which you conduct most of your business. Such a bank may be able to keep you updated on economic conditions overseas and supply you with the names of important contacts as well as tailor import/export financing and provide letters of credit. You can locate international banks in your city by looking in the classified telephone directory or by contacting your state banking associations, which can provide a listing.

As you can see, the requirements for applying for private or commercial financing are not unlike the requirements set forth for SBA financing applications. The one major difference is that the SBA requires you be turned down by one or more of these commercial financing sources.

TIMING THE SUBMISSION OF YOUR SBA APPLICATION

The government's fiscal year begins October 1 and ends September 30, but government budgets are rarely approved before December. Because the SBA must have budgeted allocations and/or funds available before it can guarantee or fund a loan request, a good time to submit a loan proposal would be in December, January, or February.

THE SBA: HOW IT WORKS

Now that we have covered how banks and the private financial industry work, let's look at how government financing in the world of the SBA works. When dealing with the Small Business Administration, always keep in mind that you are dealing with a huge, politically motivated bureaucracy, not a commercial financing organization. What this means is that whereas a bank has lending officers who work with you to provide the financing you need, the SBA loan officer has no such desire or incentive. The bank lending officer wants to make the loan because his or her incentive commission is involved—there will be a reward if your loan goes through. In contrast, the SBA loan officer has an incentive to do just the opposite—to stop the loan—because if the loan progresses, it merely means more work to do for no more pay, and the work load is already oppressive. Because of this you should expect to encounter many "stall" tactics, especially if you attempt to get a direct loan from the SBA.

The SBA is organized to function as a loan guarantor, not as a loan grantor. Participating banking organizations are expected to do the legwork involved in processing the loan request. A typical SBA loan officer has little experience in loan or risk analysis. His or her expertise is in ensuring that the procedures, as set forth by the SBA, have been followed and that all forms are properly completed. And when dealing with a certified or preferred lender—those authorized by the SBA to act in its behalf—a loan officer is not even involved. These lenders do everything from processing to approval to funding. The SBA has trained the personnel of these organizations and feels sufficiently confident to automatically back their loans.

To get an even better perspective on the SBA and its personality, let's look at some of its organizational problems. Remember, it's a political bureaucracy, with more than 40 politically appointed jobs and 4,000 to 5,000 employees; it has one of the highest proportions of political posts of any federal agency.

Organizational Problems of the SBA

The SBA was created in 1953 out of a wartime agency, the Small Defense Plants Administration, to provide government loans and to serve as an advocate for small business concerns. Its loan programs are credited with helping thousands of businesses get started, and over the past four decades the agency has promoted programs to aid businesses owned by minorities, women, and the disabled. The SBA also runs the nation's disaster-relief system.

As mentioned earlier, the primary loan program, 7(a), lets small companies borrow up to $750,000 from private lenders, with as much as 90 percent guaranteed by the government. Nearly 90,000 companies now have such loans. According to the National Association of Government Guaranteed Lenders, the SBA's guaranteed loans account for fewer than 1 percent of all small business loans made annually, including family loans, although they make up about 40 percent of all long-term loans for small businesses. Those who watch the SBA say the 7(a) loan program is generally successful and doing its job.

But some minority-aid and other programs have been embroiled in scandals. And it has been charged that the SBA, despite a $382 million annual budget, is a useless bureaucracy that touches the lives of very few small business owners.

When one new SBA administrator was appointed, the stated "immediate mission" was to find a permanent chief counsel for the SBA's office of advocacy as well as a deputy administrator for the parent agency. In fact, small business representatives, in meetings with White House aides, strongly urged that the long-vacant posts be filled with appointees having relevant business backgrounds. However, while this was going on, SBA officials were embroiled in internal disputes over the lines of authority within the agency.

It must be realized, however, that the organization had become so low in morale that staffers joked sarcastically about bringing back Charles Heatherly, the official whom President Reagan sent to head the agency—and kill it. A former budget director called the SBA "a billion-dollar rat hole." During the 1980s, President Reagan twice tried to kill the SBA as a prime example of government waste. Congress wouldn't go along, and President Bush, in turn, supported the agency.

Needless to say, with these attitudes to deal with the administrator was unable to fully realize the stated "immediate mission," let alone make a substantive, positive change in the other areas of concern.

Today, some critics are still questioning the SBA's role. One problem, it's said, is that the SBA has often been treated as a dumping ground for unemployed politicians.

Lawmakers' use of the SBA for patronage and pork is an example of their meddling and has further complicated the agency's effectiveness. For instance, for years the appropriations bill for the SBA has prohibited it from reducing the staffing level of its Charleston, West Virginia, office; the powerful Democratic senator Robert Byrd is from that state. In all, 63 lawmakers sit on the SBA's House and Senate oversight committees, making it practically impossible for the SBA to ignore political influence.

The SBA has lacked a deputy administrator for almost a year, and an inspector general was named after the post had been vacant for eight months. It has been without a permanent chief counsel for its advocacy office since November 1989. The advocate, one of four presidentially appointed posts at the SBA, is supposed to speak for the SBA independently of the administration or Congress. This has led to gridlock on issues like capital gains and health care. The only nominee for the position to date was withdrawn after he ran into resistance at the Senate Small Business Committee. However, President Clinton has (at the time of this writing) compiled a list of top candidates for this post. One is California attorney Margaret Smith, who represents small and midsize Silicon Valley concerns and exporters. Another is Jere Glover, general counsel of the National Association for the Self-Employed in Washington.

Meanwhile, one of the agency's biggest troubles continues: its Small Business Investment Company (mentioned earlier) and minority procurement programs. During the 1989–91 time frame, about 200 of these concerns went out of business, and the government could lose over $800 million on their failed deals.

In fiscal year 1990, 50 people were convicted of defrauding SBA programs. This was up from 28 in all of the previous years. About half of the cases involved the agency's minority procurement program, and a third involved SBA loan programs. One Indiana woman applied for an SBA-backed loan while on a prison-release program, falsely claiming she had no criminal record despite 12 convictions for violating federal financial laws.

One reason given for the rise in convictions was SBA Inspector General Charles Gillum, who took over in mid-1987. He took a more aggressive stance than his predecessors. He persuaded Congress to allow the SBA to audit agency-licensed small business investment firms less frequently so that it could spend more time checking loan programs, which have about 15 times more money at risk. Congress agreed because it was felt that in the investment program SBA auditors "generally know who the bad actors are."

This indicates, of course, that the problems within the SBA are correctable. It merely requires that people with the desire to pursue its mission very aggressively be placed in specific positions.

New Directions

President Clinton has now nominated and Congress has confirmed Erskine Bowles, a North Carolina investment banker and a fund-raiser for the Clinton presidential campaign, to head the Small Business Administration. Mr. Bowles is an investment banker by profession, serving an unglamorous side of American business: smaller, low-technology firms with extensive but often-overlooked needs.

There has been some speculation that the SBA could take a new direction under the Clinton administration to match some of his campaign themes. Small business owners and groups have said that the person selected to head the SBA would indicate whether the president will follow through on promises to give small business issues a higher priority.

The president has stressed the importance of access to capital for growing companies that create jobs, encouraging those who want to see more emphasis on aggressive young concerns. But Mr. Clinton also has stressed the importance of community-based development banks to aid tiny startup businesses.

Mr. Bowles takes over from the SBA's acting administrator, Mr. Dayton Watkins. And as can be seen from the above, the new administrator will inherit an agency that was nearly eliminated by the Reagan administration and that has been used as a dumping ground for political appointees by several other presidents. Employee morale remained low as each of a series of administrators stayed on for relatively short periods.

The agency's main loan guarantee program, however, is growing at a rate of about 37 percent annually because banks are reluctant to make loans to small companies without the assurance that the federal government will stand behind 75 to 90 percent of the loan amount. The program is also considered a well-managed one.

But the SBA is under continued criticism for its management of the federally licensed investment companies that operate as venture capital firms and for its government-contracting program for minority-owned and disadvantaged businesses.

Now the administrations' deficit reduction program has the guaranteed loan program facing yet more turmoil. The Clinton administration and Congress are supposed to draw up a compromise to revise the program to keep it from running out of money.

This new turmoil stems from an administration proposal to reduce the government guarantees and impose a surcharge if the loans are sold in secondary financial markets. Private lenders say this would force them to make fewer SBA-backed loans. Clinton administration officials contend that the proposed changes would actually let the government help more small companies by spreading the loan funds more widely, but they would force banks to bear a larger share of the costs and risks involved in small business loans. Extra funding needed for the program was part of the Clinton economic stimulus package that failed to pass Congress.

The Clinton plan would reduce the average percentage of a loan backed by the SBA to about 75 percent from the current 81 percent. It also would impose an annual fee of one half of a percentage point on those SBA-guaranteed loans that lenders sell to investors. The goal is to reduce the government's cost of supporting the program.

The SBA program will guarantee more than $6 billion in loans in fiscal 1993 if Congress approves the extra funds. Under current rules, Congress must appropriate $50 million to stand behind every $1 billion of guaranteed loans. But if Congress agrees to shrink the size of the guaranteed share and add the proposed fees, the administration would need only $23.5 million to back $1 billion of loans. According to SBA estimates, with the administration's proposed changes, Congress would need to appropriate only $155 million in fiscal 1994 to support about $6 billion worth of lending.

Some SBA-lending specialists have commented that the government could cut program costs by placing a smaller surcharge on all SBA loans, instead of just those sold in the secondary market. This approach would encourage smaller lenders—which need to use the secondary markets—to continue doing so.

Bankers have also strongly suggested that longer-term proposed changes and the short-term funding threat would hinder their loans to small businesses. Reducing the guaranteed percentage means the bank carries more of the loan. This would affect the amount of lending done because of the increased amount of risk on the bank's books. But, on the other hand, Mr. Clinton has asked federal bank regulators to be a little more lenient in their oversight audits of small business loans to encourage lending.

The White House budget office contends the changes will help more small firms rather than hamper lending. And administration officials say selling the guaranteed portion of the loan brings a handsome profit to most banks.

This dispute highlights the critical new role that the SBA loan guarantee program plays in today's economy. With the current credit freeze and more strict banking regulations, the program has become an increasingly important source of small business financing, having doubled in size since 1989.

The Small Business Administration Offers Financing Advice

Again, if your business doesn't qualify for an SBA loan or bank guarantee or if for one reason or another you don't want to become involved with SBA financing, most SBA offices can still provide guidance. Volunteers from the Service Corps of Retired Executives (SCORE) are there to help SBA applicants pinpoint their objectives, prepare business and financing plans, and assist as business consultants wherever their talents are needed. And their work is free of charge.

Unfortunately, this looks better on paper than in reality. Most SCORE members have no consulting background and come from lower management positions in large and mid-sized companies. Although these people are well intentioned, their advice tends to be superfluous at best and erroneous at worst. On the other hand, SCORE members might point you to financing options outside of the SBA. And some "volunteers" working through SBA offices are active consultants trying to get new clients. They are quick to offer their services, and they do charge consulting fees. However, most have no experience in the financing game and tend to lead clients down the wrong paths. Caution is recommended, and it's probably best to stay away from them.

In one particular case about 22 years ago, a private investigator was approached by an attorney, who was a client of the investigator, to join a process-serving business he was opening. They couldn't reach an understanding and went their separate ways, each starting the same type of business. The attorney failed at it, and the investigator struggled. A couple of years after closing the operation, the investigator went to an SBA office for assistance. They sat down and counseled, and then the SBA staff said they would put the investigator in touch with an expert. The "expert," one of the SBA's SCORE counselors, turned out to be that same lawyer who had failed in his own business.

The reality of the situation is that the value of the advice you get from SCORE depends on what you already know and whether you're fortunate enough to be assigned to an advisor who meets your needs. According to some, if this program has any value, it is best for people who are completely uninitiated in the ways of business. A good mechanic who knows how to fix cars and wants to run his or her own gas station could probably get good advice from the SBA on keeping books, managing employees, and so on. But the general recommendation is that a small business person can get better advice on the Working From Home Forum on CompuServ.

Yes, the SBA Does Have Grants . . . Well—Sort Of

Wouldn't it be nice if you had a rich uncle to start you out in your own business and bail you out every time you made a bad decision? Yes, that would be great. But don't despair because you don't have such an uncle, not even in Uncle Sam. Federal grants are available, but they are not easily obtained. If you desire to be the one out of ten whose proposal is accepted, you will have to demonstrate a higher level of planning, preparation, and presentation than your competition. The most reliable way to do so is to hire a grant consultant, a person who already knows the right answers to the questions.

Prospects best qualified for government grants are those who can submit proposals for researching the potential for a new product, new technology, new process, and so on. Private sector funding is very difficult, if not impossible, to obtain for these high-risk research and development projects due to their expense, their long-term payoff, and the uncertainty of their success.

Because of American businesses' reluctance to commit to long-term research and development, these government grants play a major role in helping the United States maintain a technological edge over other countries. These grants range from $50,000 to $500,000 and are supervised by the Small Business Innovations Research Program (SBIR) with funding distribution controlled by the SBA.

Velda Sue—The New Lady of the SBA House

Frequently the government, through congressional action, creates new financing programs that add to those currently offered by the SBA or assist the SBA funding process. Velda Sue (Venture Enhancement and Loan Development Administration for Smaller Undercapitalized Enterprises) is one of these. This program would create a federally chartered corporation to support loans to small businesses. It also would help create a secondary market for these loans. House hearings on the bill began in February 1993, and the measure's chances of passing look better than in the past.

So far, Velda Sue exists as about 90 pages of controversial federal legislation that mimics the successful approach of government-sponsored enterprises such as Fannie Mae and Freddie Mac. Fannie Mae is the name used for the Federal National Mortgage Association; Freddie Mac is the Federal Home Loan Mortgage Corp. Both are federally sponsored corporations that do business in the secondary mortgage market.

A bill to create Velda Sue died in the last Congress because of opposition from the Bush administration. But U. S. Representative John J. LaFalce, a New York Democrat heading the House Small Business Committee, reintroduced the proposal in January 1993.

In theory, Velda Sue would make it easier for small companies to borrow money, especially for real estate, plant and equipment, and other needs that require long-term borrowing. Banks would be encouraged to make such loans to credit-worthy companies, knowing they could then sell the loan to Velda Sue. Without secondary markets such as these, banks have to hold the loans to maturity. Because banks have government-imposed limits on overall lending, the inability to sell off loans makes them reluctant to lend to long-term situations. Loans that are sold in the secondary market don't count against a bank's limit on lending to individual borrowers.

Government-sponsored enterprises are not considered part of the federal budget, but they carry the implicit warranty of government aid in case of a loan default. This makes their securities attractive to investors. Velda Sue's individual securities wouldn't carry a government guarantee as such, but the bill permits the Treasury Department to buy as much as $1.5 billion of Velda Sue loans, subject to congressional appropriation, in a funding crisis.

These quasi-government guarantees are a sensitive issue, especially in the wake of the multibillion-dollar savings and loan industry bailout. The recently signed S&L reorganization act requires the Treasury Department, no fan of government-sponsored corporations, to make a new study of these enterprises.

Major differences exist between bank and thrift regulation—in which deposits are guaranteed and federal and state regulators keep track of an institution's health—and the arm's-length relationship that exists between the government and federally chartered corporations.

To be eligible for Velda Sue, according to the bill, loans would have to be generated by small businesses with a net worth of $8 million or less and have annual, after-tax income of $2.5 million or less. Loans would have to be fully amortized and secured by a first mortgage on the firms' collateral. Banks would have to be shareholders in Velda Sue before they could sell loans to it. Velda Sue, as a corporation, wouldn't start until it had sold $30 million in stock to participating financial institutions.

The bill also would create a Velda Sue subsidiary, the Corporation for Small Business Investment (COSBI), which would perform a parallel secondary market function for debentures sold by some 300 privately capitalized small business investment companies licensed by the Small Business Administration to invest in minority-owned companies or other small firms. COSBI has been debated in Congress for several years but has failed to win approval as an entity of its own.

BUREAUCRACY AT ALL LEVELS

To keep all this in perspective, the federal government is not alone in its problems of bureaucratic impropriety. There are many stories of bureaucratic blunders at the state, county, and city levels. As one story goes, a Massachusetts maker of precision metal parts handed some paperwork in a sealed envelope to a state environmental regulator. The regulator lifted it and without opening it handed it back, saying it wasn't heavy enough.

In today's world of bureaucratic red tape, strange things happen. Watchdog groups as well as business owners who consider strong regulation essential shrug off the horror stories as irregularities. Others see them as further evidence that regulators are eating entrepreneurs alive.

Another story is of a New York city businessman who applied for a low-interest $400,000 loan from New York City's Small Business Growth Fund early in 1991. His successful scrap-metal processing firm had more than enough fixed-asset collateral to cover a $400,000 obligation, and he thought all he had to do was to furnish the city information.

But that was the problem. The city definitely wanted information—lots and lots of information. The city required the applicant to fill out paperwork reportedly two or three inches thick. They wanted a history of the company back to 1910 as well as five-year forecasts for the business and for the entire U.S. economy. During the fall of 1992, he was going to quit, but the city urged that the application be resubmitted, saying all it needed were some "updates." The paperwork continued. The loan was finally granted. But in the meantime, market interest rates had come down. The applicant had also spent $20,000 for outside help in filling out forms. It was finally calculated that his savings would be only $5,000 in lower interest payments—or about one-tenth of his original projection of $50,000.

The agency running the Small Business Growth Fund for the city of New York acknowledges that the program is not perfect. This is due partly to the cumbersome paperwork required and partly to the fact that it cannot accept receivables or inventory as collateral. But the program has achieved a distinction of sorts: In its two years of existence, it has made only one loan.

These are merely a couple of "war stories" about dealing with bureaucracies, of which the SBA is one. When you decide to deal with it, be prepared for the type of inaction you've just read about. As was stated at the beginning of this section, there is no incentive for the employees of these organizations to be responsive to you (the customer). In fact, there is incentive to do just the opposite and hope you will go away. But you can be thankful that the vast majority of the SBA's employees are sincere, hard-working individuals who truly want to help.

However, it may be just your luck to run into and get stuck with that minority that creates the infamous reputation of the organization as a whole. If this occurs, demand the name of the suspected offender's supervisor and continue to go up the chain of command until you get answers to your questions and action on your request. Document your case thoroughly, including telephone conversations, and send copies of that documentation to the SBA administrator—currently Mr. Erskine Bowles—in Washington, D.C., your regional SBA director, and your congressional representatives. Ask for their intervention in your case to get the answers you desire. This will inform them of the problems at the field office level—and put pressure on the field office officials to look into your specific case. You still may not get the answer(s) you wanted, but you will likely get results.

SBA PUBLICATIONS

Home-based businesses can benefit from the SBA's numerous publications and videotapes, which are produced by local offices as well as the Washington headquarters. Though they are sometimes elementary (a pamphlet called *Small Business Start-up Information Package* reads, "Business ownership can be challenging, fun, and exciting. But it's also a lot of work. Can you face 12-hour workdays six or seven days a week?"), the publications do cover an array of topics. SBA publications begin with such basics as writing a business plan and the ABCs of borrowing and then progress through venture capital, accounting and bookkeeping, cash management, choosing a retail location, leasing equipment, and managing a small construction company.

Many of these pamphlets are free; others carry charges ranging from 50 cents to a few dollars. Unfortunately, you often have to work to get the pamphlets mailed to you. Some people have reported it taking as many as three attempts to secure a single SBA publication.

The agency operates a toll-free Small Business Answer Desk in Washington, D.C. (see "How to Contact the SBA" on page 17), but dialing it can land you in a voicemail runaround. You can also order a list of publications as well as information on various services. But calling the SBA office nearest you is probably the best first step.

All in all, because many SBA publications are free, they are a good starting point. According to some people, the SBA publications are the best buy in the country and are likely better written than many business texts.

SBDCs

The SBA's Small Business Development Centers (SBDCs), a cooperative effort by universities, the federal government, state and local governments, and the private sector, are probably the best service the SBA offers small businesses. Started as a pilot program at one university in 1976, it has expanded to 650 SBDC branches nationwide, most of them on college campuses. Unfortunately, if you don't live near a college with an SBDC, you generally won't be able to take advantage of their services, which range from low-cost seminars, workshops, and instructional courses to individualized consulting by the business school's faculty and students. The goal of SBDCs is to provide management training, as the SBA estimates that "managerial deficiencies cause 9 out of 10 business failures."

SBDCs have a databank of talent. When you need help in finance, marketing, legal issues, government procurement, or exporting, go to them and they will assign you an expert who charges a modest fee. SBDCs are prepared to help with all aspects of a small-business start-up, including financing, business plan, marketing plan, cash flow, and so on.

THE SBA DOES HAVE COMPETITION

The federal government is a treasure chest of business information, but for most businesses seeking help, the chest may seem locked. However, more and more inquirers are discovering an easy-to-use key: OBL, short for the Office of Business Liaison in the U.S. Department of Commerce. If you're planning to call the federal government about a business matter but have no idea where to begin, OBL is a good start.

Seasoned government officials everywhere have heard pleas like the following many times from desperate callers: "You're the tenth person to whom I've been transferred—I hope you can help." OBL was created to help in cases such as these. It functions as a conduit between the business community and the Commerce Department. One call to its staff, and you will be referred to the right source or provided with the answer and materials you need.

The answers are usually simple. Finding the right person to ask is not. Most requests reaching OBL are for information having to do with government procurement, exporting, marketing, statistical sources, and regulatory matters. And although inquiries do come from small firms without Washington offices, larger companies can also have difficulty in understanding the complexities of the government. For example, a major food processing company needed help in labeling products for export. OBL researched this question and provided the company with the proper information. It was found that the office charged with reviewing and approving labels was not the Commerce Department but the Food and Drug Administration.

The business assistance staff in OBL maintains a network of interagency contacts so that it can quickly provide current information on a wide range of subjects. OBL can also give direction regarding some private sector programs.

For instance, OBL regularly takes calls from business officials who want to put bar codes on their products. They are usually surprised to learn that the Universal Product Code (UPC) symbols, which are used for computerized checkouts and inventory control, are not a government program but are managed by the Uniform Code Council, Inc., of Dayton, Ohio.

Researchers call OBL for market share information once they discover the cost of buying it from private market research firms. Although the government does not compete with private business, it does provide market forecast information at the industry level, which is published each year in the *U.S. Industrial Outlook*, a comprehensive volume sold by the U.S. Government Printing Office and available at most libraries.

These are just a few examples of information available from the Department of Commerce's Business Assistance Program. People with specific questions about government programs can find the answers by writing to:

Business Assistance Staff
U.S. Department of Commerce
Office of Business Liaison, Room H5898C
Washington, DC 20230
(202) 482-2000

THE SBA COOPERATES WITH OUTSIDE GROUPS TO SERVE YOU

New software programs developed by the National Business Association (NBA) in partnership with the U.S. Small Business Administration can give you a good idea of whether or not you qualify for an SBA-guaranteed loan.

THE FIRST STEP REVIEW is an orientation to the SBA-guaranteed loan program and will assist you in determining the likelihood of obtaining a loan backed by the SBA. The purpose of FIRST STEP is to provide you with information about where you stand at present in terms of receiving an SBA-guaranteed loan. By knowing what a lender is looking for, you can move forward with confidence and improve your chances of success. The program requests information on five critical areas and then evaluates and scores the responses. You can usually complete the program in less than half an hour, even if you have never worked on a computer before. A total score of 70 or more suggests that you have a good chance of receiving an SBA-guaranteed loan; however, it does not guarantee that you will be approved. It does mean that you are in a very favorable position to apply. If you get below 70, you can play around with your score in areas where you are weak to see what it would take to get a 70 and then develop a plan to improve your score. If you score 70 or above and need a lender, the NBA can be contacted to put you in touch with one that is working with the NBA under the guaranteed loan program. The program diskette is available on a Macintosh 3½″ diskette as well as DOS 3½″ or 5¼″ diskettes. This program is free to all requesting it.

The FIRST STEP PROJECTED PROFIT OR LOSS STATEMENT has been designed to assist you in securing an SBA loan. This program will obviate endless hours of manually figuring, erasing, and revising your profit or loss statements; now all the figuring can be done on a user-friendly IBM-compatible (DOS-based) computer (the program requires a hard disk drive to operate). The profit or loss statement generated by this program is an exact duplicate of the SBA Plan Forecast form used as part of the loan eligibility process. This program is available for $5.00 to the general public and is free to NBA members.

The FIRST STEP PROJECTED CASH FLOW ANALYSIS duplicates the SBA Cash Flow form. Based on reasonable predictions of monthly levels of sales, costs, and expenses, this forecast enables you to develop a preview of the amount of profit or loss that can be expected either month to month or for the business year. This program is available for IBM-compatible computers; it can be yours for $5.00 or for free if you are an NBA member.

To order these programs, send your request to:

National Business Association
P.O. Box 870728
Dallas, TX 75287

or call the NBA at (800)456-0440 and order with your American Express, VISA, or Mastercard. Be sure to include the following information in your request: Your name, NBA member certificate number (if applicable), street address, telephone, city, state, and zip code.

SUMMARY

Regardless of whatever proclamations the SBA or like government agencies (state or local) make regarding the benefits they can offer fledgling and/or small businesses, be prepared to work hard to obtain them. These agencies are political in nature, and it is in their best interest to play the game of politics and not necessarily to fulfill their supposed obligations. They will do their jobs, but only if they have no other choice—meaning that you must struggle through all the required paperwork and legwork and be properly qualified for the benefit(s) you wish to receive without any help from them. (They can't give you direct help because that might be interpreted as showing favoritism toward one person or group over another, which is outside the limits of their defined role.)

So do your part diligently and patiently, and you, too, will reap the benefits your government has made available to you.

3 Participating Lenders

The Small Business Administration works with banks that are interested in its loan participation program. Training programs are available that teach these banks the lending procedures and criteria of the SBA. Some banks are content merely to maintain their status as an SBA lender. However, other banks will make the extra effort of having an in-house specialist who is fully trained in these procedures and evaluation criteria; they are designated as "preferred SBA lenders." These lenders can evaluate your loan package and speak for the SBA regarding its acceptance or rejection as a participation loan. However, only the SBA can accept or reject a direct SBA loan. Later in this chapter you will find a listing of SBA preferred lenders and certified lending institutions.

Banks looking for an SBA specialist are quite selective. For example, this ad seeking such a specialist appeared in the 26 January 1993 issue of the *Wall Street Journal*:

> Seeking highly qualified SBA lending professionals in various strategic locations in the US (eg. Dallas, L.A., Seattle, San Francisco, Washington D.C. etc.) to solicit targeted SBA 7(a) business within assigned area. Use effective sales & marketing plan to fully develop area and achieve goals for portfolio characteristics. Effectively screen & structure transactions to assure approval & negotiate with customer to provide proposals w/competitive rates, terms & conditions conducive with achieving the common goals & objectives of the Small Business Lending Corporation (SBLC). Coordinate transaction packaging & submission to SBLC credit/operations for processing & ensure transactions managed timely & smoothly. Develop & maintain strong relations with SBA district offices and act as [XXX] SBLC's local representative in SBA district. Stay current in SBA industry trends, product changes, emerging customers and present recommendations to Regional Sales Team Leader/Product Manager. Candidate must have a minimum of 5 to 10 years experience in commercial business development and SBA lending. Knowledge of cash flow and real estate lending strongly preferred in addition to strong communication & negotiation skills and good understanding of financial analysis & credit principles.

The SBA, in most cases, will only guarantee 75 percent of each loan made by a preferred lender instead of the 85 to 90 percent guarantee for loans made by nonpreferred lenders. This is justified because of the reduced costs to the preferred lender of processing the loan, which is the result of the SBA allowing the lender to circumvent standard procedures that would extend the lending process an average of ten days. However, a recent law has denied the SBA authority to limit loan guarantees for preferred lenders.

Any district or regional office of the SBA can provide a current list of such lenders and their status.

A SOMETIMES ROCKY RELATIONSHIP

The cooperative relationship between the SBA and participating lenders is not always a cordial one. There are times when the lenders do not participate as much as meets the political desires of the SBA officials. For example, a regional head of the SBA recently addressed a group of bankers, publicly taking them to task for their low volume of lending under the SBA's guaranteed loan program. The comments confused, angered, and exasperated the bankers with whom the regional head had to work.

Briefly, the bankers were told that the area's banking institutions were playing a public relations game, advertising their commitment to small business but in reality setting unrealistic thresholds that don't help small business. The regional head went on to say that as advocates on behalf of small businesses, the banks had a moral and public responsibility to do more lending. (SBA lending volume in this particular region is among the lowest in the country.)

The banks defended their record, saying the weak local economy made many companies bad credit risks, even for loans largely backed by the government. They added that they would do more lending if the SBA created better lending products, products that meet the needs of the nineties. Many said that the regional office needed to develop more ways to deliver lines of credit to businesses.

So as you can see, the relationship between the SBA and its participating lenders is not always smooth, but overall the program is successful and beneficial to the small business entrepreneur.

SBA PREFERRED AND CERTIFIED LENDING INSTITUTIONS

The following is a listing of SBA preferred and certified lenders by state.
*Indicates preferred lending participants.

ALABAMA (19)

Anniston	First Alabama Bank
Birmingham	AmSouth Bank, N.A.
Birmingham	Central Bank of the South
Birmingham	First Alabama Bank of Birmingham
Birmingham	National Bank of Commerce of Birmingham
Birmingham	SouthTrust Bank of Alabama-Birmingham, N.A.
Dothan	Southland Bancorporation
Dothan	Southtrust Bank of Dothan
Florence	First National Bank of Florence
Guntersville	The Home Bank
Huntsville	South Trust Bank of Huntsville
Mobile	Southtrust Bank of Mobile
Montgomery	The First Alabama Bank of Montgomery, N.A.
Montgomery	First Montgomery Bank
Montgomery	South Trust Bank, N.A.
Opelika	Farmers National Bank
Opp	Southtrust Bank of Covington County
Selma	Peoples Bank & Trust Co.
Sylacauga	The First National Bank in Sylacauga

ALASKA (3)

Anchorage	First National Bank of Anchorage
Anchorage	Key Bank of Alaska
Anchorage	National Bank of Alaska

ARIZONA (7)

Phoenix	First Interstate Bank of Arizona, N.A.
Phoenix	ITT Small Business Finance Corporation
Phoenix	*M&I Thunderbird Bank
Phoenix	*The Money Store Investment Corporation
Phoenix	Valley National Bank
Tempe	Rio Salado Bank
Tucson	*The Money Store Investment Corporation

ARKANSAS (13)

Arkadelphia	Elk Horn Bank & Trust
Batesville	First National Bank
Fayetteville	McIlroy Bank & Trust
Fort Smith	City National Bank of Fort Smith
Hot Springs	Worthern National Bank of Hot Springs
Jonesboro	Citizens Bank of Jonesboro
Little Rock	First Commercial Bank, N.A.
Little Rock	Metropolitan National Bank
Little Rock	Worthen National Bank
North Little Rock	The Twin City Bank
Pine Bluff	Simmons First National Bank
Rogers	First National Bank
Texarkana	Commercial National Bank of Texarkana

CALIFORNIA (66)

Alhambra	General Bank
Anaheim	Landmark Bank
Auburn	*The Bank of Commerce, N.A.
Bakersfield	*San Joaquin Bank
Carlsbad	Bank of LaCosta
Carlsbad	*Capital Bank of Carlsbad
Chula Vista	First International Bank
Chula Vista	Pacific Commerce Bank
Concord	*Bank of America State Bank
Concord	Tracy Federal Bank
Covina	*California State Bank
El Centro	Valley Independent Bank
Encino	*The Money Store Investment Corporation
Escondido	North County Bank
Eureka	*U.S. Bank of California
Fairfield	Suisun Valley Bank
Fallbrook	Fallbrook National Bank
Fresno	Bank of Fresno
Fresno	*The Money Store Investment Corporation
Huntington Beach	Liberty National Bank
Irvine	*The Money Store Investment Corporation
La Mesa	First California Bank
LaPalma	Frontier Bank
Los Angeles	*Government Funding CALBIDCO
Los Angeles	Liberty National Bank
Los Angeles	*Mid City Bank
Los Angeles	*National Bank of California

Modesto	Pacific Valley National Bank
Modesto	Modesto Banking Co.
Monterey	Monterey County Bank
North Hollywood	Val Ven California Business & Industrial Deve. Corp.
Ontario	*The Money Store Investment Corporation
Orange	El Dorado Bank
Paramount	*Mechanics National Bank
Red Bluff	Mid Valley Bank
Redding	North Valley Bank
Sacramento	American River Bank
Sacramento	*Sacramento Commercial Bank
Sacramento	*The Money Store Investment Corporation
Salinas	First National Bank of Central CA
San Diego	*Bank of Commerce
San Diego	*Bank of San Diego
San Diego	Bank of Southern California
San Diego	First National Bank
San Diego	*ITT Small Business Finance Corp.
San Diego	*The Money Store Investment Corporation
San Diego	*San Diego Trust & Savings Bank
San Diego	Union Bank
San Francisco	*Bank of America
San Francisco	*Commercial Bank of San Francisco
San Francisco	*Heller First Capital
San Francisco	*The Money Store Investment Corporation
San Jose	California Business Bank
San Jose	*Pacific Western
San Jose	*The Money Store Investment Corporation
San Leandro	*Bay Bank of Commerce
San Luis Obispo	*First Bank of San Luis Obispo
Santa Cruz	*Coast Commercial Bank
Santa Rosa	*National Bank of Redwoods
Santa Rosa	Sonoma National Bank
Santee	Cuyamaca Bank
Sherman Oaks	*American Pacific State Bank
Truckee	*Truckee River Bank
Tustin	Eldorado Bank
Van Nuys	Industrial Bank
Walnut Creek	*The Money Store Investment Corporation

COLORADO (11)

Alamosa	The First National Bank in Alamosa
Aurora	*The Money Store Investment Corp.
Boulder	Colorado National Bank
Colorado Springs	*The Money Store Investment Corp.
Denver	First Commercial Bank, N.A. dba
Denver	First Commercial Capital Corp.
Englewood	*Republic National Bank of Englewood
Hotchkiss	The First State Bank of Hotchkiss
Littleton	United Bank of Littleton
Montrose	United Bank of Montrose, N.A.
Pueblo	Pueblo Bank & Trust Co.

CONNECTICUT (2)

Hamden	American National Bank
Hartford	First National Bank of Hartford

DELAWARE (2)

Wilmington	Delaware Trust Company
Wilmington	Mellon Bank (DE), N.A

DISTRICT OF COLUMBIA
(Washington, D.C. SMSA) (1)

Washington, D.C.	*Allied Lending Corporation

FLORIDA (17)

Boca Raton	First United Bank
Ft. Myers	Sun Bank of Lee County
Ft. Walton Beach	First National Bank and Trust
Jacksonville	Community Savings Bank
Jacksonville	First Guaranty Bank & Trust Company
Lake Worth	Nova Savings Bank
Longwood	Liberty National Bank
Macon	First South Bank, N.A.
North Miami Beach	First Western SBLC, Inc.
Orlando	The Money Store Investment Corporation
Panama City	*Bay Bank & Trust Company
Panama City	First National Bank
Panama City	Peoples First Financial Savings
Panama City	Security Federal Savings Bank of Florida
Port Charlotte	Charlotte State Bank
Tampa	Southern Commerce Bank
West Palm Beach	Bay Savings Bank

GEORGIA (31)

Atlanta	Bank South, N.A.

Atlanta	The Business Development Corporation of Georgia	Benton	*United Illinois Bank of Benton
Atlanta	The Citizens & Southern National Bank	Chicago	*Albany Bank and Trust Company, N.A.
Atlanta	*Commercial Bank of Georgia	Chicago	Colonial Bank
Atlanta	Decatur Federal Savings & Loan	Chicago	ITT Small Business Finance Corporation
Atlanta	The Enterprise Bank	Chicago	Seaway National Bank of Chicago
Atlanta	First National Bank	Chicago	South Central Bank & Trust
Atlanta	Fulton Federal Savings & Loan Association	Chicago	The Money Store Investment Corporation
Atlanta	*Georgia Bankers Bank	Chicago	*The South Shore Bank of Chicago
Atlanta	Metro Bank		
Atlanta	Standard Chartered Bank	Collinsville	*United Illinois Bank of Collinsville
Atlanta	*The Money Store Investment Corporation	Danville	Palmer American National Bank
Atlanta	The Summit National Bank	East Peoria	*Community Bank of Greater Peoria
Atlanta	Trust Company Bank		
Augusta	Bankers First Savings & Loan Association	Elgin	Union National Bank & Trust of Elgin
Byron	Middle Georgia Bank	Maywood	Maywood-Proviso State Bank
Cordele	First State Bank & Trust	Naperville	Firstar Naper Bank, NA
Decatur	Decatur Federal Savings Bank	Pekin	*First State Bank of Pekin
Decatur	Fidelity National Bank	Rockford	First National Bank & Trust
Decatur	Prime Bank, FSB	Schaumburg	The Money Store Investment Corp.
Fort Valley	First South Bank		
Lawrenceville	Gwinnett Federal Savings & Loan	Springfield	First of American Bank
		Springfield	Marine Bank of Springfield
Mableton	Community Bank & Trust	Urbana	*Busey First National Bank
Macon	*First South Bank	West Frankfort	Banterra Bank of West Frankfort
Marietta	*The Chattahoochee Bank		
Richmond	*The Money Store Investment Corp.	Wilmette	Edens Plaza State Bank
Riverdale	Tara State Bank		
Roswell	The Northside Bank & Trust	**INDIANA (12)**	
Savannah	AmeriBank	Covington	Bank of Western Indiana
Savannah	*The Coastal Bank	Evansville	Citizens National Bank of Evansville
Snellville	Eastside Bank & Trust	Fort Wayne	Lincoln National Bank & Trust Company of Fort Wayne
HAWAII (4)			
Honolulu	Bank of Hawaii	Fort Wayne	Summit Bank
Honolulu	Central Pacific Bank	Indianapolis	Bank One Indianapolis
Honolulu	City Bank	Indianapolis	Huntington National Bank of Indiana
Honolulu	First Hawaiian Bank		
		Indianapolis	The Indiana National Bank
		Merrillville	Bank One, Merrillville
IDAHO (4)		South Bend	First Source Bank of Southbend
Boise	American Bank of Commerce		
Boise	*First Security Bank of Idaho	South Bend	Society Bank, Indiana
		South Bend	Trustcorp Bank
Boise	Key Bank of Idaho	Whiting	Centier Bank
Boise	*West One Bank		
		IOWA (25)	
		Ames	Firstar Bank Ames
ILLINOIS (23)		Cedar Rapids	*Firstar Bank Cedar Rapids
Bellwood	The Bank of Bellwood		

Davenport	*Davenport Bank and Trust Company
Davenport	Northwest Bank and Trust Company
Des Moines	Bankers Trust Company
Des Moines	Brenton National Bank of Des Moines
Des Moines	First Interstate Bank of Des Moines
Des Moines	Hawkeye Bank & Trust of Des Moines
Des Moines	*Norwest Bank Iowa, N.A.
Des Moines	*Firstar Bank Des Moines
Dubuque	Dubuque Bank and Trust Company
Fort Dodge	First American State Bank
Fort Dodge	Norwest Bank Iowa, N.A.
Iowa City	Iowa State Bank and Trust Company
Maquoketa	Maquoketa State Bank
Marion	Farmers State Bank
Newton	Jasper County Savings Bank
Sergeant Bluff	Pioneer Bank
Sioux Center	American State Bank
Sioux City	Norwest Bank Iowa N.A.
Sioux City	*Security National Bank
Spencer	Boatman's National Bank
Urbandale	First Interstate Bank of Urbandale
West Des Moines	First National Bank of West Des Moines
West Des Moines	*West Des Moines State Bank

KANSAS (20)

Abilene	Citizens Bank & Trust Co.
Dodge City	Fidelity State Bank & Trust Company
Dodge City	First National Bank and Trust Company in Dodge City
Great Bend	Farmers Bank & Trust
Hayes	Emprise Bank
Hutchinson	Emprise Bank, N.A.
Kansas City	Guaranty State Bank & Trust
Liberal	*First National Bank
Newton	Midland National Bank
Neodesha	First National Bank of Neodesha
Olathe	Bank IV Olathe
Olathe	First National Bank
Overland Park	Metcalf State Bank
Overland Park	Overland Park State Bank & Trust Co.
Shawnee	*United Kansas Bank & Trust
Ulysses	Grant County State Bank
Wichita	American National Bank
Wichita	First National Bank in Wichita
Wichita	*Bank IV Wichita
Wichita	Kansas State Bank & Trust Co.

KENTUCKY (17)

Ashland	First American Bank
Bowling Green	American National Bank & Trust
Bowling Green	Citizens National Bank of Bowling Green
Bowling Green	Trans Financial Bank
Covington	Star Bank, N.A.
Danville	Bank of Danville
Florence	The Fifth Third Bank
Hopkinsville	Sovran Bank
Lexington	Central Bank
Lexington	First Security National Bank & Trust Co.
Louisville	First National Bank of Louisville (10)
Louisville	Citizens Fidelity Bank & Trust Company
Louisville	First National Bank of Louisville
Mount Sterling	Exchange Bank of Kentucky
Murray	Peoples Bank of Murray
Pikeville	Pikeville National Bank & Trust Company
Somerset	First & Farmers Bank

LOUISIANA (12)

Abbeville	Gulf Coast Bank
Baton Rouge	City National Bank
Baton Rouge	Premier Bank, N.A.
Eunice	Tri-Parish Bank
Lafayette	First National Bank
Metairie	Hibernia National Bank in Jefferson Parish
Monroe	First American Bank
New Orleans	First National Bank of Commerce
Plattenville	Bayoulands Bank
Port Allen	Bank of West Baton Rouge
Shreveport	Commercial National Bank
Zachary	Guaranty Bank & Trust Company

MAINE (5)

Augusta	*Key Bank of Central Maine
Bar Harbor	The First National Bank of Bar Harbor
Portland	Casco Northern Bank, N.A. (Southern Division)
Portland	Key Bank of Southern Maine
Portland	Fleet Bank of Maine

MARYLAND (4)

Baltimore	*First National Bank of Maryland
Baltimore	*Maryland National Bank
Baltimore	*Signet Bank
Baltimore	*The Money Store Investment Corporation

MASSACHUSETTS (10)

Boston	*First National Bank of Boston
Boston	Massachusetts Business Development Corp.
Boston	*Shawmut Bank of Boston
Danvers	*Danvers Savings Bank
Fitchburg	First Safety Fund National Bank
Hyannis	*Cape Cod Bank and Trust Company
Lawrence	Shawmut Arlington Trust Co.
Springfield	Bank of Western Massachusetts
Worcester	Commerce Bank and Trust Company
Worcester	Shawmut Worcester County Bank

MICHIGAN (7)

Flint	The Citizens Commercial Savings Bank
Grand Rapids	*United Bank of Michigan
Kalamazoo	First of America Bank–Michigan, N.A.
Kalamazoo	Old Kent Bank of Kalamazoo
Midland	*Chemical Bank & Trust Company
Owosso	Key State Bank
Traverse City	*The Empire National Bank of Traverse City

MINNESOTA (7)

Bloomington	Firstar Bank of Minnesota
Minneapolis	*First Bank National Association
Rochester	Norwest Bank Rochester
St. Cloud	*First American National Bank of St. Cloud
St. Cloud	Zapp National Bank
St. Louis Park	Firstar Shelard Bank, N.A.
Young America	State Bank of Young America

MISSISSIPPI (8)

Batesville	Batesville Security Bank
Biloxi	The Jefferson Bank
Gulfport	Hancock Bank
Jackson	Deposit Guaranty National Bank
Jackson	Trustmark National Bank
Picayune	First National Bank of Picayune
Starkville	National Bank of Commerce of Mississippi
Tupelo	*Bank of Mississippi

MISSOURI (18)

Carthage	Boatman's Bank of Carthage
Clayton	The Money Store Investment Corporation
Columbia	Boone County National Bank of Columbia
Columbia	*First National Bank & Trust Company
Jefferson City	The Central Trust Bank
Joplin	Mercantile Bank and Trust Co. of Joplin
Kansas City	Boatmen's First National Bank of Kansas City
Kansas City	United Missouri Bank of Kansas City, N.A.
Springfield	*The Boatmen's National Bank of Springfield
Springfield	*Commerce Bank of Springfield
Springfield	*First City National Bank
Springfield	Mercantile Bank of Springfield
St. Louis	American Bank of St. Louis
St. Louis	Boatmen's National Bank of St. Louis
St. Louis	Commerce Bank of St. Louis
St. Louis	ITT Small Business Finance Corporation
St. Louis	*Mercantile Trust Company, N.A.
St. Louis	United Missouri Bank of St. Louis, N.A.

MONTANA (18)

Billings	First Bank Montana, NA
Billings	*First Interstate Bank
Billings	Norwest Bank Billings
Bozeman	First Bank Montana, NA
Bozeman	First Security Bank of Bozeman
Bozeman	Montana Bank of Bozeman
Great Falls	Norwest Bank Great Falls
Helena	First Bank Montana, National
Helena	Valley Bank of Helena
Kalispell	*Norwest Bank Kalispell, NA
Kalispell	Valley Bank of Kalispell
Livingston	First National Park Bank

Missoula	Bank of Montana
Missoula	First Interstate Bank
Missoula	*First Security Bank of Missoula
Missoula	Montana Bank of South Missoula
Whitefish	The First National Bank of Whitefish
Whitefish	*Mountain Bank

NEBRASKA (9)

Bellevue	First National Bank of Bellevue
Lincoln	*FirsTier Bank, Lincoln
Lincoln	National Bank of Commerce
Lincoln	Norwest Bank Nebraska Lincoln N.A.
Lincoln	*Union Bank & Trust Company
Omaha	FirsTier Bank, Omaha
Omaha	First National Bank of Omaha
Omaha	Northern Bank
Omaha	Norwest Bank Nebraska

NEVADA (2)

Las Vegas	*Valley Bank of Nevada
Las Vegas	*First Interstate Bank of Nevada, N.A.

NEW HAMPSHIRE (5)

Bedford	The Money Store Investment Corporation
Concord	First NH Bank
Manchester	BankEast
Manchester	Merchants National Bank of Manchester
Nashua	N.F.S. Savings Bank

NEW JERSEY (10)

Burlington	*First Fidelity Bank, N.A. South Jersey
Clark	ITT Small Business Finance Corporation
Flemington	Prestige State Bank
Hasbrouch	*National Community Bank of New Jersey
Jackson	*Garden State Bank
North Plainfield	*Rock Bank
Pennington	New Jersey National Bank
Somerset	New Era Bank
Union	*The Money Store Investment Corporation
Wayne	The Ramapo Bank

NEW MEXICO (10)

Albuquerque	*The First National Bank of Albuquerque
Albuquerque	National Bank of Albuquerque
Albuquerque	Sunwest Bank of Albuquerque
Albuquerque	United New Mexico Bank at Albuquerque
Carlsbad	Western Commerce Bank
Clovis	Western Bank of Clovis
Las Cruces	*Bank of the Rio Grande, N.A.
Las Cruces	Citizens Bank of Las Cruces
Las Cruces	*United New Mexico Bank at Las Cruces
Las Cruces	Western Bank Las Cruces

NEW YORK (28)

Albany	Key Bank, N.A.
Albany	New York Business Development Corporation
Albany	Norstar Bank of Upstate, N.Y.
Albany	The Money Store of New York, Inc.
Bath	The Bath National Bank
Buffalo	Manufacturers and Traders Trust Co.
Buffalo	Marine Midland Bank
Buffalo	Norstar Bank
Cortland	First National Bank of Cortland
Elmira	Chemung Canal Trust Co.
Geneva	The National Bank of Geneva
Glens Falls	Glens Falls National Bank and Trust Company
Ithaca	Thompkins County Trust Company
Long Island City	*Citibank, N.A.
Newburgh	Key Bank of Southeastern NY
New York City	*Chase Manhattan Bank, N.A.
New York City	*National Westminster Bank
New York City	*The Money Store of New York, Inc.
New York City	Republic National Bank
Norwich	The National Bank and Trust Co. of Norwich
Rochester	Chase Lincoln First Bank, N.A.
Rosslyn Heights	*The Money Store of New York, Inc.
Schenectady	TrustCo Bank NY
Syracuse	*Marine Midland Bank
Syracuse	Onbank & Trust Co.
Syracuse	Norstar Bank of Central NY
Warsaw	Wyoming County Bank

Watertown	Key Bank of Northern New York, N.A.

NORTH CAROLINA (9)

Charlotte	First Union National Bank of North Carolina
Charlotte	NCNB National Bank of North Carolina
Charlotte	The Money Store Investment Corporation
Durham	Central Carolina Bank & Trust Company
Lumberton	Southern National Bank of North Carolina
Rocky Mount	Centura Bank
Whiteville	United Carolina Bank
Wilson	Branch Banking & Trust Company
Winston-Salem	*Wachovia Bank & Trust Company, N.A.

NORTH DAKOTA (11)

Bismarck	United Bank of Bismarck
Dickinson	Liberty National Bank and Trust
Fargo	First Interstate Bank
Fargo	State Bank of Fargo
Grand Forks	First National Bank in Grand Forks
Grand Forks	Valley Bank and Trust Company
Mandan	First Southwest Bank of Mandan
Minot	First American Bank West
Minot	First Western Bank of Minot
West Fargo	West Fargo State Bank
Williston	American State Bank and Trust Company

OHIO (18)

Akron	First National Bank of Ohio
Beachwood	Commerce Exchange Bank
Bowling Green	*Mid-American National Bank & Trust Company
Cincinnati	The Central Trust Bank, N.A.
Cincinnati	Star Bank
Cleveland	AmeriTrust Company, N.A.
Cleveland	Society Bank
Columbus	BancOhio National Bank
Columbus	*Bank One, Columbus, N.A.
Columbus	*The Huntington National Bank
Columbus	Society Bank
Dayton	Bank One, Dayton, N.A.
Dayton	*The First National Bank
Delaware	The Delaware County Bank
Dublin	The Money Store Investment Corporation

Lorain	Lorain National Bank
Piqua	*The Fifth Third Bank of Western Ohio
Worthington	Star Bank

OKLAHOMA (7)

Oklahoma City	BancFirst
Oklahoma City	Boatman's First National
Oklahoma City	Rockwell Bank, N.A.
Poteay	Central National Bank
Stillwater	*Stillwater National Bank and Trust Company
Tonkawa	*First National Bank of Tonkawa
Tulsa	*Security Bank

OREGON (6)

Coos Bay	Western Bank
Portland	*First Interstate Bank of Oregon, N.A.
Portland	Key Bank of Oregon
Portland	*The Money Store Investment Corp.
Portland	U.S. National Bank of Oregon
Salem	The Commercial Bank

PENNSYLVANIA (17)

Bethlehem	Lehigh Valley Bank
Erie	*Integra National Bank/ North
Erie	*Marine Bank
Ft. Washington	*The Money Store Investment
Hermitage	*First National Bank of Mercer County
Laceyville	Grange National Bank of Wyoming County
Morrisville	*Bucks County Bank & Trust Company
Philadelphia	Corestate Bank, NA
Philadelphia	Mellon Bank (East), National Association
Pittsburgh	Equibank, N.A.
Pittsburgh	Mellon Bank, N.A.
Pittsburgh	*Pittsburgh National Bank
Pittston	First Bank of Greater Pittston
Pottsville	Pennsylvania National Bank
Reading	*Meridian Bank
Scranton	Northeastern Bank of Pennsylvania
Sharon	*McDowell National Bank of Sharon

RHODE ISLAND (6)

Providence	The Citizens Trust Company
Providence	*Fleet National Bank

Providence	Old Stone Bank, a Federal Savings Bank
Providence	Peoples Bank, NA
Providence	Rhode Island Hospital Trust National Bank
Providence	Shawmut Bank of Rhode Island

SOUTH CAROLINA (5)

Columbia	*Business Development Corporation of South Carolina
Columbia	*First Citizens Bank
Columbia	*NCNB South Carolina
Lexington	The Lexington State Bank
Mullins	Anderson Brothers Bank

SOUTH DAKOTA (20)

Belle Fourche	*Pioneer Bank and Trust
Brookings	First National Bank
Burke	First Fidelity Bank
Custer	First Western Bank
Huron	Farmers & Merchants Bank
Huron	Community First State Bank of Huron
Milbank	Dakota State Bank
Mitchell	Commercial Trust & Savings Bank
Philip	First National Bank
Pierre	American State Bank
Pierre	BankWest, N.A.
Pierre	First National Bank
Rapid City	*Rushmore State Bank
Sioux Falls	First Bank of South Dakota, N.A.
Sioux Falls	First National Bank in Sioux Falls
Sioux Falls	Norwest Bank Sioux Falls, N.A.
Sioux Falls	*Western Bank
Wagner	Commercial State Bank
Winner	Farmers State Bank
Yankton	First Dakota National Bank

TENNESSEE (8)

Chattanooga	American National Bank & Trust Company
Columbia	First Farmers & Merchants National Bank
Elizabethton	*Citizens Bank
Memphis	Union Planters National Bank
Memphis	United American Bank
Nashville	*First American National Bank, N.A.
Nashville	*Sovran Bank/Central South
Nashville	*Third National Bank

TEXAS (71)

Amarillo	The First National Bank of Amarillo
Austin	Bank of the Hills
Austin	Cattlemen's State Bank
Austin	*Horizon Savings Association
Austin	Liberty National Bank
Austin	*The Money Store Investment Corporation
Beaumont	Parkdale Bank
Bellaire	Independence Mortgage, Inc.
Brownsville	International Bank of Commerce, N.A.
Brownsville	Texas Commerce Bank–Brownsville
Bryan	First City Texas
Carrollton	City National Bank of Carrollton
Carrollton	First Western National Bank
Cleburne	First National Bank of Cleburne
Corpus Christi	American National Bank
Corpus Christi	Bank of Corpus Christi
Corpus Christi	First City–Texas
Corpus Christi	First Commerce Bank
Corpus Christi	First National Bank of Corpus Christi
Dallas	Bank One
Dallas	Comerica Bank–Texas
Dallas	Equitable Bank
Dallas	First Texas Bank
Dallas	First Western SBLC, Inc.
Dallas	The Money Store Investment Corporation
El Paso	The Bank of El Paso
El Paso	State National Bank of El Paso
El Paso	Montwood National Bank
Fort Worth	Bank of North Texas
Garland	Central Bank
Harlingen	Harlingen National Bank
Harlingen	The Harlingen State Bank
Highland Village	United Commerce Bank (17)
Houston	Charter National Bank–Colonial
Houston	Charter National Bank–Houston
Houston	Enterprise Bank
Houston	Fidelity Bank
Houston	Houston Independent Bank
Houston	Independence Bank
Houston	Lockwood National Bank
Houston	Metrobank, N.A.
Houston	Park National Bank
Houston	QuestStar Bank

Houston	Texas Guaranty Bank
Houston	The Money Store Investment Corporation
Irving	*Bank of the West
Kilgore	Kilgore First National Bank
LaPorte	Bayshore National Bank of LaPorte
Longview	Longview Bank and Trust Company
Los Fresnos	FirstBank Los Fresnos
Lubbock	American State Bank
Lubbock	First National Bank at Lubbock
Lubbock	Lubbock National Bank
Lubbock	Plains National Bank
McAllen	Inter National Bank of McAllen
McAllen	Texas State Bank
Missouri City	*First National Bank of Missouri City
Navasoto	First Bank
Odessa	First State Bank of Odessa
Odessa	Texas Bank
San Antonio	First Western SBLC
San Antonio	*ITT Small Business Finance Corp.
San Antonio	*The Money Store Investment Corp.
San Antonio	Nationsbank of Texas, N.A.
Seguin	First Commercial Bank
Stephenville	Stephenville Bank & Trust
Temple	First National Bank of Temple
Tomball	Tomball National Bank
Waco	American Bank, N.A.
Weatherford	Texas Bank
Wolfforth	American Bank of Commerce

UTAH (9)

Logan	Cache Valley Bank
Salt Lake City	Brighton Bank
Salt Lake City	Key Bank
Salt Lake City	West One Bank–Utah
Salt Lake City	First Interstate Bank of Utah
Salt Lake City	*First Security Bank
Salt Lake City	*Guardian State Bank
Salt Lake City	*Valley Bank and Trust Company
Salt Lake City	*Zions First National Bank, N.A.

VERMONT (14)

Barre	Granite Savings Bank & Trust
Bellow Falls	Bellow Falls Trust Company
Brattleboro	First Vermont Bank & Trust
Brattleboro	*Vermont National Bank
Burlington	Bank of Vermont
Burlington	*Chittenden Trust Company
Burlington	The Howard Bank
Burlington	*The Merchant's Bank
Burlington	Vermont Federal Bank
Manchester	Center Factory Point National Bank
Morrisville	*Union Bank
Randolph	The Randolph National Bank
Rutland	*Green Mountain Bank
St. Albans	*Franklin Lamoille Bank

VIRGINIA (4)

Richmond	Crestar
Richmond	Dominion National Bank of Richmond
Richmond	*The Money Store Investment Corporation
Vienna	The Money Store Investment Corporation

WASHINGTON (21)

Bellingham	Bellingham National Bank
Bellevue	*The Money Store Investment Corporation
Chelan	North Cascades National Bank
Ferndale	Whatcom State Bank
Kennewick	American National Bank
Lacey	*First Community Bank of Washington
Lynnwood	*City Bank
Everett	Frontier Bank
Olympia	Centennial Bank
Seattle	First Interstate Bank of Washington, N.A.
Seattle	Key Bank of Puget Sound
Seattle	Pacific Northwest Bank
Seattle	Puget Sound National Bank
Seattle	*Security Pacific Bank
Seattle	*Seattle–First National Bank
Seattle	*The Money Store Investment Corporation
Seattle	*US Bank of Washington
Snohomish	*First Heritage Bank
Spokane	*Washington Trust Bank
Spokane	The Money Store Investment Corporation
Yakima	Pioneer National Bank

WEST VIRGINIA (2)

Huntington	*The First Huntington National Bank
Wheeling	Wheeling National Bank

WISCONSIN (23)

Appleton	First Wisconsin Bank of Appleton

Appleton	*Valley Bank	WYOMING (8)	
Brookfield	Bank One, Waukesha	Casper	First Interstate Bank of Casper, N.A.
Brookfield	*M & I Northern Bank		
Brown Deer	First Bank, Brown Deer	Casper	Key Bank
Eau Claire	*First Wisconsin National Bank	Casper	Norwest Casper Bank
		Cheyenne	American National Bank
Fond du Lac	*First Wisconsin National Bank of Fond du Lac	Cheyenne	*Key Bank
		Laramie	Key Bank
Green Bay	Associated Kellogg	Rawlins	Key Bank
Green Bay	First Wisconsin Bank of Green Bay	Sheridan	First Interstate Bank of Commerce
Green Bay	University Bank		
Madison	*First Wisconsin National Bank of Madison	GUAM	
		No Data Found	
Madison	Bank One, Madison		
Madison	Valley Bank Madison	PUERTO RICO (2)	
Manitowoc	Associated Manitowoc Bank	San Juan	Banco Popular de Puerto Rico
Menomonee	F&M Bank of Menomonee		
Milwaukee	*Associated Commerce Bank	San Juan	Government Development Bank of Puerto Rico
Milwaukee	*First Wisconsin National Bank of Milwaukee		
Milwaukee	*Bank One, Milwaukee	TRUST TERRITORY OF THE PACIFIC ISLANDS	
Sheboygan	Norwest Bank Wisconsin, East Central	No Data Found	
Sheboygan	*First Wisconsin National Bank of Sheboygan	VIRGIN ISLANDS	
Sturgeon Bay	Bank of Sturgeon Bay	No Data Found	
Wausau	*First American National Bank of Wausau		
		AMERICAN SAMOA	
Wausau	M&I First American National Bank	No Data Found	

SBA VENTURE CAPITAL PROGRAM (SBICs AND MESBICs)

Although this 33-year-old program provided startup capital for companies such as Apple Computer and Federal Express and also helped create the private venture capital industry, it has experienced some hard times in recent years. The most recent recession, the inherent risk of venture capital investments, and derelict SBA regulation has helped create a high failure rate for SBICs in recent years.

Take, for example, River Capital Corp. of Springfield, Virginia, and First Connecticut Small Business Investment Co. of Bridgeport. Both failed in 1990, owing the SBA nearly $30 million each. Another SBIC, Royal Business Funds, Inc., of New York, failed in the late 1980s, leaving the SBA with the Colorado ski resort mentioned previously. Last year, a review conducted for the Senate Small Business Committee concluded that the SBIC program is in danger of self-destructing as a result of structural and regulatory problems.

Despite these recent difficulties, the SBIC program has been an overall success. The historic proof is that the program doesn't lose money. And with the use of borrowed funds to make equity investments, the SBICs have financed a nice crop of big companies. The issue is to make that universe of companies bigger.

A Small Business Administration task force released a report in 1992 that calls for drastically revamping the financing of this troubled federal program. The panel has advocated a new kind of long-term backing for SBIC programs that would let SBICs raise part of their venture capital by selling preferred stock to the government. Currently, SBICs borrow federal funds and add them to private money to invest in ventures that can't obtain financing elsewhere.

The task force's main recommendation for improving the program is aimed at its most serious structural problem: the fact that SBICs have to make equity or long-term investments in venture-oriented companies by using borrowed funds. Reviews of the program suggest that many SBICs ran into trouble because they had to repay those loans on a regular basis, even though their investment wouldn't show any short-term profits. The SBA already has stiffened its oversight of the program by changing some rules and adding staff to review the investment companies.

The report goes on to say that under the task force proposal the government would benefit not only from receiving the eventual dividends paid on its preferred stock but also from sharing with other investors in a company's profits. This could mean that the government's return on its investment in SBICs could reach about 10 percent under the new system, compared with an average of 7 percent in past years. This new financing proposal for the investment companies also would probably attract pension fund investors. Pension funds, which provide about half of all the money used by the venture capital industry, haven't invested in SBICs because the old operating system would have forced them to file complicated tax returns.

The private venture capital industry also shrank in size during the latest recession. It now handles about $1 billion a year, compared with about $4 billion annually in the late 1980s. At the time, the Bush administration said it wanted to spur investment in businesses with high potential, and the SBA administrator backed the task force's recommendations. But the fate of the proposal is uncertain because the proposal is new and relatively complex.

A report prepared for the Senate Small Business Committee says that the SBA's venture capital program is in a "free fall of crisis proportions" and will become extinct unless it is overhauled immediately. It goes on to compare the program's problems to those of the savings and loan industry, though on a much smaller scale. According to the report, SBICs in liquidation proceedings are expected to owe the government $645 million by the end of 1992, or 41 percent of the government money invested in the entire program. That total would be up 36 percent from $476 million in 1991. The report also maintains that poor regulation and understaffing at the SBA are among the principal causes of the current problems. The study refers to semiannual reports from the office of the SBA's inspector general in 1986 and 1987 that reveal the office couldn't examine 63 SBICs because of staff limitations. Budget requests for the inspector general's office were reduced by a total of 45 percent in 1985 and 1986. When the SBIC crisis was first uncovered, the five staffers handling SBIC liquidations had a caseload that experts said would have required 50 people to handle effectively by private industry standards.

The report precipitated the call for a stronger reregulation of the investment firms, noting a close analogy between what had happened in the savings and loan industry and what was happening in the SBIC program. It stated that unless the program was managed more effectively, the best plan of action might be to exercise benign neglect and let the program slowly rust away—or to gut it outright. The previous lack of oversight meant that the value placed on the investment of company assets often wasn't challenged by either the SBA or private accounting firms under contract to perform audits.

Whether the SBIC program lives or dies is of enormous importance to many business start-ups. The program was started to create long-term funding for risky startup businesses in high-technology industries and in manufacturing. Defenders of the program argue that tax revenues from such success stories as Apple Computer and Federal Express more than cover the program's losses.

The report goes on to state that at present 368 SBICs are operating with $1 billion in SBA-backed funds, including totally guaranteed loans and debentures. But assets from a further 165 SBICs are being liquidated, with 94 of those company failures having occurred since 1986. About 30 more SBIC failures are expected.

A year earlier, when SBICs held about $1.4 billion in SBA-backed funds, an SBA estimate showed that potential losses from its investment firms could reach $800 million over the next few years. Officials that are close to the problem have commented that it's hard to have faith in a program that could possibly lose half of the money it's borrowed. However, the SBA generally expects to lose about half of all the funds that go into liquidation, and it will be years before the money owed by companies that have gone into liquidation recently is charged off as a loss.

To be licensed as an SBIC, investors need at least $1 million in private capital. They can borrow up to four times that amount from the SBA in government debentures or 100 percent loan commitments, which can be renewed. The result, say some critics, can be continuous, rolling loans that last until a company's investments run into trouble. The government's venture capital program has run into trouble partly because of poor investment decisions by the companies themselves. Some critics also argue that too many SBICs operate as lenders instead of venture capitalists.

Some 38 percent of SBICs are bank-owned, but they represent 74 percent of the private capital used in the entire program and make 61 percent of the investments and loans. The bank-led investment firms are also more likely to make equity investments in small firms, like traditional venture capitalists, whereas the individually owned SBICs often simply act as lenders. In fact, the report suggests that one of the biggest problems is that SBIC lenders need a relatively quick return on their investments to cover their own loan payments, while their clients need very long-term investors.

The report concludes that the SBIC industry is in the process of self-destructing. The investment companies financed 29 percent fewer companies in 1990 than in 1989, and the number of new SBICs being licensed is at its lowest point in 21 years. But it is recommended that Congress save the program by making the regulatory and structural changes needed.

Horror stories aside, the SBIC program is essentially a success and represents a viable alternative for some financing needs. If you intend to approach the SBICs for such financing, be prepared to complete an Application Information and Personal Histories form as the first step in the application process. An example of such forms follows.

APPLICATION INFORMATION

APPLICANT COMPANY

Business Name: _____

Address: _____

_____

Telephone: _____

Key Contact: _____ Title: _____

Tax I.D. Number: _____ Form: Corporation _____

Date Established: _____ Partnership _____

Type of Business: _____ Proprietorship _____

USE OF PROCEEDS

Land and/or Building Acquisition $ _____

New Building Construction $ _____

Leasehold Improvements, Expansion/Repair $ _____

Acquisition of Machinery & Equipment $ _____

Inventory Purchase $ _____

Working Capital, Including A/P Payment $ _____

Payoff of SBA Loan $ _____

Payoff of Bank Debt (Non-SBA) $ _____

Payoff of Other Debt (Non-SBA) $ _____

Total Loan Requested $ _____

OWNERSHIP & MANAGEMENT

List all officers, directors, owners, partners, and key managers. 100% of ownership must be shown. Use added sheets if necessary.

Name	Title	% Owned	Compensation

BUSINESS SERVICE & ADVISORS

Bank of Business Account: _____

Account Officer: _____ Phone: _____

Branch Address: _____

CPA Firm: _____

Contact:_____ Phone: _____

Address: _____

Law Firm: _____

Contact: _____ Phone: _____

Address: _____

Business Insurance Broker: _____

Broker/Agent: _____ Phone: _____

Address: _____

Personal Insurance Broker: _____

Broker/Agent: _____ Phone: _____

Address: _____

Does this business, its officers or directors, or any 20 percent or more owner also own or have a controlling interest in any other businesses? (yes) (no) If so, please provide their names and the relationship with your company, along with a current balance sheet and operating statement for each.

_____

_____

Do you buy from, sell to, or use the services of any concern in which any officer, director, key manager, or 20 percent or more owner of this company have a significant financial interest? (yes) (no) If so, provide details as attachments.

_____

_____

Have you or any officers of this company ever been involved in bankruptcy or insolvency proceedings? (yes) (no) If so, please provide additional details as attachments.

Are you or your business involved in any pending lawsuits? (yes) (no) If so, please provide details as attachments.

Is any officer, director, key manager, or 20 percent or more owner of this company presently under indictment, or on parole or probation? (yes) (no) If so, please provide details as attachments.

PERSONAL HISTORIES

Please provide the following information for every officer, director, owner of 20% or more of the company, and any other person who has authority to speak for and commit the company in the management of the business:

Full Name: _____

Any Former Names: _____   Dates Used: _____

_____   _____

Social Security No.: _____   U.S. Citizen? Yes _____ No _____

Date of Birth: _____   If no, give Alien Registration Number:

Place of Birth: _____   _____

Current Home Address: _____

_____

Current Phone: home _____ business _____

Dates Here: from _____ until _____

Immediate Past Home: _____

_____

Dates There: from _____ until _____

****

When you provide the SBIC the above information, the SBIC Loan Officer can proceed to efficiently complete the SBA loan package forms and do the credit and background checks in the shortest amount of time (as short as ten days in ideal situations).

_____

Because of the problems of the SBIC program, there has been a constant change in qualified participant companies. For a current list of the Small Business Investment Corporations in your area, contact your regional SBA office.

When contacting these companies you should discuss some very pertinent items before making a decision to proceed with your loan or investment request. The following is a general checklist.

Name: _____

Address: _____

_____

City: _____ State: _____ Zip: _____

Phone No.: _____

FAX No.: _____

Contact person: _____

Preferred level of loans or investments: _____

Preferred types of loans or investments: _____

Investment types: _____

Industry preference: _____

Geographical lending/investing preference: _____

The blanks for name, address, phone and fax numbers, and contact person are self-explanatory. However, some people may have trouble understanding what is meant by the last five items, so here's an explanation of each.

- **Preferred level of loans or investments:** Here you fill in the amount and type of funding the organization would like to receive, such as loans between $250,000 and $500,000 or equity investment up to $1 million, and so on.

- **Preferred types of loans or investments:** Does the organization prefer to make loans or equity investments or both?

- **Investment types:** Does the organization prefer to invest in startup companies, early stage companies, expansion stage companies, or seasoned companies?

- **Industry preference:** What types of companies does the organization prefer to finance— for example, communications, medical/health related, transportation?

- **Geographical preference:** Where in the world does the organization prefer to invest—locally, statewide, regionally, nationally, or worldwide?

Fill out this information for each of the SBICs you contact. In this manner you can evaluate those SBICs that present the best potential for success in obtaining the financing you desire.

For additional and more current lists of capital sources, refer to *Pratt's Guide to Venture Capital Sources* (New York: Venture Economics Publishing, 1993).

4 Direct Loan Application Approval and Denial

LOAN EVALUATION GUIDELINES

To apply for a direct loan, you must provide proof that funds are not available on reasonable terms elsewhere. You must show evidence of refusal from your bank, if any, or a lending institution with capacity to provide the kind of funding requested. In cities where the population is more than 200,000, you must be refused by at least two such institutions. Each bank must provide a letter stating its reasons for refusal of credit, the date of refusal, and the requested terms and amount.

Also, you do not qualify for a direct loan if the owner, manager(s), partner(s), or principal shareholders of the applicant company can reasonably use personal credit resources. SBA policy is intended for the stimulation and promotion of maximum lending by banks and similar lending institutions.

LOAN AMOUNTS AND DETAILS

You should first try to obtain a loan through all available lending services. The SBA, at this time, seldom makes its own monies available through direct loans. (These are mainly used for disaster and emergency situations.) Thus, this book concentrates mainly on guarantee or participation type loans. These loans are usually made in cooperation with a private lender that provides the funds, with the SBA guaranteeing up to 90 percent of the loan's value. This SBA guarantee enables many private lenders to approve a loan that they otherwise would have denied.

The interest rate for a guaranteed loan is the same as that charged by banks all over the country. It is based on the prime rate. For instance, if the prime rate is 9 percent, then the bank may charge you an interest rate of 10.5 percent on your loan. Even though loans can run for 1 to 2 years and even 20 years (such as for construction), most loans are made with 5- to 8-year repayment terms.

INCREASING YOUR CHANCES OF GETTING A DIRECT LOAN

After meeting eligibility requirements, you have completed only the first step, particularly if you are a new business seeking funds and have no previous business history to present. Of course, close attention will be given to your personal financial record, including whether you have ever declared bankruptcy or defaulted on a financial obligation. Be cautioned that the possibility of your obtaining a loan is minimized if you have at any time been a principal in a business bankruptcy proceeding.

Also considered will be your ability and willingness to provide as collateral anything of value in addition to whatever amount of money (if any) you intend to put into the new business. Even though your responses to these questions will not in themselves cause approval or denial, they certainly will carry a lot of weight in determining how favorably the SBA views your loan request.

TEN REASONS FOR DENYING YOUR SBA DIRECT LOAN REQUEST

1. You are able to obtain funds from private lenders on reasonable terms.
2. Your loan is intended to pay off existing debt, to pay off the principal(s) of the business, as in a management or partnership buyout, or to replace capital already used for such purposes.
3. The applicant is a nonprofit organization.
4. The loan is intended to be used for lending or investing.
5. The loan is used in the speculation of any kind of property.
6. The loan is intended for the relocation of a business for other than sound business reasons.
7. The applicant is a newspaper, book publishing company, magazine, or similar enterprise with the exception of TV, radio, or cable broadcasting firms.
8. The loan promotes a monopoly or is not consistent with the accepted free competitive standards of the American system of government.
9. Some of the applicant's (or principal owners' or shareholders') gross income is derived from gambling, except for those small concerns that obtain less than one-third of their income from the sale of state lottery tickets in a state where such activities are legal.
10. You are acquiring or starting another business (if you already own a business) or expanding to an additional location. However, you may use funds to buy out and/or expand an existing business in its current location. In addition to the preceding requirements, you must be directly involved in your business. Absentee ownership is not allowed.

One of the ways in which the SBA will judge your competence is by the various financial statements that must be included with your loan application. If more than a few inaccuracies appear in your cash-flow statements, cost estimates, and profit projections, your application will very likely be disapproved on the grounds that your management ability is questionable.

The SBA's aim is to promote sound business enterprises. You will certainly hurt your chances with the SBA if you purposely underestimate costs or overstate sales and profits.

5 Preparing a Loan Proposal

Preparing a loan request and application for an SBA loan is not difficult. It involves three simple steps:

1. Collect the necessary information.
2. Utilize the information to prepare the application and forms.
3. Present your application to your bank.

If you need an SBA loan, you either prepare the loan application and additional forms yourself or retain a professional financial analyst to prepare everything for you. Analyst's fees could range from $500 to $10,000 or more.

The loan proposal that has the best chance of being approved is the one you prepare yourself, because in the process of working through the documents you gain better understanding of all the managerial and financial aspects of your enterprise. You learn exactly what the loan request is all about. If you have someone do it for you, you miss gaining knowledge that can be crucial to managing your business. Furthermore, preparing the papers for your loan impresses the lender that you are capable of doing it yourself, and it is often several thousand dollars cheaper.

Following is the recommended procedure for completing an SBA loan application:

I. Contact the commercial (SBA) banking officer of your bank and request an SBA loan package.

II. Review the SBA requirements for a loan proposal, which are printed as items 1 through 20 of the Application for Business Loan (SBA Form 4), and familiarize yourself with the requirements as they pertain to your loan request.

III. Prepare the business plan narrative (operating plan forecast).

IV. Prepare the financial exhibits:
   1. 12-month income statement (profit and loss statement).
   2. 12-month cash flow forecast.
   3. Other relevant financial projections.

V. Complete the loan application documents as required. Pay special attention to required signatures and documents. This is important in expediting your loan request.

VI. Schedule an appointment with the commercial (SBA) banking officer of your bank to review the loan application and discuss your loan request.

In determining your eligibility for a loan, the SBA will investigate your character and your standing in the community. Written character references from friends, business associates, and community leaders will carry much weight.

The SBA will investigate your background, including whether you have a criminal record. Do not lie about your past. Having a criminal record does not in itself disqualify you for a loan, but deliberately misrepresenting facts in your application will.

An ideal way to provide the SBA with a crystal-clear picture of your character is through a professional-style résumé attached to your loan application. In Chapter 8 are a sample résumé and examples of character reference letters that you can use.

A clear SBA requirement is that a business enterprise seeking SBA assistance should be a full-time and primary income source for the owner(s).

Note: When completing forms that do not provide sufficient space for typing in information, you may, wherever you find it necessary, fill in such forms and/or charts by hand, in ink. The SBA allows you to type or write your application and supporting documents—or you can combine these methods.

STEP-BY-STEP PROCEDURES FOR NEW BUSINESSES (START-UPS)

1. Explain in detail the type of business you want to establish.
2. Point out your experience and management capabilities.
3. Prepare an up-to-date personal balance sheet; indicate all personal assets and liabilities.
4. Estimate in writing how much money you or others have to invest in the business. Decide exactly how much you will need to borrow to get off to a good start.
5. Prepare a detailed statement projecting the business's first-year earnings.
6. List whatever collateral (if any) you intend to offer as security for the loan. Indicate what you think the current market value of each item is.
7. Present the documentation to your banker or any bank of your choosing to support a request for a private commercial loan. If your application is denied, ask the bank to make the loan in accordance with SBA's loan guarantee plan or to participate with the SBA in a loan. If the bank is interested, ask the loan officer to contact the SBA regarding your loan application. The SBA usually deals directly with the bank concerning guaranteed or participation loans.
8. If the SBA guarantees or participates in your loan, you will be required

to complete SBA Form 4, Application for Loan (see Chapter 3) and other related forms. Also, you will be required to provide certain exhibits as supplementary information. Included in this book is a detailed explanation of these forms and exhibits with sample fill-in documents and line-by-line explanations.

9. If you are unable to find a bank to participate, then you should immediately write or visit the nearest SBA office. The SBA has many field offices, and its officers visit many small cities on a regular basis. (A list of SBA offices and phone numbers is provided in Appendix K.) For faster results, when you first write or visit the SBA, provide them with all your carefully prepared financial information.

STEP-BY-STEP PROCEDURES FOR ESTABLISHED BUSINESSES

1. Prepare a current balance sheet, indicating all *business* assets and liabilities. Do not include personal assets or debt on this statement.
2. Provide an earnings (profit and loss) statement for the previous full year of operation as well as for the current (up-to-date) period.
3. Prepare a personal financial statement for each principal, partner, or shareholder holding 20 percent or more of the business.
4. List collateral to be offered as security along with your estimate of the current market value of each item.
5. Indicate the exact amount of loan needed and clearly specify just how it will be used.
6. Present the documentation to your banker or any bank of your choosing to support a request for a private commercial loan. If your application is denied, ask the bank to make the loan in accordance with the SBA's loan guarantee plan or to participate with the SBA in a loan. If the bank is interested, ask the loan officer to contact the SBA regarding your loan application. The SBA usually deals directly with the bank concerning guaranteed or participation loans.
7. If the SBA guarantees or participates in your loan, it will require you to complete SBA Form 4, Application for Loan, (see Chapter 3) and other related forms. Also, you will be required to provide certain exhibits as supplementary information. Included in this book is a detailed explanation of these forms and exhibits with sample fill-in documents and line-by-line explanations.
8. If you are unable to find a bank to participate, then you should immediately write or visit the nearest SBA office. The SBA has many field offices, and SBA officers visit many small cities on a regular basis. (A list of SBA offices and phone numbers is provided in Appendix K.) For faster results, when you first write or visit the SBA, provide them with all your carefully prepared financial information.

THE BUSINESS PLAN

Whether you plan to seek financing for a new business or expand an established one, it is essential to develop a detailed business plan. It should include a history of the company and details about its facilities and equipment, technology, products and/or services, production capabilities, markets, competition, sales strategies, management, employees, and company goals. You should also supply complete pro forma financial projections for three years, plus financial statements and tax returns for the past three years if the company has such a history.

A business plan is two things: First, it is your presentation of the positive attributes of your business to lenders or suppliers from whom you are requesting credit. It should tell the whole story about your business (past, present, and future) as briefly as possible. Second, a business plan is also your guide to your business. It organizes, on paper, your thoughts as to why you are in business, who your customers and competition are, your strengths and weaknesses, and your plans for the future. It is a very good idea to update the business plan at the beginning of each year.

Some businesses do not have a business plan, but those that do are in a better position to succeed. Business plans show potential lenders and suppliers that you have thought about the basics of business in general and your business in particular. It also shows that you plan for the future. Business plans are required by the SBA and are strongly preferred by private lenders. The business plan describes the current and planned operations of your business and demonstrates how the desired loan will further your business goals. In the following list are key elements that should be addressed. When compiled, this information will become a written description of your business and should be included in the narrative section of your loan proposal. Carefully think about each area and be realistic in your description. Although you may wish to seek professional help in preparing your plan, you should be familiar with every detail. Your knowledge and understanding of all aspects of your business will help the bank to understand your business and work with you to evaluate your plan and your SBA loan request.

Why a Business Plan Is Important

1. For the entrepreneur seeking business financing, a plan is required to obtain a loan or attract venture capital.
2. For any startup company, whether or not financing is needed, a plan will help keep the business on track during its critical first months and years of operation. One of the principal reasons why businesses fail is that their managers did not develop or follow a plan.
3. If prepared each year, complete with monthly goals, the plan can serve as a valuable management tool for monitoring the progress of all areas of any business.

The Components of a Plan

Certainly there are many forms a plan can take, but if one is searching for a loan or equity funding, it should include the following components.

Executive Summary

The executive summary should be brief (no more than 2 to 5 pages) and provide:

1. The name, address, and telephone number of the business and the contact person.
2. The purpose for requesting a loan or investment and the amount required.
3. A brief description of the company's history, facilities, equipment, products, services, or project.
4. A brief description of the company's markets, competition, and sales strategies.
5. A brief description of management's expertise and background.
6. A brief description of how the funds requested, once received, will be used.
7. A short paragraph about the company's goals.

This summary is nothing more than a condensed version of the more detailed business plan. Very often it is mailed to a prospective lender or investor along with a cover letter to determine if there is interest in the company or project. When submitted with a formal business plan, the summary is intended to give the reader a quick overview and encourage a thorough reading of the plan itself.

The Company

This opening section of the plan should fully describe the historical development of the company. Include its formal name, date of formation, legal structure, significant changes in ownership, business industry, its products and/or services (or those planned), acquisitions and subsidiaries (if any), and the dates when they occurred. Also include your investment and percentage of ownership plus that of others and each owner's role in the formation and operation of the company. If you are seeking financing for a nonoperating business in the development stage, give as many of the above details as possible and describe the investment you and/or others intend to contribute to the enterprise.

In short—what kind of business is it: construction, manufacturing, retailing, service, and so on? What is your legal form of organization: corporation, partnership, or proprietorship? How many owners? What are their names and addresses, and what percentage of ownership does each hold? In what capacity will they function in the business?

Products and Services

In this section, provide information about the company's products and/or services sold or those it proposes to offer. Include inventories in stock or to be purchased, their costs, current or estimated production costs, and selling prices. Briefly present a sales forecast for the next three years. When possible, list some of your suppliers and any credit terms they may offer. A good way to approach this section is to present all of the information you would want to know about the products or services of a company if it were asking you for money.

If you are a manufacturer, describe the products you plan to produce. If you are a retailer, list the various types of goods sold, some major brand names, and so forth. If yours is a service business, describe the services provided. Include a statement telling how this loan will affect the product or service you provide.

Location. Where will your business be located? If it's a retail business, describe the area and the people. Describe your business location's advantages and disadvantages. What are the local zoning requirements? What kind of licensing will be needed?

Facilities. Describe the company's offices, building, warehouse, store, or other facilities; the type of construction (wood frame, concrete, or steel); size of space in square feet; mortgage or lease and utility costs; and condition of the building. What are the purchase or rental terms? What improvements are needed? Describe the types and quality of existing equipment, furniture, and fixtures. What do you want to change? If new quarters and equipment are required, describe the company's needs fully.

Success. Why did you pick this type of business? What makes your chances of success unusually good? What have been your past problems with the business?

Marketing and Sales

This important section must furnish the details concerning your marketing, advertising, and sales plans, complete with projected annual expenses for each category. Include any marketing research and analysis data that will support your sales projections. Describe who your competitors are and explain how the company will be able to compete favorably in the marketplace.

Who are your customers: retailers, wholesalers, or the public? How are your sales made? Do you have to bid? What problems have you experienced in bidding? Do you use sales representatives? How much do you pay them? Who are your suppliers? How do you determine the price of your product or service? What is your estimated cost of sales and net profit margin? How will you advertise or what promotional activities will you conduct to generate sales?

Briefly describe your major competitors. What competitive edge will your business have over your competitor's operation?

Ownership

Furnish the names, addresses, and business affiliations of all principal owners of the company's stock or those who have an equity interest in the business. Explain the degree to which these individuals are involved in the company's management. Include the names and addresses of the board of directors (if incorporated) and the areas of their expertise. Describe the amount of stock (common or preferred shares) authorized (if incorporated) and the number of shares issued and outstanding. If the enterprise is in the development stage, present the details about the planned ownership and include a personal financial statement (assets less liabilities) for each individual who will own equity in the company.

Technology

Describe the technical aspects of your products or services and mention any patents or copyrights you or your company may own. Include any new technology you intend to develop in the near future and the associated costs for same. If you own the rights to a unique technology, this is the section where the details should be disclosed.

Management

In this section, discuss the company's management. List their individual job responsibilities, employment histories, and education. Résumés may be substituted but should be limited to one page or less for each manager. Include management's current salaries plus any other forms of intended compensation. Fully describe any additions in management that may be contemplated and the salaries to be paid.

Employees

On a spread sheet, list all other employees by job title and tabulate the projected wages plus benefits for each over a three-year period. Always indicate the total number of employees the company plans to employ each year (both full-time and part-time), because a number of federal and state loan programs use this information to determine the total loan amount they can provide. In some cases, the limit is $10,000 to $15,000 per job created or retained.

How many employees will you hire? Outline any special skills your employees need and briefly describe their responsibilities. What wages will you pay? Is a union involved?

Other

What kind of business insurance will you carry? What kind of financial records will be prepared, how frequently, and by whom? What are your future growth plans? Are there any other relevant topics or issues of which the bank should be aware?

Finance

In this section, list the names and addresses of your business/personal banker, credit references, legal counsel, and accountant or auditor.

When financing is needed to fund a new business or a project, use this section to describe how the money will be used (product development, inventories, equipment, marketing, working capital, and so on) complete with cost figures for each line item. Be sure the funds requested are adequate to finance the business start-up or expansion planned. If you are requesting a loan, explain the repayment schedule desired and refer the reader to the cash flow projections or demonstrate how the loan will be repaid, with interest, in context with the company's other operating expenses. This is important because all lenders want to know when and how you will repay a loan.

SAMPLE BUSINESS PLAN OUTLINE

I. Cover letter
   A. Dollar amount requested.
   B. Terms and timing.
   C. Purpose of the loan.

II. Executive summary
   A. Business description.
      1. Name.
      2. Location and plan description.
      3. Product/service.
      4. Market competition.
      5. Management expertise.
   B. Business goals.
   C. Summary of financial needs and breakdown of how loan funds will be used.
   D. Earnings projections.

III. Market analysis
   A. Description of total market.
   B. Industry trends.
   C. Target market.
   D. Competition.

IV. Products/services
   A. Description of product/service line.
   B. Proprietary position: patents, copyrights, and legal and technical considerations.
   C. Comparison to competitors' products.

V. Manufacturing process (if applicable)
   A. Materials.
   B. Source of supply.
   C. Production methods.

VI. Marketing strategy
   A. Overall strategy.
   B. Pricing policy.
   C. Method of selling, distributing, and servicing products.

VII. Management plan
   A. Form of business organization.

B. Composition of board of directors.
C. Officers: organization chart and responsibilities.
D. Résumés of key personnel.
E. Staffing plan/number of employees.
F. Facilities plan/planned capital improvements.
G. Operating plan/schedule of upcoming work for next one to two years.

VIII. **Financial data**
A. Financial statements (two to three years to present, if this is an existing business).
B. Financial projections.
   1. 12-month profit and loss (income) statement.
   2. 12-month cash flow forecast.
   3. Balance sheet assuming funding of loan.
C. Explanation of projects.
D. Key business ratios.
   1. Current ratio (current assets/current liabilities).
   2. Working capital (current assets − current liabilities).
   3. Acid-test ratio (cash + securities + receivables/current liabilities).
   4. Return on owner's equity (net profit/equity).
   5. Return on investment (net profit/total assets).

IMPORTANT: When seeking a business loan or venture capital, the plan must include pro forma projected financial statements for up to three years into the future. The statements normally required are a balance sheet; a profit and loss statement; a sales forecast; an inventory schedule; marketing, payroll, and overhead expense sheets; and a cash flow forecast for each year of operation. If your company has an operating history, submit the above pro formas and your business financial statements (audited and unaudited) for the previous three years and the company's tax returns. Some lenders and investors may also want to see your personal tax returns for the same period.

Keep It Brief but Informative

You may wish to include other items with the plan such as drawings, photographs of the facilities, equipment, patents, and so on, but when possible, attempt to keep the total document length to 50 pages or less (30 pages is the best count). One way to look at this "short plan" philosophy is to imagine that your desk is piled high with 100 plans or more and your job is to read and evaluate each one! It is only human nature to select the thin ones first. If your plan is easy to read, realistic, and factual and contains the information required by a lender or investor, it does not have to be the size of an encyclopedia to gain a favorable response. Although some may argue the point, my advice is to keep it brief unless the project is exceptionally large and warrants the detail. The other exception would be if the plan is to be used internally as a monitoring tool. Then you would modify the plan and include considerably more detail about your goals and so on.

Additional Tips

Consider double-spacing the text for easy reading. The financial projections should not be double-spaced. Number each page and include a table of contents for quick reference to the individual sections. Make several copies of your plan for submission to prospective lenders and venture capital companies and keep the original in a safe place. Fancy cover jackets are not required. It's what the reader finds between the covers that counts! Always enclose a brief cover letter with each one you distribute.

Unsure About Your Writing Ability?

Preparing a good business plan does require a certain flair for writing, considerable planning, and some accounting knowledge and patience, but many entrepreneurs do write their own. Check with your local library to determine what books they have available on the subject. *The Total Business Plan* by this author (previously mentioned) offers step-by-step guides that can help you. Should you still have doubts about your ability to write a good presentation, contact a business consultant or accountant in your community who specializes in preparing business plans or proposals. Ask for samples of their work, and if you like what you see, negotiate a reasonable fee for his or her services. It will be money well spent! But remember—the plan must come from you. You must know the meaning and intent of every word and proposition in the plan. The lender, be it the SBA or a bank, will demand this.

6 Completing the SBA Loan Application—SBA Forms 4, 160, 160A, 652, and 601

An SBA loan application package is normally obtained by request from a SBA participating lender (bank). Contact the commercial banking accounts officer. Forms 160, 160A, 652, and 601, which are part of the same package, must be filled out by the business in accordance with the particulars of the business/organization that is applying for the loan.

INSTRUCTIONS FOR PREPARING SBA FORM 4

For illustration, refer to the forms in Figure 6.1a–f.

Information About You

Individual: Fill in (type or print clearly) YOUR legal name (not the name of your business).

Full Address: Use your personal residence address (include the street, city, county, state, and zip code of your personal residence).

Tax I.D. No.: If you have a federal tax I.D. number, include it here. If yours is a new business and you plan to hire employees, you must request an Employer's Identification Number from the Internal Revenue Service. In this case, note that the number has been "applied for." If you do not currently have any employees, do not intend to hire any in the planned future of the business, and are a single proprietorship, it is not necessary to have an I.D. number. Therefore, merely indicate "none" in the space provided.

Telephone: Use your personal and complete telephone number, including the area code.

126

U.S. Small Business Administration
APPLICATION FOR BUSINESS LOAN

Individual	Full Address

Name of Applicant Business	Tax I.D. No. or SSN

Full Street Address of Business	Tel. No. (inc. A/C)

City	County	State	Zip	Number of Employees (Including subsidiaries and affiliates)
Type of Business		Date Business Established		At Time of Application _____
Bank of Business Account and Address				If Loan is Approved _____
				Subsidiaries or Affiliates _____ (Separate from above)

Use of Proceeds: (Enter Gross Dollar Amounts Rounded to the Nearest Hundreds)	Loan Requested		Loan Requested
Land Acquisition		Payoff SBA Loan	
New Construction/ Expansion Repair		Payoff Bank Loan (Non SBA Associated)	
Acquisition and/or Repair of Machinery and Equipment		Other Debt Payment (Non SBA Associated)	
Inventory Purchase		All Other	
Working Capital (Including Accounts Payable)		Total Loan Requested	
Acquisition of Existing Business		Term of Loan - (Requested Mat.)	_____ Yrs.

PREVIOUS SBA OR OTHER FEDERAL GOVERNMENT DEBT: If you or any principals or affiliates have 1) ever requested Government Financing or 2) are delinquent on the repayment of any Federal Debt complete the following:

Name of Agency	Original Amount of Loan	Date of Request	Approved or Declined	Balance	Current or Past Due
	$			$	
	$			$	

ASSISTANCE   List the names(s) and occupations of any who assisted in the preparation of this form, other than applicant.

Name and Occupation	Address	Total Fees Paid	Fees Due
Name and Occupation	Address	Total Fees Paid	Fees Due

PLEASE NOTE: The estimated burden hours for the completion of this form is 19.8 hours per response. If you have any questions or comments concerning this estimate or any other aspect of this information collection please contact, Chief Administrative Information Branch, U.S. Small Business Administration, Washington, D.C. 20416 and Gary Waxman, Clearance Officer, Paperwork Reduction Project (3245-0016), Office of Management and Budget, Washington, D.C. 20503.

SBA Form 4 (5-92) Previous Edition is Obsolete   Page 1

Figure 6.1a

ALL EXHIBITS MUST BE SIGNED AND DATED BY PERSON SIGNING THIS FORM

BUSINESS INDEBTEDNESS: Furnish the following information on all installment debts, contracts, notes, and mortgages payable. Indicate by an asterisk(*) items to be paid by loan proceeds and reason for paying same (present balance should agree with the latest balance sheet submitted).

To Whom Payable	Original Amount	Original Date	Present Balance	Rate of Interest	Maturity Date	Monthly Payment	Security	Current or Past Due
Acct. #	$		$			$		
Acct. #	$		$			$		
Acct. #	$		$			$		
Acct. #	$		$			$		

MANAGEMENT (Proprietor, partners, officers, directors all holders of outstanding stock - <u>100% of ownership must be shown</u>). Use separate sheet if necessary.

Name and Social Security Number and Position Title	Complete Address	% Owned	*Military Service From	To	*Race	*Sex

*This data is collected for statistical purpose only. It has no bearing on the credit decision to approve or decline this application.

THE FOLLOWING EXHIBITS MUST BE COMPLETED WHERE APPLICABLE . ALL QUESTIONS ANSWERED ARE MADE A PART OF THE APPLICATION.

For Guaranty Loans please provide an original and one copy (Photocopy is Acceptable) of the Application Form, and all Exhibits to the participating lender. For Direct Loans submit one original copy of the application and Exhibits to SBA.

1. Submit SBA Form 912 (Personal History Statement) for each person e.g. owners, partners, officers, directors, major stockholders, etc.; the instructions are on SBA Form 912.

2. If your collateral consists of (A) Land and Building, (B) Machinery and Equipment, (C)Furniture and Fixtures, (D) Accounts Receivable (E) Inventory, (F) Other, please provide an itemized list (labeled Exhibit A) that contains serial and identification numbers for all articles that had an original value greater than $500. Include a legal description of Real Estate offered as collateral.

3. Furnish a signed current personal balance sheet (SBA Form 413 may be used for this purpose) for each stockholder (with 20% or greater ownership), partner, officer, and owner. Social Security number should be included on personal financial statement. It should be as of the same date as the most recent business financial statements. Label this Exhibit B.

4. Include the statements listed below: 1,2,3 for the last three years; also 1,2,3, 4 as of the same date, which are current within 90 days of filing the application; and statement 5, if applicable. This is Exhibit C (SBA has Management Aids that help in the preparation of financial statements.) All information must be **signed and dated**.

1. Balance Sheet   2. Profit and Loss Statement
3. Reconciliation of Net Worth
4. Aging of Accounts Receivable and Payable
5. Earnings projects for a least one year where financial statements for the last three years are unavailable or where requested by District Office.
   (If Profit and Loss Statement is not available, explain why and substitute Federal Income Tax Forms.)

5. Provide a brief history of your company and a paragraph describing the expected benefits it will receive from the loan. Label it Exhibit D.

6. Provide a brief description similar to a resume of the education, technical and business background for all the people listed under Management. Please mark it Exhibit E.

Figure 6.1a (*continued*)

7. Do you have any co-signers and/or guarantors for this loan? If so, please submit their names, addresses, tax Id Numbers, and current personal balance sheet(s) as Exhibit F.

8. Are you buying machinery or equipment with your loan money? If so, you must include a list of equipment and cost as quoted by the seller and his name and address. This is Exhibit G.

9. Have you or any officer of your company ever been involved in bankruptcy or insolvency proceedings? If so, please provide the details as Exhibit H. If none, check here: ☐ Yes ☐ No

10. Are you or your business involved in any pending lawsuits? If yes, provide the details as Exhibit I. If none, check here: ☐ Yes ☐ No

11. Do you or your spouse or any member of your household, or anyone who owns, manages, or directs your business or their spouses or members of their households work for the Small Business Administration, Small Business Advisory Council, SCORE or ACE, any Federal Agency, or the participating lender? If so, please provide the name and address of the person and the office where employed. Label this Exhibit J. If none, check here: ☐ Yes ☐ No

12. Does your business, its owners or majority stockholders own or have a controlling interest in other businesses? If yes, please provide their names and the relationship with your company along with a current balance sheet and operating statement for each. This should be Exhibit K.

13. Do you buy from, sell to, or use the services of any concern in which someone in your company has a significant financial interest? If yes, provide details on a separate sheet of paper labeled Exhibit L.

14. If your business is a franchise, include a copy of the franchise agreement and a copy of the FTC disclosure statement supplied to you by the Franchisor. Please include it as Exhibit M.

CONSTRUCTION LOANS ONLY

15. Include a separate exhibit (Exhibit N) the estimated cost of the project and a statement of the source of any additional funds.

16. Provide copies of preliminary construction plans and specifications. Include them as Exhibit O. Final plans will be required prior to disbursement.

DIRECT LOANS ONLY

17. Include two bank declination letters with your application. (In cities with 200,000 people or less, one letter will be sufficient.) These letters should include the name and telephone number of the persons contacted at the banks, the amount and terms of the loan, the reason for decline and whether or not the bank will participate with SBA.

EXPORT LOANS

18. Does your business presently engage in Export Trade?
Check here: ☐ Yes ☐ No

19. Do you have plans to begin exporting as a result of this loan?
Check here: ☐ Yes ☐ No

20. Would you like information on Exporting?
Check here: ☐ Yes ☐ No

AGREEMENTS AND CERTIFICATIONS

Agreements of non-employment of SBA Personnel: I agree that if SBA approves this loan application I will not, for at least two years, hire as an employee or consultant anyone that was employed by the SBA during the one year period prior to the disbursement of the loan.

Certification: I certify: (a) I have not paid anyone connected with the Federal Government for help in getting this loan. I also agree to report to the SBA office of the Inspector General, Washington, D.C. 20416 any Federal Government employee who offers, in return for any type of compensation, to help get this loan approved.

(b) All information in this application and the Exhibits are true and complete to the best of my knowledge and are submitted to SBA so SBA can decide whether to grant a loan or participate with a lending institution in a loan to me. I agree to pay for or reimburse SBA for the cost of any surveys, title or mortgage examinations, appraisals credit reports, etc., performed by non-SBA personnel provided I have given my consent.

(c) I understand that I need not pay anybody to deal with SBA. I have read and understand SBA Form 159 which explains SBA policy on representatives and their fees.

(d) As consideration for any Management, Technical, and Business Development Assistance that may be provided, I waive all claims against SBA and its consultants.

If you make a statement that you know to be false or if you over value a security in order to help obtain a loan under the provisions of the Small Business Act, you can be fined up to $5,000 or be put in jail for up to two years, or both.

If Applicant is a proprietor or general partner, sign below.

By: _____
                                                      Date

If Applicant is a Corporation, sign below:

Corporate Name and Seal   Date

_____

By: _____
                        Signature of President

Attested by: _____
                        Signature of Corporate Secretary

Figure 6.1a (*continued*)

APPLICANT'S CERTIFICATION

By my signature I certify that I have read and received a copy of the "STATEMENTS REQUIRED BY LAW AND EXECUTIVE ORDER" which was attached to this application. My signature represents my agreement to comply with the approval of my loan request and to comply, whenever applicable, with the hazard insurance, lead-based paint, civil rights or other limitations in this notice.

Each Proprietor, each General Partner, each Limited Partner or Stockholder owning 20% or more, and each Guarantor must sign. Each person should sign only once.

Business Name _____

_____   By _____
Date   Signature and Title

_____   _____
Date   Signature

_____   _____
Date   Signature

_____   _____
Date   Signature

_____   _____
Date   Signature

Figure 6.1a (*continued*)

U.S. Small Business Administration
SCHEDULE OF COLLATERAL
Exhibit A

OMB Approval No. : 3245-0016
Expiration Date: 6/30/94

Applicant		
Street Address		
City	State	Zip Code

LIST ALL COLLATERAL TO BE USED AS SECURITY FOR THIS LOAN

Section I—REAL ESTATE

Attach a copy of the deed(s) containing a full legal description of the land and show the location (street address) and city where the deed(s) is recorded. Following the address below, give a brief description of the improvements, such as size, type of construction, use, number of stories, and present condition (use additional sheet if more space is required).

LIST PARCELS OF REAL ESTATE

Address	Year Acquired	Original Cost	Market Value	Amount of Lien	Name of Lienholder

Description(s):

SBA Form 4 Schedule A (8-91) Use 4-87 Edition until exhaused

Figure 6.1b

SECTION II—PERSONAL PROPERTY

All items listed herein must show manufacturer or make, model, year, and serial number. Items with no serial number must be clearly identified (use additional sheet if more space is required).

Description - Show Manufacturer, Model, Serial No.	Year Acquired	Original Cost	Market Value	Current Lien Balance	Name of Lienholder

All information contained herein is TRUE and CORRECT to the best of my knowledge. I understand that FALSE statements may result in forfeiture of benefits and possible fine and prosecution by the U.S. Attorney General (Ref. 18 U.S.C. 100).

_____   Date _____

_____   Date _____

SBA Form 4 Schedule A (8-91) Use 4-87 Edition until exhaused   *U.S. Government Printing Office: 1991 — 282-429/45515

Figure 6.1b (*continued*)

132

(For Corporate Applicants)

U.S. Small Business Administration

RESOLUTION OF BOARD OF DIRECTORS OF

_____

(Name of Applicant)

(1) RESOLVED, that the officers of this corporation named below, or any one of them, or their, or any one of their, duly elected or appointed successors in office, be and they are hereby authorized and empowered in the name and on behalf of this corporation and under its corporate seal to execute and deliver to the _____
(hereinafter called "Lender") or the Small Business Administration (hereinafter called "SBA"), as the case may be, in the form required by Lender or SBA, the following documents: (a) application for a loan or loans, the total thereof not to exceed in principal amount $ _____ , maturing upon such date or dates and bearing interest at such rate or rates as may be prescribed by Lender or SBA; (b) applications for any renewals or extensions of all or any part of such loan or loans and of any other loans, heretofore or hereafter made by Lender or SBA to this corporation; (c) the promissory note or notes of this corporation evidencing such loan or loans or any renewals or extensions thereof; and (d) any other instruments or agreements of this corporation which may be required by Lender or SBA in connection with such loans, renewals, and/or extensions; and that said officers in their discretion may accept any such loan or loans in installments and give one or more notes of this corporation therefor, and may receive and endorse in the name of this corporation any checks or drafts representing such loan or loans or any such installments;

(2) FURTHER RESOLVED, that the aforesaid officers or any one of them, or their duly elected or appointed successors in office, be and they are hereby authorized and empowered to do any acts, including but not limited to the mortgage, pledge, or hypothecation from time to time with Lender or SBA of any or all assets of this corporation to secure such loan or loans, renewals and extensions, and to execute in the name and on behalf of this corporation and under its corporate seal or otherwise, any instruments or agreements deemed necessary or proper by Lender or SBA, in respect of the collateral securing any indebtedness of this corporation;

(3) FURTHER RESOLVED, that any indebtedness heretofore contracted and any contracts or agreements heretofore made with Lender or SBA on behalf of this corporation, and all acts of officers or agents of this corporation in connection with said indebtedness or said contracts or agreements, are hereby ratified and confirmed;

(4) FURTHER RESOLVED, that the officers referred to in the foregoing resolutions are as follows:

_____	_____	_____
(Typewrite name)	(Title)	(Signature)
_____	_____	_____
(Typewrite name)	(Title)	(Signature)
_____	_____	_____
(Typewrite name)	(Title)	(Signature)
_____	_____	_____
(Typewrite name)	(Title)	(Signature)
_____	_____	_____
(Typewrite name)	(Title)	(Signature)

(5) FURTHER RESOLVED, that Lender or SBA is authorized to rely upon the aforesaid resolutions until receipt of written notice of any change.

CERTIFICATION

I HEREBY CERTIFY that the foregoing is a true and correct copy of a resolution regularly presented to and adopted by the Board of Directors of _____ at a meeting duly called and held at _____
(Name of Applicant)
on the _____ day of _____ , 19 _____ , at which a quorum was present and voted, and that such resolution is duly recorded in the minute book of this corporation; that the officers named in said resolution have been duly elected or appointed to, and are the present incumbents of, the respective offices set after their respective names; and that the signatures set opposite their respective names are their true and genuine signatures.

(Seal)   _____
                                          Secretary

Figure 6.1c

SBA LOAN NO.

U.S. SMALL BUSINESS ADMINISTRATION
CERTIFICATE AS TO PARTNERS

We, the undersigned, are general partners doing business under the firm name and style of _____ _____ and constitute all the partners thereof.

Acts done in the name of or on behalf of the firm, by any one of us shall be binding on said firm and each and all of us.

This statement is signed and the foregoing representations are made in order to induce the _____ _____ (hereinafter called "Lender") or the Small Business Administration (hereinafter called "SBA"):

1. To consider applications for a loan or loans to said firm when signed by any one of us.
2. To make a loan or loans to said firm against a promissory note or promissory notes signed in the firm name by any one of.us.
3. To accept as security for the payment of such note or notes any collateral which may be offered by any one of us.
4. To consider applications signed in the firm name by any one of us for any renewals or extensions for all or any part of such loan or loans and any other loan or loans heretofore or hereafter made by Lender or SBA to said firm.
5. To accept any other instruments or agreements of said firm which may be required by Lender or SBA in connection with such loan, renewals, or extensions when signed by any one of us.

Any indebtedness heretofore contracted and any contracts or agreements heretofore made with Lender or SBA on behalf of said firm and all acts of partners or agents of said firm in connection with said indebtedness or said contracts or agreements are hereby ratified and confirmed, and we do hereby certify that THERE IS ATTACHED HERETO A TRUE COPY OF OUR AGREEMENT OF PARTNERSHIP.

Each of the undersigned is authorized to mortgage and/or pledge all or any part of the property, real, personal, or mixed, of said firm as security for any such loan.

This statement and representations made herein are in no way intended to exclude the general authority of each partner as to any acts not specifically mentioned or to limit the power of any one of us to bind said firm and each and every one of us individually.

Lender or SBA is authorized to rely upon the aforesaid statements until receipt of written notice of any change.

Signed this _____ day of _____ , 19 ____

(Typewrite Name)	_(Signature)_
(Typewrite Name)	_(Signature)_
(Typewrite Name)	_(Signature)_
(Typewrite Name)	_(Signature)_
(Typewrite Name)	_(Signature)_
(Typewrite Name)	_(Signature)_
(Typewrite Name)	_(Signature)_
(Typewrite Name)	_(Signature)_

State of _____)

County of _____)ss:

On this _____ day of _____ , 19 ____ , before me personally appeared

_____ and _____ and _____ and

_____ and _____ and _____ and

_____ and _____ and

to be known to be the persons described in and who executed the foregoing instrument, and acknowledged that they executed the same as their free act and deed.

_____
Notary Public

My commission expires _____

NOTE: If this form of notarial certificate cannot be used in the State in question, the form should be properly modified.

SBA Form 160A(11-87)
Use 12-84 edition until exhausted

Figure 6.1d

U.S. Small Business Administration
ASSURANCE OF COMPLIANCE FOR NONDISCRIMINATION

_____, Applicant/Licensee/Recipient/Subrecipient, (hereinafter referred to as applicant) in consideration of Federal financial assistance from the Small Business Administration, herewith agrees that it will comply with the nondiscrimination requirements of 13 CFR Parts 112 and 113 of the Regulations issued by the Small Business Administration (SBA).

13 CFR Parts 112 and 113 require that no person shall on the grounds of age, color, handicap, marital status, national origin, race, religion or sex, be excluded from participation in, be denied the benefits of or otherwise be subjected to discrimination under any program or activity for which the applicant received Federal financial assistance from SBA.

Applicant agrees to comply with the recordkeeping requirements of 13 CFR 112.9 and 113.5 as set forth in SBA Form 793, "Notice to New SBA Borrowers", to permit effective enforcement of 13 CFR 112 and 113. Such recordkeeping requirements have been approved under OMB Number 3245-0076. Applicant further agrees to obtain or require similar Assurance of Compliance for Nondiscrimination from subrecipients, contractors/subcontractors, successors, transferees and assignees as long as it/they receive or retain possession of any Federal financial assistance from SBA. In the event the applicant fails to comply with any provision or requirement of 13 CFR Parts 112 and 113, SBA may call, cancel, terminate, accelerate repayment or suspend any or all Federal financial assistance provided by SBA.

Executed the _____ day of _____ 19 _____ .

_____
Name, Address & Phone No. of Applicant

By _____
Typed Name & Title of Authorized Official

Corporate Seal

_____
Signature of Authorized Official

_____
Name, Address & Phone No. of Subrecipient

By _____
Typed Name & Title of Authorized Official

Corporate Seal

_____
Signature of Authorized Official

SBA FORM 652 (8-85) SOP 90 30
PREVIOUS EDITIONS OBSOLETE

Figure 6.1e

135

U.S. Small Business Administration

AGREEMENT OF COMPLIANCE

In compliance with Executive Order 11246, as amended (Executive Order 11246, as amended prohibits discrimination because of race, color, religion, sex, or national origin, and requires affirmative action to ensure equality of opportunity in all aspects of employment by all contractors and subcontractors, performing work under a Federally assisted construction contract in excess of $10,000, regardless of the number of employees), the applicant/recipient, contractor or subcontractor agrees that in consideration of the approval and as a condition of the disbursement of all or any part of a loan by the Small Business Administration (SBA) that it will incorporate or cause to be incorporated into any contract or subcontract in excess of $10,000 for construction work, or modification thereof, as defined in the regulations of the Secretary of Labor, at 41 CFR Chapter 60, which is paid for in whole or in part with funds obtained from the Federal Government or borrowed on the credit of the Federal Government pursuant to a grant, contract, loan, insurance or guarantee, or undertaken pursuant to any Federal program involving such grant, contract, loan, insurance or guarantee, the following equal opportunity clause:

During the performance of this contract, the contractor agrees as follows:

(1) The contractor will not discriminate against any employee or applicant for employment because of race, color, religion, sex or national origin. The contractor will take affirmative action to insure that applicants are employed, and that employees are treated during employment without regard to their race, color, religion, sex or national origin. Such action shall include, but not be limited to the following: employment, upgrading, demotion or transfer; recruitment or advertising; layoff or termination; rates of pay or other forms of compensation; and selection for training, including apprenticeship. The contractor agrees to post in conspicuous places, available to employees and applicants for employment, notices to be provided setting forth the provisions of this nondiscrimination clause.

(2) The contractor will, in all solicitations or advertisements for employees placed by or on behalf of the contractor, state that all qualified applicants will receive consideration for employment without regard to race, color, religion, sex or national origin.

(3) The contractor will send to each labor union or representative of workers with which he has a collective bargaining agreement or other contract or understanding, a notice to be provided advising the said labor union or workers' representative of the contractor's commitments under Executive Order 11246, as amended, and shall post copies of the notice in conspicuous places available to employees and applicants for employment.

(4) The contractor will comply with all provisions of Executive Order 11246, as amended, and the rules and relevant orders of the Secretary of Labor created thereby.

(5) The contractor will furnish all information and reports required by Executive Order 11246, as amended, and by the rules, regulations and orders of the Secretary of Labor, or pursuant thereto, and will permit access to books, records and accounts by SBA (See SBA Form 793) and the Secretary of Labor for purposes of investigation to ascertain compliance with such rules, regulations and orders. (The information collection requirements contained in Executive Order 11246, as amended, are approved under OMB No. 1215-0072.)

(6) In the event of the contractor's noncompliance with the nondiscrimination clause or with any of the said rules, regulations or orders, this contract may be cancelled, terminated or suspended in whole or in part and the contractor may be declared ineligible for further Government contracts or federally assisted construction contracts in accordance with procedures authorized in Executive Order 11246, as amended, and such other sanctions may be imposed and remedies invoked as provided in the said Executive Order or by rule, regulation or order of the Secretary of Labor, or as otherwise provided by law.

The contractor will include the portion of the sentence immediately preceding paragraph (1) and the provisions of paragraphs (1) through (6) in every subcontract or purchase order unless exempted by rules, regulations or orders of the Secretary of Labor issued pursuant to Executive Order 11246, as amended, so that such provisions will be binding upon each subcontractor or vendor. The contractor will take such action with respect to any subcontract or purchase order as SBA may direct as a means of enforcing such provisions, including sanctions for noncompliance: Provided, however that in the event a contractor becomes involved in or is threatened with litigation with a subcontractor or vendor as a result of such direction by SBA, the contractor may request the United States to enter into such litigation to protect the interest of the United States.

SBA Form 601 (10-85) REF: SOP 9030 Previous editions are obsolete

Figure 6.1f

The Applicant further agrees that it will be bound by the above equal opportunity clause with respect to its own employment practices when it participates in federally assisted construction work.

The Applicant agrees that is will assist and cooperate actively with SBA and the Secretary of Labor in obtaining the compliance of contractors and subcontractors with the equal opportunity clause and the rules, regulations and relevant orders of the Secretary of Labor, that it will furnish SBA and the Secretary of Labor such information as they may require for the supervision of such compliance, and that it will otherwise assist SBA in the discharge of the Agency's primary responsibility for securing compliance. The Applicant further agrees that it will refrain from entering into any contract or contract modification subject to Executive Order 11246, as amended, and will carry out such sanctions and penalties for violation of the equal opportunity clause as may be imposed upon contractors and subcontractors by SBA or the Secretary of Labor or such other sanctions and penalties for violation thereof as may, in the opinion of the Administrator, be necessary and appropriate.

In addition, the Applicant agrees that it if fails or refuses to comply with these undertakings SBA may take any or all of the following actions: cancel, terminate or suspend in whole or in part the loan; refrain from extending any further assistance to the applicant under the programs with respect to which the failure or refusal occurred until satisfactory assurance of future compliance has been received from such applicant; and refer the case to the Department of Justice for appropriate legal proceedings.

In consideration of the approval by the Small Business Administration of a loan to _____ _____ Applicant, said Applicant and _____ the general contractor, mutually promise and agree that the(y) will comply with all nondiscrimination provisions and requirements of Executive Order 11246, as amended.

Executed the _____ day of _____ 19___.

Name, Address, & Phone No. of Applicant

By _____
   Typed Name & Title of Authorized Official

Corporate Seal

Signature of Authorized Official

Name, Address, & Phone No. of Subrecipient

By _____
   Typed Name & Title of Authorized Official

Corporate Seal

Signature of Authorized Official

Figure 6.1f (*continued*)

Information About Your Business

Name of Applicant Business: Fill in the legal name of your business. If incorporated, use the name indicated on the corporate seal.

Full Street Address of Business: Use business street address.

City: Name of city where business is located.

County: County, if any, where business is located.

State: State where business is located.

Zip: Business location zip code.

Number of Employees (including subsidiaries and affiliates) at Time of Application: Indicate current number of employees. If Loan Is Approved: Indicate total number of employees you intend to have immediately upon loan approval. If you do not intend to add employees at this time, indicate the same number as indicated in ''At Time of Application.''

Subsidiaries or Affiliates: Indicate the current number of employees at locations other than the primary business address, if any.

Type of Business: Fill in the name of the general classification of your business, such as sporting goods or auto repair. (Refer to the SIC manual at your local public library.)

Date Business Established: If a sole proprietorship, use the date you first started doing business. If a partnership, use the date your partnership agreement was signed. If a corporation, use the date of incorporation as noted on the corporate seal.

Bank of Business Account and Address: Indicate the name and full street of the bank where your business account is kept.

How Do You Plan to Use the Loan Amount?

Use of Proceeds: Enter gross dollar amounts rounded to the nearest hundred. The SBA will place particular emphasis on this section. It is very important that you demonstrate in your business plan how you arrived at these requirements. Your managerial ability will be judged by how well you deal with the presentation of this item.

Land Acquisition: If you plan to acquire land to use in the operation of your business—to build an office or to use for display of your product—the purchase value of that land must be indicated here. Be prepared to describe all details pertaining to land acquisition, including a discussion of why purchasing is more advantageous than leasing.

New Construction/Expansion/Repair: Indicate the amount of the loan that will be used for the construction/purchase of the building *only*. This can include construction, leasehold improvements, or fixtures to be erected. Be prepared to show why you chose a particular contractor by demonstrating that you got several bids and communicated with people who had previously used the contractor's service.

Acquisition and/or Repair of Machinery and Equipment: Indicate the amount of the loan that will be used for the purchase/repair of capital equipment. Have written quotes available from suppliers for any machinery, equipment, and motor vehicles you plan to purchase in your initial stage of operation.

Inventory Purchase: Indicate the amount of the loan that will be used to establish an inventory of items necessary for the transaction of your business.

Working Capital (including Accounts Payable): Indicate the amount of the loan that will be used as working capital, defined as the money held to meet day-to-day expenses of the business. SBA Form 1099, Operating Plan Forecast (Profit and Loss Projection) and Form 1100, Monthly Cash Flow Projection, should be used as a guideline in developing working capital needs.

Acquisition of Existing Business: If you intend to use any portion of the proceeds of the loan for the purchase of an existing business, that amount must be indicated here. If you are not purchasing an existing business, indicate that this item is not applicable (n/a).

Payoff SBA Loan: Indicate any amount that will be used to satisfy an existing SBA loan. If this doesn't apply to your situation, indicate so (n/a).

Payoff Bank Loan (Non SBA Associated): Indicate any amount that will be used to satisfy an existing bank loan. If this doesn't apply to your situation, indicate so (n/a).

All Other: Indicate the amount of the loan that will be used for any purposes other than those already noted. If any amount is indicated here, be sure to include a list of the items included along with their respective values. This section should include a factor of unplanned expenses that may occur (contingencies), which can be anywhere from 5 percent to 20 percent of the loan amount.

Total Loan Requested: The amount shown here must equal the sum of the amounts of all listed items.

Term of Loan: Indicate here the total number of years and months you want the loan to cover. If your plan is to pay the loan off in 10 years, indicate "10 years." SBA business loans may be for as long as 25 years. However, working capital loans are usually limited to five to seven years. If you use the loan funds for purposes that do not fit these categories or if you use the "All Other" category, provide details in a separate schedule and label it "Exhibit A_1". A sample of such a schedule follows on page 140.

Collateral

The collateral you will offer (if any) must be listed on the Schedule of Collateral (Exhibit A of SBA Form 4—Application for Business Loan) and will be scrutinized closely by the SBA and your bank. Keep in mind that collateral for a loan may include any one or more of the following items:

- Transference of inventory receipts for salable merchandise.
- A mortgage on equipment and/or building(s).

EXHIBIT A₁

How the Loan Money Will Be Used

Store Fixtures	$ 7,000
Equipment	5,000
Starting Inventory	15,000
Rent Deposit (2 months)	3,000
Deposit with Utilities	725
Legal and Accounting Fees	800
Licenses and Permits	200
Advertising and Opening Promotions	1,750
Insurance (Initial Premiums)	400
Printing and Stationery	325
Motor Vehicle	6,200
Working Capital	10,000
Contingency Reserve	5,000
Total Capital Required	$55,400
Less: Applicant's Investment	12,200
Total Loan Requested	$43,200

- Personal endorsements, guarantees, and, in certain cases, current receivables that can be signed over.

- Chattel mortgage on your automobile and/or other items of value.

Only when inventories are being kept in a bonded or acceptable storage area or warehouse will a mortgage or pledge on inventories be considered as adequate collateral. Indicate the current market value and current mortgage value and cost minus depreciation of assets you plan to use as collateral in these categories:

- Land and building(s)
- Machinery and equipment
- Furniture and fixtures
- Accounts receivable
- Inventory
- Other

Should you make an entry in the "Other" category in Item 2(f) at the bottom of page 2 of SBA Form 4, attach a separate list marked "Exhibit A₂" indicating each identification and serial number of each article with an original value of more than $500.

EXHIBIT A$_2$

Other Collateral

1979 Plymouth (Horizon) $4,895.00
Serial Number BNL3621A

Previous SBA or Other Federal Government Debt: In the event that any of the principals of the business have applied for any government financing, whether through the SBA or any other agency, the details of such applications must be indicated here. If more space is needed, attach a separate sheet titled "Exhibit A$_3$."

Business Indebtedness: List here all installment debts of the principals of the business. This should include contracts, notes payable, and mortgages payable. An asterisk (*) should be used to indicate any debt that is to be paid off by the loan proceeds. In each of these cases, a full explanation of the reason for paying the debt must be included. If more space is needed, attach a separate list titled "Exhibit A$_4$—Indebtedness."

Information About Management

Name and Social Security Number and Position Title: Fill in the name of the primary owner/officer of the business (the person holding the majority interest in the business). Indicate that person's title, such as chief executive officer or president, and include that person's social security number.

Complete Address: Fill in the complete residential address of the person noted above.

% Owned: Indicate this person's percentage of ownership of the business. If the person being described has served in any military organization, the term of that service must be noted for statistical purposes as well as the race and sex of the person.

These last two items have no credit implications regarding the loan being applied for except in the case of U.S. veterans. In this case any benefits accruing because of veteran status will be applied. Complete the same information for all persons owning an interest in the business. One hundred percent of the ownership of the business must be shown.

Assistance

This section requires you to provide details on professional services used in the preparation of the application. Anyone assisting the applicant in the preparation of the application for a fee must provide all information requested here and sign where indicated.

SBA Form 159, "Compensation Agreement for Services in Connection with Application and Loan" (see Chapter 11), must also be completed if this section applies to the loan being requested. This form should be completed in responding to requirements of this section. It refers to provisions of the Code of Federal Regulations pertaining to appearance and compensation of persons representing SBA applicants, which includes the following regulations.

Representatives are prohibited by articles in the Code of Federal Regulations from charging fees in connection with the application of an SBA loan unless the amount of such fee bears necessary and reasonable relationship to the services actually performed; charging any fee that is deemed by the SBA to be unreasonable for the services actually performed; or charging for any expenses that are not deemed by the SBA to have been necessary in connection with the application. The regulations (part 122, Sec. 122 19) prohibit payment of any bonuses, commissions, or brokerage fees in connection with SBA loans.

In accordance with these regulations, the SBA will not approve placement or finder's fees for the use or attempted use of influence in obtaining or trying to obtain an SBA loan or fees predicated solely upon a percentage of the loan or any part of such loan. Approved fees will be limited to reasonable sums for services actually rendered in connection with the application or the closing, based upon the time and effort required, the qualifications of the representative, and the nature and extent of the services rendered in connection with said loan.

It is the responsibility of the applicant to set forth in the appropriate section of the application the names of all persons or firms engaged by or on behalf of the applicant. Applicants are required to advise the SBA Regional Officer *in writing* of the names and fees of any representative(s) engaged by the applicant subsequent to the filing of the application. Any loan applicant who has any question regarding the payment of fees or whether a fee is reasonable should communicate with the field office with which the application is filed.

Name and Occupation: Write the name of the person assisting in the preparation of your loan application (if any) and note that person's occupation (for example, CPA, attorney, or financial advisor).

Address: Indicate the complete address of the assisting person's business location: street, city, state, and zip code.

Total Fees Paid: Note the total of all fees paid to the assisting person up to and including the date of the application.

Fees Due: Note any balance of fees due and yet to be paid to the assisting person as of the date of the application.

Checklist for Application Package

Beginning on the bottom of page 2 of SBA Form 4 and continuing to page 3, there are 20 questions requiring a yes or no answer. Questions 1 through 14 apply to all applicants. Questions 15 and 16 must be answered solely by those applicants requesting loans relating to construction. Question 17 concerns applicants applying for a direct SBA loan, and questions 18–20 apply only to those in the export business. All of the questions must be answered by placing a mark in the appropriate yes or no box. The applicant should place a mark in the no box if the question does not apply to the applicant's loan situation.

Question 1 requires that you provide the SBA with a completed SBA Form 912, Personal History Statement.

Question 2 refers to material previously covered for Exhibits A through A_4.

Question 3 requires that you include with your loan application a personal balance sheet as Exhibit B and advises that SBA Form 413 may be used.

Question 4 requires that you submit the following as Exhibit C:

1. Balance sheet.
2. Profit and loss statement.
3. Reconciliation of net worth.
4. Aging of accounts receivable and payable.
5. Earnings projections.

Question 5 requires that if you have submitted a brief history of your company, you must also indicate as Exhibit D the benefits you expect to receive if the SBA approves your loan request.

Question 6 asks that you provide the SBA with a brief outline, marked as Exhibit E, of the technical education and business background of the persons indicated in the Management section of Form 4.

Question 7 requires you to provide the names, addresses, and personal balance sheets of any cosigners and/or guarantors connected with your loan request as Exhibit F.

Question 8: If you anticipate purchasing equipment or machinery with SBA loan funds, submit a list itemizing each piece of machinery and its cost as Exhibit G.

Question 9: If you or any of your officers and/or partners were ever associated with a bankruptcy action or an insolvency proceeding, a summary of each action/proceeding must be attached as Exhibit H.

Question 10: Submit details of any lawsuit in which either you or your business are involved as Exhibit I.

Question 11: Provide names and addresses of members of your family or of your business associates who are employed by the SBA, Active Corps of Executives (ACE), or Service Corps of Retired Executives (SCORE). If applicable, also indicate the office where employed and attach as Exhibit J.

Question 12: Submit as Exhibit K information regarding all affiliates or subsidiaries. Such information should consist of the affiliate's or subsidiary's financial statements.

Question 13: If you either sell to, purchase from, or utilize the products and/or services of any firm in which someone in or connected with your firm has a vested or financial interest, furnish such information to the SBA as Exhibit L.

Question 14: If you presently have a franchise agreement, provide it as Exhibit M.

Question 15 (applicable to construction loans only): Provide the projected cost of the construction project along with a statement indicating the source of any additional moneys as Exhibit N.

When you answer question 15, the SBA will require that you make certain that all appropriate compliance forms are properly filed. If you are not sure whether this applies to your case, then consult with a loan officer regarding which forms are required. (Because these are special case forms, they have not been provided here. However, your bank loan officer will provide the applicable forms and assist in their completion.)

Question 16: Include copies of preliminary specifications and construction plans. Final plans will be required prior to the disbursement of funds. Label these Exhibit O.

Question 17 (applicable to direct loans only): Attach loan denial letters from two (2) banks stating that your loan request has been denied. The following information should be included in each letter:

1. Names and telephone number of officers or persons contacted at the banks.

2. Amounts and terms of the requested loans.

3. Reasons the loan was denied.

4. An indication as to whether or not the bank will participate with the SBA in a loan to the applicant.

(**NOTE:** In towns with a population of 200,000 persons or less, only a single letter will be required.)

Questions 18 through 20 (applicable to export loans): Merely check the appropriate yes or no box that indicates your particular business operation and plans.

Agreements and Certifications

Be sure to read this section. It contains agreements and certifications by the individual(s) signing the loan application regarding compliance with the appropriate government regulations, particularly those pertaining to discriminatory practices and payments to and employment of certain federal employees. When executing each form, the signatories are attesting to the fact that any answers and/or statements submitted are, to the best of their knowledge, true.

Important Note: Improperly prepared loan applications will cause unnecessary delay in the prompt processing of your loan application. See that all items can stand up under an inspection by SBA appraisers and lending officers.

7 Personal Financial Statement—SBA Form 413

Each bank or participating SBA lending organization will have some variation on Form 413. The format might be different, but it will require the same information for the most part. The sample form presented as Figure 7.1a is one used by a major banking organization. By completing it, you will be able to transfer the information to most forms provided by other banking institutions to which you apply. Again, remember that the SBA may not approve your loan application if sloppy, incorrect entries appear on any form.

A Form 413 must be completed for each proprietor (owner); each limited partner owning 20 percent or more interest in the business; each general partner; each stockholder owning 20 percent or more of voting stock; each corporate officer and director; or any other person or entity providing a guarantee on the loan.

Form 4506, which is ancillary to Form 413, is a release for additional information from the IRS that the SBA can use if necessary. (See Figure 7.1b.)

PERSONAL DATA

As of: Enter the date the application is being completed.

Name: Indicate the name of the person to which the form information applies.

Business Phone: Indicate the business or daytime phone number at which you can be reached.

Residence Address: Indicate your complete residential address (street, city, state, and zip code).

Residence Phone: Enter the phone number at your primary residence.

145

OMB Approval No. 3245-0188

PERSONAL FINANCIAL STATEMENT

U. S. SMALL BUSINESS ADMINISTRATION

As of_____, 19_____

Complete this form for: (1) each proprietor, or (2) each limited partner who owns 20% or more interest and each general partner, or (3) each stockholder owning 20% or more of voting stock and each corporate officer and director, or (4) any other person or entity providing a guaranty on the loan.

Name	Business Phone ( )
Residence Address	Residence Phone ( )
City, State, & Zip Code	
Business Name of Applicant/Borrower	

ASSETS	(Omit Cents)	LIABILITIES	(Omit Cents)
Cash on hands & in Banks . . . . $_____		Accounts Payable . . . . $_____	
Savings Accounts . . . . $_____		Notes Payable to Banks and Others . . . . $_____	
IRA or Other Retirement Account . . . . $_____		(Describe in Section 2)	
Accounts & Notes Receivable . . . . . . $_____		Installment Account (Auto) . . . . $_____	
Life Insurance–Cash Surrender Value Only $_____		Mo. Payments $_____	
(Complete Section 8)		Installment Account (other) . . . . $_____	
Stocks and Bonds . . . . $_____		Mo. Payments $_____	
(Describe in Section 3)		Loan on Life Insurance . . . . $_____	
Real Estate . . . . $_____		Mortgages on Real Estate . . . . $_____	
(Describe in Section 4)		(Describe in Section 4)	
Automobile–Present Value . . . . $_____		Unpaid Taxes . . . . $_____	
Other Personal Property . . . . $_____		(Describe in Section 6)	
(Describe in Section 5)		Other Liabilities . . . . $_____	
Other Assets . . . . $_____		(Describe in Section 7)	
(Describe in Section 5)		Total Liabilities . . . . $_____	
		Net Worth . . . . $_____	
Total . . $_____		**Total** . . $_____	

Section 1. Source of Income		Contingent Liabilities	
Salary . . . . $_____		As Endorser or Co-Maker. . . . . $_____	
Net Investment Income . . . . $_____		Legal Claims & Judgments . . . . $_____	
Real Estate Income . . . . $_____		Provision for Federal Income Tax . . . . $_____	
Other Income (Decribe below)* . . . . . $_____		Other Special Debt . . . . $_____	

Description of Other Income in Section 1.

*Alimony or child support payments need not be disclosed in "Other Income" unless it is desired to have such payments counted toward total income.

Section 2. Notes Payable to Bank and Others. (Use attachments if necessary. Each attachment must be identified as a part of this statement and signed.).

Name and Address of Noteholder(s)	Original Balance	Current Balance	Payment Amount	Frequency (monthly,etc.)	How Secured or Endorsed Type of Collateral

SBA Form 413 (5-91) Previous Editions Obsolete. Ref: SOP 50-10 and 50-30 (tumble)

Figure 7.1a

Section 3. **Stocks and Bonds.** (Use attachments if necessary. Each attachment must be identified as a part of this statement and signed).

Number of Shares	Name of Securities	Cost	Market Value Quotation/Exchange	Date of Quotation/Exchange	Total Value

Section 4. **Real Estate Owned.** (List each parcel separately. Use attachments if necessary. Each attachment must be identified as a part of this statement and signed).

	Property A	Property B	Property C
Type of Property			
Name & Address of Title Holder			
Date Purchased			
Original Cost			
Present Market Value			
Name & Address of Mortgage Holder			
Mortgage Account Number			
Mortgage Balance			
Amount of Payment per Month/Year			
Status of Mortgage			

Section 5. **Other Personal Property and Other Assets.** (Describe, and if any is pledged as security, state name and address of lien holder, amount of lien, terms of payment, and if delinquent, describe delinquency).

Section 6. **Unpaid Taxes.** (Describe in detail, as to type, to whom payable, when due, amount, and to what property, if any, a tax lien attaches).

Section 7. **Other Liabilities.** (Describe in detail).

Section 8. **Life Insurance Held.** (Give face amount and cash surrender value of policies – name of insurance company and beneficiaries).

I authorize SBA/Lender to make inquiries as necessary to verify the accuracy of the statements made and to determine my creditworthiness. I certify the above and the statements contained in the attachments are true and accurate as of the stated date(s). These statements are made for the purpose of either obtaining a loan or guaranteeing a loan. I understand FALSE statements may result in forfeiture of benefits and possible prosecution by the U.S. Attorney General (Reference 18 U.S.C. 1001).

Signature:	Date:	Social Security Number:
Signature:	Date:	Social Security Number:

PLEASE NOTE: The estimated average burden hours for the completion of this form is 1.5 hours per response. If you have questions or comments concerning this estimate or any other aspect of this information, please contact Chief, Administrative Branch, U.S. Small Business Administration, Washington, D.C. 20416, and Clearance Office, Paper Reduction Project (3245–0188), Office of Management and Budget, Washington, D.C. 20503.

* U.S Government Printing Office1992- 312-624/62831

Figure 7.1a (*continued*)

Form 4506

(Rev. January 1987)

Department of the Treasury
Internal Revenue Service

Request for Copy of Tax Form

Please read instructions before completing this form.

OMB No. 1545-0423

Expires 12-31-89

Important: Full payment must accompany your request.

1 Name of taxpayer(s) as shown on tax form (husband's and wife's, if joint return)	**6** Social security number as shown on tax form (if joint return, show husband's number)
2 Current name and address	**6a** Wife's social security number as shown on tax form
	7 Employer identification number as shown on tax form
	8 Tax form number (Form 1040, 1040A, etc.)
3 If copy of form is to be mailed to someone else, show the third party's name and address	**9** Tax period(s) (1983, etc.) (No more than 4 per request)
3a If we cannot find a record of your return, check here if you want the payment refunded to the third party. ☐	**10** Amount due for copy of tax form:
4 If name in third party's records differs from item 1 above, show name here. (See instructions for items 3, 3a, and 4.)	**a** Cost for each period . . . . . . $ 4.25
	b Number of periods requested in item 9 . . . .
	c Total cost (multiply item 10a by item 10b). . . . . . . $
	Make check or money order payable to Internal Revenue Service

5 Check the box to show what you want:

☐ Copy of tax form and all attachments. The charge is $4.25 for each period requested.

Note: If you need these copies for court or administrative proceedings, also check here ☐

☐ Copy of Form W-2 only. There is no charge for this.

Please Sign Here

Signature _____ Date _____

Telephone number of requester ( )

Convenient time for us to call

Title (if item 1 above is a corporation, partnership, estate, or trust)

Instructions

Privacy Act and Paperwork Reduction Act Notice.—We ask for this information to carry out the Internal Revenue laws of the United States. We need the information to gain access to your return in our files and properly respond to your request. If you do not furnish the information, we may not be able to fill your request.

Purpose of Form.—Use this form to request a copy of a tax return or Form W-2.

Note: If you had your return filled out by a paid preparer, check first to see if you can get a copy from the preparer. This may save you both time and money.

If you are not the taxpayer shown in item 1, you must send a copy of your authorization to receive the copy of the form. This will generally be a power of attorney, tax information authorization, or evidence of entitlement (for Title 11 Bankruptcy or Receivership Proceeding). If the taxpayer is deceased, you must send enough evidence to establish that you are authorized to act for the taxpayer's estate.

Copies of joint returns may be furnished to either the husband or the wife. Only one signature is required. If your name has changed, sign Form 4506 exactly as your name appeared on the return and also sign with your current name.

Please allow at least 45 days for delivery. Be sure to furnish all the information asked for on this form to avoid any delay in our sending your requested copies. (You must allow at least 6 weeks processing time after a return is filed before requesting a copy.)

Corporations, Partnerships, Estates, and Trusts.—For rules on who may obtain tax information on the entity, see Internal Revenue Code section 6103.

Items 3, 3a, and 4.—If you have named someone else to receive the tax form (such as a CPA, scholarship board, or mortgage lender), you must include the name of an individual with the address in item 3. Also, be sure to write the name of the client, student, or applicant in item 4 if it is different from the name shown in item 1. For example, item 1 may be the parents of a student applying for financial aid. Show the student's name in item 4 so the scholarship board will know what file to associate the return with. If we cannot find a record of your return, we will notify the third party directly that we cannot fill the request. If you checked the box in 3a, we will refund the payment for the copies to the third party.

Item 5.—If you want a copy of your Form W-2 only and not a copy of your tax return, be sure to check the box for Copy of Form W-2 only and in item 8 show "Form W-2 only"; in item 10c show "no charge."

If you need only tax account information and not a copy of your tax return or Form W-2, do not complete this form. See the instructions on the back under "Tax Account Information Only."

Items 6 and 6a.—For individuals, enter the social security number as shown on the tax form. For joint returns, show the husband's social security number in item 6 and the wife's in item 6a. If you do not furnish this information, there may be a delay in processing your request.

(Continued on back)

Form 4506 (Rev. 1-87)

Figure 7.1b

148

Item 9.—Enter the year(s) of the tax form you are requesting. For fiscal-year filers or requests for quarterly returns, enter the date the period ended. If you need more than four different periods, use additional request forms. Returns which were filed six or more years ago may not be available for making copies. However, tax account information is generally still available for these periods.

Item 10.—Write your social security number or Federal employer identification number and "Form 4506 Request" on your check or money order. If we cannot fill your request, we will refund your payment.

Where To File.—After you have completed this form, send it to the service center at the address shown in the last column for the location where you lived when the requested tax form was filed.

Note: *You must use a separate form for each service center from which you are requesting a copy of your tax form.*

Tax Account Information Only.—In addition to a copy of a tax form, we can provide a listing of certain tax account information, which is available free of charge and can be obtained by contacting your local IRS office. Generally, tax account information is needed because students applying for financial aid may be required to give the college a copy of their tax return. The school may, however, permit you to use tax return information provided by the IRS instead. If so, the following information will be sent:

(a) Name and social security number.
(b) Type of return filed.
(c) Marital status.
(d) Tax shown on return.
(e) Adjusted gross income.
(f) Taxable income.
(g) Self-employment tax, and
(h) Number of exemptions.

Form 1040A or 1040EZ Verification for Mortgage Revenue Bonds.—States issuing mortgage revenue bonds are required to verify that the mortgage applicant did not own a home during the 3 previous years. As part of this verification, the mortgage lender may want proof that you did not claim interest or real estate tax deductions for a residence on your return. If you have kept a copy of your return, or if it was filled out by a paid preparer and you can get a copy, the mortgage lender can accept your signed copy.

If you do not have a copy of your return and filed Form 1040A or 1040EZ, you can request tax account information, which will provide sufficient information to satisfy the mortgage lender. To get tax account information, do not complete this form. Instead, contact your local IRS office for this information.

If you filed Form 1040, you will have to get a copy of your return to verify that you did not claim any itemized deductions for a residence. To get a copy, please complete this form. Write "Mortgage Revenue Bond" across the top.

If you lived in	Please mail to the following Internal Revenue Service Center
New Jersey, New York (New York City and counties of Nassau, Rockland, Suffolk, and Westchester)	P.O. Box 400 Holtsville, NY 11742
New York (all other counties), Connecticut, Maine, Massachusetts, Minnesota, New Hampshire, Rhode Island, Vermont	P.O. Box 3006 Woburn, MA 01801
Alabama, Florida, Georgia, Mississippi, South Carolina	P.O. Box 47412 Doraville, GA 30362
Kentucky, Michigan, Ohio, West Virginia	P.O. Box 145500 Cincinnati, OH 45214
Kansas, Louisiana, New Mexico, Oklahoma, Texas	3651 South International Highway Photocopy Unit Stop 6716 Austin, TX 73301
Alaska, Arizona, Colorado, Idaho, Montana, Nebraska, Nevada, North Dakota, Oregon, South Dakota, Utah, Washington, Wyoming	TPR/Photocopy 3B P.O. Box 9956 Mail Stop 6734 Ogden, UT 84409
Illinois, Iowa, Missouri, Wisconsin	Photocopy Unit Stop 56 Kansas City, MO 64999
California, Hawaii	5045 E. Butler Avenue Photocopy Unit Stop 53260 Fresno, CA 93888
Arkansas, Indiana, North Carolina, Tennessee, Virginia	P.O. Box 2501 Memphis, TN 38101
Delaware, District of Columbia, Maryland, Pennsylvania, outside the United States	P.O. Box 920 Photocopy Unit Drop Point 536 Bensalem, PA 19020

Figure 7.1b (*continued*)

Business Name of Applicant/Borrower: Enter the formal name used when signing legal and business documents (this may be the same as entered in the "Name" section above).

Assets: List all personal assets as asked for on each line of the form. Round all figures to the nearest dollar. Give details as asked for in the appropriate sections. If more space for these details is needed, use a separate page and title it as an "addendum" to the applicable section, such as "Addendum to section 8." If a line item does not apply in your case, merely note N/A on its blank line. Add these asset items up and write that total figure across from the word "Total" on its blank line.

Liabilities: List all personal liabilities (all items you owe) in dollar amounts only, giving details as requested and described under "Assets" above. Add these liability items up and write that total figure across from "Total Liabilities." Subtract the total liabilities from the total assets figure and enter the difference across from the "Net Worth" entry. Add the total liabilities and the net worth figures and enter that total across from the "Total" entry. The total entry under assets and the total entry under liabilities must be equal.

Section 1. Source of Income: List all sources of income and their respective dollar amounts (omit cents). Alimony or child support payments need not be entered unless it is desired to have such payments counted toward total income.

Contingent Liabilities: List all situations you are currently involved in that constitute a possible monetary liability on your part. If you have cosigned a note for a relative, that must be noted here. If there is a pending court case in which you are either the plaintiff or defendant, note that here. Any other potential liabilities also must be noted here.

Section 2. Notes Payable to Bank and Others: List the names and addresses of any bank(s) or other lending institutions to which you owe money and indicate the original amount of the loan, its current balance, what you pay each period, what the payment period (frequency) is, and what type of security is given—an auto, furniture, or merely your signature.

Section 3. Stocks and Bonds: List all stock, bonds, and like securities you own; the quantity (number of shares) of each; the name of each security; its original cost per share; market value per share; the date the market value was determined; and the total value of each security.

Section 4. Real Estate Owned: List all real property owned by you. This includes any interest in condominium(s), time-share(s), and so forth.

Section 5. Other Personal Property and Other Assets: Describe all assets. And if any are pledged as security for a loan, state the name and address of the lien holder, amount of lien, and terms of payment; if delinquent, describe the conditions of the delinquency.

Section 6. Unpaid Taxes: Describe in detail the type of tax unpaid, to whom it's payable, when it was due, the amount, and on what property (if any) it constitutes a lien.

Section 7. Other Liabilities: Describe all liabilities. And, if any, state the name and address of the person or organization to which you owe the liability and the conditions of the liability.

Section 8. Life Insurance Held: List the name of the insurance company for each policy, the beneficiary(s), the face amount of each policy, and its surrender value.

Thoroughly read and understand the authorizing paragraph. This paragraph authorizes the SBA and/or lender to verify all the above information, and false statements (not mistakes or errors) can result in penalization. So when you are comfortable with all the information you've provided, sign and date the form and provide your social security number.

REQUEST FOR COPY OF TAX FORM(S)—FORM 4506

This is an ancillary form to Form 413. If you have a tax preparer complete your tax returns to the government, contact that person and request a copy of your last two years' tax returns. If these are not available, you must complete the 4506 form and send it to the appropriate IRS office with the proper payment ($4.25 per form) to get the necessary copies. These tax return copies must accompany Form 413 when you submit your loan application.

8 Statement of Personal History—SBA Form 912

A sample of this form (Figure 8.1) is provided at the end of this chapter. It must be filed in triplicate by each party to the loan request. This means:

- If the business is a sole proprietorship, it must be filed by the owner. A statement must also be filed by the owner's spouse and/or any person employed to supervise the operation of the business.
- If the business is a partnership, it must be filed by each partner. A statement must also be filed by the owner's spouse and/or any person employed to supervise the operation of the business.
- If the business is a corporation or a development company, it must be filed by each officer, director, and holder of 20 percent or more of the voting stock.
- This form must be filed by any other person, including a hired manager who has authority to speak for, enter into obligations on behalf of, or in any manner can act for or commit the borrower in the management of the business.

Name and Address of Applicant: Enter the name of your company and the proposed company's address. Use your home address if a location has not been located.

SBA District Office and City: The SBA office handling your application will complete this section.

Amount Applied for: Indicate the amount of loan money requested. This should agree with the sum of money noted on SBA Form 4.

1. Personal Statement of: List the exact and complete name of the individual whose personal history is being presented. Indicate former name(s) used, if any, and the dates each name was used.
2. Date of Birth: Indicate the date of birth of the person completing this statement.

3. Place of Birth: Indicate birthplace. Note whether the applicant is a U.S. citizen and provide alien registration number if not.

4. Percentage of ownership: For the individual whose personal history statement is be presented, indicate that individual's percentage of ownership in the company requesting the loan. Provide that individual's Social Security Number.

5. Present residence address: Provide the individual's present address and both home and business telephone numbers, including area code for each. Indicate his or her previous address and the dates he or she resided at that address.

6. Is the individual completing this form presently under indictment or on parole or probation? If so, provide details in a separate exhibit.

7. Has the individual ever been charged with or arrested for any criminal offense? If he or she has ever been officially charged with and/or arrested for any criminal offense besides a minor traffic or motor vehicle–related offense, supply specifics in a separate exhibit.

8. Did any of these charges result in a conviction? If so, supply specifics in a separate exhibit.

9. Name and address of participating bank. Indicate the name and address of the bank that has agreed to participate in your loan. However, if no bank or lending institution has agreed to do so, then note that fact in this space. In the space under this item, include all details you wish to provide the SBA to assist in an evaluation of your character and indicate supporting documents attached, such as:

    - Letters of recommendation.

    - Membership in charitable and civic organizations.

    - Achievement awards.

    - Résumé.

The employment section of the résumé should reflect a history of experience in the field in which your business venture is related. It is also to your advantage if your educational background reflects studies in areas related to the business.

OMB APPROVAL NO. 3245-0178
Expiration Date: 5-31-93

Please Read Carefully - Print or Type

Each member of the small business concern requesting assistance or the development company must submit this form in TRIPLICATE for filing with the SBA application. This form must be filled out and submitted by:

1. If a sole proprietorship by the proprietor.
2. If a partnership by each partner.
3. If a corporation or a development company, by each officer, director, and additionally by each holder of 20% or more of the voting stock.
4. Any other person including a hired manager, who has authority to speak for and commit the borrower in the management of the business.

United States of America

SMALL BUSINESS ADMINISTRATION

STATEMENT OF PERSONAL HISTORY

Name and Address of Applicant (Firm Name) (Street, City, State and ZIP Code)

SBA District Office and City

Amount Applied for:

1. Personal Statement of: (State name in full, if no middle name, state (NMN), or if initial only, indicate initial). List all former names used, and dates each name was used. Use separate sheet if necessary.

   First   Middle   Last

2. Date of Birth: (Month, day and year)

3. Place of Birth: (City & State or Foreign Country).

   U.S. Citizen? ☐ YES ☐ NO
   If no, give alien registration number:

4. Give the percentage of ownership or stock owned or to be owned in the small business concern or the Development Company.

   Social Security No.

5. Present residence address: City   State

   From: To: Address:

   Home Telephone No. (Include A/C):   Business Telephone No. (Include A/C):

   Immediate past residence address:

   From: To: Address:

BE SURE TO ANSWER THE NEXT 3 QUESTIONS CORRECTLY BECAUSE THEY ARE IMPORTANT.

THE FACT THAT YOU HAVE AN ARREST OR CONVICTION RECORD WILL NOT NECESSARILY DISQUALIFY YOU. BUT AN INCORRECT ANSWER WILL PROBABLY CAUSE YOUR APPLICATION TO BE TURNED DOWN.

6. Are you presently under indictment, on parole or probation?

   ☐ Yes ☐ No   If yes, furnish details in a separate exhibit. List name(s) under which held, if applicable.

7. Have you ever been charged with or arrested for any criminal offense other than a minor motor vehicle violation?

   ☐ Yes ☐ No   If Yes, furnish details in a separate exhibit. List name(s) under which charged, if applicable.

8. Have you ever been convicted of any criminal offense other than a minor vehicle violation?

   ☐ Yes ☐ No   If Yes, furnish details in a separate exhibit. List name(s) under which convicted, if applicable.

9. Name and address of participating bank

The information on this form will be used in connection with an investigation of your character. Any information you wish to submit, that you feel will expedite this investigation should be set forth.

Whoever makes any statement knowing it to be false, for the purpose of obtaining for himself or for any applicant, any loan, or loan extension by renewal, deferment or otherwise, or for the purpose of obtaining, or influencing SBA toward, anything of value under the Small Business Act, as amended, shall be punished under Section 16(a) of that Act, by a fine of not more than $5000, or by imprisonment for not more than 2 years, or both.

Signature   Title   Date

It is against SBA's policy to provide assistance to persons not of good character and therefore consideration is given to the qualities and personality traits of a person, favorable and unfavorable, relating thereto, including behavior, integrity, candor and disposition toward criminal actions. It is also against SBA's policy to provide assistance not in the best interests of the United States, for example, if there is reason to believe that the effect of such assistance will be to encourage or support, directly of indirectly, activities inimical to the Security of the United States. Anyone concerned with the collection of this information, as to its voluntariness, disclosure of routine uses may contact the FOIA Office, 1441 "L" Street, N.W., and a copy of §9 "Agency Collection of Information" from SOP 40 04 will be provided

SBA FORM 912 (5-87) SOP 9020 USE 6-85 EDITION UNTIL EXHAUSTED

1. SBA FILE COPY

Please Note: The estimated burden hours for completion of this form is 15 minutes per response. If you have any questions or comments concerning this estimate or any other aspect of this information collection please contact, Chief Administrative Information Branch, U.S. Small Business Administration 409 Third Street, S.W. Washington, D.C. 20416 or Gary Waxman, Clearance Officer, Paperwork Reduction Project (3245-0178), Office of Management and Budget, Washington, D.C. 20503

Figure 8.1

9 Monthly Cash Flow Projections—SBA Form 1100

The small business owner can realize numerous benefits by completing an operating plan forecast, an essential business planning aid. After the planning stage has been completed, the forecast aids management in guiding the business to perform in accordance with the plan. (See Figure 9.1.)

A PLANNING TOOL

Utilizing the forecast, you can gain valuable insight into the amount of profit or loss to be realized monthly and yearly, based on reasonable estimates of monthly sales levels, expenses, and costs. By having such insight into future events, you can measure the anticipated yearly profits or losses against the profit results, aims, and requirements of the business. Should the profit goals, as estimated, not be realized, there will be ample time to find a remedy and, by doing so, turn an imminent setback into a profitable outcome.

A CONTROL TOOL

Using the completed forecast, you can compare the actual figures as they arrive with the estimates for that month. Proper steps can subsequently be initiated to right any part of the operation that may get off course. Time and money are saved, thus insuring a generally more profitable enterprise.

SOME CASH FLOW CONSIDERATIONS

Don't expect the forecast to provide accurate information about cash flow. Profits and cash are not the same thing. To reasonably estimate the company's cash needs in the future, it is essential that you prepare a separate cash-flow schedule—one designed especially for that purpose. However,

154

some of the information needed to produce a cash-flow plan—namely, projections of monthly sales, costs of sales, and expenses—can be found in the completed projected profit and loss forecast. See ''Manpower Budget'' and ''Budget Worksheet'' in Appendix H of this book for examples of a cash flow projection.

INDUSTRY AVERAGES

Before you begin to make projections, it is advantageous to determine the average operating percentages of your particular industry. This information may be obtained from accountants, banks, trade associations, or with the help of the reference librarian in your public library, who can lead you to documents containing the percentage figures. Industry averages can be used as a guide in establishing your initial budget figures and comparing your firm's actual costs of doing business at some future date.

DEVELOPING THE ESTIMATES

For forecasts to be useful, projections should be made for all facets of the operation (expenses, sales, and cost of sales) on a monthly basis. Where a company's business cycle contains more elements affecting the firm's operations than indicated on the form (for instance, long-term construction contracts), the forecast should be modified to reflect these elements.

WHERE TO BEGIN

Although the process of developing projections can start with expenses or with sales, the majority of people prefer to begin by projecting expenses. By starting this way, you can more easily estimate break-even points, project whether sales will produce a sufficient margin of profit, and determine assets. This method allows you to check the validity of such break-even points. Some people prefer to project the sales potential first, particularly in regards to the anticipated amount of monthly sales.

Regardless of where you begin your projections, it is essential that you give adequate attention to both sales and expenses. You may begin doing this by making a complete projection of expenses and then estimating a feasible amount of sales, considering the marketing strategies and prices involved.

To estimate expenses, first determine the cost of materials and direct labor required for each unit produced or sold. Such costs are called *variable expenses*—those costs that relate directly to the number of units produced and/or sold. This includes packaging costs, delivery fees, sales commissions, and so on. The resulting variable expenses, based on the projected number of units to be produced and/or sold, is added to the total fixed expenses such as telephone, rent, insurance, interest, basic utilities, depreciation, and the like.

MONTHLY CASH FLOW PROJECTION

See Reverse Side for Instructions and Public Comment Information

Form Approval:
OMB No. 3245-0019
Expires: 8-31-91

NAME OF BUSINESS | ADDRESS | OWNER | TYPE OF BUSINESS | PREPARED BY | DATE

YEAR / MONTH	Pre-Start-up Position	1	2	3	4	5	6	7	8	9	10	11	12	TOTAL Columns 1—12	
	Estimate / Actual	Estimate / Actual	Estimate / Actual	Estimate / Actual	Estimate / Actual	Estimate / Actual	Estimate / Actual	Estimate / Actual	Estimate / Actual	Estimate / Actual	Estimate / Actual	Estimate / Actual	Estimate / Actual	Estimate / Actual	
1. CASH ON HAND (Beginning of month)															1.
2. CASH RECEIPTS															2.
(a) Cash Sales															(a)
(b) Collections from Credit Accounts															(b)
(c) Loan or Other Cash Injection (Specify)															(c)
3. TOTAL CASH RECEIPTS (2a + 2b + 2c = 3)															3.
4. TOTAL CASH AVAILABLE (Before cash out) (1 + 3)															4.
5. CASH PAID OUT															5.
(a) Purchases (Merchandise)															(a)
(b) Gross Wages (Excludes withdrawals)															(b)
(c) Payroll Expenses (Taxes, etc.)															(c)
(d) Outside Services															(d)
(e) Supplies (Office and operating)															(e)
(f) Repairs and Maintenance															(f)
(g) Advertising															(g)
(h) Car, Delivery and Travel															(h)
(i) Accounting and Legal															(i)
(j) Rent															(j)
(k) Telephone															(k)
(l) Utilities															(l)
(m) Insurance															(m)
(n) Taxes (Real estate, etc.)															(n)
(o) Interest															(o)
(p) Other Expenses (Specify each)															(p)
(q) Miscellaneous (Unspecified)															(q)
(r) Subtotal															(r)
(s) Loan Principal Payment															(s)
(t) Capital Purchases (Specify)															(t)
(u) Other Start-up Costs															(u)
(v) Reserve and/or Escrow (Specify)															(v)
(w) Owner's Withdrawal															(w)
6. TOTAL CASH PAID OUT (Total 5a thru 5w)															6.
7. CASH POSITION (End of month) (4 minus 6)															7.
ESSENTIAL OPERATING DATA (Non-cash flow information)															
A. Sales Volume (Dollars)															A.
B. Accounts Receivable (End of month)															B.
C. Bad Debt (End of month)															C.
D. Inventory on Hand (End of month)															D.
E. Accounts Payable (End of month)															E.
F. Depreciation															F.

SBA FORM 1100 (1-83) REF: SOP 60 10 Previous Edition Are Obsolete

Figure 9.1

MONTHLY CASH FLOW PROJECTION

NAME OF BUSINESS   ADDRESS   OWNER   TYPE OF BUSINESS   PREPARED BY   DATE

YEAR

Pre–Start–Up Position

	Est.	Act.	MONTH 1 Est.	Act.	2 Est.	Act.	3 Est.	Act.	4 Est.	Act.	5 Est.	Act.	6 Est.	Act.	7 Est.	Act.	8 Est.	Act.	9 Est.	Act.	10 Est.	Act.	11 Est.	Act.	12 Est.	Act.	TOTAL Est.	Act.

1. CASH ON HAND
2. CASH RECEIPTS
  a. Cash Sales
  b. Collections from Credit Accounts
  c. Loan or Other Cash Injection (Specify)
3. TOTAL CASH RECEIPTS
4. TOTAL CASH AVAILABLE
5. CASH PAID OUT
  a. Purchases (Merchandise)
  b. Gross Wages (Excludes withdrawals)
  c. Payroll Expenses (Taxes, etc.)
  d. Outside Services
  e. Supplies (Office & operating)
  f. Repairs and Maintenance
  g. Advertising
  h. Car, Delivery, and Travel
  i. Accounting and Legal
  j. Rent
  k. Telephone
  l. Utilities
  m. Insurance
  n. Taxes (Real Estate, etc.)
  o. Interest
  p. Other Expenses (Specify each)

  q. Miscellaneous (Unspecified)
    r. PAID OUT SUBTOTAL
  s. Loan Principal Payment
  t. Capital Purchases (Specify)
  u. Other Start–up Costs
  v. Reserve and/or Escrow (Specify)
  w. Owner's Withdrawal
6. TOTAL CASH PAID OUT
7. CASH POSITION

ESSENTIAL OPERATING DATA
  A. Sales Volume (Dollars)
  B. Accounts Receivable (End of month)
  C. Bad Debt (End of month)
  D. Inventory on Hand (End of month)
  E. Accounts Payable (End of month)
  F. Depreciation

Figure 9.1 (*continued*)

157

A selling price for each unit can be determined based on the above stated factors; the number of units that can be marketed at that price can also be reasonably projected. Dollar sales volume projections can be made by multiplying the expected unit sales times the unit price.

REVENUES (SALES)

First, determine the overall current condition of each department; then, decide on the number of products or the quantity of services you reasonably anticipate selling each month at the projected prices.

This is an ideal time to review your pricing strategies. Ask yourself these questions:

- Have all potential markets been carefully considered?
- Have I carefully weighed what customers will pay and the sales volume desired?
- Do the selected prices reflect such findings?
- What are the expected markdowns and returns?

Your total projected sales figure should be net of markdowns and returns.

COST OF SALES

Project the cost of sales for each of your sales categories. Do not omit freight in your cost projections where materials (inventory items) are involved. Summarize the information in the schedule and transfer these figures to the company's monthly cash-flow projection under "Cost of sales."

EVALUATING THE ESTIMATES

You can compare the estimated results with the profit aims for the company immediately after the estimates have been made and entries added up. Thus, if the forecast indicates that expenses will not be realized (or if realized, that sufficient profit will not be left), there will be ample time to make changes. For instance, are services priced too low? Or should you develop new sales promotion efforts or innovative marketing strategies to increase sales volume?

If expenses and costs are not out of harmony with estimated sales volume (compared with industry averages) but interest expense is, consider whether there is any surplus equipment, inventory, or other commercial property that can be sold in order to pay off creditors and reduce debt service. If the forecast results show that certain changes are required, then new projections must be made. A forecast is flexible and can be modified as frequently as needed to indicate what reasonably can be anticipated in future developments.

When operating projections have been made and included in the forecast, utilize them as targets for controlling business operations. Each month as the operating totals are tallied, include them in the forecast and compare them with the projections.

EVALUATING ACTUAL RESULTS

Company performance in the areas of expenses, actual sales, and cost of sales can be determined by comparing each figure with these standards:

1. The industry's operating averages.
2. The previous year's results.
3. The company's targets for the month.

These regular comparisons will enable you to zero in on the problem should sales go below target or expenses exceed their target. For instance, is the payroll too large in comparison with total sales? Has time on each job been correctly indicated? Is travel time appropriately accounted for? Has the customer been charged when employee overtime is paid? Does actual time on the job exceed the estimate if work was performed on a guaranteed-charge basis? In the estimate, are fringe benefits costs being omitted? By combining jobs or making other changes, can labor time be reduced? These are just a few of many ways this management tool can be used to control the company's activities.

FURTHER ANALYSIS

Comparative analysis of individual units of business activity can help determine performance patterns for more profitable operations, control of sales, cost of sales, and expenses. The more profitable departments of the operation sometimes reveal expansion possibilities. At other times, less-productive departments will invite closer scrutiny and perhaps require scaling down.

CALCULATE PERCENTAGES

If you convert the dollar figures to percentages, your evaluation of the results will be more efficient. For example, try calculating:

- Each sales classification (department) as a percentage of total sales.
- The cost of sales for each sales category converted to a percentage of that category's (or department's) sales.
- Total gross profit as a percentage of total sales.
- Each expense category as a percentage of total sales.

Percentages can be figured by using an inexpensive calculator. Or capture your business financial picture at a glance through the use of a personal computer spreadsheet program. Such figures will produce valid comparisons for business planning.

GENERAL CONSIDERATIONS

A cash flow projection is a forecast of cash funds (funds, for the purpose of this projection, are defined as cash on hand, checks, or money orders, paid out or received) that a business anticipates receiving, on the one hand, and disbursing, on the other hand, throughout the course of a given span of time. It also predicts the anticipated cash position at set times during the period being projected.

The purpose of preparing a cash-flow projection is to determine deficiencies or excesses in cash from that necessary to operate the business during the time for which the projection is prepared. If deficiencies are revealed in the cash flow, financial plans must be altered to provide for more cash, for example, by obtaining more equity capital and loans or increasing selling prices of products; to reduce expenditures including inventory; or to allow fewer credit sales until a proper cash flow balance is obtained. If excesses of cash are revealed, it might indicate excessive borrowing or idle money that could be put to work. The objective is to develop a plan that, if followed, will provide a well-managed flow of cash.

The cash flow projection form provides a systematic method of recording estimates of cash receipts and expenditures, which can be compared with actual receipts and expenditures as they become known—hence the two columns, "Estimate" and "Actual." The entries listed on the form will not necessarily apply to every business, and some entries that would be pertinent to specific businesses may not be included. It is suggested, therefore, that the form be adapted to the particular business for which the projection is being made, with appropriate changes in the entries as required. Before the cash flow projection can be completed and the pricing structure established, it is necessary to know or to estimate various important factors of the business, for example: What are the direct costs of the product or services per unit? What are the monthly or yearly costs of operation? What is the sales price per unit of the product or service? Determine that the pricing structure provides this business with reasonable break-even goals (including a reasonable net profit) when conservative sales goals are met. What are the available sources of cash, other than income from sales—for example, loans, equity capital, rent, or other sources?

Most of the entries on the form are self-explanatory; however, the following suggestions are offered to simplify the procedure:

1. Round off figures to the nearest dollar.
2. If this is a new business or an existing business undergoing significant changes or alterations, the cash flow part of the column marked "Pre-Start-Up Position" should be completed. (Fill in appropriate blanks only.) Costs involved here are, for example, rent, telephone, and utilities

deposits before the business is actually open. Other items might be equipment purchases, alterations, the owner's cash injection, and cash from loans received before actual operations begin.

3. Next, fill in the Pre-Start-Up position of the essential operating data (non-cash flow information), where applicable.

4. Complete the form using the suggestions in the partial form below for each entry.

Checking

To ensure that the figures are properly calculated and balanced, they must be checked. Several methods may be used, but the following four checks are suggested as a minimum:

1. Item 1 (Beginning Cash on Hand—1st month)
   plus Item 3 (Total Cash Receipts—total column)
   minus Item 6 (Total Cash Paid Out—total column)
   equals Item 7 (Cash Position at End of 12th month).

2. Item A (Sales Volume—total column)
   plus Item B (Accounts Receivable—Pre-Start-Up Position)
   minus Item 2(a) (Cash Sales—total column)
   minus Item 2(b) (Accounts Receivable Collection—total column)
   minus Item C (Bad Debt—total column)
   equals Item B (Accounts Receivable at End of 12th month).

3. The horizontal total of Item 6 (Total Cash Paid Out) is equal to the vertical total of all items under Item 5 in the total column at the right of the form.

4. The horizontal total of Item 3 (Total Cash Receipts) is equal to the vertical total of all items under Item 2 in the total column at the right of the form.

Analyze the correlation between the cash flow and the projected profit during the period in question. The estimated profit is the difference between the estimated change in assets and the estimated change in liabilities before such things as any owner withdrawal, appreciation of assets, change in investments, and the like. The change may be positive or negative. The change in assets can be computed by adding the results of each of the following calculations:

1. Item 7 (Cash Position—End of Last Month)
   minus Item 1 (Cash on Hand at the Beginning of the First Month).

2. Item 5(t) (Capital Purchases—total column)
   minus Item 7F (Depreciation—total column).

3. Item 7B (Accounts Receivable—End of 12th Month)
   minus Item 7B (Accounts Receivable—Pre-Start-Up Position).

4. Item 7D (Inventory on Hand—End of 12th Month)
   minus Item 7D (Inventory on Hand—Pre-Start-Up Position).

5. Item 5(w) (Owner's Withdrawal—total column or dividends) minus such things as an increase in investment.
6. Item 5(v) (Reserve and/or Escrow—total column).

The change in liabilities before items noted in "Change in Assets" can be computed by adding the results of each of these calculations:

1. Item 2(c) (Loans—total column)
    minus 5(s) (Loan Principal Payment—Total Column)
2. Item 7E (Accounts Payable—End of 12th Month)
    minus 7E (Accounts Payable—Pre-Start-Up Position)

Analysis

1. The cash position at the end of each month should be adequate to meet the cash requirements for the following month. If too little cash, then additional cash will have to be injected or cash paid out must be reduced. If there is too much cash on hand, the money is not working for your business.
2. The cash flow projection, the profit and loss projection, the break-even analysis, and good cost control information are tools which, if used properly, will be useful in making decisions that can increase profits to insure success.
3. The projection becomes more useful when the estimated information can be compared with actual information as it develops. It is important to follow through and complete the actual columns as the information becomes available. Utilize the cash flow projection to assist in setting new goals and planning operations for more profit.

THE FORM

The following will help you understand what is expected to be included in each entry area of the Monthly Cash Flow Projection, Form 1100.

Name of Business: Enter the complete name of the business as it appears on the business license, agreement of partnership, or article of incorporation.

Address: Enter the street address of the business.

Owner: Enter the name of the owner, loan applicant, or senior officer of the business.

Type of Business: Enter the type of business as it was stated in the loan application.

Prepared By: The name of the person preparing this form must be entered here. That could be the owner, loan application preparer, CPA, and so on.

Date: Enter the date the form is completed and ready for submission to the lender.

Year: Enter the year the form is being prepared.

Month: Enter the name of the first month for which the projection is prepared under the column numbered 1. Then enter the succeeding months across the page under each of the column numbers. This allows the projection to start at any month of the year, but the form will cover 12 successive months, or one complete year.

Pre-Start-Up Position: This column should contain an estimate of the value of each of the items prior to the real start of the projection period. A startup business will have entries under the listings for Item 1—cash on hand, Item 2(c)—loan or other cash injection, Item 3—total cash receipts (the same as Item 2(c) because there would be no sales and probably no credit collections), and Item 4—total cash available (the sum of Items 1 and 3). Item 7 would also be filled in with the figure from Item 4 as there would be no cash paid out because the business hadn't started. But these are general suppositions. Each business situation is unique, so you must enter whatever will give a complete and accurate picture of the financial condition that exists prior to the starting date of the projected period.

1. Cash on Hand: This will be the same as Item 7 (Cash Position) at the end of the previous month. Merely carry the figure from Item 7 of the previous month up to this entry space.

2. Cash Receipts
   a. Cash Sales: Omit credit sales unless cash is actually received.
   b. Collections from Credit Accounts: Amount to be expected from all credit accounts.
   c. Loan or Other Cash Injection (Specify): Indicate here all cash injections not shown in 2a or 2b above. See Item 1 of Analysis, page 162.

3. Total Cash Receipts: The added total of Items 2a through 2c.

4. Total Cash Available: The added total of Items 1 and 3.

5. Cash Paid Out: Here all cash expenditures are broken down and listed, starting with:
   a. Purchases (Merchandise): Purchases of merchandise for resale or for use in the product paid for in the current month.
   b. Gross Wages (Exclude Owner's Withdrawal): Base pay of your employees plus overtime (if any).
   c. Payroll Expenses (Taxes, etc.): Include paid vacations, paid sick leave, health insurance, unemployment insurance, and so on. This might be 10 percent to 45 percent of 5b.
   d. Outside Services: This could include outside contracted labor and/or material for specialized overflow work, including subcontracting.
   e. Supplies (Office and Operating): Items purchased for use in the business (not for resale).
   f. Repairs and Maintenance: Include periodic large expenditures such as painting or decorating.
   g. Advertising: This amount should be adequate to maintain sales volume—include costs for Yellow Page listings in phone directories.
   h. Car, Delivery, and Travel: If a personal car is used, include related charges in this column, such as parking.
   i. Accounting and Legal: Outside services, including, for example, bookkeeping.

j. Rent: Real estate only—see 5p for other rentals.

k. Telephone: Include all costs of telephone services.

l. Utilities: Water, heat, lights, and/or power (electric and gas)

m. Insurance: Coverage on business property and products, for example, fire liability; also worker's compensation, fidelity, and the like. Exclude executive life (include this in 5w).

n. Taxes (Real Estate, etc.): Plus inventory tax, sales tax, excise tax, if applicable.

o. Interest: Remember to add interest on loan as it is injected (see 2c).

p. Other Expenses (Specify each): Unexpected expenditures may be included here as a safety factor. Equipment expenses during the month should be included here (noncapital equipment).

q. Miscellaneous (unspecified): Small expenditures for which separate accounts would not be practical.

r. Subtotal (operations): This subtotal indicates cash out for all above stated operating costs.

s. Loan Principal Payment: Include payment on all loans, including vehicle and equipment purchases on time-payment.

t. Capital Purchases (Specify): Nonexpensed (depreciable) expenditures such as equipment, building, vehicle purchases, and leasehold improvements.

u. Other Start-up Costs: Expenses incurred prior to the first month's projection and paid for after the "Start-up" position.

v. Reserve and/or Escrow (Specify): Examples: Insurance, tax, or equipment escrow to reduce impact of large periodic payments.

w. Owner's Withdrawal: Should include payment for such things as owner's income tax, social security, health insurance, "executive" life insurance premiums, and so on.

6. Total Cash Paid Out: The added total of items 5r through 5w.

7. Cash Position: Item 4 minus Item 6. Enter this amount in Item 1 (Cash on Hand) for the next month. See Item 1 of "Analysis."

Essential Operating Data (Non-cash flow information): This is basic information necessary for proper planning and for proper cash flow projection. In conjunction with this data, the cash flow can be evolved and shown in the above form.

A. Sales Volume (Dollars): This is a very important figure and should be estimated carefully, taking into account the size of the facility and employee output as well as realistic anticipated supplier response. This should be an estimate of sales completed, not merely orders received.

B. Accounts Receivable (End of month): Previous unpaid credit sales plus current month's credit sales, less amounts received during current month (deduct C below).

C. Bad Debt (End of month): Bad debts should be subtracted from B in the month anticipated.

D. Inventory on Hand (End of month): Last month's inventory plus merchandise received and/or manufactured during the current month minus the amount sold during the current month.

E. Accounts Payable (End of month): Previous month's payable plus the current month's payable, minus any amount paid during the current month.

F. Depreciation: As established by your accountant or the value of all your equipment divided by useful life (in months) as allowed by the Internal Revenue Service.

10 Operating Plan Forecast

An operating plan forecast, though not required as part of the SBA loan package, can yield multiple benefits to the small business owner/operator. First, the forecast, sometimes called a pro forma profit and loss statement, is a valuable business planning tool. Second, when the planning phase has been completed, the forecast becomes a key management tool in controlling the business operations to achieve the results for which you have planned. (See Figure 10.1.)

AS A PLANNING TOOL

The forecast enables you to develop a preview of the amount of profit or loss that can be expected to be generated each month and over the course of the business year based on reasonable predictions of monthly levels of sales, costs, and expenses. In this way you can compare, ahead of time, the year's expected profits or loss against the profit goals and needs established for the business. If the results as forecasted are not satisfactory, there is time to identify what must be done to maximize profit that year.

AS A CONTROL TOOL

A completed forecast enables you to compare the figures for the actual results, as they become known, with the estimated figures, or targets, projected for that month. Where the results are out of line, steps can be taken to correct undesired deviations. By being able to see quickly where the trouble is, less time and money will be lost in getting back on track toward overall profit goals.

LIMITATIONS REGARDING CASH FLOW

Valuable as the operating plan forecast is as both a planning tool and a management tool, it does not provide information about cash. Profits and cash are not the same thing. To project the firm's future cash require-

OPERATING PLAN FORECAST (Profit and Loss Projection)

NAME OF BUSINESS   ADDRESS   OWNER   TYPE OF BUSINESS   PREPARED BY   DATE

FISCAL YEAR

		Month 1				Month 2				Month 3				Month 4				Month 5				Month 6				Month 7				Month 8				Month 9				Month 10				Month 11				Month 12				TOTAL			
	Ind. %	Est.	Act.	%	Est.	Act.	%	Est.	Act.	%	Est.	Act.	%	Est.	Act.	%	Est.	Act.	%	Est.	Act.	%	Est.	Act.	%	Est.	Act.	%	Est.	Act.	%	Est.	Act.	%	Est.	Act.	%	Est.	Act.	%	Est.	Act.	%	Est.	Act.	%

Revenue (sales)

TOTAL Revenue (sales)
Cost of Sales

TOTAL Cost of Sales
GROSS PROFIT
Expenses
Salary expenses: Sales, office and other
Payroll Expenses (taxes, etc.)
Outside Services
Supplies (office and operating)
Repairs and Maintenance
Advertising
Car, Delivery and Travel
Accounting and Legal
Rent
Telephone
Utilities
Insurance
Taxes (Real Estate, etc.)
Interest
Other Expenses (Specify each)

Miscellaneous (Unspecified)
TOTAL Expenses
NET PROFIT

Figure 10.1

167

ments—as well as to project the amount of cash it will have available to meet those requirements—you will need to complete a separate schedule specifically designed for that purpose. (See SBA Form 1100 in Chapter 9.) However, monthly estimates of sales, costs of sales, and expenses that are needed for a cash-flow projection can be easily obtained from the operating plan forecast when it is completed.

INDUSTRY AVERAGES

In starting the estimating process, it may be desirable to enter the average operating percentages for your industry into the "Industry Percentage" column of the forecast. These percentages may be obtained from various sources such as trade associations, accountants, or banks. Also, the reference librarian in your nearest public library can refer you to appropriate documents containing the percentage figures. Industry averages can serve as a useful benchmark against which to compare cost and expense estimates being developed for your firm. Later, they will be useful for comparing the firm's actual operations.

DEVELOPING THE ESTIMATES

To get the most out of an operating plan forecast, estimates should be developed for each operating element (sales, costs of sales, and expenses) for each month of the firm's business year. When a firm's business cycle covers more than 12 months or where special factors influencing the firm's activities will not properly be reflected within that period—for example, long-term construction contracts—the forecast should be extended for the appropriate additional period.

WHERE TO BEGIN

The work of developing the estimates can begin with either sales or expenses: Most businesspeople find it valuable to begin by estimating expenses first. In this way the user can project break-even points, assess their reasonableness, and determine if projected sales will yield an adequate profit margin. However, if a forecast has not been previously prepared for the firm and unit cost information is not readily available, some will prefer to estimate the market potential first, in terms of the expected dollar amount of monthly sales. No matter which way the estimates are started, it is important to pay attention to both categories. This is done by developing a complete estimate of expenses and projecting a reasonable estimate of sales that are attainable based on the prices and marketing methods to be used.

Expenses can be estimated by unit costs. To do so, determine the cost of materials and direct labor required for each unit produced or sold. These costs are part of the variable expenses, which include any cost that varies directly with the number of units produced and sold, such as sales commissions, packaging cost, delivery fees, and so on. Depending on the number of units to be produced and sold, the resulting variable expense is added to the total fixed expenses—those that go on regardless of the volume of business done, like phones, basic utilities, insurance, interest, and depreciation.

Based on the above, a selling price can be determined for the unit and an estimate made of the number of units can be sold at that price. Multiplying the expected sales times the price yields dollar sales volume.

REVENUE (SALES)

Look at each department of the firm. Determine the number of units of products or services you realistically expect to sell each month in each department at the prices you expect to get. Use this phase of the estimating process to review your pricing practices. Do the selected prices reflect the best balance between what customers will pay and the volume of sales to be attained, considering the nature and type of competition? Have all potential markets been considered? What returns and markdowns can be expected? (Final sales estimates should be net of returns and markdowns.)

COST OF SALES

Estimate the cost of sales for each of the sales categories listed under "Revenue (sales)." When considering materials (inventory), do not overlook transportation cost. Include any direct labor. Careful development of the cost of materials for each department can be used not only for this forecast but also for calculating the firm's monthly cash-flow projection. The figures are also useful as tools for controlling operations.

EVALUATING THE ESTIMATES

After the estimates have been made and entries totaled, you can compare the projected results with the profit goals for the firm. If the forecast shows that expenses will not be covered or that profit will be scanty, there is time to plan for changes. For example, are services or merchandise priced too low? If costs and expenses are not out of line with predicted sales volume (compare them with industry averages), attention can be given to increasing sales through new promotional efforts or improving merchandising techniques. If interest expense, for example, is out of line, is there any excess equipment, inventory, or other business property that could be disposed of so that indebtedness and interest payments could be reduced with the proceeds?

Where the results of the forecast indicate changes to be made, new estimates are calculated. A forecast is not rigid. It is revised as often as necessary to reflect what realistically can be expected in the future.

USING THE FORECAST FOR CONTROLLING TARGETS

Once operating estimates have been developed and entered on the forecast, they can serve as definite targets for controlling business operation. As the actual operating results become known each month, they are entered on the forecast for comparison with the targets.

EVALUATING ACTUAL RESULTS

Actual sales, cost of sales, and expense performance can be evaluated against several standards: to the targets for the month, to the operating average for the industry, or to last year's performance. Where actual sales are below target, or actual costs or expenses are above target, you will be able to pinpoint the cause(s).

For example, if payroll has been identified as overly large in relation to total sales, is time for each job being accurately recorded? Is travel time being properly accounted for? When employee overtime is paid, has the customer been charged? If work was done on a guaranteed-charge basis, does actual time on the job exceed the estimate? Are fringe benefit costs being omitted in the estimate? Can labor time be reduced by combining jobs or other changes? These are only a few illustrations of the value of this management tool for controlling the firm's operation.

FURTHER ANALYSIS

Comparative analysis using units of business activity can be of further help in gauging performance trends for better operations, control of sales, costs of sales, and expenses. Perhaps the more profitable departments of the operation suggest expansion possibilities, just as the less productive invite close review.

CALCULATE PERCENTAGES

Evaluating actual results will be quicker if dollar amounts are converted to percentages. You should obtain the following figures: each sales category (department) as a percentage of total sales, the cost of sales for each sales category converted to a percentage of that category's sales, the total gross profit as a percent of total sales, and each expense category as a percent of total sales. An inexpensive calculator allows for rapid calculation of these percentage figures, which will help you make useful comparisons for business decisions.

COMPLETING THE FORECAST FORM

Date: Enter the date of the forecast.

Revenue (sales): List here the various sales avenues or departments within the business. For example, in an appliance sales and service business, there might be new appliance sales, used appliance sales, parts sales, in-shop service sales, and on-site service sales.

In the "Estimate" columns, enter a reasonable projection of the sales to be made each month for each department of the business. Include both cash and on-account sales. In the "Actual" columns, enter figures for actual sales for the month as they become available.

Exclude from the "Revenue (sales)" section any revenue that is not strictly related to the business, for example, rental income derived from an apartment or excess space in the business property. (Correspondingly, estimates for business expenses should be net of expenses associated with the production of that nonbusiness revenue.) Excluding nonbusiness revenue from business revenue (sales) will make for a more meaningful analysis of the firm's operations and comparison with industry averages.

Total Revenue (sales): Add the "Estimate" and "Actual" columns (down the page) and enter their totals in their respective columns.

Cost of Sales: Cite costs by department of the business, the same as listed for Revenue (sales). In the "Estimate" columns, enter the cost of sales estimated for each month for each department of the business. For product inventory, calculate the cost of the goods sold for each department (beginning inventory plus purchases and transportation costs during the month, minus the ending inventory). Enter "Actual" costs each month when known.

Total Cost of Sales: Add the "Estimate" and "Actual" columns (down the page) for cost of sales and enter their totals in their respective columns.

Gross Profit: Enter the column total of estimated and actual total revenue (sales) minus total cost of sales.

Expenses: List here the various expenses of the business, such as the following:

- Salary expense: Salespeople, office workers, and others. Figure gross base pay plus overtime.
- Payroll expenses (taxes, etc.): Include paid vacations, sick leave, health insurance, unemployment insurance, and social security taxes.
- Outside services: This could include costs of subcontractors, overflow work farmed out, and special or one-time services.
- Supplies (office and operating): Services and items purchased for use in the business, not for resale.
- Repairs and maintenance: Regular maintenance and repair, including periodic large expenditures for services such as painting or decorating.
- Advertising: Should be sufficient to support desired sales volume. Include Yellow Pages expense.
- Car, delivery, and travel: Include charges if a personal car is used in the business. Include parking, tolls, buying trips, etc.
- Accounting and legal: Outside professional services.
- Rent: Real estate used in the business; list equipment and other rentals under "Other Expense."

- Telephone: Business telephone costs.
- Utilities: Water, heat, light, etc.
- Insurance: Fire or liability on property or products, worker's compensation; exclude executive life insurance.
- Taxes (real estate, etc.): Inventory tax, sales tax, excise tax, and others as applicable.
- Interest: Business borrowed money expense.
- Depreciation: Amortization of capital expenses.
- Other expenses (specify each): Tools "Expensed" on purchase—not set up on depreciation schedule. Monthly payments for leased or rented equipment are shown here.
- Miscellaneous (unspecified): Include small expenditures for which separate accounts would not be prepared.

Total Expenses: Enter the column totals for estimated and actual expenses here.

Net Profit: Enter the column totals for estimated and actual gross profit minus total expenses.

Ind. %: Enter the industry percentage average for each respective revenue, cost of sales, and expense item.

%: Refer to the "Calculate Percentages" on page 170. Also, the diskette accompanying this book computes these percentages automatically as the actual entries are made.

Totals: Add the estimate and actual items across the page and enter their totals in the respective estimate and actual columns under this heading. Where the "Total Revenue (sales)," "Total Cost of Sales," and "Total Expenses" items meet the "Totals" columns, the figures entered should be the result of adding the figures down the "Totals" columns and across the form. If it is the same for both the up/down and across-the-page additions, the form is said to be in balance. If it is not in balance, check each of the items on the form to find the discrepancy and correct it until balance is obtained. (Do not attempt to add the % columns. The result will not be meaningful.)

11 Finishing Touches—Forms 159, 641, and 1624

COMPENSATION AGREEMENT FOR SERVICES IN CONNECTION WITH APPLICATION AND LOAN FROM THE SMALL BUSINESS ADMINISTRATION—SBA FORM 159

An applicant for an SBA loan may obtain the assistance of any attorney, accountant, engineer, appraiser, or other representative toward the preparation and presentation of the application; however, such representation is not mandatory. In the event that a loan is approved, the services of an attorney may be necessary to assist in the preparation of closing documents, title abstracts, and the like. The SBA will allow the payment of reasonable fees or other compensation for services performed by such representatives on behalf of the applicant.

There are no "authorized representatives" of the SBA other than its regular salaried employees. Payment of any fee or gratuity to SBA employees is illegal and will subject the parties to such a transaction to prosecution.

SBA regulations (Part 103, Sec. 103.13-5(c)) prohibit applicant representatives from charging or proposing to charge any contingent fee for any services performed in connection with an SBA loan unless the amount of such fee bears a necessary and reasonable relationship to the services actually performed or to charge for any expenses that are not deemed by the SBA to have been necessary in connection with the application. The regulations (Part 120, Sec. 120.104-2) also prohibit the payment of any bonus, brokerage fee, or commission in connection with SBA loans.

In accord with these regulations, the SBA will not approve placement or finder's fees for the use or attempted use of influence in obtaining or trying to obtain an SBA loan or fees based solely upon a percentage of the approved loan or any part thereof.

Approved fees will be limited to reasonable sums for services actually rendered in connection with the application or the closing, based on the time and effort required, the qualifications of the representatives, and the nature and extent of the services rendered by such representatives. Representatives of loan applicants will be required to execute an agreement detailing their compensation for services rendered in connection with said loan.

It is the responsibility of the applicant to set forth in the appropriate section of the application the names of all persons or firms engaged by or on behalf of him or her. Applicants are required to advise the regional office of the SBA in writing of the names and fees of any representatives engaged by the applicant subsequent to the filing of the application. This reporting requirement is approved under OMB Approval Number 2345-0016.

Any loan applicant having any question concerning the payments or reasonableness of fees should communicate with the SBA field office with which the application is filed.

Should the loan applicant retain anyone to provide services or assistance in connection with the loan application, a "Compensation Agreement," Form 159, must be prepared and submitted with the loan application. (See Figure 11.1). In instances where there is more than a single individual or firm providing such services, it is required that a separate Form 159 be completed and signed for each individual or firm and submitted with the loan application.

The Appendixes in this book have been included to give you additional information and examples that may assist in the creation of a specific loan package and the initiation of a proposed business venture.

REQUEST FOR COUNSELING—SBA FORM 641

The SBA provides technical and management assistance free of charge to those who request it. Should you require such assistance, complete Form 641 and submit it to your regional SBA office. A sample of this form appears as Figure 11.2.

A. Name of company: Enter the full name of the company/business. Leave blank if you are not yet in business.

B. Your name (last, first, middle): Enter your name. If the business is a partnership or corporation, enter only one name.

C. through H.
Telephone, street, city, state, county, zip: Enter both the home (H) and business (B) telephone numbers of the person and business named; enter the street address, city, state, county, and zip code of the residence of the person named.

I. Type of business (check one): Check the item that reflects the applicant's primary business.

J. Bus. ownshp./gender: Check the box that applies to the person named in the form, whether he or she already owns the business or wants to start one. The third box, "Male/Female," applies to joint ownership of a business. Check only one of the boxes.

K. Veteran status: Check any and all boxes that apply to the applicant.

L. Complete as indicated. When answering the "Type of Business" question, use three to five words to describe the business's general field of interest (i.e., bicycle repair or auto parts resale).

SBA LOAN NUMBER

COMPENSATION AGREEMENT FOR SERVICES IN CONNECTION WITH APPLICATION AND LOAN
FROM (OR IN PARTICIPATION WITH) SMALL BUSINESS ADMINISTRATION

The undersigned representative (attorney, accountant, engineer, appraiser, etc.) hereby agrees that the undersigned has not and will not, directly or indirectly, charge or receive any payment in connection with the application for or the making of the loan except for services actually performed on behalf of the Applicant. The undersigned further agrees that the amount of payment for such services shall not exceed an amount deemed reasonable by SBA (and, if it is a participation loan, by the participating lending institution), and to refund any amount in excess of that deemed reasonable by SBA (and the participating institution). This agreement shall supersede any other agreement covering payment for such services.

A general description of the services performed, or to be performed, by the undersigned and the compensation paid or to be paid are set forth below. If the total compensation in any case exceeds $1,000 (or $300 for: (1) regular business loans of $15,000 or less; or (2) all disaster home loans) or if SBA should otherwise require, the services must be itemized on a schedule attached showing each date services were performed, time spent each day, and description of service rendered on each day listed.

The undersigned Applicant and representative hereby certify that no other fees have been charged or will be charged by the representative in connection with this loan, unless provided for in the loan authorization specifically approved by SBA.

GENERAL DESCRIPTION OF SERVICES

Paid Previously $ _____
Additional Amount to be Paid $ _____
Total Compensation $ _____

(Section 13 of the Small Business Act (15 USC 642) requires disclosures concerning fees. Parts 103, 108 and 120 of Title 13 of the Code of Federal Regulations contain provisions covering appearances and compensation of persons representing SBA applicants. Section 103.13-5 authorizes the suspension or revocation of the privilege of any such person to appear before SBA for charging a fee deemed unreasonable by SBA for services actually performed, charging of unreasonable expenses, or violation of this agreement. Whoever commits any fraud, by false or misleading statement or representation, or by conspiracy, shall be subject to the penalty of any applicable Federal or State statute.)

Dated _____, 19 _____

_____
(Representative)

By _____

The Applicant hereby certifies to SBA that the above representations, description of services and amounts are correct and satisfactory to Applicant.

Dated _____, 19 _____

_____
(Applicant)

By _____

The participating lending institution hereby certifies that the above representations of service rendered and amounts charged are reasonable and satisfactory to it.

Dated _____, 19 _____

_____
(Lender)

By _____

NOTE: Foregoing certification must be executed, if by a corporation, in corporate name by duly authorized officer and duly attested; if by a partnership, in the firm name, together with signature of a general partner.

PLEASE NOTE: The estimated burden hours for the completion of SBA Form 147, 148, 159, 160, 160A, 529B, 928, and 1059 is 6 hrs. per response. If you have any questions or comments concerning this estimate or any other aspect of this information collection please contact, William Cline, Chief Administrative Information Branch, U.S. Small Business Administration, 409 3 rd st. S. W. Washington, D.C. 20416 and Gary Waxman, Clearance Officer, Paperwork Reduction Project (3245-0201), Office of Management and Budget, Washington, D.C. 20503.

SBA FORM 159 (1-91) REF SOP 70 50 Use 7-89 Edition Until Exhausted

Figure 11.1

POLICY AND REGULATIONS CONCERNING REPRESENTATIVES AND THEIR FEES

An applicant for a loan from SBA may obtain the assistance of any attorney, accountant, engineer, appraiser or other representative to aid him in the preparation and presentation of his application to SBA; however, such representation is not mandatory. In the event a loan is approved, the services of an attorney may be necessary to assist in the preparation of closing documents, title abstracts, etc. SBA will allow the payment of reasonable fees or other compensation for services performed by such representatives on behalf of the app'icant.

There are no "authorized representatives" of SBA, other than our regular salaried employees. Payment of any fee or gratuity to SBA employees is illegal and will subject the parties to such a transaction to prosecution.

SBA Regulations (Part 103, Sec. 103.13-5(c)) prohibit representatives from charging or proposing to charge any contingent fee for any services performed in connection with an SBA loan unless the amount of such fee bears a necessary and reasonable relationship to the services actually performed; or to charge for any expenses which are not deemed by SBA to have been necessary in connection with the application. The Regulations (Part 120, Sec. 120.104-2) also prohibit the payment of any bonus, brokerage fee or commission in connection with SBA loans.

In line with these Regulations SBA will not approve placement or finder's fees for the use or attempted use of influence in obtaining or trying to obtain an SBA loan, or fees based solely upon a percentage of the approved loan or any part thereof.

Fees which will be approved will be limited to reasonable sums of services actually rendered in connection with the application or the closing, based upon the time and effort required, the qualifications of the representative and the nature and extent of the services rendered by such representatives. Representatives of loan applicants will be required to execute an agreement as to their compensation for services rendered in connection with said loan.

It is the responsibility of the applicant to set forth in the appropriate section of the application the names of all persons or firms engaged by or on behalf of the applicant. Applicants are required to advise the Regional Office in writing the names and fees of any representatives engaged by the applicant subsequent to the filing of the application. This reporting requirement is approved under OMB Approval Number 2345-0016.

Any loan applicant having any question concerning the payments of fees, or the reasonableness of fees, should communicate with the Field Office where the application is filed.

*U.S. Government Printing Office: 1991 — 282-429/45506

Figure 11.1 (*continued*)

U.S. Small Business Administration

REQUEST FOR COUNSELING

A. NAME OF COMPANY	B. YOUR NAME (Last, First, Middle)	C. TELEPHONE (H) (B)

D. STREET	E. CITY	F. STATE	G. COUNTY	H. ZIP

I. TYPE OF BUSINESS (Check one) 1. ☐ Retail 4. ☐ Manufacturing 2. ☐ Service 5. ☐ Construction 3. ☐ Wholesale 6. ☐ Not in Business	J. BUS. OWNSHP./GENDER 1. ☐ Male 2. ☐ Female 3. ☐ Male/Female	K. VETERAN STATUS 1. ☐ Veteran 2. ☐ Vietnam-Era Veteran 3. ☐ Disabled Veteran

L.
- INDICATE PREFERRED DATE AND TIME FOR APPOINTMENT
  DATE _____ TIME _____
- ARE YOU CURRENTLY IN BUSINESS? YES ____ NO ____
- IF YES, HOW LONG? _____
- TYPE OF BUSINESS (USE THREE TO FIVE WORDS)
  _____

M. ETHNIC BACKGROUND

a. *Race:*
1. ☐ American Indian or Alaskan Native
2. ☐ Asian or Pacific Islander
3. ☐ Black
4. ☐ White

b. *Ethnicity:*
1. ☐ Hispanic Origin
2. ☐ Not of Hispanic Origin

N. INDICATE, BRIEFLY, THE NATURE OF SERVICE AND/OR COUNSELING YOUR ARE SEEKING

_____

O.
- IT HAS BEEN EXPLAINED TO ME THAT I MAY USE FURTHER SERVICES SPONSORED BY THE U.S. SMALL BUSINESS ADMINISTRATION YES ____ NO ____
- I HAVE ATTENDED A SMALL BUSINESS WORKSHOP YES ____ NO ____
- CONDUCTED BY _____

P. HOW DID YOU LEARN OF THESE COUNSELING SERVICES?
1. ☐ Yellow Pages 3. ☐ Radio 5. ☐ Bank 7. ☐ Word-of-Mouth
2. ☐ Television 4. ☐ Newspapers 6. ☐ Chamber of Commerce 8. ☐ Other ____

Q. SBA CLIENT (To Be Filled Out By Counselor)
1. ☐ Borrower 2. ☐ Applicant 3. ☐ 8(a) Client 4. ☐ COC 5. ☐ Surety Bond

R. AREA OF COUNSELING PROVIDED (To Be Filled Out By Counselor) ☐

1. Bus. Start-Up/Acquisition	5. Accounting & Records	9. Personnel
2. Source of Capital	6. Finan. Analysis/Cost Control	10. Computer Systems
3. Marketing/Sales	7. Inventory Control	11. Internat'l Trade
4. Government Procurement	8. Engineering R&D	12. Business Liq./Sale

I request business management counseling from the Small Business Administration. I agree to cooperate should I be selected to participate in surveys designed to evaluate SBA assistance services. I authorize SBA to furnish relevant information to the assigned management counselor(s) although I expect that information to be held in strict confidence by him/her.

I further understand that any counselor has agreed not to: (1) recommend goods or services from sources in which he/she has an interest and (2) accept fees or commissions developing from this counseling relationship. In consideration of SBA's furnishing management or technical assistance, I waive all claims against SBA personnel, SCORE, SBDC and its host organizations, SBI, and other SBA Resource Counselors arising from this assistance.

SIGNATURE AND TITLE OF REQUESTER	DATE

FOR USE OF THE SMALL BUSINESS ADMINISTRATION		
RESOURCE	DISTRICT	REGION

SBA FORM 641 (2-91) PREVIOUS EDITION IS OBSOLETE

WHITE: COUNSELOR
YELLOW: SBI OR SCORE OR SBDC SUB.
PINK: DO OR NSO OR SBDC LEAD

Figure 11.2

M. Ethnic background: Check the boxes that apply to the primary applicant. This requires two answers: one for race and one for ethnicity.

N. Indicate, briefly, the nature of service and/or counseling you are seeking.

O. Complete as indicated. Be sure to include the name of the person conducting the SBA workshop you attended, which is required before receiving counseling.

P. Answer as indicated. Check any and all boxes that apply.

Q. SBA client: This item is to be completed by the assigned counselor. Check all that apply. "Q2. Applicant" refers to applicants for SBA financial assistance. "Q4. COC" refers to applicants who have applied for a certificate of competence.

R. Area of counseling provided: This item is to be completed by the assigned counselor. Determine the area for which you will provide assistance. Check only one.

The applicant must sign and date the request form and submit it to the SBA field office to which the loan application will be submitted.

CERTIFICATION REGARDING DEBARMENT, SUSPENSION, INELIGIBILITY, AND VOLUNTARY EXCLUSION LOWER TIER COVERED TRANSACTIONS—SBA TEMPORARY FORM 1624

1. By signing and submitting this proposal (see Figure 11.3), the prospective lower tier participant is providing the certification set out below.

2. The certification in this clause is a material representation of fact upon which reliance was placed when this transaction was entered into. If it is later determined that the prospective lower tier participant knowingly rendered an erroneous certification, in addition to other remedies available to the Federal Government, the department or agency with which this transaction originated may pursue available remedies, including suspension and/or debarment.

3. The prospective lower tier participant shall provide immediate written notice to the person to which this proposal is submitted if at any time the prospective lower tier participant learns that its certification was erroneous when submitted or has become erroneous by reason of changed circumstances.

4. The terms "covered transaction," "debarred," "suspended," "ineligible," "lower tier covered transaction," "participant," "person," "primary covered transaction," "principal," "proposal," and "voluntarily excluded," as used in this clause, have the meaning set out in the Definitions and Coverage sections of the rules implementing Executive Order 12549. You may contact the person to which this proposal is submitted for assistance in obtaining a copy of those regulations (13 CFR Part 145).

5. The prospective lower tier participant agrees by submitting this proposal that, should the proposed covered transaction be entered into, it shall not knowingly enter into any lower tier covered transaction with a person

**Certification Regarding
Debarment, Suspension, Ineligibility and Voluntary Exclusion
Lower Tier Covered Transactions**

This certification is required by the regulations implementing Executive Order 12549, Debarment and Suspension, 13 CFR Part 145. The regulations were published as Part VII of the May 26, 1988 *Federal Register* (pages 19160-19211). Copies of the regulations may be obtained by contacting the person to which this proposal is submitted.

(BEFORE COMPLETING CERTIFICATION, READ INSTRUCTIONS ON REVERSE)

(1) The prospective lower tier participant certifies, by submission of this proposal, that neither it nor its principals are presently debarred, suspended, proposed for debarment, declared ineligible, or voluntarily excluded from participation in this transaction by any Federal department or agency.

(2) Where the prospective lower tier participant is unable to certify to any of the statements in this certification, such prospective participant shall attach an explanation to this proposal.

Business Name _____

Date _____   By _____
                                            Name and Title of Authorized Representative

                                            _____
                                            Signature of Authorized Representative

SBA Temporary Form 1624 (10-88)

Figure 11.3

who is debarred, suspended, declared ineligible, or voluntarily excluded from participating in this covered transaction, unless authorized by the department or agency with which this transaction originated.

6. The prospective lower tier participant further agrees by submitting this proposal that it will include the clause titled "Certification Regarding Debarment, Suspension, Ineligibility and Voluntary Exclusion—Lower Tier Covered Transaction," without modification, in all lower tier covered transactions and in all solicitations for lower tier covered transactions.

7. A participant in a covered transaction may rely upon a certification of a prospective participant in a lower tier covered transaction that it is not debarred, suspended, ineligible, or voluntarily excluded from the covered transaction, unless it knows that the certification is erroneous. A participant may decide the method and frequency by which it determines the eligibility of its principals. Each participant may, but is not required to, check the Nonprocurement List.

8. Nothing contained in the foregoing shall be construed to require establishment of a system of records in order to render in good faith the certification required by this clause. The knowledge and information of a participant is not required to exceed that which is normally possessed by a prudent person in the ordinary course of business dealings.

9. Except for transactions authorized under paragraph 5 of these instructions, if a participant in a covered transaction knowingly enters into a lower tier covered transaction with a person who is suspended, debarred, ineligible, or voluntarily excluded from participation in this transaction, in addition to other remedies available to the Federal Government, the department or agency with which this transaction originated may pursue available remedies, including suspension and/or debarment.

APPENDIX A

Statements Required by Law and Executive Order

Federal executive agencies, including the Small Business Administration (SBA), are required to withhold or limit financial assistance, to impose special conditions on approved loans, to provide special notices to applicants or borrowers, and to require special reports and data from borrowers in order to comply with legislation passed by Congress and Executive Orders issued by the president and by the provisions of various interagency agreements. The SBA has issued regulations and procedures that implement these laws and executive orders, and they are contained in Parts 112, 113, 116, and 117, Title 13, Code of Federal Regulations Chapter 1, of Standard Operating Procedures.

FREEDOM OF INFORMATION ACT (5 U.S.C. 552)

This law provides, with some exceptions, that the SBA must supply information reflected in agency files and records to persons requesting it. Information about approved loans that will be automatically released includes, among other things, statistics on its loan programs (individual borrowers are not identified in the statistics) and other information such as the names of the borrowers (and their officers, directors, stockholders or partners), the collateral pledged to secure the loan, the amount of the loan, its purpose in general terms, and the maturity. Proprietary data on a borrower would not routinely be made available to third parties. All requests under this act are to be addressed to the nearest SBA office and identified as a Freedom of Information request.

RIGHT TO FINANCIAL PRIVACY ACT OF 1978 (12 U.S.C. 3401)

According to this act, the SBA has access rights to records held by financial institutions that are or have been doing business with you or your business, including any financial institutions participating in a loan or loan guarantee, in connection with its consideration or administration of assistance to you in the form of a government loan or loan guarantee agreement. The SBA is required to provide a certificate of its compliance with the act to a financial institution in connection with its first request for access to your financial records, after which no further certification is required for subsequent accesses. The law provides that the SBA's access rights continue for the term of any approved loan or loan guarantee agreement. No further notice to you of the SBA's access rights is required during the term of any such agreement.

The law also authorizes the SBA to transfer to another government authority any financial records included in an application for a loan or concerning an approved loan or loan guarantee as necessary to process, service, or foreclose on a loan or loan guarantee or to collect on a defaulted loan or loan guarantee. No other transfer of your financial records to another government authority will be permitted by the SBA except as required or permitted by law.

FLOOD DISASTER PROTECTION ACT (42 U.S.C. 4011)

Regulations have been issued by the Federal Insurance Administration (FIA) and by the SBA implementing this act and its amendments, which prohibit the SBA from making certain loans in an FIA-designated floodplain unless federal flood insurance is purchased as a condition of the loan. Failure to maintain the required level of flood insurance makes the applicant ineligible for any future financial assistance from the SBA under any program, including disaster assistance.

EXECUTIVE ORDERS—FLOODPLAIN MANAGEMENT AND WETLAND PROTECTION (42 F.R. 26951 and 42 F.R. 26961)

The SBA discourages any settlement in or development of a floodplain or a wetland. This statement is to notify all SBA loan applicants that such actions are hazardous to both life and property and should be avoided. The additional cost of flood preventive construction must be considered in addition to the possible loss of all assets and investments in future floods.

OCCUPATIONAL SAFETY AND HEALTH ACT (15 U.S.C. 651 et seq.)

This legislation authorizes the Occupational Safety and Health Administration in the Department of Labor to require businesses to modify facilities and procedures to protect employees or else pay penalty fees. In some instances the business can be forced to cease operations or be prevented from starting operations in a new facility. Therefore, the SBA may sometimes require additional information from an applicant to determine whether the business will be in compliance with OSHA regulations and allowed to operate its facility after the loan is approved and disbursed.

Signing this form as a borrower is a certification that the OSHA requirements that apply to the borrower's business have been determined and that the borrower to the best of its knowledge is in compliance.

CIVIL RIGHTS LEGISLATION

All businesses receiving SBA financial assistance must agree not to discriminate in any business practice, including employment practices and services to the public, on the basis or categories cited in 13 C.F.R., Parts 112, 113, and 117, or SBA Regulations. This includes making their goods and services available to handicapped clients or customers. All business borrowers will be required to display the "Equal Employment Opportunity Poster" prescribed by the SBA.

EQUAL CREDIT OPPORTUNITY ACT (15 U.S.C. 1691)

The Federal Equal Credit Opportunity Act prohibits creditors from discriminating against credit applicants on the basis of race, color, religion, national origin, sex, marital status, or age (provided that the applicant has the capacity to enter into a binding contract); because all or part of the applicant's income derives from any public assistance program; or because the applicant has, in good faith, exercised any right under the Consumer Credit Protection Act. The federal agency that administers compliance with this law concerning this creditor is the Federal Trade Commission, Equal Credit Opportunity, Washington, D.C. 20580.

EXECUTIVE ORDER 11738—ENVIRONMENTAL PROTECTION (38 F.R. 25161)

This order charges the SBA with administering its loan program in a manner that will result in effective enforcement of the Clean Air Act, the Federal Water Pollution Act and other environmental protection legislation. The SBA must, therefore, impose conditions on some loans. By acknowledging receipt of this form and presenting the application, the principals of all small businesses borrowing $100,000 or more in direct funds agree to the following stipulations:

1. That any facility used or to be used by the subject firm is not cited on the EPA list of Violating Facilities.
2. That the subject firm will comply with all the requirements of Section 114 of the Clean Air Act (42 U.S.C. 7414) and Section 308 of the Water Act (33 U.S.C. 1318) relating to inspection, monitoring, entry, reports and information, as well as all other requirements specified in Section

114 and Section 308 of the respective acts and all regulations and guidelines issued thereunder.

3. That the subject firm will notify the SBA of the receipt of any communication from the director of the Environmental Protection Agency indicating that a facility utilized or to be utilized by the subject firm is under consideration to be listed on the EPA List of Violating Facilities.

DEBT COLLECTION ACT OF 1982; DEFICIT REDUCTION ACT OF 1984 (31 U.S.C. 3701 et seq. and other titles)

These laws require the SBA to aggressively collect any loan payments that become delinquent. The SBA must obtain your taxpayer identification number when you apply for a loan. If you receive a loan and do not make payments as they come due, the SBA may take one or more of the following actions:

1. Report the status of your loan(s) to credit bureaus.
2. Hire a collection agency to collect your loan.
3. Offset your income tax refund or other amounts due to you from the federal government.
4. Suspend or debar you or your company from doing business with the federal government.
5. Refer your loan to the Department of Justice or other attorneys for litigation.
6. Foreclose on collateral or take other action permitted in the loan instruments.

IMMIGRATION REFORM AND CONTROL ACT OF 1986 (PUB. L. 99-603)

If you are an alien who was in this country illegally since before January 1, 1982, you may have been granted lawful temporary resident status by the United States Immigration and Naturalization Service pursuant to the Immigration Reform and Control Act of 1986 (Pub. L 99-603). For five years from the date you are granted such status, you are not eligible for financial assistance from the SBA in the form of a loan or guarantee under section 7(a) of the Small Business Act unless you are disabled or a Cuban or Haitian entrant. When you sign this document, you are certifying that the Immigration Reform and Control Act of 1986 does not apply to you or, if it does apply, that more than five years have elapsed since you have been granted lawful temporary resident status pursuant to such legislation.

LEAD-BASED PAINT POISONING PREVENTION ACT (42 U.S.C. 4821 et seq.)

Borrowers using SBA funds for the construction or rehabilitation of a residential structure are prohibited from using lead-based paint (as defined in SBA regulations) on all interior surfaces, whether accessible or not, and exterior surfaces, such as stairs, decks, porches, railings, windows, and doors, that are readily accessible to children under seven years of age. A "residential structure" is any home, apartment, hotel, motel, orphanage, boarding school, dormitory, day care center, extended care facility, college or other school housing, hospital, group practice or community facility, and all other residential or institutional structures where persons reside.

APPENDIX B

Some Things to Do in Starting Your Own Business

What follows is intended to be a guide for the newly forming business, indicating the various federal, state, and county/city government agencies to be contacted prior to opening the doors and taking in the first sales dollar. Be sure to contact the appropriate agencies at the state, county, and city levels because local regulations can and will vary and you will be held responsible for abiding by them.

FEDERAL AGENCIES

Internal Revenue Service (IRS)

If you plan to take on employees, you must contact the IRS and apply for an Employer Identification Number by filing a Form SS-4. After you have filed this form, you, as an employer, will be held responsible and liable for federal withholding taxes, FICA, and FUTA. Rates and due dates appear in the *Employers' Tax Guide* (IRS Circular E). IRS will also compile a kit for you that contains samples of all the forms that you will be working with in complying with federal tax laws.

For the location of the IRS office nearest you, look under "U.S. Government" in your local telephone directory.

STATE AGENCIES

State Department of Employment Development

If you intend to take on employees, most states require that you file and/ or register with the Department of Employment. After you have filed, you will be responsible and liable for withholding and payment of State Payroll Tax.

For the location of your nearest Department of Employment office, look under "State Government" in your local telephone directory.

State Board of Equalization

States with sales tax provisions require all persons, firms, partnerships, corporations, and so on intending to engage in selling tangible personal property of a kind ordinarily subject to taxation to apply for a Seller's Permit. Wholesalers as well as retailers must secure a separate permit for each place of business. Application must be made to the state taxing authority on forms supplied by that agency. There may or may not be a fee required for such a Seller's Permit.

The taxing authority may require a security deposit for payment of taxes on estimated sales. The amount of security required is determined at the time of application. The applicant should be prepared to furnish estimated monthly operating expenses for the business, such as rent, payroll, and payments on equipment as well as anticipated average monthly sales and the amount of these sales that is not taxable. Security may be posted in any of the forms authorized by the taxing authority.

Applicants may be expected to furnish their social security number; name and location of bank; address of property owned, its value, amount owed, and to whom payments are made; names of suppliers; name of record keeper; and names and addresses of personal references. Other information may be required.

Any seller required to hold a Seller's Permit as defined above must file sales tax returns regardless of whether or not a permit has been received.

Returns must be completed and filed on or before the last day of the month following the reporting period, regardless of whether or not there were any sales during that period. The returns are normally filed on the basis of calendar quarters unless otherwise required by the taxing authority. A remittance of the tax must accompany the sales tax return.

Complete records of all business transactions, including sales, receipts, purchases, and other expenditures, must be maintained and made available at all times for inspection by the representatives of the taxing authority.

State Department of Industrial Relations

If your business is to hire employees, this department should be contacted for particulars on Worker's Compensation Insurance. Your own insurance company or broker may also be able to handle this requirement. Private insurance companies as well as the state offer this coverage.

Some states have enacted an Occupational Safety and Health Act. It is essential that a business owner intending to take on employees become familiar with this act if the state has one. The requirements are normally stringent, and fines for noncompliance can be steep. Special permits are required for those engaged in the construction business.

For the location of your nearest Department of Industrial Relations Office, look under "State" in your local telephone directory.

LOCAL (MUNICIPAL/COUNTY) AGENCIES

Licenses and permits to operate a business are controlled at the county and municipal levels. Your city and/or county offices should be contacted for information regarding fees and requirements. Certain types of businesses (restaurants and food services, for example) may be subject to special permits from health authorities, fire and police departments, etc.

If you plan to do business under a "fictitious name," this must be formally filed, published, and recorded with the Recorder's Office of the county in which you are to do business. Contact the applicable County (Township) Recorder's Office for details. This procedure may not apply if you are incorporating.

If your business is building its own building or plant, local zoning ordinances that govern construction in the area must be thoroughly investigated at your city/county offices. A building permit is normally required for both new construction and remodeling.

If you intend to do business from your home, make certain that your business activity falls within the purview of current zoning regulations.

SOME SOURCES OF HELP

An accountant should be consulted who can set up a good pattern of record keeping for your business. Inadequate record keeping continues to plague small business and is a leading factor in small business failure.

An attorney's services may be essential in helping you cope with legal complexities and procedures that arise during the formative stages of your business.

Your banker is an excellent source of information regarding your capital requirements and your ability to obtain financing.

Your insurance broker or insurance company will advise you as to the types and amounts of coverage that are available or necessary. These include fire, hazard, theft, product, and life insurance.

Your chamber of commerce usually has area statistics involving local commercial and population patterns that can be useful in establishing your market area and location.

A good summary of federal tax aspects that you will be facing is found in the *Tax Guide for Small Business,* available from the Internal Revenue Service at a nominal fee. (Ask for Publication Number 334.)

APPENDIX C
10 Rules of Advertising

1. **Stick to your purpose.** Ask yourself: Whom am I trying to reach? What are they like? What's the best way to reach them?

2. **Remember what interests people most.** What interests people most is themselves. Remember to personalize your advertisement and direct it towards the people you want to reach. What's important to them about your product or service?

3. **Differentiate your product.** If you adopt a comparative sales strategy, develop distinct competitive benefits, establish a distinctive image, and/or develop a strong position strategy.

4. **Match your program to your budget.** Don't try to do too much with too few dollars. Be clear on what you want to accomplish so you can evaluate the effectiveness of your program.

5. **Evaluate costs wisely.** Don't choose what seems to be the least expensive media—how does it rate when you consider the retention of consumer usage compared to the cost per thousand viewers, listeners, or readers?

6. **Advertise frequently.** Even with the most comprehensive program, very few viewers, listeners, and readers will remember your ad the next day. Advertising is what motivates your customers to buy.

7. **Avoid imitation.** It may be the sincerest form of flattery, but what if your competition's ads aren't very effective? And what if you end up helping their business?

8. **Don't be overly creative.** Ask yourself: Is it easy to read? Is it easy to understand? What message is it getting across?

9. **Concentrate on key emotions.** Develop advertising that reflects people's key emotions: hope, admiration, and fear.

10. **Motivate and direct your customer.** Balance your advertising between motivational and directional advertising so that your customers can find you once they've decided to buy.

APPENDIX D
Media Options

DIRECTIVE ADVERTISING		CREATIVE ADVERTISING				
	YELLOW PAGES	METRO-POLITAN NEWSPAPER	LOCAL NEWSPAPER	RADIO	TELEVISION	LOCAL MAGAZINES
USE	Shopping decisions	Entertainment news	Entertainment news	News, traffic info., entertainment	Entertainment news	Entertainment news
SHELF LIFE	1 year	1 day	1 day, week, month	60 seconds	30 seconds	1 month
HOUSEHOLDS REACHED	606,000	700,000	55,000	27,000 adults ages 25–54	450,000 adults ages 25–54	60,000
COST	$1,082	$7,140 per 1/2 page	$1,090 per 1/2 page	$230 (average of day parts)	$11,250 av. for prime time	$1,435 per 1/2 page
PRODUCTION COST	Free	$100–$5,000	$100 (appx.)	$100–$5,000	$5,000– $300,000	$1,000– $5,000
MOST EFFECTIVE USE	Direct: consumer to you	Product/ service identity	Announce special offer	Announce special offer	Product demonstration	Product/ service identity

NOTE: This chart reflects sample San Francisco Bay Area media options. Source: Pacific Bell Directory Research, 1987.

The above chart provides a comparison of advertising media options. The data is regionally specific and should not be relied upon as valid data for your specific region. Contact your local telephone company and chamber of commerce for current data directly applicable to your area.

APPENDIX E
Advertising-to-Sales Ratios

INDUSTRY	AD DOLLAR AS PERCENT OF SALES	AD DOLLAR AS PERCENT OF MARGIN
Agriculture Production—Crops	2.1	7.0
Crude Petroleum & Natural Gas	.2	.2
Gen. Bldg. Contractors—Nonresidential	.3	2.4
Construction—Special Contractors	1.9	6.4
Food & Kindred Products	5.2	17.4
Bakery Products	1.5	3.3
Candy & Other Confectionery	6.5	16.3
Bottled & Canned Soft Drinks	6.6	12.4
Apparel	2.3	7.8
Lumber & Wood Products	3	1.7
Wood Buildings—Mobile Homes	1.4	7.8
Household Furniture	2.6	9.0
Office Furniture	1.6	4.2
Books—Publishing & Printing	4.0	7.1
Commercial Printing	1.2	3.4
Drugs	8.9	14.2
Soap & Other Detergents	7.9	19.9
Perfumes & Cosmetics	13.1	21.3
Paints, Varnishes & Lacquers	2.8	7.9
Paving & Roofing Materials	1.2	6.7
Footwear (Except Rubber)	4.5	12.2
Leather Goods	6.7	16.7
Glass Containers	2.2	5.7
Hardware	6.3	12.6
Construction Machinery & Equipment	.6	2.1
Household Appliances	4.3	15.3
Electrical Lighting & Wiring Equipment	1.1	3.3
Radio & TV Receiving Sets	2.4	6.4
Phonograph Records	9.1	19.0
Semiconductors & Related Devices	1.1	2.7
Computers—Mini & Micro	6.5	15.7
Computers—Mainframe	1.5	2.5

INDUSTRY	AD DOLLAR AS PERCENT OF SALES	AD DOLLAR AS PERCENT OF MARGIN
Office Automation Systems	2.0	4.5
Motor Vehicles & Car Bodies	1.6	0.0
Motor Homes	1.1	6.7
Aircraft & Parts	1.3	5.5
Ship or Boat Building & Repairing	1.8	8.0
Motorcycles, Bicycles & Parts	1.9	9.8
Watches, Clocks & Parts	1.6	5.4
Jewelry & Precious Metals	1.8	6.4
Musical Instruments	3.9	21.6
Toys & Amusement Sports Goods	10.0	23.0
Pens, Pencils & Other Office Materials	5.3	12.2
Trucking—Local & Long Distance	2.4	12.4
Transportation Services	4.5	13.1
Radio & TV Broadcasters	3.8	9.9
Sanitary Services	.7	2.3
Wholesale Durable Goods	5.0	17.8
Wholesale Nondurable Goods	1.8	8.9
Retail Lumber & Building Materials	2.7	12.7
Retail Department Stores	3.5	14.6
Retail Grocery Stores	1.4	5.7
Retail Auto Dealers & Gas Stations	1.6	6.1
Retail Apparel & Accessory Stores	2.5	6.4
Retail Shoe Stores	2.2	6.1
Retail Furniture Stores	5.8	14.9
Retail Eating Places	3.7	17.4
Retail Jewelry Stores	6.2	13.7
Retail Mail Order Houses	13.2	36.7
Retail Computer Stores	2.9	10.7
Savings & Loan Associations	.7	1.9
Personal Credit Institutions	1.6	3.1
Business Credit Institutions	.2	.3
Finance Services	2.5	10.4
Insurance Agents, Brokers & Services	.8	2.9
Real Estate	1.5	5.1
Hotels & Motels	3.5	12.7
Services—Advertising Agencies	.1	.2
Services—Cleaning & Maintenance to Building	1.5	8.5
Personnel Supply Services	1.9	8.1
Services—Computer & Data Processing	1.4	3.3
Services—C.M.P. Program & Software	2.8	7.2
Services—Research & Development Lab	1.3	15.0
Services—Management Consultation & PR	.2	.8
Photofinishing Laboratories	4.7	11.7
Services—Misc. Amusement & Recreation	4.7	15.7
Services—Hospitals	3.2	12.0
Medical & Dental Labs	.6	1.5
Outpatient Care Facilities	1.6	10.5
Services—Educational	4.1	10.2
Services—Engineering & Architectural	1.1	3.6

Source: "Advertising-to-sales ratios, 1985 (By Industry)," *Advertising Age* 15 September 1986.

How to Write a Successful Yellow Pages Ad

STEP ONE: PLAN YOUR AD WITH YOUR MARKET IN MIND

- Decide what elements will make your ad stand out. Ad size has a definite impact on effectiveness—studies show that a half-page ad gets 15 times the results of a small ad.
- Take a look at what your competition is doing. It will help you select the approach that will make the biggest splash in your market.
- Boost your impact by using an illustration or highlighting in red—a device that can triple your ad's drawing power.

STEP TWO: USE YOUR AD TO HELP BUYERS FIND YOU IN THE DIRECTORY

- Include your logo and slogan in your ad for fast identification.
- Advertise under all the headings where potential buyers might look for you.

STEP THREE: USE YOUR AD TO ANSWER QUESTIONS CUSTOMERS MIGHT HAVE ABOUT YOUR BUSINESS

- List your product line and services prominently. Give your location with a cross street or map if necessary. If you offer parking, say so. List which credit cards you honor, whether you deliver, and your hours of business.
- Highlight the strengths that differentiate you from your competitors—emphasize your affiliation with regulating agencies, longevity in the industry, or reputation for low costs.

- Provide the information that consumers need to make an intelligent choice.

STEP FOUR: MAKE YOUR AD ATTRACTIVE

- Include the information you need to highlight your business, but don't let the ad appear cluttered.

STEP FIVE: COVER THE GEOGRAPHIC AREA YOUR BUSINESS CAN SERVE

- If you expect to draw customers from outside your own community, expand your advertising to include directories for those areas.
- Use toll-free 800 numbers and Remote Call Forwarding to give you the equivalent of a branch office anywhere in your servicing area.

APPENDIX G
Advertising Considerations

Analyze your market. Decide the best way to approach your potential customers. Do you need to build excitement quickly? If so, go with television advertising. Do you want to expand your client base or increase sales from your existing customers? Direct mail could be the answer. The type of advertising you need is tied directly to your marketing objectives.

Target your audience. Identify whom you are trying to reach. Is it a diverse, mass audience or a very select group? Once you know who's likely to use your services, you'll be able to choose the best means of reaching those people.

Identify your competition. Know your competition. Is your industry highly competitive, meaning that your approach to advertising needs to be attention-grabbing? And, how are your local competitors attempting to reach customers?

Advertise within your budget. Put your advertising budget to use where it will have the most impact—but stay within your budget.

Ask an expert. Consult the Small Business Administration. Call SCORE, the SBA's corps of retired executives, for free advice. Utilize local libraries and bookstores. Consult free-lance talent, consultants, or even public relations or advertising agencies, who are often available on an hourly basis.

Evaluate the effectiveness of your advertising. Determine how you'll measure the effects of your advertising. Will you measure your company's sales against industry levels or your own figures from last year? Or will you evaluate the effects of different ad campaigns tested in different sales regions? Assess your results and be prepared to revise your advertising accordingly.

APPENDIX H
The Business Plan

The business plan describes the current and planned operations of your business and demonstrates how the desired loan will further your business goals. Listed below are key elements that should be addressed; this information should be incorporated into a written description of your business plan and included in the narrative section of your loan proposal. Carefully think about each area and be realistic in your description. Although you may wish to seek professional help in preparing your plan, you should be familiar with every detail. Your knowledge and understanding of all aspects of your business will help the lender to understand and work with you to evaluate your plan and your loan request. The sample business plan outline can be used to assist you in organizing your plan.

Type of Organization: What kind of business is it—construction, manufacturing, retailing, service, etc.? What is your legal organizational status—corporation, partnership, or proprietorship? How many owners? What are their names and addresses, and what percentage of ownership does each hold? In what capacity will they function in the business?

Product/Service or Description of Business Activity: If you are a manufacturer, describe the products you plan to make. If you are a retailer, talk about the various types of goods sold, some major brand names, etc. If you are a service business, talk about the services given. How will this loan affect the product/service you provide?

Success: Why did you pick this type of business? What makes your chances of success unusually good? What have been your past problems with the business?

Sales/Marketing Activity: To whom will you sell—retailers, wholesalers, or the public? How are your sales made? Do you have to bid? What problems have you experienced in bidding? Do you use a sales representative? How much do you pay him/her? Who are your suppliers? How do you determine the price of your product or service? What is your estimated cost of sales and net profit margin? How will you advertise or what promotional activities will you conduct to generate sales?

Competition: Briefly describe your major competitors. What competitive edge will your business have over your competitor's operation?

Location: Where will your business be located? If it's a retail business, describe the area and the people. Describe your business location's advantages and disadvantages. What are the local zoning requirements? What kind of licensing will be needed?

Facilities: Describe the type and condition of the building. What are the purchase or rental terms? What improvements are needed? Describe the types and quality of existing equipment, furniture, and fixtures. What do you want to change?

Employees: How many employees will you hire? What kind of special skills do your employees need? Briefly describe their responsibilities. What wages will you pay? Is a union involved?

Other: What kind of business insurance will you carry? What kind of financial records will be prepared, how frequently, and by whom? What are your future plans for growth? Are there any relevant topics or issues the bank should be aware of?

THE BUSINESS PLAN OUTLINE

   I. **Cover Letter.**
      A. Dollar amount requested.
      B. Terms and timing.
      C. Purpose of the loan.

  II. **Summary.**
      A. Business description.
         1. Name.
         2. Location and plan description.
         3. Product.
         4. Market and competition.
         5. Management expertise.
      B. Business goals.
      C. Summary of financial needs and breakdown of how loan funds will be used.
      D. Earnings projections.

 III. **Market Analysis.**
      A. Description of total market.
      B. Industry trends.
      C. Target market.
      D. Competition.

  IV. **Products and Services.**
      A. Description of product line.
      B. Proprietary position: patents, copyrights, and legal and technical considerations.
      C. Comparison to competitor's products.

   V. **Manufacturing Process (if applicable).**
      A. Materials.
      B. Source of supply.
      C. Production methods.

  VI. **Marketing Strategy.**
      A. Overall strategy.
      B. Pricing policy.
      C. Method of selling, distributing, and servicing products.

 VII. **Management Plan.**
      A. Form of business organization.
      B. Board of directors' composition.
      C. Officers: organization chart and responsibilities.
      D. Résumés of key personnel.
      E. Staffing plan/number of employees.
      F. Facilities plan/planned capital improvements.
      G. Operating plan/schedule of upcoming work for next one to two years.

VIII. **Financial Data.**
      A. Financial statements (two to three years to present, if this is an existing business).

    B. Financial projections.
        1. 12-month profit and loss statement.
        2. 12-month cash-flow forecast.
        3. Balance sheet upon funding of loan.
    C. Explanation of projects.
    D. Key business ratios.

SAMPLE BUSINESS PLAN

James Sanders, Gen. Mgr.
434 Any Ave.
Anytown, XA 95635
(796) 444-6666

Executive Summary

The business venture described in this plan is an automobile fleet maintenance service to be known as "XYZ Auto Repair" and will be located in the city of Anytown, State.

Growth plans include engine rebuilding and automobile restoration services.

Mission Statements

- To provide those businesses within a 25-mile radius of the city of Anytown a fleet maintenance service that is scheduled, reliable, and cost effective.

- To provide the general public a cost-effective engine rebuilding service.

- To locate and acquire popular vintage-model automobiles for the purpose of restoring and reselling, specializing in model years prior to 1970.

The target market is those businesses with fleets of 5 to 15 vehicles (i.e., Motorola Service Co., 8 vehicles; Tiffany Plant Rentals, 10 vehicles).

A review of the local (Anytown) auto mechanic businesses reveals that no members are targeting a specific customer area. Instead, they rely on the general public to respond to local advertising or merely "drop in" as the need occurs. Thus, the proposed market is without any real competition in the planned area of service.

The two principals of the business, James Sanders and Fred Smith, are well experienced in their respective areas. Jim has been active for over 20 years in the design, development, implementation, and management of service support programs for electronic and electromechanical systems. Fred has over 5 years experience in the automotive repair industry in general mechanics: tune-ups, lube, oil changes, tire rotation, transmission service, road testing, differential service, and engine rebuilding.

The purpose of the loan funds is to provide working capital until the business is past the break-even point—approximately 6 to 9 months. It will also provide funds for the purchase of some major items of capital equipment over the first 5 months of operation.

The amount being requested is $150,000, which will be paid back over 15 years at prime plus 2%. The funds are to be secured by the assets of the business, which include over $92,000 worth of hand tools and heavy equipment such as an air compressor, engine hoist, and engine rack.

Table of Contents

1. Name of Firm

The business will be known as "XYZ Auto Repair."

2. Ownership

The business is to be formed as a partnership consisting of two partners: James Sanders, as to an undivided fifty-one percent (51%) interest, and Fred Smith, as to an undivided forty-nine percent (49%) interest.

3. Information on the Business

a. Type of business and product or service.

The proposed business venture is an automobile fleet maintenance service targeting those businesses with fleets of 5 to 15 vehicles. The owners plan to also engage in engine rebuilding and automobile restoration services after sufficient growth has occurred.

Mission Statements:

- To provide those businesses within a 25-mile radius of the city of Anytown a fleet maintenance service that is scheduled, reliable, and cost effective.
- To provide the general public a cost-effective engine rebuilding service.
- To locate and acquire popular vintage-model automobiles for the purpose of restoring and reselling, specializing in model years prior to 1970.

b. History

This is a start-up business venture and as such has no history of previous operation to relate. However, both principals forming the business have histories in the maintenance business. The general manager (James Sanders) has been in computer maintenance management for the past 20 years (refer to résumé attached), and the operations manager (Fred Smith) has been in the automobile repair industry for over 5 years. Both of these people have demonstrated progressive success in their respective areas of expertise and feel that by combining their talents, a new automotive repair niche market can be profitably addressed.

c. Office hours.

Business hours: 10:00 a.m. to 9:00 p.m. Thursday through Tuesday.

These hours are considered best for the convenience of the target customer, who does not want to be bothered with fleet unit "shuffling" during the busy morning hours when trying to dispatch deliveries, etc. In some cases, customers cannot deliver vehicles for servicing during normal working hours of 8:00 a.m. to 5:00 p.m. and/or during the normal workdays of Monday through Friday. Thus, 4-hour availability during the week from 5:00 p.m. to 9:00 p.m. and weekend (Saturday and Sunday) availability provides the most convenient time for fleet maintenance needs.

d. Economic/Accounting.

The business will make revenue by providing a cost-effective vehicle service facility for businesses with fleet maintenance needs. These services will be provided under a semiannual or annual contract basis at a stated monthly charge for the fleet. Repair items not included in the contract will be provided at extra charge, which will provide revenue over and above the contract revenue.

Prices will be determined by the general manager with consultation from the operations manager and will initially be determined by estimate using industry standards and later, once a history has been obtained, by experience. The general formula for pricing will be: all costs (parts, labor, overhead) plus 50%. This may be modified depending on what the market will bear.

Full accounting records will be kept by the administrative manager (Jane Smith—wife of Fred) for all supplies purchased, parts purchased and sold, and labor and overhead costs. This complete recording system will be implemented as a computerized system specific to the auto repair industry.

e. Inventory, supplies, suppliers, and equipment.

Inventory will consist primarily of consumable office supplies (forms, pens, etc.). Very little inventory of high-cost parts will be kept on hand because there are many parts stores in the general area that can supply most needed parts within one working day or less. Therefore, it is the intent to practice the "JIT" inventory strategy with only a few specific exceptions relating to signed contract obligations.

f. Legal.

The business is to be formed as a partnership consisting of two partners: James Sanders, as to an undivided fifty-one percent (51%) interest, and Fred Smith, as to an undivided forty-nine percent (49%) interest.

Responsibilities of the business will be divided into two general areas: administration and operation. James Sanders will be responsible for the administration and general management of the business, and Fred Smith will be responsible for managing the day-to-day shop operations.

g. Future plans.

The company mission will be accomplished in three phases, starting with the operation that provides the greatest opportunity for immediate cash flow and profit and, once the first phase has proven stable and profitable, adding the necessary resources to incorporate the objectives of the second phase. Then, using the same criteria of stability and profitability, the business will expand to the third phase of operation. Each progressive phase will require greater human, capital, and time resources.

4. Market Analysis

The target market is those businesses with fleets of 5 to 15 vehicles (i.e., Motorola Service Co., 8 vehicles; Tiffany Plant Rentals, 10 vehicles)

A review of the local (Anytown) auto mechanic businesses reveals that no members are targeting a specific customer area. Instead, they rely on the general public to respond to local advertising or merely "drop in" as the need occurs.

The objective of this targeting is to attract and retain a group of 40–45 accounts averaging 8 vehicles each. The vehicles will require servicing (tune-up, lube, oil change) twice per year (minimum) and will use approximately 2 hours to service. ($43 \times 8 = 347$ vehicles, $347 \times 2 = 693$ servicings, 693×2 hours $= 1396$ hours per year, 1396 hours/1980 total working hours per year $= .70$, or 70% annual capacity.)

(1980 wkg. hrs./yr. $\times .7 = 1386$; 1386/4 vehicles per day per mechanic $= 347$ vehicles per year per mechanic at 70% efficiency.)

(Servicing price: $127.00. Servicing cost: $92.00. Gross net per service: $35.00. $35.00 \times 347 = \$12,128.00$ at 70% eff.)

The target market will be attracted to the service being offered because they will no longer need to track the service record of each vehicle. That will be provided for them via a computer printout. Also, a reminder call will be made when the estimated time for service is near. Thus, they can plan for a vehicle or series of vehicles to be out of service, reducing the impact on their work scheduling. The yearly vehicle maintenance cost will also be a known, easily budgeted figure, because the service will be provided under a contract agreement and not, as potential competition would offer, a no-contract variable rate.

Any problems found that require work beyond that agreed to under contract would be first recommended after which a cost bid would be submitted. The customer would then have the option to go ahead with the work or check the general market for competitive bids.

Anytown Chamber of Commerce information indicates that industry is moving into the Anytown area encouraged by the fact that the city government has set aside 7,000 acres for industrial purposes. 4,000 acres are currently zoned for industrial use and have 50 industrial parks and districts at different levels of development.

As of 1992 there were in excess of 400 plants in the city of Anytown. Leading group classes of products are electronics, fabricated metal products, automobiles, metal container fabricating, roofing, and printing.

Job growth rate during the past year has been 4% and is expected to continue.

The initial growth rate of the business is expected to be 15% per month. This is justified by the facts that the service offered has virtually no competition in the area and that there is already a potential large customer base established in the area. This potential must first be addressed, then the expected growth rate of 19% factored into the projections. (Telephone Company Yellow Pages demographic study indicates a 19% area growth rate.)

5. Products and Services

a. XYZ Auto Repair will provide fleet maintenance service to surrounding businesses in the Anytown area. This will include:

Tune-up	Wheel replacement
Lubrication	Engine analysis
Oil change	Engine repair
Brake rebuilding	Exhaust maintenance
Tire replacement/balancing	Transmission repair/service

Wheel alignments and smog checks are to be subcontracted.

b. Comparison to competitors' products.

The service being proposed is a standard automotive service but will be offered to a specific target market in an attractive package (contract form), which no other organization offering this type of service is now doing.

Competition remains the standard auto repair service, which is "location" bound to attract the transient customer, normally a single-vehicle owner with standard maintenance needs. Thus, there is no competition for the service being offered by XYZ Auto Repair.

6. Marketing Strategy

a. Promotion strategy.

The service will be promoted by targeted telemarketing methods. This means that via a demographic study, specific businesses will be identified as fleet owners. These businesses will be contacted and the person responsible for fleet management will be identified. That person will be contacted with a description of the service and its benefits. An interview will be arranged in which a full discussion and explanation of the service will be presented and specific information on the fleet will be obtained. A bid contract will then be generated and presented for the person (customer) to read and sign.

Other promotional aids will be mailings directed to the specific person responsible for fleet management (or the general manager if that person cannot be identified) explaining the benefits of the service and with a return-mail inquiry card enclosed.

Initial promotion will be kept to the Anytown area to accomplish the market test and contain costs. Budgeted promotion costs will approximate, at maturity, the industry averages. These are:

Auto Dealers and Gas Station Advertising to Sales Ratios:

  1.6% Ad $ as % of Sales
  6.1% Ad $ as % of Margin

(Source: "Advertising-to-sales ratios, 1985 (By Industry), *Advertising Age,* 15 September 1987.)

b. Pricing policy.

Pricing will be established to encourage multiple vehicle maintenance contracts. The advantage to the customer is a constant set monthly cost for ease in budgeting. The advantage to the business is a constant, dependable cash flow.

c. Sales strategy.

Sales will be accomplished by personal interviews with people responsible for fleet maintenance. These interviews will be generated by telemarketing and/or direct-mail response. During these interviews the full range of services provided and their cost will be discussed. A contract will be drafted to address the customer's specific needs that includes prices and conditions of payment. The contract will then be presented for signature.

7. Management Plan

a. Form of business organization.

A partnership consisting of two (2) partners:

  James Sanders
  Fred Smith

b. Board of directors' composition.

Board of Directors:

Chairman— James Sanders, owner/general manager
  Fred Smith, owner/operations manager
  Betty Jones
  Jane Smith

Advisory Board:

Chairman— James Sanders, owner/general manager
  Fred Smith, owner/operations manager
Attorney— Dave Neverwantsto, advise as needed.

CPA—   Eugene Tohightomuch, advise as needed, audit accounts, and prepare tax filings

Insurance— Paul Notenough, Ins. Broker, advise as needed.

c. Officers: organization chart and responsibilities.

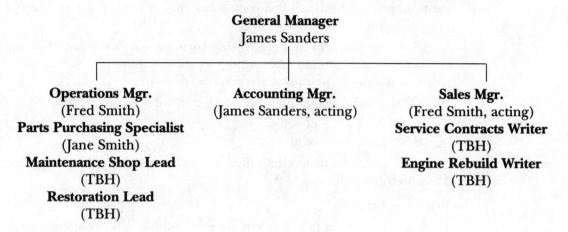

General Manager
James Sanders

Operations Mgr.	**Accounting Mgr.**	**Sales Mgr.**
(Fred Smith)	(James Sanders, acting)	(Fred Smith, acting)
Parts Purchasing Specialist		**Service Contracts Writer**
(Jane Smith)		(TBH)
Maintenance Shop Lead		**Engine Rebuild Writer**
(TBH)		(TBH)
Restoration Lead		
(TBH)		

d. Résumés of key personnel

RESUME

JAMES SANDERS, Ph.D.
General Manager

BACKGROUND SUMMARY

Over 20 years experience in the design, development, and implementation of sales support programs for electronic and electromechanical systems.

Director of Technical Support, Technical Sales Support Manager, and Project Manager for microcomputer and peripheral computer products.

SPECIFIC AREAS OF EXPERTISE

Technical Support Administration
Maintainability Engineering
Reliability Engineering
Program Management
Field Technical Operations Management
Material Control Systems
Customer Relations
Technical Training
Technical Documentation

EXPERIENCE APPLIED TO THE FOLLOWING SYSTEMS

Microcomputers and Word Processors
Computer peripherals—matrix and drum printers, disk and tape storage devices
Telecommunications
Networks

EDUCATION

B.S., Business Management; LaSalle University
B.S.E.E.; Loyola University
B.S., Business Administration; Columbia Pacific University
Ph.D. Business Administration; Columbia Pacific University

COMPANY AFFILIATIONS

E.D.P. Div. Honeywell, Inc.
Hewlett-Packard Co.
Microform Data Systems, Inc.
Osborne Computer Corp.
Ferix Corp.

RESUME

FRED SMITH
Operations Manager

BACKGROUND SUMMARY

Over 5 years experience in the automotive repair industry, apprenticing in general mechanics: tune-ups, lube, oil changes, tire rotation, transmission service, road testing, and differential service.

Completed journeyman work in engine rebuilding, transmission repair, and clutch replacement of most foreign and domestic automobiles and 4-wheel drive trucks.

SPECIFIC AREAS OF EXPERTISE

Engine Rebuilding
Transmission Rebuilding
Clutch Replacement

EDUCATION

Reynolds High School; Graduated 1983
Sequoia Institute
Chabot Jr. College

COMPANY AFFILIATIONS

Mowry Automotive, Anytown, CA.
Winner Chevrolet, Tracy, CA.
Anytown Ford, Anytown, CA.
Shamrock Ford, Dublin, CA.
Dan's Car Repair, Anytown, CA.
Osborne Computer Corporation, Hayward, CA.
Southerland Construction Co., Anytown, CA.

e. **Staffing plan/number of employees.**

Initially staffing will consist of James Sanders and Fred Smith, who will be responsible for assuring that the accounting books are in order and that the job flow is maintained through the shop, respectively. These two people will share the responsibility of soliciting business, answering the telephone, and taking care of necessary correspondence.

This will be the mode of operation until on-going cash flow justifies the hiring of additional personnel. The first to be hired will be a maintenance shop apprentice. The intent will be for Fred Smith to supervise and train the individual in the proper shop processes so as to allow his or her promotion to maintenance shop lead. When this occurs, Fred will begin setting up the engine rebuilding facility. When that department's cash flow justifies hiring another person, that person will be hired as an apprentice and trained by Fred in the proper procedures of rebuilding engines. Fred will then move on to the third and last operation of establishing the restoration shop. The same rules for hiring will apply here: cash flow justification and apprentice-to-journeyman progression.

The primary source of apprentice-type personnel will be the Sequoia Institute. However, other sources will not necessarily be refused.

Additional personnel that may be necessary (again, justified by cash flow) will be a service contract writer, engine rebuild writer, and restored auto salesperson. As these positions are primarily sales oriented, workers will be paid through a combination of salary and commissions.

The basic philosophy of personnel management will be to hire from outside the company but promote from within the company. This assures a career growth path not offered by many in the industry. This will promote loyalty and longevity of the individual employee.

8. Financial Plan

a. **Explanation of key financial points.**

b. **Financial projections.**

1. Manpower Budget—Administration.
2. Budget Worksheet—Administration.
3. Manpower Budget—Operations.
4. Budget Worksheet—Operations.
5. Projection of Financial Statement—First Running Year.
6. Pro Forma Balance Sheets—First Running Year.
7. Projection of Financial Statements—3 Continuing Years.
8. Pro Forma Balance Sheets—3 Continuing Years.
9. Pricing Strategy.

a. **Explanation of key financial points.**

Manpower Budgets

There are 2 budgeted departments: administration and operations. It is indicated that the initial manpower will consist of 1 primary person in each department with a part-time person assisting with the clerical and data entry duties in administration. This will continue for approximately 6 months or until the business growth justifies additional help in each department.

Budget Worksheets

Again, there are 2 budgeted departments, each showing the projected cash flow needs of that specific department. The major expenses for capital equipment are called out, being:

$10,000   Computer system for accounting purposes in administration
$ 5,000   Chassis lift
$ 4,500   Tire-mounting equipment and brake lathe
$ 5,000   Engine-analyzing equipment

These purchases are spread through the first 6 months of operation.

Cash Flow Projections

This is a combined projection for XYZ Auto Repair operations and includes the budgeted items mentioned above.

Cash receipts reflects what is expected from miscellaneous repair work, which is outside the targeted market of maintenance contract work. This is expected to increase at the same rate as the maintenance contract work, which is 15% per month.

Cash disbursements includes all disbursements of both the administrative and operations departments.

Depreciation is based on the 5-year straight-line method against the capital equipment purchases mentioned above.

Accounts receivable reflects the income from the sale of fleet maintenance contracts and the expected increase at a 15% per month rate.

Accounts payable are expenses for fleet maintenance contract parts purchases.

Payment of other expenses reflects the cost of parts purchases for work other than fleet maintenance accounts.

Purchase of equipment shows the expected expenditures for capital equipment.

Increase in funds invested reflects the average of the long-term loan principal payback of approx. $500 per month.

At the back of the financials, for additional information, a pricing strategy sheet has been included.

MANPOWER BUDGET

DEPT. NAME: ADMINISTRATION
DEPT. NO:

		$/hr	Emp. Cnt.	1	2	3	4	5	6	7	8	9	10	11	12	YR END TOTAL
MONTH				1	2	3	4	5	6	7	8	9	10	11	12	TOTAL
EMPLOYEES				1	1	1	1	1	2	2	2	2	3	3	3	2
TEMP. EMP.	WK HRS/MO 167							1	1	· 1	1	1				0
ADDITIONS									1	1	1	1	1	1	1	1
HIRE/PROM.																
DATE	POSITION	$/hr	Emp. Cnt.													
Mo. 1	Admin. Mgr.	15	1	15	15	15	15	15	15	15	15	15	15	15	15	
Mo. 1	Data Entry/Recept	5.5	1	5.5	5.5	5.5	5.5	5.5								
Mo. 6	DE merit inc.	6.5	1						6.5	6.5	6.5	6.5	6.5	6.5	6.5	
TOTAL SALARIES & WAGES				3417	3417	3417	3417	3417	3584	3584	3584	3584	3584	3584	3584	42175
MERIT INCREASE (10% ANN)																
	OVERTIME															
	TEMP.															
TOTAL SALARY & WAGES				3417	3417	3417	3417	3417	3584	3584	3584	3584	3584	3584	3584	42175

BUDGET WORKSHEET		ADMINISTRATION													
ACCT	DESCRIPTION		MONTH 1	2	3	4	5	6	7	8	9	10	11	12	TOTAL
0100	SALARIES & WAGES		3417	3417	3417	3417	3417	3584	3584	3584	3584	3584	3584	3584	42175
0110	OVERTIME PREMIUM														0
0150	ENGINEERING PROJECT														0
0200	PAYROLL BENEFITS	23% of hrly	786	786	786	786	786	824	824	824	824	824	824	824	9700
0210	EMPLOYEE DEVELOPMENT	5% of hrly	171	171	171	171	171	179	179	179	179	179	179	179	2109
0450	ADVERT PRINTING SERV	1.6% of Sales													0
0460	CONTRACT LABOR – TEMP	$5.50/hr													0
0500	OFFICE SUPPLIES	$20.00/mo	20	20	20	20	20	20	20	20	20	20	20	20	240
0510	EXPENSED EQUIPMENT	$500/qtr	500			500			500			500			2000
0530	EQUIPMENT RENTAL														0
0540	EQUIPMENT MAINT.	$50.00/mo	50	50	50	50	50	50	50	50	50	50	50	50	600
0560	OPERATING SUPPLIES														0
0700	TRAVEL & ENTERTAIN														0
0790	MISC. EXPENSE	5% of Sales													0
	CAPITAL EQUIPMENT		10000												10000
0830	DEPRECIATION & AMORT	5yr st line		−167	−167	−167	−167	−167	−167	−167	−167	−167	−167	−167	−1833
0890	OTHER	$50.00/mo	50												50
	DEPARTMENT TOTAL		14994	4278	4278	4778	4278	4491	4991	4491	4491	4991	4491	4491	65041

212

MANPOWER BUDGET

DEPT. NAME: OPERATIONS

DEPT. NO:

DATE	POSITION	$/hr	Emp. Cnt.	MONTH 1	2	3	4	5	6	7	8	9	10	11	12	YR END TOTAL
EMPLOYEES				1	1	1	1	1	1	2	2	2	3	3	3	3
TEMP.EMP.	WK HRS/MO 166.7							1	1	1	1	1				0
ADDITIONS										1			1			2
HIRE/PROM.																
Mo. 1	Oper.Mgr.	20	1	20	20	20	20	20	20	20	20	20	20	20	20	
Mo. 5	Flt Maint App	5.5	1					5.5	5.5							
Mo. 7	Flt Maint Lead	6.5	1							6.5	6.5	6.5	6.5	6.5	6.5	
Mo. 8	Flt Maint App	5.5	1								5.5	5.5				
Mo. 8	Flt Maint Lead	6.5	1										6.5	6.5	6.5	
Mo. 10	Eng Rebld App	7.5	1										7.5	7.5	7.5	
TOTAL SALARIES & WAGES				3334	3334	3334	3334	4251	4251	4418	5334	5334	6751	6751	6751	57178
MERIT INCREASE (10% ANN)																
OVERTIME																
TEMP.																
TOTAL SALARY & WAGES				3334	3334	3334	3334	4251	4251	4418	5334	5334	6751	6751	6751	57178

BUDGET WORKSHEET — OPERATIONS

ACCT	DESCRIPTION		MONTH 1	2	3	4	5	6	7	8	9	10	11	12	TOTAL
0100	SALARIES & WAGES		3334	3334	3334	3334	4251	4251	4418	5334	5334	6751	6751	6751	57178
0110	OVERTIME PREMIUM														0
0150	ENGINEERING PROJECT														0
0200	PAYROLL BENEFITS	23% of hrly	767	767	767	767	978	978	1016	1227	1227	1553	1553	1553	13151
0210	EMPLOYEE DEVELOPMENT	5% of hrly	167	167	167	167	213	213	221	267	267	338	338	338	2859
0450	PRINTING SERVICES														0
0460	CONTRACT LABOR – TEMP	$5.50/hr													0
0470	OTHER PURCHASED SERV	$100.00/mo	100	100	100	100	100	100	100	100	100	100	100	100	1200
0500	OFFICE SUPPLIES	$20.00/mo	20	20	20	20	20	20	20	20	20	20	20	20	240
0510	EXPENSED EQUIPMENT	$500/qtr	500			500			500			500			2000
0520	SMALL TOOLS	$20.00/mo	20	20	20	20	20	20	20	20	20	20	20	20	240
0530	EQUIPMENT RENTAL														0
0540	EQUIPMENT MAINT.	$50.00/mo	50	50	50	50	50	50	50	50	50	50	50	50	600
0560	OPERATING SUPPLIES														0
0700	TRAVEL & ENTERTAIN														0
0710	DUES & SUBSCRIPTIONS	$200.00/yr	20			20	20	20	20	20	20	20	20	20	200
0790	MISC. EXPENSE	5% of Sales													0
0800	JANITORIAL & MAINT.	$5.50/hr.6hr/wk	143	143	143	143	143	143	143	143	143	143	143	143	1716
0810	INSURANCE	$3500.00/yr	292	292	292	292	292	292	292	292	292	292	292	292	3500
0820	FREIGHT & POSTAGE	Eng rbld $50/mo								50	50	50	50	50	250
	CAPITAL EQUIPMENT		5000	4500			5000								14500
0830	DEPRECIATION & AMORT	5yr st line		-83	-158	-158	-158	-242	-242	-242	-242	-242	-242	-242	-2250
0840	TELEPHONE & TELEX	$60.00/mo	60	60	60	60	60	60	60	60	60	60	60	60	720
0850	RENT	1325ft/$600/mo	600	600	600	600	600	600	600	600	600	600	600	600	7200
0860	UTILITIES	$100.00/mo	100	100	100	100	100	100	100	100	100	100	100	100	1200
0870	TAXES	28% of Sales													0
0890	OTHER	$100.00/mo	100	100	100	100	100	100	100	100	100	100	100	100	1200
	DEPARTMENT TOTAL		11272	10169	5594	6114	11787	6704	7417	8141	8141	10455	9955	9955	105704

PROJECTION OF FINANCIAL STATEMENTS
FIRST OPERATION YEAR

(1=1000)

	MONTH 1	2	3	4	5	6	7	8	9	10	11	12	TOTAL
PROFITS AND LOSS													
Direct Sales	1.95	2.24	2.58	2.97	3.41	3.92	4.51	5.19	5.97	6.86	7.89	9.07	56.55
Contract Sales	0.00	5.75	6.61	7.60	8.75	10.06	11.57	13.30	15.30	17.59	20.23	23.26	140.01
NET SALES	1.95	7.99	9.19	10.57	12.16	13.98	16.08	18.49	21.26	24.45	28.12	32.33	196.56
Less: Material Used	0.92	1.01	1.11	1.22	1.35	1.48	1.63	1.79	1.97	2.17	2.39	2.62	19.67
Direct Labor	3.33	3.33	3.33	3.33	4.25	4.25	4.42	5.33	5.33	6.75	6.75	6.75	57.18
Other Oper. Expense	0.10	0.10	0.10	0.10	0.10	0.10	0.10	0.10	0.10	0.10	0.10	0.10	1.20
COST OF GOODS SOLD	4.35	4.45	4.55	4.66	5.70	5.83	6.15	7.23	7.41	9.02	9.24	9.48	78.05
GROSS PROFIT	−2.40	3.55	4.64	5.91	6.46	8.15	9.93	11.26	13.85	15.43	18.88	22.86	118.51
Less: Sales Expense (8% sales)	0.16	0.64	0.74	0.85	0.97	1.12	1.29	1.48	1.70	1.96	2.25	2.59	15.72
Warranty (.1% sales)	0.00	0.01	0.01	0.01	0.01	0.01	0.02	0.02	0.02	0.02	0.03	0.03	0.20
Gen. and Admin. Exp.	3.42	3.42	3.42	3.42	3.42	3.58	3.58	3.58	3.58	3.58	3.58	3.58	42.17
Burden (50% labor)	1.67	1.67	1.67	1.67	2.13	2.13	2.21	2.67	2.67	3.38	3.38	3.38	28.59
													0.00
OPERATING PROFIT	−7.65	−2.18	−1.18	−0.03	−0.07	1.30	2.83	3.51	5.88	6.49	9.64	13.28	31.83
Less: Other Exp. or Inc. (Net)	0.00	0.00	0.00	0.00	0.00	0.00	0.00	0.00	0.00	0.00	0.00	0.00	0.00
Income Tax Provision (28%)	−2.14	−0.61	−0.33	−0.01	−0.02	0.37	0.79	0.98	1.65	1.82	2.70	3.72	8.91
													0.00
NET PROFIT	−5.51	−1.57	−0.85	−0.02	−0.05	0.94	2.04	2.53	4.23	4.67	6.94	9.56	22.92

215

P & L RATIO ANALYSIS													
Sales	1.00	1.00	1.00	1.00	1.00	1.00	1.00	1.00	1.00	1.00	1.00	1.00	1.00
Cost of Goods Sold	2.23	0.56	0.49	0.44	0.47	0.42	0.38	0.39	0.35	0.37	0.33	0.29	0.40
Gross Margin	-1.23	0.44	0.51	0.56	0.53	0.58	0.62	0.61	0.65	0.63	0.67	0.71	0.60
Net Profit on Sales	-2.82	-0.20	-0.09	0.00	0.00	0.07	0.13	0.14	0.20	0.19	0.25	0.30	0.12
Marketing (Sales Exp + Wty)	0.08	0.08	0.08	0.08	0.08	0.08	0.08	0.08	0.08	0.08	0.08	0.08	0.08
Admin. (Gen and Admin + Burden)	2.61	0.64	0.55	0.48	0.46	0.41	0.36	0.34	0.29	0.28	0.25	0.22	0.36
CASH PROJECTION													
CASH BALANCE (Opening)	1.00	129.57	113.34	106.82	100.59	93.71	82.12	75.80	71.09	62.52	59.89	58.59	
Plus RECEIPTS: Receivable Coll.	0.00	0.00	5.75	6.61	7.60	8.75	10.06	11.57	13.30	15.30	17.59	20.23	
Interest Inc (cash bal. x .06/12)	0.01	0.65	0.57	0.53	0.50	0.47	0.41	0.38	0.36	0.31	0.30	0.29	
Return of Net Profit	0.00	0.00	0.00	0.00	0.00	0.00	0.00	2.04	2.53	4.23	4.67	6.94	
Bank Ln Proceeds	150.00												
Total receipts	151.01	130.22	119.66	113.96	108.69	102.92	92.59	89.78	87.27	82.37	82.45	86.05	
Less: DISBURSEMENTS: Trade Payables	0.00	0.92	1.01	1.11	1.22	1.35	1.48	1.63	1.79	1.97	2.17	2.39	
Direct Labor	3.33	3.33	3.33	3.33	4.25	4.25	4.42	5.33	5.33	6.75	6.75	6.75	
Other Manuf. Exp.	0.00	0.00	0.00	0.00	0.00	0.00	0.00	0.00	0.00	0.00	0.00	0.00	
Sales, Gen & Admin Exp	5.24	5.73	5.83	5.94	6.53	6.84	7.10	7.75	7.97	8.94	9.24	9.58	
Fixed Asset Adds	15.00	4.50	0.00	0.00	0.00	5.00	0.00	0.00	5.00	0.00	0.00	0.00	
Income Taxes	-2.14	-0.61	-0.33	-0.01	-0.02	0.37	0.79	0.98	1.65	1.82	2.70	3.72	
Dividends or Withdrawals	0.00	0.00	0.00	0.00	0.00	0.00	0.00	0.00	0.00	0.00	0.00	0.00	
Bank Ln Repayment	0.00	3.00	3.00	3.00	3.00	3.00	3.00	3.00	3.00	3.00	3.00	3.00	
Total disbursements	21.44	16.87	12.84	13.38	14.98	20.81	16.79	18.70	24.75	22.48	23.86	25.43	
CASH BALANCE (Closing)	129.57	113.34	106.82	100.59	93.71	82.12	75.80	71.09	62.52	59.89	58.59	60.62	

BALANCE SHEET

(1=1000)	MONTH 1	2	3	4	5	6	7	8	9	10	11	12
ASSETS:												
Cash	1.00	129.57	113.34	106.62	100.59	93.71	82.12	75.80	71.09	62.52	59.89	58.59
Marketable Securities			5.75	6.61	7.60	8.75	10.06	11.57	13.30	15.30	17.59	20.23
Receivables (Net)	19.00	19.00	19.00	19.00	19.00	19.00	19.00	19.00	19.00	19.00	19.00	19.00
Inventory (Net)	34.00	34.00	34.00	29.00	29.00	29.00	29.00	5.00	0.00	0.00	0.00	0.00
Spec. Auto Inventory												
Total Current Assets	54.00	182.57	172.09	161.23	156.19	150.46	140.18	111.37	103.39	96.82	96.48	97.82
Fixed Assets (Net)	37.50	52.50	57.00	57.00	57.00	57.00	62.00	62.00	67.00	72.00	72.00	72.00
Deferred Charges												
TOTAL ASSETS	91.50	235.07	229.09	218.23	213.19	207.46	202.18	173.37	170.39	168.82	168.48	169.82
LIABILITIES												
Notes Payable – Banks	150.00	129.47	116.16	108.94	102.22	95.52	84.34	78.79	73.99	67.34	66.43	70.10
Trade Payables	0.92	1.01	1.11	1.22	1.35	1.48	1.63	1.79	1.97	2.17	2.39	2.62
Income Tax	-2.14	-0.61	-0.33	-0.01	-0.02	0.37	0.79	0.98	1.65	1.82	2.70	3.72
Accruals (ins. $3500/yr)	0.29	0.29	0.29	0.29	0.29	0.29	0.29	0.29	0.29	0.29	0.29	0.29
Total Current Liabilities	149.07	130.16	117.23	110.45	103.84	97.66	87.05	81.85	77.90	71.62	71.81	76.74
Capital Stock – Net Worth Surplus	-57.57	104.91	111.86	107.79	109.36	109.79	115.13	91.51	92.49	97.19	96.67	93.08
TOTAL LIABILITIES AND NET WORTH	91.50	235.07	229.09	218.23	213.19	207.46	202.18	173.37	170.39	168.82	168.48	169.82
BALANCE SHEET RATIO ANALYSIS												
Current Ratio	0.36	1.40	1.47	1.46	1.50	1.54	1.61	1.36	1.33	1.35	1.34	1.27
Debt-to-Equity	-2.59	1.24	1.05	1.02	0.95	0.89	0.76	0.89	0.84	0.74	0.74	0.82
Return on Assets	-1.59	2.24	2.05	2.02	1.95	1.89	1.76	1.89	1.84	1.74	1.74	1.82
Return on Equity	-0.02	1.24	1.06	1.05	0.99	0.93	0.80	0.95	0.91	0.80	0.80	0.85
Return on Investment (ROI)	0.01	0.55	0.52	0.52	0.51	0.49	0.46	0.50	0.50	0.46	0.46	0.46
Working Capital (acid test)	-95.07	52.41	54.86	50.79	52.36	52.79	53.13	29.51	25.49	25.19	24.67	21.08

BALANCE SHEET RATIO ANALYSIS												
Current Ratio	0.36	1.40	1.47	1.46	1.50	1.54	1.61	1.36	1.33	1.35	1.34	1.27
Debt-to-Equity	-2.59	1.24	1.05	1.02	0.95	0.89	0.76	0.89	0.84	0.74	0.74	0.82
Return on Assets	-1.59	2.24	2.05	2.02	1.95	1.89	1.76	1.89	1.84	1.74	1.74	1.82
Return on Equity	-0.02	1.24	1.06	1.05	0.99	0.93	0.80	0.95	0.91	0.80	0.80	0.85
Return on Investment (ROI)	0.01	0.55	0.52	0.52	0.51	0.49	0.46	0.50	0.50	0.46	0.46	0.46
Working Capital (acid test)	-95.07	52.41	54.86	50.79	52.36	52.79	53.13	29.51	25.49	25.19	24.67	21.08

PROJECTION OF FINANCIAL STATEMENTS
THREE RUNNING YEARS

(1 = 1000)

	BY QUARTER 1	2	3	4	TOTAL	QUARTER 1	2	3	4	TOTAL	QUARTER 1	2	3	4	TOTAL
PROFITS AND LOSS															
Direct Sales	31.29	35.98	41.38	47.59	156.24	54.73	62.94	72.38	83.23	273.27	95.72	110.07	126.59	145.57	477.95
Contract Sales	80.25	92.29	106.13	122.05	400.72	140.36	161.41	185.62	213.47	700.86	245.49	282.31	324.66	373.35	1225.81
NET SALES	111.54	128.27	147.51	169.64	556.96	195.08	224.35	258.00	296.70	974.13	341.20	392.38	451.24	518.93	1703.76
Less: Material Used	7.86	8.65	9.51	10.46	36.48	11.51	12.66	13.92	15.32	53.41	16.85	18.53	20.39	22.43	78.19
Direct Labor	20.25	20.25	20.25	20.25	81.00	20.25	20.25	22.28	22.28	85.05	22.28	22.28	22.28	22.28	89.10
Other Oper. Expense	0.30	0.30	0.30	0.30	1.20	0.50	0.50	0.50	0.50	2.00	0.50	0.50	0.50	0.50	2.00
COST OF GOODS SOLD	28.41	29.20	30.06	31.01	118.68	32.26	33.41	36.70	38.09	140.46	39.62	41.31	43.16	45.20	169.29
GROSS PROFIT	83.13	99.07	117.45	138.63	438.28	162.83	190.94	221.30	258.61	833.67	301.58	351.08	408.08	473.73	1534.46
Less: Sales Expense (8% sales)	8.92	10.26	11.80	13.57	44.56	15.61	17.95	20.64	23.74	77.93	27.30	31.39	36.10	41.51	136.30
Warranty (.1% sales)	0.11	0.13	0.15	0.17	0.56	0.20	0.22	0.26	0.30	0.97	0.34	0.39	0.45	0.52	1.70
Gen. and Admin. Exp.	10.74	10.74	10.74	10.74	42.96	10.74	10.74	11.81	11.81	45.11	11.81	11.81	11.81	11.81	47.26
Burden (50% labor)	10.13	10.13	10.13	10.13	40.50	10.13	10.13	11.14	11.14	42.53	11.14	11.14	11.14	11.14	44.55
					0.00					0.00					0.00
OPERATING PROFIT	53.23	67.82	84.64	104.02	309.71	126.16	151.90	177.45	211.62	667.13	250.99	296.34	348.58	408.74	1304.65
Less: Other Exp. or Inc. (Net)	0.00	0.00	0.00	0.00	0.00	0.00	0.00	0.00	0.00	0.00	0.00	0.00	0.00	0.00	0.00
Income Tax Provision (28%)	14.90	18.99	23.70	29.13	86.72	35.32	42.53	49.69	59.25	186.80	70.28	82.98	97.60	114.45	365.30
					0.00					0.00					0.00
NET PROFIT	38.33	48.83	60.94	74.90	222.99	90.83	109.37	127.76	152.37	480.34	180.71	213.37	250.98	294.29	939.35
		check sum			222.99		check sum			480.34		check sum			939.35
P & L RATIO ANALYSIS															
Sales	1.00	1.00	1.00	1.00		1.00	1.00	1.00	1.00		1.00	1.00	1.00	1.00	1.00
Cost of Goods Sold	0.25	0.23	0.20	0.18		0.17	0.15	0.14	0.13		0.12	0.11	0.10	0.09	0.10
Gross Margin	0.75	0.77	0.80	0.82		0.83	0.85	0.86	0.87		0.88	0.89	0.90	0.91	0.90
Net Profit on Sales	0.34	0.38	0.41	0.44		0.47	0.49	0.50	0.51		0.53	0.54	0.56	0.57	0.55
Marketing (Sales Exp + Wty)	0.08	0.08	0.08	0.08		0.08	0.08	0.08	0.08		0.08	0.08	0.08	0.08	0.08
Admin. (Gen and Admin + Burden)	0.19	0.16	0.14	0.12		0.11	0.09	0.09	0.08		0.07	0.06	0.05	0.04	0.05
CASH PROJECTION															
CASH BALANCE (Opening)	58.59	15.04	46.19	93.29		158.97	244.51	349.10	483.65		647.52	843.63	1086.03	1379.73	
Plus RECEIPTS: Receivable Coll.	20.23	80.25	92.29	106.13		122.05	140.36	161.41	185.62		213.47	245.49	282.31	324.66	
Interest Inc (cash bal. x .06/12)	0.88	0.23	0.69	1.40		0.79	1.22	1.75	2.42		3.24	4.22	5.43	6.90	
Return of Net Profit	16.60	38.33	48.83	60.94		74.90	90.83	109.37	127.76		152.37	180.71	213.37	250.98	
Bank Ln Proceeds															
Total receipts	96.30	133.85	188.00	261.76		356.71	476.92	621.62	799.46		1016.59	1274.05	1587.14	1962.26	
Less: DISBURSEMENTS: Trade Payables	6.90	7.86	8.65	9.51		10.46	11.51	12.66	13.92		15.32	18.53	18.53	20.39	
Direct Labor	20.25	20.25	20.25	20.25		20.25	20.25	22.28	22.28		22.28	22.28	22.28	22.28	
Other Oper. Exp.	0.30	0.30	0.30	0.30		0.50	0.50	0.50	0.50		0.50	0.50	0.50	0.50	
Sales, Gen & Admin Exp	29.90	31.25	32.81	34.61		36.67	39.04	43.85	46.98		50.59	54.73	59.50	64.98	
Fixed Asset Adds	14.90	0.00	0.00	0.00		0.00	5.00	0.00	0.00		5.00	0.00	0.00	0.00	
Income Taxes	14.90	18.99	23.70	29.13		35.32	42.53	49.69	59.25		70.28	82.98	97.60	114.45	
Dividends or Withdrawals	0.00	0.00	0.00	0.00		0.00	0.00	0.00	0.00		0.00	0.00	0.00	0.00	
Bank Ln Repayment	9.00	9.00	9.00	9.00		9.00	9.00	9.00	9.00		9.00	9.00	9.00	9.00	
Total disbursements	81.25	87.65	94.71	102.79		112.20	127.83	137.97	151.94		172.96	188.02	207.41	231.59	
CASH BALANCE (Closing)	15.04	46.19	93.29	158.97		244.51	349.10	483.65	647.52		843.63	1086.03	1379.73	1730.66	

BALANCE SHEET
(Three Running Years)

(1=1000)	BY QUARTER 1	2	3	4	TOTAL	QUARTER 1	2	3	4	TOTAL	QUARTER 1	2	3	4	TOTAL
ASSETS:															
Cash	58.59	15.04	46.19	93.29	213.11	158.97	244.51	349.10	483.65	1236.23	647.52	843.63	1086.03	1379.73	3956.91
Marketable Securities					0.00					0.00					0.00
Receivables (Net)	20.23	80.25	92.29	106.13	298.90	122.05	140.36	161.41	185.62	609.44	213.47	245.49	282.31	324.66	1065.93
Inventory (Net)	19.00	19.00	19.00	19.00	76.00	19.00	19.00	19.00	19.00	76.00	19.00	19.00	19.00	19.00	76.00
Spec. Auto Inventory	0.00	34.00	34.00	29.00	97.00	29.00	29.00	5.00	0.00	63.00	0.00	0.00	0.00	0.00	0.00
Total Current Assets	97.82	148.29	191.48	247.42	685.01	329.02	432.87	534.51	688.27	1984.67	879.99	1108.12	1387.34	1723.39	5098.84
Fixed Assets (Net)	67.00	67.00	71.50	71.50	277.00	71.50	71.50	76.50	76.50	296.00	76.50	81.50	81.50	81.50	321.00
Deferred Charges					0.00					0.00					0.00
TOTAL ASSETS	164.82	215.29	262.98	318.92	962.01	400.52	504.37	611.01	764.77	2280.67	956.49	1189.62	1468.84	1804.89	5419.84
LIABILITIES															
Notes Payable – Banks	129.00	127.50	126.00	124.50	507.00	123.00	121.50	120.00	118.50	483.00	117.00	115.50	114.00	112.50	459.00
Trade Payables	7.86	8.65	9.51	10.46	36.48	11.51	12.66	13.92	15.32	53.41	16.85	18.53	20.39	22.43	78.20
Income Tax	14.90	18.99	23.70	29.13	86.72	35.32	42.53	49.69	59.25	186.79	70.28	82.98	97.60	114.45	365.31
Accruals (Ins. $3500/yr)	875.00	875.00	875.00	875.00	3500.00	875.00	875.00	875.00	875.00	3500.00	875.00	875.00	875.00	875.00	3500.00
Total Current Liabilities	1026.76	1030.14	1034.21	1039.09	4130.20	1044.83	1051.69	1058.61	1068.07	4223.20	1079.13	1092.01	1106.99	1124.38	4402.51
Capital Stock – Net Worth	-861.94	-814.85	-771.23	-720.17	-3168.19	-644.31	-547.32	-447.60	-303.30	-1942.53	-122.64	97.61	361.85	680.51	1017.33
Surplus					0.00					0.00					0.00
TOTAL LIABILITIES AND NET WORTH	164.82	215.29	262.98	318.92	962.01	400.52	504.37	611.01	764.77	2280.67	956.49	1189.62	1468.84	1804.89	5419.84
BALANCE SHEET RATIO ANALYSIS															
Current Ratio	0.10	0.14	0.19	0.24		0.31	0.41	0.50	0.64		0.82	1.01	1.25	1.53	
Debt-to-Equity	-1.19	-1.26	-1.34	-1.44		-1.62	-1.92	-2.37	-3.52		-8.80	11.19	3.06	1.65	
Return on Assets	-0.19	-0.26	-0.34	-0.44		-0.62	-0.92	-1.37	-2.52		-7.80	12.19	4.06	2.65	
Return on Equity	-0.09	-0.12	-0.18	-0.28		-0.44	-0.70	-1.14	-2.21		-7.02	11.16	3.78	2.50	
Return on Investment (ROI)	0.48	0.44	0.53	0.63		0.70	0.76	0.84	0.88		0.90	0.92	0.93	0.94	
Working Capital (acid test)	-928.94	-881.85	-842.73	-791.67		-715.81	-618.82	-524.10	-379.80		-199.14	16.11	280.35	599.01	

PRICING STRATEGY									
SINGLE VEHICLE									
	TIME	TIME	PARTS	TOTAL	LABOR	PARTS			GROSS
ITEM	REQ.	COST	COST	COST	CHARGE	CHARGE	PRICE		MARGIN
Tune-up	1.50	30.00	30.00	60.00	60.00	45.00	105.00		0.57
Chassis Lube	0.50	10.00	2.00	12.00	20.00	3.00	23.00		0.52
Oil Change	0.50	10.00	10.00	20.00	20.00	15.00	35.00		0.57
Brake Rebuild	4.00	80.00	65.00	145.00	160.00	97.50	257.50		0.56
Tire Replace	1.50	30.00	5.00	35.00	60.00	7.50	67.50		0.52
Wheel Replace	1.50	30.00		30.00	60.00	0.00	60.00	Plus Pts	0.50
Engine Anal.	1.00	20.00		20.00	40.00	0.00	40.00	Plus Pts	0.50
Engine Repair	16.00	320.00	300.00	620.00	340.00	450.00	790.00		0.78
Exhaust Maint.	3.00	60.00		60.00	120.00	0.00	120.00	Plus Pts	0.50
Trans Service	1.00	20.00		20.00	40.00	0.00	40.00	Plus Pts	0.50
Trans Repair	8.00	160.00		160.00	320.00	0.00	320.00	Plus Pts	0.50
* Wheel alignment to be subcontracted									
Smog checks to be subcontracted									
MULTIPLE VEHICLE DISCOUNT SCHED. (3 TO 6)									
Tune-up	1.20	24.00	30.00	54.00	48.00	45.00	93.00		0.58
Chassis Lube	0.40	8.00	2.00	10.00	16.00	3.00	19.00		0.53
Oil Change	0.40	8.00	10.00	18.00	16.00	15.00	31.00		0.58
Brake Rebuild	3.20	64.00	65.00	129.00	128.00	97.50	225.50		0.57
Tire Replace	1.20	24.00	5.00	29.00	48.00	7.50	55.50		0.52
Wheel Replace	1.20	24.00		24.00	48.00	0.00	48.00	Plus Pts	0.50
Engine Anal.	0.00	16.00		16.00	32.00	0.00	32.00	Plus Pts	0.50
Engine Repair	12.00	256.00	300.00	556.00	512.00	450.00	962.00		0.58
Exhaust Maint.	2.40	48.00		48.00	96.00	0.00	96.00	Plus Pts	0.50

Trans Service	0.80	16.00		16.00	32.00	0.00	32.00	Plus Pts	0.50
Trans Repair	6.40	128.00		128.00	256.00	0.00	256.00	Plus Pts	0.50
MULTIPLE VEHICLE DISCOUNT SCHED. (7 TO 10)									
Tune-up	0.96	19.20	30.00	49.20	38.40	45.00	83.40		0.59
Chassis Lube	0.32	6.40	2.00	8.40	12.80	3.00	15.80		0.53
Oil Change	0.32	6.40	10.00	16.40	12.80	15.00	27.80		0.59
Brake Rebuild	2.56	51.20	65.00	116.20	102.40	97.50	199.90		0.58
Tire Replace	0.96	19.20	5.00	24.20	38.40	7.50	45.90		0.53
Wheel Replace	0.96	19.20		19.20	38.40	0.00	38.40	Plus Pts	0.50
Engine Anal.	0.64	12.80		12.80	25.60	0.00	25.60	Plus Pts	0.50
Engine Repair	10.24	204.80	300.00	504.80	409.60	450.00	859.60		0.59
Exhaust Maint.	1.92	38.40		38.40	76.80	0.00	76.80	Plus Pts	0.50
Trans Service	0.64	12.80		12.80	25.60	0.00	25.60	Plus Pts	0.50
Trans Repair	5.12	102.40		102.40	204.80	0.00	204.80	Plus Pts	0.50

Typical Loan Package as Provided by a Participating Bank

SBA 7(a) PROGRAM

PURPOSE   Loan funds may be used for any acceptable business purpose

- business expansion or acquisition
- working capital
- machinery and equipment
- leasehold improvements
- owner occupied real estate

We are not currently encouraging applications from businesses that are less than one year old.

FINANCING   Funds are provided by Bank of America with an SBA guarantee.

INTEREST   Loans are priced within SBA guidelines and are based on loan size, loan term, and the borrower. Rates never exceed New York Prime plus 2.75%.

FEES   SBA fee of 2% of the guaranteed portion. Bank processing fee of between $250.00 to $500.00 plus out-of-pocket expenses.

MATURITY   The loan purpose is the basis for the term

- working capital   up to 7 years
- machinery and equipment   up to 10 years
- leasehold improvements   up to 15 years
- real estate purchase   up to 25 years

PREPAYMENT   No prepayment penalty

COLLATERAL   Business or personal assets as necessary. Often real estate acquisitions can be financed for up to 90% with only the support of the 1st deed of trust and the owner's personal guarantee.

ELIGIBILITY   Manufacturing   Wholesale   Retail/Service

(generally)   up to 500 employees   up to 100 employees   up to $3.5 million
                                                                   in annual sales

LOAN AMOUNT   From $25,000. up to $1,000,000.

(sba7a.pgm)

224

SBA 504 LOAN PROGRAM

PURPOSE   For the purchase of existing buildings or modernization of commercial property to be owner occupied.

90% FINANCING

Project Cost	Source of Funds	Interest Rates	Maturity/Collateral
50%	Bank of America	Market rates and terms*	10 year maturity and 25-30 amortization 1st deed of trust
40%	SBA Debenture	Fixed rate* (often below market rates)	20 years fully amortizing 2nd deed of trust

*The overall blended rate is often below the market rate for comparable financing.

ELIGIBILITY   The business must be a for profit concern with a net worth of less than $6 million and after tax profits averaging less than $2 million over the last two years. The business must also show the ability to generate at least one new job for each $35,000. of SBA Debenture funds over the next two years.

LOAN AMOUNT $250,000. to $2,000,000. or more.

(SBA504.pgm)

U.S. Small Business Administration
APPLICATION FOR BUSINESS LOAN

Individual	Full Address

Name of Applicant Business	Tax I.D. No. or SSN

Full Street Address of Business	Tel. No. (inc. A/C)

City	County	State	Zip	Number of Employees (Including subsidiaries and affiliates)
Type of Business		Date Business Established		At Time of Application _____
Bank of Business Account and Address				If Loan is Approved _____
				Subsidiaries or Affiliates _____ (Separate from above)

Use of Proceeds: (Enter Gross Dollar Amounts Rounded to the Nearest Hundreds)	Loan Requested		Loan Requested
Land Acquisition		Payoff SBA Loan	
New Construction/ Expansion Repair		Payoff Bank Loan (Non SBA Associated)	
Acquisition and/or Repair of Machinery and Equipment		Other Debt Payment (Non SBA Associated)	
Inventory Purchase		All Other	
Working Capital (Including Accounts Payable)		Total Loan Requested	
Acquisition of Existing Business		Term of Loan - (Requested Mat.)	_____ Yrs.

PREVIOUS SBA OR OTHER FEDERAL GOVERNMENT DEBT: If you or any principals or affiliates have 1) ever requested Government Financing or 2) are delinquent on the repayment of any Federal Debt complete the following:

Name of Agency	Original Amount of Loan	Date of Request	Approved or Declined	Balance	Current or Past Due
	$			$	
	$			$	

ASSISTANCE   List the names(s) and occupations of any who assisted in the preparation of this form, other than applicant.

Name and Occupation	Address	Total Fees Paid	Fees Due
Name and Occupation	Address	Total Fees Paid	Fees Due

PLEASE NOTE: The estimated burden hours for the completion of this form is 19.8 hours per response. If you have any questions or comments concerning this estimate or any other aspect of this information collection please contact, Chief Administrative Information Branch, U.S. Small Business Administration, Washington, D.C. 20416 and Gary Waxman, Clearance Officer, Paperwork Reduction Project (3245-0016), Office of Management and Budget, Washington, D.C. 20503.

SBA Form 4 (5-92) Previous Edition is Obsolete

ALL EXHIBITS MUST BE SIGNED AND DATED BY PERSON SIGNING THIS FORM

BUSINESS INDEBTEDNESS: Furnish the following information on all installment debts, contracts, notes, and mortgages payable. Indicate by an asterisk(*) items to be paid by loan proceeds and reason for paying same (present balance should agree with the latest balance sheet submitted).

To Whom Payable	Original Amount	Original Date	Present Balance	Rate of Interest	Maturity Date	Monthly Payment	Security	Current or Past Due
Acct. #	$		$			$		
Acct. #	$		$			$		
Acct. #	$		$			$		
Acct. #	$		$			$		

MANAGEMENT (Proprietor, partners, officers, directors all holders of outstanding stock - <u>100% of ownership must be shown</u>). Use separate sheet if necessary.

Name and Social Security Number and Position Title	Complete Address	% Owned	*Military Service From	To	*Race	*Sex

*This data is collected for statistical purpose only. It has no bearing on the credit decision to approve or decline this application.

THE FOLLOWING EXHIBITS MUST BE COMPLETED WHERE APPLICABLE . ALL QUESTIONS ANSWERED ARE MADE A PART OF THE APPLICATION.

For Guaranty Loans please provide an original and one copy (Photocopy is Acceptable) of the Application Form, and all Exhibits to the participating lender. For Direct Loans submit one original copy of the application and Exhibits to SBA.

1. Submit SBA Form 912 (Personal History Statement) for each person e g. owners, partners, officers, directors, major stockholders, etc.; the instructions are on SBA Form 912.

2. If your collateral consists of (A) Land and Building, (B) Machinery and Equipment, (C)Furniture and Fixtures, (D) Accounts Receivable (E) Inventory, (F) Other, please provide an itemized list (labeled Exhibit A) that contains serial and identification numbers for all articles that had an original value greater than $500. Include a legal description of Real Estate offered as collateral.

3. Furnish a signed current personal balance sheet (SBA Form 413 may be used for this purpose) for each stockholder (with 20% or greater ownership), partner, officer, and owner. Social Security number should be included on personal financial statement. It should be as of the same date as the most recent business financial statements. Label this Exhibit B.

4. Include the statements listed below: 1,2,3 for the last three years; also 1,2,3, 4 as of the same date, which are current within 90 days of filing the application; and statement 5, if applicable. This is Exhibit C (SBA has Management Aids that help in the preparation of financial statements.) All information must be <u>signed and dated</u>.

1. Balance Sheet   2. Profit and Loss Statement
3. Reconciliation of Net Worth
4. Aging of Accounts Receivable and Payable
5. Earnings projects for a least one year where financial statements for the last three years are unavailable or where requested by District Office.
    (If Profit and Loss Statement is not available, explain why and substitute Federal Income Tax Forms.)

5. Provide a brief history of your company and a paragraph describing the expected benefits it will receive from the loan. Label it Exhibit D.

6. Provide a brief description similar to a resume of the education, technical and business background for all the people listed under Management. Please mark it Exhibit E.

ALL EXHIBITS MUST BE SIGNED AND DATED BY PERSON SIGNING THIS FORM

7. Do you have any co-signers and/or guarantors for this loan? If so, please submit their names, addresses, tax Id Numbers, and current personal balance sheet(s) as Exhibit F.

8. Are you buying machinery or equipment with your loan money? If so, you must include a list of equipment and cost as quoted by the seller and his name and address. This is Exhibit G.

9. Have you or any officer of your company ever been involved in bankruptcy or insolvency proceedings? If so, please provide the details as Exhibit H. If none, check here: ☐ Yes ☐ No

10. Are you or your business involved in any pending lawsuits? If yes, provide the details as Exhibit I. If none, check here: ☐ Yes ☐ No

11. Do you or your spouse or any member of your household, or anyone who owns, manages, or directs your business or their spouses or members of their households work for the Small Business Administration, Small Business Advisory Council, SCORE or ACE, any Federal Agency, or the participating lender? If so, please provide the name and address of the person and the office where employed. Label this Exhibit J. If none, check here: ☐ Yes ☐ No

12. Does your business, its owners or majority stockholders own or have a controlling interest in other businesses? If yes, please provide their names and the relationship with your company along with a current balance sheet and operating statement for each. This should be Exhibit K.

13. Do you buy from, sell to, or use the services of any concern in which someone in your company has a significant financial interest? If yes, provide details on a separate sheet of paper labeled Exhibit L.

14. If your business is a franchise, include a copy of the franchise agreement and a copy of the FTC disclosure statement supplied to you by the Franchisor. Please include it as Exhibit M.

CONSTRUCTION LOANS ONLY

15. Include a separate exhibit (Exhibit N) the estimated cost of the project and a statement of the source of any additional funds.

16. Provide copies of preliminary construction plans and specifications. Include them as Exhibit O. Final plans will be required prior to disbursement.

DIRECT LOANS ONLY

17. Include two bank declination letters with your application. (In cities with 200,000 people or less, one letter will be sufficient.) These letters should include the name and telephone number of the persons contacted at the banks, the amount and terms of the loan, the reason for decline and whether or not the bank will participate with SBA.

EXPORT LOANS

18. Does your business presently engage in Export Trade?
Check here: ☐ Yes ☐ No

19. Do you have plans to begin exporting as a result of this loan?
Check here: ☐ Yes ☐ No

20. Would you like information on Exporting?
Check here: ☐ Yes ☐ No

AGREEMENTS AND CERTIFICATIONS

Agreements of non-employment of SBA Personnel: I agree that if SBA approves this loan application I will not, for at least two years, hire as an employee or consultant anyone that was employed by the SBA during the one year period prior to the disbursement of the loan.

Certification: I certify: (a) I have not paid anyone connected with the Federal Government for help in getting this loan. I also agree to report to the SBA office of the Inspector General, Washington, D.C. 20416 any Federal Government employee who offers, in return for any type of compensation, to help get this loan approved.

(b) All information in this application and the Exhibits are true and complete to the best of my knowledge and are submitted to SBA so SBA can decide whether to grant a loan or participate with a lending institution in a loan to me. I agree to pay for or reimburse SBA for the cost of any surveys, title or mortgage examinations, appraisals credit reports, etc., performed by non-SBA personnel provided I have given my consent.

(c) I understand that I need not pay anybody to deal with SBA. I have read and understand SBA Form 159 which explains SBA policy on representatives and their fees.

(d) As consideration for any Management, Technical, and Business Development Assistance that may be provided, I waive all claims against SBA and its consultants.

If you make a statement that you know to be false or if you over value a security in order to help obtain a loan under the provisions of the Small Business Act, you can be fined up to $5,000 or be put in jail for up to two years, or both.

If Applicant is a proprietor or general partner, sign below.

By: _____

Date

If Applicant is a Corporation, sign below:

_____
Corporate Name and Seal   Date

_____

By: _____
Signature of President

Attested by: _____
Signature of Corporate Secretary

SBA Form 4 (5-92) Previous Edition is Obsolete

Page 3

228

APPLICANT'S CERTIFICATION

By my signature I certify that I have read and received a copy of the "STATEMENTS REQUIRED BY LAW AND EXECUTIVE ORDER" which was attached to this application. My signature represents my agreement to comply with the approval of my loan request and to comply, whenever applicable, with the hazard insurance, lead-based paint, civil rights or other limitations in this notice.

Each Proprietor, each General Partner, each Limited Partner or Stockholder owning 20% or more, and each Guarantor must sign. Each person should sign only once.

Business Name _____

_____   By _____
Date   Signature and Title

_____
Date   Signature

_____
Date   Signature

_____
Date   Signature

_____
Date   Signature

Equal Credit Opportunity Act (15 U S C 1691)

The Federal Equal Credit Opportunity Act prohibits creditors from discriminating against credit applicants on the basis of race, color, religion, national origin, sex, marital status or age (provided that the applicant has the capacity to enter into a binding contract); because all or part of the applicant's income derives from any public assistance program, or because the applicant has in good faith exercised any right under the Consumer Credit Protection Act. The Federal agency that administers compliance with this law concerning this creditor is the Federal Trade Commission, Equal Credit Opportunity, Washington, D C 20580

Executive Order 11738 -- Environmental Protection (38 F.R. 25161)

The Executive Order charges SBA with administering its loan programs in a manner that will result in effective enforcement of the Clean Air Act, the Federal Water Pollution Act and other environmental protection legislation. SBA must, therefore, impose conditions on some loans. By acknowledging receipt of this form and presenting the application, the principals of all small businesses borrowing $100,000 or more in direct funds stipulate to the following:

1. That any facility used, or to be used, by the subject firm is not cited on the EPA list of Violating Facilities.

2. That subject firm will comply with all the requirements of Section 114 of the Clean Air Act (42 U.S.C. 7414) and Section 308 of the Water Act (33 U.S.C. 1318) relating to inspection, monitoring, entry, reports and information, as well as all other requirements specified in Section 114 and Section 308 of the respective Acts, and all regulations and guidelines issued thereunder.

3. That subject firm will notify SBA of the receipt of any communication from the Director of the Environmental Protection Agency indicating that a facility utilized, or to be utilized, by subject firm is under consideration to be listed on the EPA List of Violating Facilities.

Debt Collection Act of 1982 Deficit Reduction Act of 1984 (31 U.S.C. 3701 et seq. and other titles)

These laws require SBA to aggressively collect any loan payments which become delinquent. SBA must obtain your taxpayer identification number when you apply for a loan. If you receive a loan, and do not make payments as they come due, SBA may take one or more of the following actions:

-Report the status of your loan(s) to credit bureaus
-Hire a collection agency to collect your loan
-Offset your income tax refund or other amounts due to you from the Federal Government
-Suspend or debar you or your company from doing business with the Federal Government
-Refer your loan to the Department of Justice or other attorneys for litigation
-Foreclose on collateral or take other action permitted in the loan instruments.

Immigration Reform and Control Act of 1986 (Pub. L. 99-603)

If you are an alien who was in this country illegally since before January 1, 1982, you may have been granted lawful temporary resident status by the United States Immigration and Naturalization Service pursuant to the Immigration Reform and Control Act of 1986 (Pub. L 99-603). For five years from the date you are granted such status, you are not eligible for financial assistance from the SBA in the form of a loan or guaranty under section 7(a) of the Small Business Act unless you are disabled or a Cuban or Haitian entrant. When you sign this document, you are making the certification that the Immigration Reform and Control Act of 1986 does not apply to you, or if it does apply, more than five years have elapsed since you have been granted lawful temporary resident status pursuant to such 1986 legislation.

Lead-Based Paint Poisoning Prevention Act (42 U.S.C 4821 et seq.)

Borrowers using SBA funds for the construction or rehabilitation of a residential structure are prohibited from using lead-based paint (as defined in SBA regulations) on all interior surfaces, whether accessible or not, and exterior surfaces, such as stairs, decks, porches, railings, windows and doors, which are readily accessible to children under 7 years of age. A "residential structure" is any home, apartment, hotel, motel, orphanage, boarding school, dormitory, day care center, extended care facility, college or other school housing, hospital, group practice or community facility and all other residential or institutional structures where persons reside.

SCHEDULE OF COLLATERAL
Exhibit A

OMB Approval No. : 3245-0016
Expiration Date: 6/30/94

Applicant		
Street Address		
City	State	Zip Code

LIST ALL COLLATERAL TO BE USED AS SECURITY FOR THIS LOAN

Section I—REAL ESTATE

Attach a copy of the deed(s) containing a full legal description of the land and show the location (street address) and city where the deed(s) is recorded. Following the address below, give a brief description of the improvements, such as size, type of construction, use, number of stories, and present condition (use additional sheet if more space is required).

LIST PARCELS OF REAL ESTATE					
Address	Year Acquired	Original Cost	Market Value	Amount of Lien	Name of Lienholder

Description(s):

SBA Form 4 Schedule A (8-91) Use 4-87 Edition until exhaused

SECTION II—PERSONAL PROPERTY

All items listed herein must show manufacturer or make, model, year, and serial number. Items with no serial number must be clearly identified (use additional sheet if more space is required).

Description - Show Manufacturer, Model, Serial No.	Year Acquired	Original Cost	Market Value	Current Lien Balance	Name of Lienholder

All information contained herein is TRUE and CORRECT to the best of my knowledge. I understand that FALSE statements may result in forfeiture of benefits and possible fine and prosecution by the U.S. Attorney General (Ref. 18 U.S.C. 100).

_____   Date _____

_____   Date _____

SBA Form 4 Schedule A (8-91) Use 4-87 Edition until exhaused   *U.S. Government Printing Office: 1991 — 282-429/45515

233

U.S. SMALL BUSINESS ADMINISTRATION

REQUEST FOR COUNSELING

A. NAME OF COMPANY	B. YOUR NAME (Last, First, Middle)	C. TELEPHONE (H) (B)

D. STREET	E. CITY	F. STATE	G. COUNTY	H. ZIP

I. TYPE OF BUSINESS (Check one)
1. ☐ Retail 4. ☐ Manufacturing
2. ☐ Service 5. ☐ Construction
3. ☐ Wholesale 6. ☐ Not in Business

J. BUS. OWNSHP./GENDER
1. ☐ Male
2. ☐ Female
3. ☐ Male/Female

K. VETERAN STATUS
1. ☐ Veteran
2. ☐ Vietnam-Era Veteran
3. ☐ Disabled Veteran

L.
- INDICATE PREFERRED DATE AND TIME FOR APPOINTMENT
  DATE _____ TIME _____
- ARE YOU CURRENTLY IN BUSINESS? YES ____ NO ____
- IF YES, HOW LONG? _____
- TYPE OF BUSINESS (USE THREE TO FIVE WORDS)
  _____

M. ETHNIC BACKGROUND

a. Race:
1. ☐ American Indian or Alaskan Native
2. ☐ Asian or Pacific Islander
3. ☐ Black
4. ☐ White

b. Ethnicity:
1. ☐ Hispanic Origin
2. ☐ Not of Hispanic Origin

N. INDICATE, BRIEFLY, THE NATURE OF SERVICE AND/OR COUNSELING YOUR ARE SEEKING

_____

_____

O.
- IT HAS BEEN EXPLAINED TO ME THAT I MAY USE FURTHER SERVICES SPONSORED BY THE U.S. SMALL BUSINESS
  ADMINISTRATION YES ____ NO ____
- I HAVE ATTENDED A SMALL BUSINESS WORKSHOP YES ____ NO ____
- CONDUCTED BY _____

P. HOW DID YOU LEARN OF THESE COUNSELING SERVICES?
1. ☐ Yellow Pages 3. ☐ Radio 5. ☐ Bank 7. ☐ Word-of-Mouth
2. ☐ Television 4. ☐ Newspapers 6. ☐ Chamber of Commerce 8. ☐ Other ____

Q. SBA CLIENT (To Be Filled Out By Counselor)
1. ☐ Borrower 2. ☐ Applicant 3. ☐ 8(a) Client 4. ☐ COC 5. ☐ Surety Bond

R. AREA OF COUNSELING PROVIDED (To Be Filled Out By Counselor)

1. Bus. Start-Up/Acquisition	5. Accounting & Records	9. Personnel	☐
2. Source of Capital	6. Finan. Analysis/Cost Control	10. Computer Systems	
3. Marketing/Sales	7. Inventory Control	11. Internat'l Trade	
4. Government Procurement	8. Engineering R&D	12. Business Liq./Sale	

I request business management counseling from the Small Business Administration. I agree to cooperate should I be selected to participate in surveys designed to evaluate SBA assistance services. I authorize SBA to furnish relevant information to the assigned management counselor(s) although I expect that information to be held in strict confidence by him/her.

I further understand that any counselor has agreed not to: (1) recommend goods or services from sources in which he/she has an interest and (2) accept fees or commissions developing from this counseling relationship. In consideration of SBA's furnishing management or technical assistance, I waive all claims against SBA personnel, SCORE, SBDC and its host organizations, SBI, and other SBA Resource Counselors arising from this assistance.

SIGNATURE AND TITLE OF REQUESTER	DATE

FOR USE OF THE SMALL BUSINESS ADMINISTRATION

RESOURCE	DISTRICT	REGION

SBA FORM 641 (2-91) PREVIOUS EDITION IS OBSOLETE

WHITE: COUNSELOR
YELLOW: SBI OR SCORE OR SBDC SUB.
PINK: DO OR NSO OR SBDC LEAD

A. Reflects the full name of the Company/Business owned. Leave blank if you are not yet in business.

B. Name. If partnership or corporation, enter only one name.

C. through H.   Complete as indicated.

I. Reflects the client's PRIMARY business.

J. Complete as indicated. (Check only one)
If in business, this box refers to owner of business. If going into business this box refers to the applicant's gender. If joint ownership, #3 refers to male and female joint ownership.

K. Complete as indicated. (Check all that apply)

L. Complete as indicated. (Requires multiple answers)

M. Requires two answers.
Select one answer for RACE and one answer for ETHNICITY.

N. Complete as indicated. (Narrative answer required)

O. Complete as indicated. (Requires multiple answers)

P. Complete as indicated.

Q. To be completed by counselor. (Check all that apply)
Q2. Applicant - refers to applicants for SBA financial assistance.
Q4. COC - refers to applicants who have applied for Certificate of Competence

R. Determine the area for which you will provide assistance. (Check only one)

PLEASE NOTE: The estimated burden hours for the completion of this form is 7 minutes per response. If you have any questions or comments concerning this estimate or any other aspect of this information collection please contact, Chief Administrative Information Branch, U.S. Small Business Administration, Washington, D.C. 20416 and Gary Waxman, Clearance Officer, Paperwork Reduction Project (3245-0096), Office of Management and Budget, Washington, D.C. 20503.

★U.S.GPO:1991-0-282-430/43627

Certification Regarding
Debarment, Suspension, Ineligibility and Voluntary Exclusion
Lower Tier Covered Transactions

This certification is required by the regulations implementing Executive Order 12549, Debarment and Suspension, 13 CFR Part 145. The regulations were published as Part VII of the May 26, 1988 *Federal Register* (pages 19160-19211). Copies of the regulations may be obtained by contacting the person to which this proposal is submitted.

(BEFORE COMPLETING CERTIFICATION, READ INSTRUCTIONS ON REVERSE)

(1) The prospective lower tier participant certifies, by submission of this proposal, that neither it nor its principals are presently debarred, suspended, proposed for debarment, declared ineligible, or voluntarily excluded from participation in this transaction by any Federal department or agency.

(2) Where the prospective lower tier participant is unable to certify to any of the statements in this certification, such prospective participant shall attach an explanation to this proposal.

Business Name _____

Date _____ By _____
Name and Title of Authorized Representative

_____
Signature of Authorized Representative

SBA Temporary Form 1624 (10-88)

236

INSTRUCTIONS FOR CERTIFICATION

1. By signing and submitting this proposal, the prospective lower tier participant is providing the certification set out below.

2. The certification in this clause is a material representation of fact upon which reliance was placed when this transaction was entered into. If it is later determined that the prospective lower tier participant knowingly rendered an erroneous certification, in addition to other remedies available to the Federal Government, the department or agency with which this transaction originated may pursue available remedies, including suspension and/or debarment.

3. The prospective lower tier participant shall provide immediate written notice to the person to which this proposal is submitted if at any time the prospective lower tier participant learns that its certification was erroneous when submitted or has become erroneous by reason of changed circumstances.

4. The terms "covered transaction," "debarred," "suspended," "ineligible," "lower tier covered transaction," "participant," "person," "primary covered transaction," "principal," "proposal," and "voluntarily excluded," as used in this clause, have the meanings set out in the Definitions and Coverage sections of the rules implementing Executive Order 12549. You may contact the person to which this proposal is submitted for assistance in obtaining a copy of those regulations (13 CFR Part 145).

5. The prospective lower tier participant agrees by submitting this proposal that, should the proposed covered transaction be entered into, it shall not knowingly enter into any lower tier covered transaction with a person who is debarred, suspended, declared ineligible, or voluntarily excluded from participation in this covered transaction, unless authorized by the department or agency with which this transaction originated.

6. The prospective lower tier participant further agrees by submitting this proposal that it will include the clause titled "Certification Regarding Debarment, Suspension, Ineligibility and Voluntary Exclusion—Lower Tier Covered Transactions," without modification, in all lower tier covered transactions and in all solicitations for lower tier covered transactions.

7. A participant in a covered transaction may rely upon a certification of a prospective participant in a lower tier covered transaction that it is not debarred, suspended, ineligible, or voluntarily excluded from the covered transaction, unless it knows that the certification is erroneous. A participant may decide the method and frequency by which it determines the eligibility of its principals. Each participant may, but is not required to, check the Nonprocurement List.

8. Nothing contained in the foregoing shall be construed to require establishment of a system of records in order to render in good faith the certification required by this clause. The knowledge and information of a participant is not required to exceed that which is normally possessed by a prudent person in the ordinary course of business dealings.

9. Except for transactions authorized under paragraph 5 of these instructions, if a participant in a covered transaction knowingly enters into a lower tier covered transaction with a person who is suspended, debarred, ineligible, or voluntarily excluded from participation in this transaction, in addition to other remedies available to the Federal Government, the department or agency with which this transaction originated may pursue available remedies, including suspension and/or debarment.

OMB Approval No 3245-0201

COMPENSATION AGREEMENT FOR SERVICES IN CONNECTION WITH APPLICATION AND LOAN FROM (OR IN PARTICIPATION WITH) SMALL BUSINESS ADMINISTRATION

The undersigned representative (attorney, accountant, engineer, appraiser, etc.) hereby agrees that the undersigned has not and will not, directly or indirectly, charge or receive any payment in connection with the application for or the making of the loan except for services actually performed on behalf of the Applicant. The undersigned further agrees that the amount of payment for such services shall not exceed an amount deemed reasonable by SBA (and, if it is a participation loan, by the participating lending institution), and to refund any amount in excess of that deemed reasonable by SBA (and the participating institution). This agreement shall supersede any other agreement covering payment for such services.

A general description of the services performed, or to be performed, by the undersigned and the compensation paid or to be paid are set forth below. If the total compensation in any case exceeds $1,000 (or $300 for: (1) regular business loans of $15,000 or less; or (2) all disaster home loans) or if SBA should otherwise require, the services must be itemized on a schedule attached showing each date services were performed, time spent each day, and description of service rendered on each day listed.

The undersigned Applicant and representative hereby certify that no other fees have been charged or will be charged by the representative in connection with this loan, unless provided for in the loan authorization specifically approved by SBA.

GENERAL DESCRIPTION OF SERVICES

Paid Previously $ _____
Additional Amount to be Paid $ _____
Total Compensation $ _____

(Section 13 of the Small Business Act (15 USC 642) requires disclosures concerning fees. Parts 103, 108 and 120 of Title 13 of the Code of Federal Regulations contain provisions covering appearances and compensation of persons representing SBA applicants. Section 103.13-5 authorizes the suspension or revocation of the privilege of any such person to appear before SBA for charging a fee deemed unreasonable by SBA for services actually performed, charging of unreasonable expenses, or violation of this agreement. Whoever commits any fraud, by false or misleading statement or representation, or by conspiracy, shall be subject to the penalty of any applicable Federal or State statute.)

Dated _____ , 19 _____

_____
(Representative)

By _____

The Applicant hereby certifies to SBA that the above representations, description of services and amounts are correct and satisfactory to Applicant.

Dated _____ , 19 _____

_____
(Applicant)

By _____

The participating lending institution hereby certifies that the above representations of service rendered and amounts charged are reasonable and satisfactory to it.

Dated _____ , 19 _____

_____
(Lender)

By _____

NOTE: Foregoing certification must be executed, if by a corporation, in corporate name by duly authorized officer and duly attested; if by a partnership, in the firm name, together with signature of a general partner.

PLEASE NOTE: The estimated burden hours for the completion of SBA Form 147, 148, 159, 160, 160A, 529B, 928, and 1059 is 6 hrs. per response. If you have any questions or comments concerning this estimate or any other aspect of this information collection please contact, William Cline, Chief Administrative Information Branch, U.S. Small Business Administration, 409 3 rd st. S. W. Washington, D.C. 20416 and Gary Waxman, Clearance Officer, Paperwork Reduction Project (3245-0201), Office of Management and Budget, Washington, D.C. 20503.

SBA FORM 159 (1-91) REF SOP 70 50 Use 7-89 Edition Until Exhausted

POLICY AND REGULATIONS CONCERNING REPRESENTATIVES AND THEIR FEES

An applicant for a loan from SBA may obtain the assistance of any attorney, accountant, engineer, appraiser or other representative to aid him in the preparation and presentation of his application to SBA; however, such representation is not mandatory. In the event a loan is approved, the services of an attorney may be necessary to assist in the preparation of closing documents, title abstracts, etc. SBA will allow the payment of reasonable fees or other compensation for services performed by such representatives on behalf of the applicant.

There are no "authorized representatives" of SBA, other than our regular salaried employees. Payment of any fee or gratuity to SBA employees is illegal and will subject the parties to such a transaction to prosecution.

SBA Regulations (Part 103, Sec. 103.13-5(c)) prohibit representatives from charging or proposing to charge any contingent fee for any services performed in connection with an SBA loan unless the amount of such fee bears a necessary and reasonable relationship to the services actually performed; or to charge for any expenses which are not deemed by SBA to have been necessary in connection with the application. The Regulations (Part 120, Sec. 120.104-2) also prohibit the payment of any bonus, brokerage fee or commission in connection with SBA loans.

In line with these Regulations SBA will not approve placement or finder's fees for the use or attempted use of influence in obtaining or trying to obtain an SBA loan, or fees based solely upon a percentage of the approved loan or any part thereof.

Fees which will be approved will be limited to reasonable sums of services actually rendered in connection with the application or the closing, based upon the time and effort required, the qualifications of the representative and the nature and extent of the services rendered by such representatives. Representatives of loan applicants will be required to execute an agreement as to their compensation for services rendered in connection with said loan.

It is the responsibility of the applicant to set forth in the appropriate section of the application the names of all persons or firms engaged by or on behalf of the applicant. Applicants are required to advise the Regional Office in writing the names and fees of any representatives engaged by the applicant subsequent to the filing of the application. This reporting requirement is approved under OMB Approval Number 2345-0016.

Any loan applicant having any question concerning the payments of fees, or the reasonableness of fees, should communicate with the Field Office where the application is filed.

*U.S. Government Printing Office: 1991 — 282-429/45506

OMB Approval No. 3245-0188

PERSONAL FINANCIAL STATEMENT

U. S. SMALL BUSINESS ADMINISTRATION

As of_____, 19_____

Complete this form for: (1) each proprietor, or (2) each limited partner who owns 20% or more interest and each general partner, or (3) each stockholder owning 20% or more of voting stock and each corporate officer and director, or (4) any other person or entity providing a guaranty on the loan.

Name	Business Phone ( )

Residence Address	Residence Phone ( )

City, State, & Zip Code

Business Name of Applicant/Borrower

ASSETS	(Omit Cents)	LIABILITIES	(Omit Cents)
Cash on hands & in Banks	$_____	Accounts Payable	$_____
Savings Accounts	$_____	Notes Payable to Banks and Others	$_____
IRA or Other Retirement Account	$_____	(Describe in Section 2)	
Accounts & Notes Receivable	$_____	Installment Account (Auto)	$_____
Life Insurance-Cash Surrender Value Only	$_____	Mo. Payments $_____	
(Complete Section 8)		Installment Account (other)	$_____
Stocks and Bonds	$_____	Mo. Payments $_____	
(Describe in Section 3)		Loan on Life Insurance	$_____
Real Estate	$_____	Mortgages on Real Estate	$_____
(Describe in Section 4)		(Describe in Section 4)	
Automobile-Present Value	$_____	Unpaid Taxes	$_____
Other Personal Property	$_____	(Describe in Section 6)	
(Describe in Section 5)		Other Liabilities	$_____
Other Assets	$_____	(Describe in Section 7)	
(Describe in Section 5)		Total Liabilities	$_____
		Net Worth	$_____
Total . . $_____		**Total . . $_____**	

Section 1. Source of Income		Contingent Liabilities	
Salary	$_____	As Endorser or Co-Maker.	$_____
Net Investment Income	$_____	Legal Claims & Judgments	$_____
Real Estate Income	$_____	Provision for Federal Income Tax	$_____
Other Income (Describe below)*	$_____	Other Special Debt	$_____

Description of Other Income in Section 1.

*Alimony or child support payments need not be disclosed in "Other Income" unless it is desired to have such payments counted toward total income.

Section 2. Notes Payable to Bank and Others. (Use attachments if necessary. Each attachment must be identified as a part of this statement and signed.).

Name and Address of Noteholder(s)	Original Balance	Current Balance	Payment Amount	Frequency (monthly,etc.)	How Secured or Endorsed Type of Collateral

SBA Form 413 (5-91) Previous Editions Obsolete. Ref: SOP 50-10 and 50-30   (tumble)

240

Section 3. Stocks and Bonds. (Use attachments if necessary. Each attachment must be identified as a part of this statement and signed).

Number of Shares	Name of Securities	Cost	Market Value Quotation/Exchange	Date of Quotation/Exchange	Total Value

Section 4. Real Estate Owned. (List each parcel separately. Use attachments if necessary. Each attachment must be identified as a part of this statement and signed).

	Property A	Property B	Property C
Type of Property			
Name & Address of Title Holder			
Date Purchased			
Original Cost			
Present Market Value			
Name & Address of Mortgage Holder			
Mortgage Account Number			
Mortgage Balance			
Amount of Payment per Month/Year			
Status of Mortgage			

Section 5. Other Personal Property and Other Assets. (Describe, and if any is pledged as security, state name and address of lien holder, amount of lien, terms of payment, and if delinquent, describe delinquency).

Section 6. Unpaid Taxes. (Describe in detail, as to type, to whom payable, when due, amount, and to what property, if any, a tax lien attaches).

Section 7. Other Liabilities. (Describe in detail).

Section 8. Life Insurance Held. (Give face amount and cash surrender value of policies – name of insurance company and beneficiaries).

I authorize SBA/Lender to make inquiries as necessary to verify the accuracy of the statements made and to determine my creditworthiness. I certify the above and the statements contained in the attachments are true and accurate as of the stated date(s). These statements are made for the purpose of either obtaining a loan or guaranteeing a loan. I understand FALSE statements may result in forfeiture of benefits and possible prosecution by the U.S. Attorney General (Reference 18 U.S.C. 1001).

Signature: Date: Social Security Number:

Signature: Date: Social Security Number:

PLEASE NOTE: The estimated average burden hours for the completion of this form is 1.5 hours per response. If you have questions or comments concerning this estimate or any other aspect of this information, please contact Chief, Administrative Branch, U.S. Small Business Administration, Washington, D.C. 20416, and Clearance Office, Paper Reduction Project (3245–0188), Office of Management and Budget, Washington, D.C. 20503.

* U.S Government Printing Office1992- 312-624/62831

241

OMB APPROVAL NO. 3245-0178
Expiration Date: 5-31-93

United States of America

SMALL BUSINESS ADMINISTRATION

STATEMENT OF PERSONAL HISTORY

Please Read Carefully - Print or Type

Each member of the small business concern requesting assistance or the development company must submit this form in TRIPLICATE for filing with the SBA application. This form must be filled out and submitted by:

1. If a sole proprietorship by the proprietor.
2. If a partnership by each partner.
3. If a corporation or a development company, by each officer, director, and additionally by each holder of 20% or more of the voting stock.
4. Any other person including a hired manager, who has authority to speak for and commit the borrower in the management of the business.

Name and Address of Applicant (Firm Name) (Street, City, State and ZIP Code)	SBA District Office and City
	Amount Applied for:

1. Personal Statement of: (State name in full, if no middle name, state (NMN), or if initial only, indicate initial). List all former names used, and dates each name was used. Use separate sheet if necessary. First Middle Last	2. Date of Birth: (Month, day and year)
	3. Place of Birth: (City & State or Foreign Country).
	U.S. Citizen? ☐ YES ☐ NO If no, give alien registration number:
4. Give the percentage of ownership or stock owned or to be owned in the small business concern or the Development Company.	Social Security No.

5. Present residence address:	City		State
From: To: Address:			
Home Telephone No. (Include A/C):	Business Telephone No. (Include A/C):		
Immediate past residence addres:			
From: To: Address:			

BE SURE TO ANSWER THE NEXT 3 QUESTIONS CORRECTLY BECAUSE THEY ARE IMPORTANT.

THE FACT THAT YOU HAVE AN ARREST OR CONVICTION RECORD WILL NOT NECESSARILY DISQUALIFY YOU. BUT AN INCORRECT ANSWER WILL PROBABLY CAUSE YOUR APPLICATION TO BE TURNED DOWN.

6. Are you presently under indictment, on parole or probation?

☐ Yes ☐ No   If yes, furnish details in a separate exhibit. List name(s) under which held, if applicable.

7. Have you ever been charged with or arrested for any criminal offense other than a minor motor vehicle violation?

☐ Yes ☐ No   If Yes, furnish details in a separate exhibit. List name(s) under which charged, if applicable.

8. Have you ever been convicted of any criminal offense other than a minor vehicle violation?

☐ Yes ☐ No   If Yes, furnish details in a separate exhibit. List name(s) under which convicted, if applicable.

9. Name and address of participating bank

The information on this form will be used in connection with an investigation of your character. Any information you wish to submit, that you feel will expedite this investigation should be set forth.

Whoever makes any statement knowing it to be false, for the purpose of obtaining for himself or for any applicant, any loan, or loan extension by renewal, deferment or otherwise, or for the purpose of obtaining, or influencing SBA toward, anything of value under the Small Business Act, as amended, shall be punished under Section 16(a) of that Act, by a fine of not more than $5000, or by imprisonment for not more than 2 years, or both.

Signature	Title	Date

It is against SBA's policy to provide assistance to persons not of good character and therefore consideration is given to the qualities and personality traits of a person, favorable and unfavorable, relating thereto, including behavior, integrity, candor and disposition toward criminal actions. It is also against SBA's policy to provide assistance not in the best interests of the United States, for example, if there is reason to believe that the effect of such assistance will be to encourage or support, directly of indirectly, activities inimical to the Security of the United States. Anyone concerned with the collection of this information, as to its voluntariness, disclosure of routine uses may contact the FOIA Office, 1441 "L" Street, N.W., and a copy of §9 "Agency Collection of Information" from SOP 40 04 will be provided

SBA FORM 912 (5-87) SOP 9020 USE 6-85 EDITION UNTIL EXHAUSTED

1. SBA FILE COPY

Please Note: The estimated burden hours for completion of this form is 15 minutes per response. If you have any questions or comments concerning this estimate or any other aspect of this information collection please contact, Chief Administrative Information Branch, U.S. Small Business Administration 409 Third Street, S.W. Washington, D.C. 20416 or Gary Waxman, Clearance Officer, Paperwork Reduction Project (3245-0178), Office of Management and Budget, Washington, D.C. 20503

The business plan describes the current and planned operations of your business and demonstrates how the desired loan will further your business goals. Listed below are key elements that should be addressed; this information will become a written description of your business plan and should be included in the narrative section of your loan proposal. Carefully think about each area and be realistic in your description. Although you may wish to seek professional help in preparing your plan, you should be familiar with every detail. Your knowledge and understanding of all aspects of your business will help us to understand and work with you to evaluate your plan and your SBA loan request. The sample business plan outline can be used to assist you in organizing your plan.

Type of Organization: What kind of business is it - construction, manufacturing, retailing, service, etc.? What is your legal entity - corporation, partnership, proprietorship? How many owners? What are their names, addresses, and what percentage of ownership does each hold? In what capacity will they function in the business?

Product/Service or Description of Business Activity: If a manufacturer, describe the products you plan to make. If you are a retailer, talk about the various types of goods sold, some major brand names, etc. If you are a service business, talk about the services given. How will this loan affect the product/service you provide?

Success: Why did you pick this type of business? What makes your chances of success unusually good? What have been your past problems with the business?

Sales/Marketing Activity: Who will you sell to - retailers, wholesalers, the public? How are your sales made? Do you have to bid? What problems have you experienced in bidding? Do you use a sales representative? How much do you pay him? Who are your suppliers? How do you determine the price of your product or service? What is your estimated cost of sales and net profit margin? How will you advertise or what promotional activities will you conduct to generate sales?

Competition: Briefly describe your major competitors. What competitive edge will your business have over your competitor's operation?

Location: Where will your business be located? If a retail business, describe the area and the people. Describe your business location's advantages and disadvantages. What are the local zoning requirements? What kind of licensing will be needed?

Facilities: Describe the type and condition of the building. What are the purchase or rental terms? What improvements are needed? Describe the types and quality of existing equipment, furniture and fixtures. What do you want to change?

0007J

1

Employees: How many employees will you hire? What kind of special skills do your employees need, and briefly describe their responsibilities. What wages will you pay? Is a union involved?

Other: What kind of business insurance will you carry? What kind of financial records will be prepared, how frequently, and by whom? What are your future plans for growth? Are there any other relevant topics or issues the bank should be aware of?

SAMPLE BUSINESS PLAN OUTLINE

I.   Cover Letter
      A.   Dollar amount requested
      B.   Terms and timing
      C.   Purpose of the loan
II.   Summary
      A.   Business Description
            1.   Name
            2.   Location and plan description
            3.   Product
            4.   Market and competition
            5.   Management expertise
      B.   Business goals
      C.   Summary of financial needs and breakdown of how loan funds will be used
      D.   Earnings projections
III. Market Analysis
      A.   Description of total market
      B.   Industry trends
      C.   Target market
      D.   Competition
IV.   Products and Services
      A.   Description of product line
      B.   Proprietary position: patents, copyrights, and legal and technical considerations
      C.   Comparison to competitors' products
V.   Manufacturing Process (if applicable)
      A.   Materials
      B.   Source of Supply
      C.   Production methods
VI.   Marketing Strategy
      A.   Overall Strategy
      B.   Pricing policy
      C.   Method of selling, distributing, and servicing products
VII. Management Plan
      A.   Form of business organization
      B.   Board of directors composition
      C.   Officers: organization chart and responsibilities

0007J

         D.   Resumes of key personnel
         E.   Staffing plan/number of employees
         F.   Facilities plan/planned capital improvements
         G.   Operating plan/schedule of upcoming work for next one to two years
VIII. <u>Financial Data</u>
         A.   Financial statements (two to three years to present, if existing
               business)
         B.   Financial projections
               1.   12 month profit and loss statement
               2.   12 month cash flow forecast
               3.   Balance sheet upon funding of loan
         C.   Explanation of projects
         D.   Key business ratios

MONTHLY CASH FLOW PROJECTION

See Reverse Side for Instructions and Public Comment Information

Form Approval:
OMB No. 3245-0019
Expires: 8-31-91

NAME OF BUSINESS

ADDRESS

OWNER

TYPE OF BUSINESS

PREPARED BY

DATE

	Pre-Start-up Position		1		2		3		4		5		6		7		8		9		10		11		12		TOTAL Columns 1—12		
YEAR MONTH	Estimate	Actual	Estimate	Actual	Estimate	Actual	Estimate	Actual	Estimate	Actual	Estimate	Actual	Estimate	Actual	Estimate	Actual	Estimate	Actual	Estimate	Actual	Estimate	Actual	Estimate	Actual	Estimate	Actual	
1. CASH ON HAND (Beginning of month)																											1.
2. CASH RECEIPTS																											
(a) Cash Sales																											(a)
(b) Collections from Credit Accounts																											(b)
(c) Loan or Other Cash Injection (Specify)																											(c)
3. TOTAL CASH RECEIPTS (2a + 2b + 2c = 3)																											3.
4. TOTAL CASH AVAILABLE (Before cash out) (1 + 3)																											4.
5. CASH PAID OUT																											5.
(a) Purchases (Merchandise)																											(a)
(b) Gross Wages (Excludes withdrawals)																											(b)
(c) Payroll Expenses (Taxes, etc.)																											(c)
(d) Outside Services																											(d)
(e) Supplies (Office and operating)																											(e)
(f) Repairs and Maintenance																											(f)
(g) Advertising																											(g)
(h) Car, Delivery, and Travel																											(h)
(i) Accounting and Legal																											(i)
(j) Rent																											(j)
(k) Telephone																											(k)
(l) Utilities																											(l)
(m) Insurance																											(m)
(n) Taxes (Real estate, etc.)																											(n)
(o) Interest																											(o)
(p) Other Expenses (Specify each)																											(p)
(q) Miscellaneous (Unspecified)																											(q)
(r) Subtotal																											(r)
(s) Loan Principal Payment																											(s)
(t) Capital Purchases (Specify)																											(t)
(u) Other Start-up Costs																											(u)
(v) Reserve and/or Escrow (Specify)																											(v)
(w) Owner's Withdrawal																											(w)
6. TOTAL CASH PAID OUT (Total 5a thru 5w)																											6.
7. CASH POSITION (End of month) (4 minus 6)																											7.
ESSENTIAL OPERATING DATA (Non-cash flow information)																											
A. Sales Volume (Dollars)																											A.
B. Accounts Receivable (End of month)																											B.
C. Bad Debt (End of month)																											C.
D. Inventory on Hand (End of month)																											D.
E. Accounts Payable (End of month)																											E.
F. Depreciation																											F.

SBA FORM 1100 (11-83) REF: SOP 60 10 Previous Editions Are Obsolete

GENERAL

Definition: A cash flow projection is a forecast of cash funds* a business anticipates receiving, on the one hand, and disbursing, on the other hand, throughout the course of a given span of time, and the anticipated cash position at specific times during the period being projected.

Objective: The purpose of preparing a cash flow projection is to determine deficiencies or excesses in cash from that necessary to operate the business during the time for which the projection is prepared. If deficiencies are revealed in the cash flow, financial plans must be altered either to provide more cash by, for example, more equity capital, loans, or increased selling prices of products, or to reduce expenditures including inventory, or allow less credit sales until a proper cash flow balance is obtained. If excesses of cash are revealed, it might indicate excessive borrowing or idle money that could be "put to work." The objective is to finally develop a plan which, if followed, will provide a well managed flow of cash.

The Form: The cash flow projection form provides a systematic method of recording estimates of cash receipts and expenditures, which can be compared with actual receipts and expenditures as they become known, hence the two columns, Estimate and Actual. The entries listed on the form will not necessarily apply to every business, and some entries may not be included which would be pertinent to specific businesses. It is suggested, therefore, that the form be adapted to the particular business for which the projection is being made, with appropriate changes in the entries as may be required. Before the cash flow projection can be completed and pricing structure established, it is necessary to know or to estimate various important factors of the business, for example. What are the direct costs of the product or services per unit? What are the monthly or yearly costs of operation? What is the sales price per unit of the product or service? Determine that the pricing structure provides this business with reasonable breakeven goals (including a reasonable net profit) when conservative sales goals are met. What are the available sources of cash, other than income from sales; for example, loans, equity capital, rent, or other sources?

Procedure: Most of the entries for the form are self explanatory; however, the following suggestions are offered to simplify the procedure:

(A) Suggest even dollars be used rather than showing cents.
(B) If this is a new business, or an existing business undergoing significant changes or alterations, the cash flow part of the column marked "Pre-Start-Up Position" should be completed. (Fill in appropriate blanks only.) Costs involved here are, for example, rent, telephone, and utilities deposits before the business is actually open. Other items might be equipment purchases, alterations, the owner's cash injection, and cash from loans received before actual operations begin.
(C) Next fill in the pre-start-up position of the essential operating data (non-cash flow information), where applicable.
(D) Complete the form using the suggestions in the partial form below for each entry.

CHECKING

In order to insure that the figures are properly calculated and balanced, they must be checked. Several methods may be used, but the following four checks are suggested as a minimum:

CHECK #1: Item #1 (Beginning Cash on Hand—1st month) plus Item #3 (Total Cash Receipts—Total Column) minus Item #6 (Total Cash Paid Out—Total Column) should be equal to Item #7 (Cash Position at End of 12th month).

CHECK #2: Item A (Sales Volume—Total Column) plus Item B (Accounts Receivable—Pre-Start-Up Position) minus Item 2(a) (Cash Sales—Total Column) minus Item 2(b) (Accounts Receivable Collection—Total Column) minus Item C (Bad Debt—Total Column) equals Item B (Accounts Receivable at End of 12th month).

CHECK #3: The horizontal total of Item #6 (Total Cash Paid Out) is equal to the vertical total of all items under Item #5 (5(a) through 5(w)) in the total column at the right of the form.

CHECK #4: The horizontal total of Item #3 (Total Cash Receipts) is equal to the vertical total of all items under Item #2 (2(a) through 2(c)) in the total column at the right of the form.

ANALYZE the correlation between the cash flow and the projected profit during the period in question. The estimated profit is the difference between the estimated change in assets and the estimated change in liabilities before such things as any owner withdrawal, appreciation of assets, change in investments, etc. (The change may be positive or negative.) This can be obtained as follows:

The **change in assets** before owner's withdrawal, appreciation of assets, change in investments, etc. can be computed by adding the following:

(1) Item #7 (Cash Position—End of Last Month) minus Item #1 (Cash on Hand at the Beginning of the First Month).
(2) Item #5(t) (Capital Purchases—Total Column) minus Item F (depreciation—Total Column).
(3) Item B (Accounts Receivable—End of 12th Month) minus Item B (Accounts Receivable—Pre-Start-Up Position).
(4) Item D (Inventory on Hand—End of 12th Month) minus Item D (Inventory on Hand—Pre-Start-Up Position).
(5) Item #5(w) (Owner's Withdrawal—Total Column) or dividends, minus such things as an increase in investment.
(6) Item #5(v) (Reserve and/or Escrow—Total Column).

The **change in liabilities** (before items noted in "change in assets") can be computed by adding the following:

(1) Item 2(c) (Loans—Total Column) minus 5(s) (Loan Principal Payment—Total Column).
(2) Item E (Accounts Payable—End of 12th Month) minus E (Accounts Payable—Pre-Start-Up Position).

ANALYSIS

A. The cash position at the end of each month should be adequate to meet the cash requirements for the following month. If too little cash, then additional cash will have to be injected or cash paid out must be reduced. If there is too much cash on hand, the money is not working for your business.

B. The cash flow projection, the profit and loss projection, the breakeven analysis, and good cost control information are tools which, if used properly, will be useful in making decisions that can increase profits to insure success.

C. The projection becomes more useful when the estimated information can be compared with actual information as it develops. It is important to follow through and complete the actual columns as the information becomes available. Utilize the cash flow projection to assist in setting new goals and planning operations for more profit.

Please note: Public reporting burden for this collection of information is estimated to average 1 hour per response, including the time for reviewing instructions, searching existing data sources, gathering and maintaining the data needed, and completing and reviewing the collection of information. Send comments regarding this burden estimate or any other aspect of this collection of information, including suggestions for reducing this burden to: Chief, Administrative Information Branch, William A. Cline, Room 200 U.S. Small Business Administration, 1111 J. St., NW, Washington, DC 20416; and to the Office of Information Regulatory Affairs, Office of Management and Budget, Washington, DC 20503.

---

* Cash funds, for the purpose of this projection, are defined as cash, checks, or money orders, paid out or received.

1. CASH ON HAND (Beginning of month)	Cash on hand same as (7), Cash Position Previous Month
2. CASH RECEIPTS	
(a) Cash Sales	All cash sales. Omit credit sales unless cash is actually received
(b) Collections from Credit Accounts	Amount to be expected from all credit accounts
(c) Loan or Other Cash injection	Indicate here all cash injections not shown in 2(a) or 2(b) above. See "A" of "Analysis"
3. TOTAL CASH RECEIPTS (2a + 2b + 2c = 3)	Self explanatory
4. TOTAL CASH AVAILABLE (Before cash out) (1 + 3)	Self explanatory
5. CASH PAID OUT	
(a) Purchases (Merchandise)	Merchandise for resale or for use in product (paid for in current month)
(b) Gross Wages (Excludes withdrawals)	Base pay plus overtime (if any)
(c) Payroll Expenses (Taxes, etc.)	Include paid vacations, paid sick leave, health insurance, unemployment insurance, etc. (this might be 10 to 45% of 5(b))
(e) Outside Services	This could include outside labor and/or material for specialized overflow work, including subcontracting
(e) Supplies (Office and operating)	Items purchased for use in the business (not for resale)
(f) Repairs and Maintenance	Include periodic large expenditures such as painting or decorating
(g) Advertising	This amount should be adequate to maintain sales volume—include telephone book yellow page cost
(h) Car, Delivery, and Travel	If personal car is used, charge in this column—include parking
(i) Accounting and Legal	Outside services, including, for example, bookkeeping
(j) Rent	Real estate only—(See 5(p) for other rentals)
(k) Telephone	Self explanatory
(l) Utilities	Water, heat, light, and/or power
(m) Insurance	Coverage on business property and products e.g. fire, liability; also workman's compensation, fidelity, etc. Exclude "executive life (include in "5W")
(n) Taxes (Real Estate, etc.)	Plus inventory tax, sales tax, excise tax, if applicable
(o) Interest	Remember to add interest on loan as it is injected (see 2(c) above)
(p) Other Expenses (Specify each)	Unexpected expenditures may be included here as a safety factor.
	Equipment expenses during the month should be included here (Non capital equipment).
	When equipment is rented or leased, record payment here
(q) Miscellaneous (Unspecified)	Small expenditures for which separate accounts would not be practical
(r) Subtotal	This subtotal indicates cash out for operating costs
(s) Loan Principal Payment	Include payment on all loans, including vehicle and equipment purchases on time payment
(t) Capital Purchases (Specify)	Non-expensed (depreciable) expenditures such as equipment, building, vehicle purchases, and leasehold improvements
(u) Other Start-up Costs	Expenses incurred prior to first month projection and paid for after the "start up" position
(v) Reserve and/or Escrow (Specify)	Example: Insurance, tax, or equipment escrow to reduce impact of large periodic payments
(w) Owner's Withdrawal	Should include payment for such things as owner's income tax, social security, health insurance, "executive" life insurance premiums, etc.
6. TOTAL CASH PAID OUT (Total 5a through 5w)	Self explanatory
7. CASH POSITION (End of month) (4 minus 6)	Enter this amount in (1) Cash on hand following month—See "A" of "Analysis"
ESSENTIAL OPERATING DATA (Non-cash flow information)	This is basic information necessary for proper planning and for proper cash flow projection. In conjunction with this data, the cash flow can be evolved and shown in the above form.
A. Sales Volume (Dollars)	This is a very important figure and should be estimated carefully taking into account size of facility and employee output as well as realistic anticipated supplier response. (Actual sales performed—not orders received)
B. Accounts Receivable (End of month)	Previous unpaid credit sales plus current month's credit sales, less amounts received current month (deduct "C" below)
C. Bad Debt (End of month)	Bad debts should be subtracted from (B) in the month anticipated
D. Inventory on Hand (End of month)	Last month's inventory plus merchandise received and/or manufactured during current month minus amount sold during current month.
E. Accounts Payable (End of month)	Previous month's payable plus current month's payable minus amount paid during current month.
F. Depreciation	Established by your accountant, or value of all your equipment divided by useful life (in months) as allowed by Internal Revenue Service.

SBA FORM 1100 (1-83)

248

Form 4506

(Rev. January 1987)

Department of the Treasury
Internal Revenue Service

Request for Copy of Tax Form

Please read instructions before completing this form.

OMB No. 1545-0423

Expires 12-31-89

Important: Full payment must accompany your request.

1 Name of taxpayer(s) as shown on tax form (husband's and wife's, if joint return)	6 Social security number as shown on tax form (if joint return, show husband's number)
	6a Wife's social security number as shown on tax form
2 Current name and address	7 Employer identification number as shown on tax form
	8 Tax form number (Form 1040, 1040A, etc.)
3 If copy of form is to be mailed to someone else, show the third party's name and address	9 Tax period(s) (1983, etc.) (No more than 4 per request)
3a If we cannot find a record of your return, check here if you want the payment refunded to the third party. ☐	10 Amount due for copy of tax form: a Cost for each period . . . . . $ 4.25 b Number of periods requested in item 9 . . . . c Total cost (multiply item 10a by item 10b). . . . . $
4 If name in third party's records differs from item 1 above, show name here. (See Instructions for Items 3, 3a, and 4.)	
	Make check or money order payable to Internal Revenue Service

5 Check the box to show what you want:

☐ Copy of tax form and all attachments. The charge is $4.25 for each period requested.

Note: If you need these copies for court or administrative proceedings, also check here. ☐

☐ Copy of Form W-2 only. There is no charge for this.

Please Sign Here

Signature	Date	Telephone number of requester ( ) Convenient time for us to call

Title (if item 1 above is a corporation, partnership, estate, or trust)

Instructions

Privacy Act and Paperwork Reduction Act Notice.—We ask for this information to carry out the Internal Revenue laws of the United States. We need the information to gain access to your return in our files and properly respond to your request. If you do not furnish the information, we may not be able to fill your request.

Purpose of Form.—Use this form to request a copy of a tax return or Form W-2.

Note: If you had your return filled out by a paid preparer, check first to see if you can get a copy from the preparer. This may save you both time and money.

If you are not the taxpayer shown in item 1, you must send a copy of your authorization to receive the copy of the form. This will generally be a power of attorney, tax information authorization, or evidence of entitlement (for Title 11 Bankruptcy or Receivership Proceeding). If the taxpayer is deceased, you must send enough evidence to establish that you are authorized to act for the taxpayer's estate.

Copies of joint returns may be furnished to either the husband or the wife. Only one signature is required. If your name has changed, sign Form 4506 exactly as your name appeared on the return and also sign with your current name.

Please allow at least 45 days for delivery. Be sure to furnish all the information asked for on this form to avoid any delay in our sending your requested copies. (You must allow at least 6 weeks processing time after a return is filed before requesting a copy.)

Corporations, Partnerships, Estates, and Trusts.—For rules on who may obtain tax information on the entity, see Internal Revenue Code section 6103.

Items 3, 3a, and 4.—If you have named someone else to receive the tax form (such as a CPA, scholarship board, or mortgage lender), you must include the name of an individual with the address in item 3. Also, be sure to write the name of the client, student, or applicant in item 4 if it is different from the name shown in item 1. For example, item 1 may be the parents of a student applying for financial aid. Show the

student's name in item 4 so the scholarship board will know what file to associate the return with. If we cannot find a record of your return, we will notify the third party directly that we cannot fill the request. If you checked the box in 3a, we will refund the payment for the copies to the third party.

Item 5.—If you want a copy of your Form W-2 only and not a copy of your tax return, be sure to check the box for Copy of Form W-2 only and in item 8 show "Form W-2 only"; in item 10c show "no charge."

If you need only tax account information and not a copy of your tax return or Form W-2, do not complete this form. See the instructions on the back under "Tax Account Information Only."

Items 6 and 6a.—For individuals, enter the social security number as shown on the tax form. For joint returns, show the husband's social security number in item 6 and the wife's in item 6a. If you do not furnish this information, there may be a delay in processing your request.

(Continued on back)

Form 4506 (Rev. 1-87)

249

Item 9.—Enter the year(s) of the tax form you are requesting. For fiscal-year filers or requests for quarterly returns, enter the date the period ended. If you need more than four different periods, use additional request forms. Returns which were filed six or more years ago may not be available for making copies. However, tax account information is generally still available for these periods.

Item 10.—Write your social security number or Federal employer identification number and "Form 4506 Request" on your check or money order. If we cannot fill your request, we will refund your payment.

Where To File.—After you have completed this form, send it to the service center at the address shown in the last column for the location where you lived when the requested tax form was filed.

Note: *You must use a separate form for each service center from which you are requesting a copy of your tax form.*

Tax Account Information Only.—In addition to a copy of a tax form, we can provide a listing of certain tax account information, which is available free of charge and can be obtained by contacting your local IRS office. Generally, tax account information is needed because students applying for financial aid may be required to give the college a copy of their tax return. The school may, however, permit you to use tax return information provided by the IRS instead. If so, the following information will be sent:

(a) Name and social security number.
(b) Type of return filed.
(c) Marital status.
(d) Tax shown on return.
(e) Adjusted gross income.
(f) Taxable income.
(g) Self-employment tax, and
(h) Number of exemptions.

Form 1040A or 1040EZ Verification for Mortgage Revenue Bonds.—States issuing mortgage revenue bonds are required to verify that the mortgage applicant did not own a home during the 3 previous years. As part of this verification, the mortgage lender may want proof that you did not claim interest or real estate tax deductions for a residence on your return. If you have kept a copy of your return, or if it was filled out by a paid preparer and you can get a copy, the mortgage lender can accept your signed copy.

If you do not have a copy of your return and filed Form 1040A or 1040EZ, you can request tax account information, which will provide sufficient information to satisfy the mortgage lender. To get tax account information, do not complete this form. Instead, contact your local IRS office for this information.

If you filed Form 1040, you will have to get a copy of your return to verify that you did not claim any itemized deductions for a residence. To get a copy, please complete this form. Write "Mortgage Revenue Bond" across the top.

If you lived in ▼	Please mail to the following Internal Revenue Service Center ▼
New Jersey, New York (New York City and counties of Nassau, Rockland, Suffolk, and Westchester)	P.O. Box 400 Holtsville, NY 11742
New York (all other counties), Connecticut, Maine, Massachusetts, Minnesota, New Hampshire, Rhode Island, Vermont	P.O. Box 3006 Woburn, MA 01801
Alabama, Florida, Georgia, Mississippi, South Carolina	P.O. Box 47412 Doraville, GA 30362
Kentucky, Michigan, Ohio, West Virginia	P.O. Box 145500 Cincinnati, OH 45214
Kansas, Louisiana, New Mexico, Oklahoma, Texas	3651 South International Highway Photocopy Unit Stop 6716 Austin, TX 73301
Alaska, Arizona, Colorado, Idaho, Montana, Nebraska, Nevada, North Dakota, Oregon, South Dakota, Utah, Washington, Wyoming	TPR/Photocopy 3B P.O. Box 9956 Mail Stop 6734 Ogden, UT 84409
Illinois, Iowa, Missouri, Wisconsin	Photocopy Unit Stop 56 Kansas City, MO 64999
California, Hawaii	5045 E. Butler Avenue Photocopy Unit Stop 53260 Fresno, CA 93888
Arkansas, Indiana, North Carolina, Tennessee, Virginia	P.O. Box 2501 Memphis, TN 38101
Delaware, District of Columbia, Maryland, Pennsylvania, outside the United States	P.O. Box 920 Photocopy Unit Drop Point 536 Bensalem, PA 19020

U.S. Small Business Administration

RESOLUTION OF BOARD OF DIRECTORS OF

_____

(Name of Applicant)

(1) RESOLVED, that the officers of this corporation named below, or any one of them, or their, or any one of their, duly elected or appointed successors in office, be and they are hereby authorized and empowered in the name and on behalf of this corporation and under its corporate seal to execute and deliver to the _____
(hereinafter called "Lender") or the Small Business Administration (hereinafter called "SBA"), as the case may be, in the form required by Lender or SBA, the following documents: (a) application for a loan or loans, the total thereof not to exceed in principal amount $ _____ , maturing upon such date or dates and bearing interest at such rate or rates as may be prescribed by Lender or SBA; (b) applications for any renewals or extensions of all or any part of such loan or loans and of any other loans, heretofore or hereafter made by Lender or SBA to this corporation; (c) the promissory note or notes of this corporation evidencing such loan or loans or any renewals or extensions thereof; and (d) any other instruments or agreements of this corporation which may be required by Lender or SBA in connection with such loans, renewals, and/or extensions; and that said officers in their discretion may accept any such loan or loans in installments and give one or more notes of this corporation therefor, and may receive and endorse in the name of this corporation any checks or drafts representing such loan or loans or any such installments;

(2) FURTHER RESOLVED, that the aforesaid officers or any one of them, or their duly elected or appointed successors in office, be and they are hereby authorized and empowered to do any acts, including but not limited to the mortgage, pledge, or hypothecation from time to time with Lender or SBA of any or all assets of this corporation to secure such loan or loans, renewals and extensions, and to execute in the name and on behalf of this corporation and under its corporate seal or otherwise, any instruments or agreements deemed necessary or proper by Lender or SBA, in respect of the collateral securing any indebtedness of this corporation;

(3) FURTHER RESOLVED, that any indebtedness heretofore contracted and any contracts or agreements heretofore made with Lender or SBA on behalf of this corporation, and all acts of officers or agents of this corporation in connection with said indebtedness or said contracts or agreements, are hereby ratified and confirmed;

(4) FURTHER RESOLVED, that the officers referred to in the foregoing resolutions are as follows:

(Typewrite name)	(Title)	(Signature)
(Typewrite name)	(Title)	(Signature)
(Typewrite name)	(Title)	(Signature)
(Typewrite name)	(Title)	(Signature)
(Typewrite name)	(Title)	(Signature)

(5) FURTHER RESOLVED, that Lender or SBA is authorized to rely upon the aforesaid resolutions until receipt of written notice of any change.

CERTIFICATION

I HEREBY CERTIFY that the foregoing is a true and correct copy of a resolution regularly presented to and adopted by the Board of Directors of _____ at a meeting duly called and held at _____
(Name of Applicant)
on the _____ day of _____ , 19 _____ , at which a quorum was present and voted, and that such resolution is duly recorded in the minute book of this corporation; that the officers named in said resolution have been duly elected or appointed to, and are the present incumbents of, the respective offices set after their respective names; and that the signatures set opposite their respective names are their true and genuine signatures.

(Seal)

_____
Secretary

SBA LOAN NO.

U.S. SMALL BUSINESS ADMINISTRATION
CERTIFICATE AS TO PARTNERS

We, the undersigned, are general partners doing business under the firm name and style of _____

_____ and constitute all the partners thereof.

Acts done in the name of or on behalf of the firm, by any one of us shall be binding on said firm and each and all of us.

This statement is signed and the foregoing representations are made in order to induce the _____

_____ (hereinafter called "Lender") or the Small Business

Administration (hereinafter called "SBA"):

1. To consider applications for a loan or loans to said firm when signed by any one of us.
2. To make a loan or loans to said firm against a promissory note or promissory notes signed in the firm name by any one of us.
3. To accept as security for the payment of such note or notes any collateral which may be offered by any one of us.
4. To consider applications signed in the firm name by any one of us for any renewals or extensions for all or any part of such loan or loans and any other loan or loans heretofore or hereafter made by Lender or SBA to said firm.
5. To accept any other instruments or agreements of said firm which may be required by Lender or SBA in connection with such loan, renewals, or extensions when signed by any one of us.

Any indebtedness heretofore contracted and any contracts or agreements heretofore made with Lender or SBA on behalf of said firm and all acts of partners or agents of said firm in connection with said indebtedness or said contracts or agreements are hereby ratified and confirmed, and we do hereby certify that THERE IS ATTACHED HERETO A TRUE COPY OF OUR AGREEMENT OF PARTNERSHIP.

Each of the undersigned is authorized to mortgage and/or pledge all or any part of the property, real, personal, or mixed, of said firm as security for any such loan.

This statement and representations made herein are in no way intended to exclude the general authority of each partner as to any acts not specifically mentioned or to limit the power of any one of us to bind said firm and each and every one of us individually.

Lender or SBA is authorized to rely upon the aforesaid statements until receipt of written notice of any change.

Signed this _____ day of _____ . 19 ____

(Typewrite Name)	(Signature)
(Typewrite Name)	(Signature)
(Typewrite Name)	(Signature)
(Typewrite Name)	(Signature)
(Typewrite Name)	(Signature)
(Typewrite Name)	(Signature)
(Typewrite Name)	(Signature)
(Typewrite Name)	(Signature)

State of _____)

County of _____)ss:

On this _____ day of _____ . 19 ____ . before me personally appeared

_____ and _____ and _____ and

_____ and _____ and _____ and

_____ and _____ and

to be known to be the persons described in and who executed the foregoing instrument, and acknowledged that they executed the same as their free act and deed.

_____
Notary Public

My commission expires _____

NOTE: If this form of notarial certificate cannot be used in the State in question, the form should be properly modified.

GPO 911-758

SBA Form 160A(11-87)
Use 12-84 edition until exhausted

U.S. Small Business Administration
ASSURANCE OF COMPLIANCE FOR NONDISCRIMINATION

_____, Applicant/Licensee/Recipient/Subrecipient, (hereinafter referred to as applicant) in consideration of Federal financial assistance from the Small Business Administration, herewith agrees that it will comply with the nondiscrimination requirements of 13 CFR Parts 112 and 113 of the Regulations issued by the Small Business Administration (SBA).

13 CFR Parts 112 and 113 require that no person shall on the grounds of age, color, handicap, marital status, national origin, race, religion or sex, be excluded from participation in, be denied the benefits of or otherwise be subjected to discrimination under any program or activity for which the applicant received Federal financial assistance from SBA.

Applicant agrees to comply with the recordkeeping requirements of 13 CFR 112.9 and 113.5 as set forth in SBA Form 793, "Notice to New SBA Borrowers", to permit effective enforcement of 13 CFR 112 and 113. Such recordkeeping requirements have been approved under OMB Number 3245-0076. Applicant further agrees to obtain or require similar Assurance of Compliance for Nondiscrimination from subrecipients, contractors/subcontractors, successors, transferees and assignees as long as it/they receive or retain possession of any Federal financial assistance from SBA. In the event the applicant fails to comply with any provision or requirement of 13 CFR Parts 112 and 113, SBA may call, cancel, terminate, accelerate repayment or suspend any or all Federal financial assistance provided by SBA.

Executed the _____ day of _____ 19 _____ .

_____
Name, Address & Phone No. of Applicant

By _____
Typed Name & Title of Authorized Official

Corporate Seal

_____
Signature of Authorized Official

_____
Name, Address & Phone No. of Subrecipient

By _____
Typed Name & Title of Authorized Official

Corporate Seal

_____
Signature of Authorized Official

SBA FORM 652 (8-85) SOP 90 30
PREVIOUS EDITIONS OBSOLETE

AGREEMENT OF COMPLIANCE

In compliance with Executive Order 11246, as amended (Executive Order 11246, as amended prohibits discrimination because of race, color, religion, sex, or national origin, and requires affirmative action to ensure equality of opportunity in all aspects of employment by all contractors and subcontractors, performing work under a Federally assisted construction contract in excess of $10,000, regardless of the number of employees), the applicant/recipient, contractor or subcontractor agrees that in consideration of the approval and as a condition of the disbursement of all or any part of a loan by the Small Business Administration (SBA) that it will incorporate or cause to be incorporated into any contract or subcontract in excess of $10,000 for construction work, or modification thereof, as defined in the regulations of the Secretary of Labor, at 41 CFR Chapter 60, which is paid for in whole or in part with funds obtained from the Federal Government or borrowed on the credit of the Federal Government pursuant to a grant, contract, loan, insurance or guarantee, or undertaken pursuant to any Federal program involving such grant, contract, loan, insurance or guarantee, the following equal opportunity clause:

During the performance of this contract, the contractor agrees as follows:

(1)   The contractor will not discriminate against any employee or applicant for employment because of race, color, religion, sex or national origin. The contractor will take affirmative action to insure that applicants are employed, and that employees are treated during employment without regard to their race, color, religion, sex or national origin. Such action shall include, but not be limited to the following: employment, upgrading, demotion or transfer; recruitment or advertising; layoff or termination; rates of pay or other forms of compensation; and selection for training, including apprenticeship. The contractor agrees to post in conspicuous places, available to employees and applicants for employment, notices to be provided setting forth the provisions of this nondiscrimination clause.

(2)   The contractor will, in all solicitations or advertisements for employees placed by or on behalf of the contractor, state that all qualified applicants will receive consideration for employment without regard to race, color, religion, sex or national origin.

(3)   The contractor will send to each labor union or representative of workers with which he has a collective bargaining agreement or other contract or understanding, a notice to be provided advising the said labor union or workers' representative of the contractor's commitments under Executive Order 11246, as amended, and shall post copies of the notice in conspicuous places available to employees and applicants for employment.

(4)   The contractor will comply with all provisions of Executive Order 11246, as amended, and the rules and relevant orders of the Secretary of Labor created thereby.

(5)   The contractor will furnish all information and reports required by Executive Order 11246, as amended, and by the rules, regulations and orders of the Secretary of Labor, or pursuant thereto, and will permit access to books, records and accounts by SBA (See SBA Form 793) and the Secretary of Labor for purposes of investigation to ascertain compliance with such rules, regulations and orders. (The information collection requirements contained in Executive Order 11246, as amended, are approved under OMB No. 1215-0072.)

(6)   In the event of the contractor's noncompliance with the nondiscrimination clause or with any of the said rules, regulations or orders, this contract may be cancelled, terminated or suspended in whole or in part and the contractor may be declared ineligible for further Government contracts or federally assisted construction contracts in accordance with procedures authorized in Executive Order 11246, as amended, and such other sanctions may be imposed and remedies invoked as provided in the said Executive Order or by rule, regulation or order of the Secretary of Labor, or as otherwise provided by law.

The contractor will include the portion of the sentence immediately preceding paragraph (1) and the provisions of paragraphs (1) through (6) in every subcontract or purchase order unless exempted by rules, regulations or orders of the Secretary of Labor issued pursuant to Executive Order 11246, as amended, so that such provisions will be binding upon each subcontractor or vendor. The contractor will take such action with respect to any subcontract or purchase order as SBA may direct as a means of enforcing such provisions, including sanctions for noncompliance: Provided, however that in the event a contractor becomes involved in or is threatened with litigation with a subcontractor or vendor as a result of such direction by SBA, the contractor may request the United States to enter into such litigation to protect the interest of the United States.

SBA Form 601 (10-85) REF: SOP 9030   Previous editions are obsolete

The Applicant further agrees that it will be bound by the above equal opportunity clause with respect to its own employment practices when it participates in federally assisted construction work.

The Applicant agrees that is will assist and cooperate actively with SBA and the Secretary of Labor in obtaining the compliance of contractors and subcontractors with the equal opportunity clause and the rules, regulations and relevant orders of the Secretary of Labor, that it will furnish SBA and the Secretary of Labor such information as they may require for the supervision of such compliance, and that it will otherwise assist SBA in the discharge of the Agency's primary responsibility for securing compliance. The Applicant further agrees that it will refrain from entering into any contract or contract modification subject to Executive Order 11246, as amended, and will carry out such sanctions and penalties for violation of the equal opportunity clause as may be imposed upon contractors and subcontractors by SBA or the Secretary of Labor or such other sanctions and penalties for violation thereof as may, in the opinion of the Administrator, be necessary and appropriate.

In addition, the Applicant agrees that it if fails or refuses to comply with these undertakings SBA may take any or all of the following actions: cancel, terminate or suspend in whole or in part the loan; refrain from extending any further assistance to the applicant under the programs with respect to which the failure or refusal occurred until satisfactory assurance of future compliance has been received from such applicant; and refer the case to the Department of Justice for appropriate legal proceedings.

In consideration of the approval by the Small Business Administration of a loan to _____ _____ Applicant, said Applicant and _____ the general contractor, mutually promise and agree that the(y) will comply with all nondiscrimination provisions and requirements of Executive Order 11246, as amended.

Executed the _____ day of _____ 19____.

_____
Name, Address, & Phone No. of Applicant

By _____
Typed Name & Title of Authorized Official

Corporate Seal

_____
Signature of Authorized Official

_____
Name, Address, & Phone No. of Subrecipient

By _____
Typed Name & Title of Authorized Official

Corporate Seal

_____
Signature of Authorized Official

SBA Form 601 (10-85) REF SOP 9030 Previous editions are obsolete

*U.S. Government Printing Office: 1991 — 312-624/51731

APPENDIX J
SBA Publications Available

FINANCIAL MANAGEMENT AND ANALYSIS

FM 1—$1.00   *ABC's of Borrowing*
FM 2—$1.00   *Profit Costing and Pricing for Manufacture*
FM 3—$0.50   *Basic Budgets for Profit Planning*
FM 4—$1.00   *Understanding Cash Flow*
FM 5—$0.50   *A Venture Capital Primer for Small Business*
FM 6—$0.50   *Accounting Services for Small Service Firms*
FM 7—$0.50   *Analyze Your Records to Reduce Costs*
FM 8—$0.50   *Budgeting in a Small Service Firm*
FM 9—$0.50   *Sound Cash Management and Borrowing*
FM 10—$1.00   *Recordkeeping in a Small Business*
FM 11—$1.00   *Simple Break-even Analysis for Small Stores*
FM 12—$0.50   *A Pricing Checklist for Small Retailers*
FM 13—$1.00   *Pricing Your Products and Services Profitably*

GENERAL MANAGEMENT AND PLANNING

MP 1—$0.50   *Effective Business Communications*
MP 2—$1.00   *Locating or Relocating Your Business*
MP 3—$0.50   *Problems in Managing a Family-Owned Business*
MP 4—$1.00   *Business Plan for Small Manufacturers*
MP 5—$1.00   *Business Plan for Small Construction Firms*
MP 6—$0.50   *Planning and Goal Setting for Small Business*
MP 8—$0.50   *Should You Lease or Buy Equipment?*
MP 9—$1.00   *Business Plan for Retailers*
MP 10—$1.00   *Choosing a Retail Location*
MP 11—$0.50   *Business Plan for Small Service Firms*
MP 12—$0.50   *Checklist for Going into Business*
MP 14—$1.00   *How to Get Started with a Small Business Computer*
MP 15—$1.00   *The Business Plan for Homebased Business*

MP 16—$1.00　*How to Buy or Sell a Business*
MP 17—$0.50　*Purchasing for Owners of Small Plants*
MP 18—$1.00　*Buying for Retail Stores*
MP 19—$1.00　*Small Business Decision Making*
MP 20—$1.00　*Business Continuation Planning*
MP 21—$1.00　*Developing a Strategic Business Plan*
MP-22—$0.50　*Inventory Management*
MP 23—$1.00　*Techniques for Problem Solving*
MP 24—$1.00　*Techniques for Productivity Improvement*
MP 25—$0.50　*Selecting the Legal Structure for Your Business*
MP 26—$0.50　*Evaluating Franchise Opportunities*
MP 28—$1.00　*Small Business Risk Management Guide*
MP 29—$2.00　*Quality Child Care Makes Good Business Sense*

CRIME PREVENTION

CP　2—$1.00　*Curtailing Crime—Inside and Out*
CP　3—$1.00　*A Small Business Guide to Computer Security*

MARKETING

MT　1—$0.50　*Creative Selling: The Competitive Edge*
MT　2—$1.00　*Marketing for Small Business: An Overview*
MT　3—$0.50　*Is the Independent Sales Agent for You?*
MT　4—$1.00　*Marketing Checklist for Small Retailers*
MT　8—$1.00　*Researching Your Market*
MT　9—$1.00　*Selling by Mail Order*
MT 10—$1.00　*Market Overseas With U.S. Government Help*
MT 11—$1.00　*Advertising*

PERSONNEL MANAGEMENT

1—$0.50　*Checklist for Developing a Training Program*
2—$1.00　*Employees: How to Find and Pay Them*
3—$1.00　*Managing Employee Benefits*

NEW PRODUCTS/IDEAS/INVENTIONS

PI 1—$2.00　*Ideas into Dollars*
PI 2—$1 00　*Avoiding Patent, Trademark, and Copyright Problems*
PI 3—$1.00　*Trademarks and Business Goodwill*

VIDEOTAPES

Each VHS videotape comes with a workbook.

VT 1—$30.00　*Marketing: Winning Customers with a Workable Plan*
VT 2—$30.00　*The Business Plan: Your Roadmap to Success*

VT 3—$30.00 *Promotion: Solving the Puzzle*

ORDERING PROCEDURE

On a separate paper write the following:

The order number and title of the publication(s) desired.
The quantity of each publication being ordered.
The dollar amount of the order.
The name and address (include the zip number) where the publication(s) is to be sent.

Write a check or money order for the total amount of the order.

Place the order and the payment in an envelope and address it to:

SBA—PUBLICATIONS
P.O. Box 30
Denver, CO 80201-0030

The following publications are MUST reading:

Help for Small Business
Business Loans from the SBA
Business Development Pamphlets
Business Development Booklets
Small Business Tax Workshops

They're available by writing:

Small Business Administration
Office of Public Communications
1441 L Street, NW
Washington, DC 20416
or call: (202) 653-6832.

You can also write the Superintendent of Documents, U.S. Government Printing Office, Washington, DC 20402 for a current price list of the following titles:

Handbook of Small Business Finance—part of Small Business Management Series No. 15.

Guides for Profit Planning—part of Small Business Management Series No. 20.

Starting and Managing a Small Business of Your Own—part of the Starting and Management Series No. 1.

Ratio Analysis for Small Business—part of Small Business Management Series No. 20.

There is still another series of publications from the SBA, Business Development Pamphlets, that are available for a nominal processing fee. Write to: Small Business Administration, P.O. Box 15434, Fort Worth, TX 76119 and ask for order form number 115A. This form will list all of the Business

Development Pamphlets under the category of Management Aids (MA) and the fees for each, including:

MA 1.010	*Accounting Services for Small Service Firms*
MA 1.004	*Basic Budgets for Profit Planning*
MA 1.011	*Analyze Your Records to Reduce Costs*
MA 1.001	*The ABC's of Borrowing*
MA 1.015	*Budgeting in a Small Business Firm*
MA 1.016	*Sound Cash Management and Borrowing*
MA 1.017	*Keeping Records in a Small Business*
MA 1.002	*What Is the Best Price?*
MA 1.020	*Profit Pricing and Costing for Services*
MA 1.018	*Checklist for Profit Watching*
MA 1.014	*Getting the Facts for Income Tax Reporting*
MA 2.016	*Checklist for Going into Business*
MA 2.025	*Thinking about Going into Business*
MA 2.004	*Problems in Managing a Family-Owned Business*
MA 2.010	*Planning and Goal-Setting for Small Business*
MA 3.010	*Techniques for Problem-Solving*
MA 2.009	*Business Life Insurance*
MA 6.004	*Selecting the Legal Structure for Your Business*
MA 4.019	*Learning about Your Market*
MA 6.003	*Incorporating a Small Business*
MA 2.027	*How to Get Started with a Small Business Computer*
MA 5	*Women's Handbook*
MA 1.019	*Simple Breakeven Analysis for Small Stores*

There is an entire library of business titles available to you simply by virtue of being a U.S. resident or citizen. If you feel you need more assistance before you decide to start your own business or want to know all there is to know about small businesses, the SBA also publishes Small Business Bibliographies, that is, lists of books available on a variety of relevant topics. Write to the SBA at P.O. Box 15434, Fort Worth, TX 76119 to find out about the bibliographies below:

SBB 89	*Marketing for Small Business*
SBB 9	*Marketing Research Procedures*
SBB 87	*Financial Management*
SBB 13	*National Directories for Use in Marketing*
SBB 2	*Home Businesses*
SBB 91	*Ideas into Dollars* (a guide for inventors)
SBB 18	*Basic Business Reference Sources*
SBB 94	*Decision-Making in Small Business*
SBB 3	*Selling by Mail Order*
SBB 15	*Recordkeeping Systems for Small Stores and Service Trade*

You can order the following informative booklets from the Minority Business Development Agency, Information Clearinghouse, Department of Commerce, Washington, DC 20230. (202) 377-1936.

HELP FOR THE HANDICAPPED

59.021: Handicapped Assistance Loans (HALs) are for disabled individuals looking to start their own businesses. There are direct loans as well as loan guarantees available.

Contact: Director, Office of Business Loans, Small Business Administration, 1441 L St., NW, Washington, DC 20416. (202) 205-6570.

VIETNAM-ERA VETERANS' DIRECT LOANS

59.038: Vietnam-era veterans and disabled veterans can get loans to help them start their own businesses through the Veterans Loan Program. As of 1988, there were several hundred loans being granted each year.

Contact: Director, Office of Business Loans, Small Business Administration, 1441 L St., NW, Washington, DC 20416. (202) 205-6570.

59.007: Economically disadvantaged businesses can receive free grants and technical assistance worth millions of dollars.

Contact: Associate Administrator for Minority Small Business, 1441 L St., NW, Room 602, Washington, DC 20416.

81.063: Minority businesses can get loans to help them prepare government proposals through the Office of Minority Economic Impact Loans.

Contact: Mr. Kenneth Workman, Office of Minority Economic Impact MI-3.2, U.S. Dept. of Energy, Forrestal Bldg., Room 5B-110, Washington, DC 20585. (202) 586-1594.

LOW-COST LITERATURE AVAILABLE

Many banking organizations offer publications that are worth obtaining and reading. For example, the Bank of America has a program called "Small Business Reporter," a series of publications on various business management subjects; each booklet costs about $3.00 to $5.00. However, one costs $9.50—the one entitled *Business Computers from A to Z.*

These publications provide a quick instruction in the specifics of business activities and are segmented to allow you to order and study only those areas of interest to you.

APPENDIX K
SBA Field Offices

The following is a listing of all SBA field offices as they pertain to each state. (Example: The regional office for Alabama is located in Atlanta, Georgia.)

ALABAMA

TYPE	CITY	STATE	ZIP CODE	ADDRESS	PHONE NUMBER
RO	ATLANTA	GA	30367	1375 PEACHTREE ST., NE	(404)347-2797
DO	ATLANTA	GA	30309	1720 PEACHTREE RD., NW	(404)347-4749
DO	BIRMINGHAM	AL	35203-2398	2121 8TH AVE. N.	(205)731-1344
DO	CHARLOTTE	NC	28202	200 N. COLLEGE ST.	(704)344-6563
DO	COLUMBIA	SC	29201	1835 ASSEMBLY ST.	(803)765-5376
DO	JACKSON	MS	39201	101 W. CAPITOL ST.	(601)965-5325
DO	JACKSONVILLE	FL	32256-7504	7825 BAYMEADOWS WAY	(904)443-1900
DO	LOUISVILLE	KY	40202	600 DR. M.L. KING JR PL	(502)582-5976
DO	CORAL GABLES	FL	33146-2911	1320 S. DIXIE HGWY.	(305)536-5521
DO	NASHVILLE	TN	37228-1500	50 VANTAGE WAY	(615)736-5881
BO	GULFPORT	MS	39501-7758	1 HANCOCK PLAZA	(601)863-4449
POD	STATESBORO	GA	30458	52 N. MAIN ST.	(912)489-8719
POD	TAMPA	FL	33602-3945	501 E. POLK ST.	(813)228-2594
POD	W. PALM BEACH	FL	33407-2044	5601 CORPORATE WAY	(407)689-3922

RO=REGIONAL OFFICE   DO=DISTRICT OFFICE   BO=BRANCH OFFICE   POD=POST OF DUTY

ALASKA

TYPE	CITY	STATE	ZIP CODE	ADDRESS	PHONE NUMBER
RO	SEATTLE	WA	98121	2615 4TH AVENUE	(206)553-5676
DO	ANCHORAGE	AK	99513	222 WEST 8TH AVENUE	(907)271-4022
DO	BOISE	ID	83702	1020 MAIN STREET	(208)334-1096
DO	PORTLAND	OR	97201	222 S.W. COLUMBIA	(503)326-5223
DO	SEATTLE	WA	98174	915 SECOND AVENUE	(206)553-1420
DO	SPOKANE	WA	99204	WEST 601 FIRST AVE	(509)353-2810

RO=REGIONAL OFFICE   DO=DISTRICT OFFICE   BO=BRANCH OFFICE
POD=POST OF DUTY   DAO=DISASTER AREA OFFICE

ARIZONA

TYPE	CITY	STATE	ZIP CODE	ADDRESS	PHONE NUMBER
DO	SAN FRANCISCO	CA	94105	71 STEVENSON STREET	(415)744-6402
DO	FRESNO	CA	93727	2719 N. AIR FRESNO DR	(209)487-5189
DO	HONOLULU	HI	96850	300 ALA MOANA BLVD	(808)541-2990
DO	LAS VEGAS	NV	89125	301 EAST STEWART ST	(702)388-6611
DO	GLENDALE	CA	91203	330 N. BRAND BLVD	(213)894-2956
DO	PHOENIX	AZ	85004	2828 N. CENTRAL AVE	(602)640-2316
DO	SAN DIEGO	CA	92188	880 FRONT STREET	(619)557-7252
DO	SAN FRANCISCO	CA	94105	211 MAIN STREET	(415)744-6820
DO	SANTA ANA	CA	92703	901 W. CIVIC CENTER DR	(714)836-2494
BO	AGANA	GM	96910	238 ARCHBISHOP FC FLORES ST	(671)472-7277
BO	SACRAMENTO	CA	95814	660 J STREET	(916)551-1426
POD	RENO	NV	89505	50 SOUTH VIRGINIA ST	(702)784-5268
POD	TUCSON	AZ	85701	300 WEST CONGRESS ST	(602)670-4759
POD	VENTURA	CA	93003	6477 TELEPHONE ROAD	(805)642-1866

RO = REGIONAL OFFICE   DO = DISTRICT OFFICE   BO = BRANCH OFFICE
POD = POST OF DUTY   DAO = DISASTER AREA OFFICE

ARKANSAS

TYPE	CITY	STATE	ZIP CODE	ADDRESS	PHONE NUMBER
RO	DALLAS	TX	75235	8625 KING GEORGE DR	(214)767-7635
DO	ALBUQUERQUE	NM	87102	625 SILVER AVENUE, SW	(505)766-1870
DO	DALLAS	TX	75242	1100 COMMERCE STREET	(214)767-0600
DO	EL PASO	TX	79935	10737 GATEWAY WEST	(915)541-5676
DO	HOUSTON	TX	77054	2525 MURWORTH	(713)660-4401
DO	LITTLE ROCK	AR	72202	2120 RIVERFRONT DRIVE	(501)324-5278
DO	HARLINGEN	TX	78550	222 EAST VAN BUREN ST	(512)427-8533
DO	LUBBOCK	TX	79401	1611 TENTH STREET	(806)743-7462
DO	NEW ORLEANS	LA	70112	1661 CANAL STREET	(504)589-2744
DO	OKLAHOMA CITY	OK	73102	200 NORTH WEST 5TH ST	(405)231-4301
DO	SAN ANTONIO	TX	78216	7400 BLANCO ROAD	(512)229-4535
BO	CORPUS CHRISTI	TX	78476	606 NORTH CARANCAHUA	(512)888-3301
BO	FT. WORTH	TX	76102	819 TAYLOR STREET	(817)334-3777
POD	AUSTIN	TX	78701	300 EAST 8TH STREET	(512)482-5288
POD	MARSHALL	TX	75670	505 EAST TRAVIS	(903)935-5257
POD	SHREVEPORT	LA	71101	500 FANNIN STREET	(318)226-5196

RO = REGIONAL OFFICE   DO = DISTRICT OFFICE   BO = BRANCH OFFICE
POD = POST OF DUTY   DAO = DISASTER AREA OFFICE

CALIFORNIA

TYPE	CITY	STATE	ZIP CODE	ADDRESS	PHONE NUMBER
DO	SAN FRANCISCO	CA	94105	71 STEVENSON STREET	(415)744-6402
DO	FRESNO	CA	93727	2719 N. AIR FRESNO DR	(209)487-5189
DO	HONOLULU	HI	96850	300 ALA MOANA BLVD	(808)541-2990
DO	LAS VEGAS	NV	89125	301 EAST STEWART ST	(702)388-6611
DO	GLENDALE	CA	91203	330 N. BRAND BLVD	(213)894-2956
DO	PHOENIX	AZ	85004	2828 N. CENTRAL AVE	(602)640-2316
DO	SAN DIEGO	CA	92188	880 FRONT STREET	(619)557-7252

DO	SAN FRANCISCO	CA	94105	211 MAIN STREET	(415)744-6820
DO	SANTA ANA	CA	92703	901 W.CIVIC CENTER DR	(714)836-2494
BO	AGANA	GM	96910	238 ARCHBISHOP FC FLORES ST	(671)472-7277
BO	SACRAMENTO	CA	95814	660 J STREET	(916)551-1426
POD	RENO	NV	89505	50 SOUTH VIRGINIA ST	(702)784-5268
POD	TUCSON	AZ	85701	300 WEST CONGRESS ST	(602)629-6715
POD	VENTURA	CA	93003	6477 TELEPHONE ROAD	(805)642-1866

RO = REGIONAL OFFICE   DO = DISTRICT OFFICE   BO = BRANCH OFFICE
POD = POST OF DUTY   DAO = DISASTER AREA OFFICE

COLORADO

TYPE	CITY	STATE	ZIP CODE	ADDRESS	PHONE NUMBER
RO	DENVER	CO	80202	999 18TH STREET	(303)294-7021
DO	CASPER	WY	82602	100 EAST B STREET	(307)261-5761
DO	DENVER	CO	80201	721 19TH STREET	(303)844-3984
DO	FARGO	ND	58108	657 2ND AVE NORTH	(701)239-5131
DO	HELENA	MT	59626	301 SOUTH PARK	(406)449-5381
DO	SALT LAKE CITY	UT	84138	125 SOUTH STATE ST.	(801)524-5800
DO	SIOUX FALLS	SD	57102	101 SOUTH MAIN AVENUE	(605)330-4231

RO = REGIONAL OFFICE   DO = DISTRICT OFFICE   BO = BRANCH OFFICE
POD = POST OF DUTY   DAO = DISASTER AREA OFFICE

CONNECTICUT

TYPE	CITY	STATE	ZIP CODE	ADDRESS	PHONE NUMBER
RO	BOSTON	MA	02110	155 FEDERAL ST.	(617)451-2023
DO	BOSTON	MA	02222-1093	10 CAUSEWAY ST.	(617)565-5590
DO	AUGUSTA	ME	04330	40 WESTERN AVE.	(207)622-8378
DO	CONCORD	NH	03302-1257	143 N. MAIN ST.	(603)225-1400
DO	HARTFORD	CT	06106	330 MAIN ST.	(203)240-4700
DO	MONTPELIER	VT	05602	87 STATE ST.	(802)828-4422
DO	PROVIDENCE	RI	02903	380 WESTMINISTER MALL	(401)528-4561
BO	SPRINGFIELD	MA	01103	1550 MAIN ST.	(413)785-0268

RO = REGIONAL OFFICE   DO = DISTRICT OFFICE   BO = BRANCH OFFICE

DELAWARE

TYPE	CITY	STATE	ZIP CODE	ADDRESS	PHONE NUMBER
RO	KING OF PRUSSIA	PA	19406	475 ALLENDALE RD.	(215)962-3700
DO	BALTIMORE	MD	21202	10 N. CALVERT ST.	(410)962-4392
DO	CLARKSBURG	WV	26301	168 W. MAIN ST.	(304)623-5631
DO	KING OF PRUSSIA	PA	19406	475 ALLENDALE RD.	(215)962-3804
DO	PITTSBURGH	PA	15222	960 PENN AVE.	(412)644-2780
DO	RICHMOND	VA	23240	400 N. 8TH ST.	(804)771-2400
DO	WASHINGTON	DC	20036	1111 18TH ST., N.W.	(202)634-1500
BO	CHARLESTON	WV	25301	550 EAGAN ST.	(304)347-5220
BO	HARRISBURG	PA	17101	100 CHESTNUT ST.	(717)782-3840
BO	WILKES-BARRE	PA	18702	20 N. PENNSYLVANIA AVE.	(717)826-6497
BO	WILMINGTON	DE	19801	920 N. KING ST.	(302)573-6295

RO = REGIONAL OFFICE   DO = DISTRICT OFFICE   BO = BRANCH OFFICE

DISTRICT OF COLUMBIA

TYPE	CITY	STATE	ZIP CODE	ADDRESS	PHONE NUMBER
RO	KING OF PRUSSIA	PA	19406	475 ALLENDALE RD.	(215)962-3700
DO	BALTIMORE	MD	21202	10 N. CALVERT ST.	(410)962-4392
DO	CLARKSBURG	WV	26301	168 W. MAIN ST.	(304)623-5631
DO	KING OF PRUSSIA	PA	19406	475 ALLENDALE RD.	(215)962-3804
DO	PITTSBURGH	PA	15222	960 PENN AVE.	(412)644-2780
DO	RICHMOND	VA	23240	400 N. 8TH ST.	(804)771-2400
DO	WASHINGTON	DC	20036	1111 18TH ST., N.W.	(202)634-1500
BO	CHARLESTON	WV	25301	550 EAGAN ST.	(304)347-5220
BO	HARRISBURG	PA	17101	100 CHESTNUT ST.	(717)782-3840
BO	WILKES-BARRE	PA	18702	20 N. PENNSYLVANIA AVE.	(717)826-6497
BO	WILMINGTON	DE	19801	920 N. KING ST.	(302)573-6295

RO = REGIONAL OFFICE   DO = DISTRICT OFFICE   BO = BRANCH OFFICE

FLORIDA

TYPE	CITY	STATE	ZIP CODE	ADDRESS	PHONE NUMBER
RO	ATLANTA	GA	30367	1375 PEACHTREE ST., NE	(404)347-2797
DO	ATLANTA	GA	30309	1720 PEACHTREE RD., NW	(404)347-4749
DO	BIRMINGHAM	AL	35203-2398	2121 8TH AVE. N.	(205)731-1344
DO	CHARLOTTE	NC	28202	200 N. COLLEGE ST.	(704)344-6563
DO	COLUMBIA	SC	29201	1835 ASSEMBLY ST.	(803)765-5376
DO	JACKSON	MS	39201	101 W. CAPITOL ST.	(601)965-5325
DO	JACKSONVILLE	FL	32256-7504	7825 BAYMEADOWS WAY	(904)443-1900
DO	LOUISVILLE	KY	40202	600 DR. M.L. KING JR PL	(502)582-5976
DO	CORAL GABLES	FL	33146-2911	1320 S. DIXIE HGWY.	(305)536-5521
DO	NASHVILLE	TN	37228-1500	50 VANTAGE WAY	(615)736-5881
BO	GULFPORT	MS	39501-7758	1 HANCOCK PLAZA	(601)863-4449
POD	STATESBORO	GA	30458	52 N. MAIN ST.	(912)489-8719
POD	TAMPA	FL	33602-3945	501 E. POLK ST.	(813)228-2594
POD	W. PALM BEACH	FL	33407-2044	5601 CORPORATE WAY	(407)689-3922

RO = REGIONAL OFFICE   DO = DISTRICT OFFICE   BO = BRANCH OFFICE   POD = POST OF DUTY

GEORGIA

TYPE	CITY	STATE	ZIP CODE	ADDRESS	PHONE NUMBER
RO	ATLANTA	GA	30367	1375 PEACHTREE ST., NE	(404)347-2797
DO	ATLANTA	GA	30309	1720 PEACHTREE RD., NW	(404)347-4749
DO	BIRMINGHAM	AL	35203-2398	2121 8TH AVE. N.	(205)731-1344
DO	CHARLOTTE	NC	28202	200 N. COLLEGE ST.	(704)344-6563
DO	COLUMBIA	SC	29201	1835 ASSEMBLY ST.	(803)765-5376
DO	JACKSON	MS	39201	101 W. CAPITOL ST.	(601)965-5325
DO	JACKSONVILLE	FL	32256-7504	7825 BAYMEADOWS WAY	(904)443-1900
DO	LOUISVILLE	KY	40202	600 DR. M.L. KING JR PL	(502)582-5976
DO	CORAL GABLES	FL	33146-2911	1320 S. DIXIE HGWY.	(305)536-5521
DO	NASHVILLE	TN	37228-1500	50 VANTAGE WAY	(615)736-5881
BO	GULFPORT	MS	39501-7758	1 HANCOCK PLAZA	(601)863-4449
POD	STATESBORO	GA	30458	52 N. MAIN ST.	(912)489-8719
POD	TAMPA	FL	33602-3945	501 E. POLK ST.	(813)228-2594
POD	W. PALM BEACH	FL	33407-2044	5601 CORPORATE WAY	(407)689-3922

RO = REGIONAL OFFICE   DO = DISTRICT OFFICE   BO = BRANCH OFFICE   POD = POST OF DUTY

HAWAII

TYPE	CITY	STATE	ZIP CODE	ADDRESS	PHONE NUMBER
DO	SAN FRANCISCO	CA	94105	71 STEVENSON STREET	(415)744-6402
DO	FRESNO	CA	93727	2719 N. AIR FRESNO DR	(209)487-5189
DO	HONOLULU	HI	96850	300 ALA MOANA BLVD	(808)541-2990
DO	LAS VEGAS	NV	89125	301 EAST STEWART ST	(702)388-6611
DO	GLENDALE	CA	91203	330 N. BRAND BLVD	(213)894-2956
DO	PHOENIX	AZ	85004	2828 N. CENTRAL AVE	(602)640-2316
DO	SAN DIEGO	CA	92188	880 FRONT STREET	(619)557-7252
DO	SAN FRANCISCO	CA	94105	211 MAIN STREET	(415)744-6820
DO	SANTA ANA	CA	92703	901 W.CIVIC CENTER DR	(714)836-2494
BO	AGANA	GM	96910	238 ARCHBISHOP FC FLORES ST	(671)472-7277
BO	SACRAMENTO	CA	95814	660 J STREET	(916)551-1426
POD	RENO	NV	89505	50 SOUTH VIRGINIA ST	(702)784-5268
POD	TUCSON	AZ	85701	300 WEST CONGRESS ST	(602)629-6715
POD	VENTURA	CA	93003	6477 TELEPHONE ROAD	(805)642-1866

RO=REGIONAL OFFICE   DO=DISTRICT OFFICE   BO=BRANCH OFFICE
POD=POST OF DUTY   DAO=DISASTER AREA OFFICE

IDAHO

TYPE	CITY	STATE	ZIP CODE	ADDRESS	PHONE NUMBER
RO	SEATTLE	WA	98121	2615 4TH AVENUE	(206)553-5676
DO	ANCHORAGE	AK	99513	222 WEST 8TH AVENUE	(907)271-4022
DO	BOISE	ID	83702	1020 MAIN STREET	(208)334-1096
DO	PORTLAND	OR	97201	222 S.W. COLUMBIA	(503)326-5223
DO	SEATTLE	WA	98174	915 SECOND AVENUE	(206)553-1420
DO	SPOKANE	WA	99204	WEST 601 FIRST AVE	(509)353-2810

RO=REGIONAL OFFICE   DO=DISTRICT OFFICE   BO=BRANCH OFFICE
POD=POST OF DUTY   DAO=DISASTER AREA OFFICE

ILLINOIS

TYPE	CITY	STATE	ZIP CODE	ADDRESS	PHONE NUMBER
RO	CHICAGO	IL	60606-6611	300 S. RIVERSIDE PLAZA	(312)353-5000
DO	CHICAGO	IL	60661-1093	500 W. MADISON ST.	(312)353-4528
DO	CLEVELAND	OH	44199	1240 E. 9TH ST.	(216)522-4180
DO	COLUMBUS	OH	43215	85 MARCONI BLVD.	(614)469-6860
DO	DETROIT	MI	48226	477 MICHIGAN AVE.	(313)226-6075
DO	INDIANAPOLIS	IN	46204-1873	429 N. PENNSYLVANIA	(317)226-7272
DO	MADISON	WI	53703	212 E. WASHINGTON AVE.	(608)264-5261
DO	MINNEAPOLIS	MN	55403-1563	100 N. 6TH ST.	(612)370-2324
BO	CINCINNATTI	OH	45202	525 VINE ST.	(513)684-2814
BO	MILWAUKEE	WI	53203	310 W. WISCONSIN AVE	(414)297-3941
BO	MARQUETTE	MI	49885	300 S. FRONT ST.	(906)225-1108
BO	SPRINGFILED	IL	62704	511 W. CAPITOL ST.	(217)492-4416

RO=REGIONAL OFFICE   DO=DISTRICT OFFICE   BO=BRANCH OFFICE

INDIANA

No Data Found

IOWA

TYPE	CITY	STATE	ZIP CODE	ADDRESS	PHONE NUMBER
RO	KANSAS CITY	MO	64106	911 WALNUT STREET	(816)426-3608
DO	CEDAR RAPIDS	IA	52402	373 COLLINS ROAD, NE	(319)393-8630
DO	DES MOINES	IA	50309	210 WALNUT STREET	(515)284-4422
DO	KANSAS CITY	MO	64105	323 WEST 8TH STREET	(816-374-6708
DO	OMAHA	NE	68154	11145 MILL VALLEY RD	(402)221-3604
DO	ST. LOUIS	MO	63101	815 OLIVE STREET	(314)539-6600
DO	WICHITA	KS	67202	100 EAST ENGLISH ST	(316)269-6273
BO	SPRINGFIELD	MO	65802	620 S. GLENSTONE ST	(417)864-7670

RO = REGIONAL OFFICE   DO = DISTRICT OFFICE   BO = BRANCH OFFICE
POD = POST OF DUTY   DAO = DISASTER AREA OFFICE

KANSAS

TYPE	CITY	STATE	ZIP CODE	ADDRESS	PHONE NUMBER
RO	KANSAS CITY	MO	64106	911 WALNUT STREET	(816)426-3608
DO	CEDAR RAPIDS	IA	52402	373 COLLINS ROAD, NE	(319)393-8630
DO	DES MOINES	IA	50309	210 WALNUT STREET	(515)284-4422
DO	KANSAS CITY	MO	64105	323 WEST 8TH STREET	(816-374-6708
DO	OMAHA	NE	68154	11145 MILL VALLEY RD	(402)221-3604
DO	ST. LOUIS	MO	63101	815 OLIVE STREET	(314)539-6600
DO	WICHITA	KS	67202	100 EAST ENGLISH ST	(316)269-6273
BO	SPRINGFIELD	MO	65802	620 S. GLENSTONE ST	(417)864-7670

RO = REGIONAL OFFICE   DO = DISTRICT OFFICE   BO = BRANCH OFFICE
POD = POST OF DUTY   DAO = DISASTER AREA OFFICE

KENTUCKY

TYPE	CITY	STATE	ZIP CODE	ADDRESS	PHONE NUMBER
RO	ATLANTA	GA	30367	1375 PEACHTREE ST., NE	(404)347-2797
DO	ATLANTA	GA	30309	1720 PEACHTREE RD., NW	(404)347-4749
DO	BIRMINGHAM	AL	35203-2398	2121 8TH AVE. N.	(205)731-1344
DO	CHARLOTTE	NC	28202	200 N. COLLEGE ST.	(704)344-6563
DO	COLUMBIA	SC	29201	1835 ASSEMBLY ST.	(803)765-5376
DO	JACKSON	MS	39201	101 W. CAPITOL ST.	(601)965-5325
DO	JACKSONVILLE	FL	32256-7504	7825 BAYMEADOWS WAY	(904)443-1900
DO	LOUISVILLE	KY	40202	600 DR. M.L. KING JR PL	(502)582-5976
DO	CORAL GABLES	FL	33146-2911	1320 S. DIXIE HGWY.	(305)536-5521
DO	NASHVILLE	TN	37228-1500	50 VANTAGE WAY	(615)736-5881
BO	GULFPORT	MS	39501-7758	1 HANCOCK PLAZA	(601)863-4449
POD	STATESBORO	GA	30458	52 N. MAIN ST.	(912)489-8719
POD	TAMPA	FL	33602-3945	501 E. POLK ST.	(813)228-2594
POD	W. PALM BEACH	FL	33407-2044	5601 CORPORATE WAY	(407)689-3922

RO = REGIONAL OFFICE   DO = DISTRICT OFFICE   BO = BRANCH OFFICE   POD = POST OF DUTY

LOUISIANA

TYPE	CITY	STATE	ZIP CODE	ADDRESS	PHONE NUMBER
RO	DALLAS	TX	75235	8625 KING GEORGE DR	(214)767-7635
DO	ALBUQUERQUE	NM	87102	625 SILVER AVENUE, SW	(505)766-1870
DO	DALLAS	TX	75242	1100 COMMERCE STREET	(214)767-0600
DO	EL PASO	TX	79935	10737 GATEWAY WEST	(915)541-5676
DO	HOUSTON	TX	77054	2525 MURWORTH	(713)660-4401
DO	LITTLE ROCK	AR	72202	2120 RIVERFRONT DRIVE	(501)324-5278
DO	HARLINGEN	TX	78550	222 EAST VAN BUREN ST	(512)427-8533
DO	LUBBOCK	TX	79401	1611 TENTH STREET	(806)743-7462
DO	NEW ORLEANS	LA	70112	1661 CANAL STREET	(504)589-2744
DO	OKLAHOMA CITY	OK	73102	200 NORTH WEST 5TH ST	(405)231-4301
DO	SAN ANTONIO	TX	78216	7400 BLANCO ROAD	(512)229-4535
BO	CORPUS CHRISTI	TX	78476	606 NORTH CARANCAHUA	(512)888-3301
BO	FT. WORTH	TX	76102	819 TAYLOR STREET	(817)334-3777
POD	AUSTIN	TX	78701	300 EAST 8TH STREET	(512)482-5288
POD	MARSHALL	TX	75670	505 EAST TRAVIS	(903)935-5257
POD	SHREVEPORT	LA	71101	500 FANNIN STREET	(318)226-5196

RO = REGIONAL OFFICE   DO = DISTRICT OFFICE   BO = BRANCH OFFICE
POD = POST OF DUTY   DAO = DISASTER AREA OFFICE

MAINE

TYPE	CITY	STATE	ZIP CODE	ADDRESS	PHONE NUMBER
RO	BOSTON	MA	02110	155 FEDERAL ST.	(617)451-2023
DO	BOSTON	MA	02222-1093	10 CAUSEWAY ST.	(617)565-5590
DO	AUGUSTA	ME	04330	40 WESTERN AVE.	(207)622-8378
DO	CONCORD	NH	03302-1257	143 N. MAIN ST.	(603)225-1400
DO	HARTFORD	CT	06106	330 MAIN ST.	(203)240-4700
DO	MONTPELIER	VT	05602	87 STATE ST.	(802)828-4422
DO	PROVIDENCE	RI	02903	380 WESTMINISTER MALL	(401)528-4561
BO	SPRINGFIELD	MA	01103	1550 MAIN ST.	(413)785-0268

RO = REGIONAL OFFICE   DO = DISTRICT OFFICE   BO = BRANCH OFFICE

MARYLAND

TYPE	CITY	STATE	ZIP CODE	ADDRESS	PHONE NUMBER
RO	KING OF PRUSSIA	PA	19406	475 ALLENDALE RD.	(215)962-3700
DO	BALTIMORE	MD	21202	10 N. CALVERT ST.	(410)962-4392
DO	CLARKSBURG	WV	26301	168 W. MAIN ST.	(304)623-5631
DO	KING OF PRUSSIA	PA	19406	475 ALLENDALE RD.	(215)962-3804
DO	PITTSBURGH	PA	15222	960 PENN AVE.	(412)644-2780
DO	RICHMOND	VA	23240	400 N. 8TH ST.	(804)771-2400
DO	WASHINGTON	DC	20036	1111 18TH ST., N.W.	(202)634-1500
BO	CHARLESTON	WV	25301	550 EAGAN ST.	(304)347-5220
BO	HARRISBURG	PA	17101	100 CHESTNUT ST.	(717)782-3840
BO	WILKES-BARRE	PA	18702	20 N. PENNSYLVANIA AVE.	(717)826-6497
BO	WILMINGTON	DE	19801	920 N. KING ST.	(302)573-6295

RO = REGIONAL OFFICE   DO = DISTRICT OFFICE   BO = BRANCH OFFICE

MASSACHUSETTS

TYPE	CITY	STATE	ZIP CODE	ADDRESS	PHONE NUMBER
RO	BOSTON	MA	02110	155 FEDERAL ST.	(617)451-2023
DO	BOSTON	MA	02222-1093	10 CAUSEWAY ST.	(617)565-5590
DO	AUGUSTA	ME	04330	40 WESTERN AVE.	(207)622-8378
DO	CONCORD	NH	03302-1257	143 N. MAIN ST.	(603)225-1400
DO	HARTFORD	CT	06106	330 MAIN ST.	(203)240-4700
DO	MONTPELIER	VT	05602	87 STATE ST.	(802)828-4422
DO	PROVIDENCE	RI	02903	380 WESTMINISTER MALL	(401)528-4561
BO	SPRINGFIELD	MA	01103	1550 MAIN ST.	(413)785-0268

RO = REGIONAL OFFICE   DO = DISTRICT OFFICE   BO = BRANCH OFFICE

MICHIGAN

TYPE	CITY	STATE	ZIP CODE	ADDRESS	PHONE NUMBER
RO	CHICAGO	IL	60606-6611	300 S. RIVERSIDE PLAZA	(312)353-5000
DO	CHICAGO	IL	60661-1093	500 W. MADISON ST.	(312)353-4528
DO	CLEVELAND	OH	44199	1240 E. 9TH ST.	(216)522-4180
DO	COLUMBUS	OH	43215	85 MARCONI BLVD.	(614)469-6860
DO	DETROIT	MI	48226	477 MICHIGAN AVE.	(313)226-6075
DO	INDIANAPOLIS	IN	46204-1873	429 N. PENNSYLVANIA	(317)226-7272
DO	MADISON	WI	53703	212 E. WASHINGTON AVE.	(608)264-5261
DO	MINNEAPOLIS	MN	55403-1563	100 N. 6TH ST.	(612)370-2324
BO	CINCINNATTI	OH	45202	525 VINE ST.	(513)684-2814
BO	MILWAUKEE	WI	53203	310 W. WISCONSIN AVE	(414)297-3941
BO	MARQUETTE	MI	49885	300 S. FRONT ST.	(906)225-1108
BO	SPRINGFILED	IL	62704	511 W. CAPITOL ST.	(217)492-4416

RO = REGIONAL OFFICE   DO = DISTRICT OFFICE   BO = BRANCH OFFICE

MINNESOTA

TYPE	CITY	STATE	ZIP CODE	ADDRESS	PHONE NUMBER
RO	CHICAGO	IL	60606-6611	300 S. RIVERSIDE PLAZA	(312)353-5000
DO	CHICAGO	IL	60661-1093	500 W. MADISON ST.	(312)353-4528
DO	CLEVELAND	OH	44199	1240 E. 9TH ST.	(216)522-4180
DO	COLUMBUS	OH	43215	85 MARCONI BLVD.	(614)469-6860
DO	DETROIT	MI	48226	477 MICHIGAN AVE.	(313)226-6075
DO	INDIANAPOLIS	IN	46204-1873	429 N. PENNSYLVANIA	(317)226-7272
DO	MADISON	WI	53703	212 E. WASHINGTON AVE.	(608)264-5261
DO	MINNEAPOLIS	MN	55403-1563	100 N. 6TH ST.	(612)370-2324
BO	CINCINNATTI	OH	45202	525 VINE ST.	(513)684-2814
BO	MILWAUKEE	WI	53203	310 W. WISCONSIN AVE	(414)297-3941
BO	MARQUETTE	MI	49885	300 S. FRONT ST.	(906)225-1108
BO	SPRINGFILED	IL	62704	511 W. CAPITOL ST.	(217)492-4416

RO = REGIONAL OFFICE   DO = DISTRICT OFFICE   BO = BRANCH OFFICE

MISSISSIPPI

TYPE	CITY	STATE	ZIP CODE	ADDRESS	PHONE NUMBER
RO	ATLANTA	GA	30367	1375 PEACHTREE ST., NE	(404)347-2797
DO	ATLANTA	GA	30309	1720 PEACHTREE RD., NW	(404)347-4749
DO	BIRMINGHAM	AL	35203-2398	2121 8TH AVE. N.	(205)731-1344
DO	CHARLOTTE	NC	28202	200 N. COLLEGE ST.	(704)344-6563
DO	COLUMBIA	SC	29201	1835 ASSEMBLY ST.	(803)765-5376
DO	JACKSON	MS	39201	101 W. CAPITOL ST.	(601)965-5325
DO	JACKSONVILLE	FL	32256-7504	7825 BAYMEADOWS WAY	(904)443-1900
DO	LOUISVILLE	KY	40202	600 DR. M.L. KING JR PL	(502)582-5976
DO	CORAL GABLES	FL	33146-2911	1320 S. DIXIE HGWY.	(305)536-5521
DO	NASHVILLE	TN	37228-1500	50 VANTAGE WAY	(615)736-5881
BO	GULFPORT	MS	39501-7758	1 HANCOCK PLAZA	(601)863-4449
POD	STATESBORO	GA	30458	52 N. MAIN ST.	(912)489-8719
POD	TAMPA	FL	33602-3945	501 E. POLK ST.	(813)228-2594
POD	W. PALM BEACH	FL	33407-2044	5601 CORPORATE WAY	(407)689-3922

RO = REGIONAL OFFICE   DO = DISTRICT OFFICE   BO = BRANCH OFFICE   POD = POST OF DUTY

MISSOURI

TYPE	CITY	STATE	ZIP CODE	ADDRESS	PHONE NUMBER
RO	KANSAS CITY	MO	64106	911 WALNUT STREET	(816)426-3608
DO	CEDAR RAPIDS	IA	52402	373 COLLINS ROAD, NE	(319)393-8630
DO	DES MOINES	IA	50309	210 WALNUT STREET	(515)284-4422
DO	KANSAS CITY	MO	64105	323 WEST 8TH STREET	(816-374-6708
DO	OMAHA	NE	68154	11145 MILL VALLEY RD	(402)221-3604
DO	ST. LOUIS	MO	63101	815 OLIVE STREET	(314)539-6600
DO	WICHITA	KS	67202	100 EAST ENGLISH ST	(316)269-6273
BO	SPRINGFIELD	MO	65802	620 S. GLENSTONE ST	(417)864-7670

RO = REGIONAL OFFICE   DO = DISTRICT OFFICE   BO = BRANCH OFFICE
POD = POST OF DUTY   DAO = DISASTER AREA OFFICE

MONTANA

TYPE	CITY	STATE	ZIP CODE	ADDRESS	PHONE NUMBER
RO	DENVER	CO	80202	999 18TH STREET	(303)294-7021
DO	CASPER	WY	82602	100 EAST B STREET	(307)261-5761
DO	DENVER	CO	80201	721 19TH STREET	(303)844-3984
DO	FARGO	ND	58108	657 2ND AVE NORTH	(701)239-5131
DO	HELENA	MT	59626	301 SOUTH PARK	(406)449-5381
DO	SALT LAKE CITY	UT	84138	125 SOUTH STATE ST.	(801)524-5800
DO	SIOUX FALLS	SD	57102	101 SOUTH MAIN AVENUE	(605)330-4231

RO = REGIONAL OFFICE   DO = DISTRICT OFFICE   BO = BRANCH OFFICE
POD = POST OF DUTY   DAO = DISASTER AREA OFFICE

NEBRASKA

No Data Found

NEVADA

TYPE	CITY	STATE	ZIP CODE	ADDRESS	PHONE NUMBER
DO	SAN FRANCISCO	CA	94105	71 STEVENSON STREET	(415)744-6402
DO	FRESNO	CA	93727	2719 N. AIR FRESNO DR	(209)487-5189
DO	HONOLULU	HI	96850	300 ALA MOANA BLVD	(808)541-2990
DO	LAS VEGAS	NV	89125	301 EAST STEWART ST	(702)388-6611
DO	GLENDALE	CA	91203	330 N. BRAND BLVD	(213)894-2956
DO	PHOENIX	AZ	85004	2828 N. CENTRAL AVE	(602)640-2316
DO	SAN DIEGO	CA	92188	880 FRONT STREET	(619)557-7252
DO	SAN FRANCISCO	CA	94105	211 MAIN STREET	(415)744-6820
DO	SANTA ANA	CA	92703	901 W.CIVIC CENTER DR	(714)836-2494
BO	AGANA	GM	96910	238 ARCHBISHOP FC FLORES ST	(671)472-7277
BO	SACRAMENTO	CA	95814	660 J STREET	(916)551-1426
POD	RENO	NV	89505	50 SOUTH VIRGINIA ST	(702)784-5268
POD	TUCSON	AZ	85701	300 WEST CONGRESS ST	(602)629-6715
POD	VENTURA	CA	93003	6477 TELEPHONE ROAD	(805)642-1866

RO = REGIONAL OFFICE   DO = DISTRICT OFFICE   BO = BRANCH OFFICE
POD = POST OF DUTY   DAO = DISASTER AREA OFFICE

NEW HAMPSHIRE

TYPE	CITY	STATE	ZIP CODE	ADDRESS	PHONE NUMBER
RO	BOSTON	MA	02110	155 FEDERAL ST.	(617)451-2023
DO	BOSTON	MA	02222-1093	10 CAUSEWAY ST.	(617)565-5590
DO	AUGUSTA	ME	04330	40 WESTERN AVE.	(207)622-8378
DO	CONCORD	NH	03302-1257	143 N. MAIN ST.	(603)225-1400
DO	HARTFORD	CT	06106	330 MAIN ST.	(203)240-4700
DO	MONTPELIER	VT	05602	87 STATE ST.	(802)828-4422
DO	PROVIDENCE	RI	02903	380 WESTMINISTER MALL	(401)528-4561
BO	SPRINGFIELD	MA	01103	1550 MAIN ST.	(413)785-0268

RO = REGIONAL OFFICE   DO = DISTRICT OFFICE   BO = BRANCH OFFICE

NEW JERSEY

TYPE	CITY	STATE	ZIP CODE	ADDRESS	PHONE NUMBER
RO	NEW YORK	NY	10278	26 FEDERAL PLAZA	(212)264-1450
DO	BUFFALO	NY	14202	111 WEST HURON ST.	(716)846-4301
DO	NEWARK	NJ	07102	60 PARK PLACE	(201)645-2434
DO	NEW YORK	NY	10278	26 FEDERAL PLAZA	(212)264-2454
DO	HATO REY	PR	00918	CARLOS CHARDON AVE.	(809)766-5572
DO	SYRACUSE	NY	13260	100 S. CLINTON ST.	(315)423-5383
BO	ELMIRA	NY	14901	333 EAST WATER ST.	(607)734-8130
BO	MELVILLE	NY	11747	35 PINELAWN RD.	(516)454-0750
BO	ROCHESTER	NY	14614	100 STATE ST.	(716)263-6700
POD	ALBANY	NY	12207	445 BROADWAY	(518)472-6300
POD	CAMDEN	NJ	08104	2600 MT. EPHRAIN DR.	(609)757-5183
POD	ST. CROIX	VI	00820	4200 UNITED SHOP. PLAZA	(809)778-5380
POD	ST. THOMAS	VI	00802	VETERANS DR.	(809)774-8530

RO = REGIONAL OFFICE   DO = DISTRICT OFFICE   BO = BRANCH OFFICE   POD = POST OF DUTY

NEW MEXICO

TYPE	CITY	STATE	ZIP CODE	ADDRESS	PHONE NUMBER
RO	DALLAS	TX	75235	8625 KING GEORGE DR	(214)767-7635
DO	ALBUQUERQUE	NM	87102	625 SILVER AVENUE, SW	(505)766-1870
DO	DALLAS	TX	75242	1100 COMMERCE STREET	(214)767-0600
DO	EL PASO	TX	79935	10737 GATEWAY WEST	(915)541-5676
DO	HOUSTON	TX	77054	2525 MURWORTH	(713)660-4401
DO	LITTLE ROCK	AR	72202	2120 RIVERFRONT DRIVE	(501)324-5278
DO	HARLINGEN	TX	78550	222 EAST VAN BUREN ST	(512)427-8533
DO	LUBBOCK	TX	79401	1611 TENTH STREET	(806)743-7462
DO	NEW ORLEANS	LA	70112	1661 CANAL STREET	(504)589-2744
DO	OKLAHOMA CITY	OK	73102	200 NORTH WEST 5TH ST	(405)231-4301
DO	SAN ANTONIO	TX	78216	7400 BLANCO ROAD	(512)229-4535
BO	CORPUS CHRISTI	TX	78476	606 NORTH CARANCAHUA	(512)888-3301
BO	FT. WORTH	TX	76102	819 TAYLOR STREET	(817)334-3777
POD	AUSTIN	TX	78701	300 EAST 8TH STREET	(512)482-5288
POD	MARSHALL	TX	75670	505 EAST TRAVIS	(903)935-5257
POD	SHREVEPORT	LA	71101	500 FANNIN STREET	(318)226-5196

RO = REGIONAL OFFICE   DO = DISTRICT OFFICE   BO = BRANCH OFFICE
POD = POST OF DUTY   DAO = DISASTER AREA OFFICE

NEW YORK

TYPE	CITY	STATE	ZIP CODE	ADDRESS	PHONE NUMBER
RO	NEW YORK	NY	10278	26 FEDERAL PLAZA	(212)264-1450
DO	BUFFALO	NY	14202	111 WEST HURON ST.	(716)846-4301
DO	NEWARK	NJ	07102	60 PARK PLACE	(201)645-2434
DO	NEW YORK	NY	10278	26 FEDERAL PLAZA	(212)264-2454
DO	HATO REY	PR	00918	CARLOS CHARDON AVE.	(809)766-5572
DO	SYRACUSE	NY	13260	100 S. CLINTON ST.	(315)423-5383
BO	ELMIRA	NY	14901	333 EAST WATER ST.	(607)734-8130
BO	MELVILLE	NY	11747	35 PINELAWN RD.	(516)454-0750
BO	ROCHESTER	NY	14614	100 STATE ST.	(716)263-6700
POD	ALBANY	NY	12207	445 BROADWAY	(518)472-6300
POD	CAMDEN	NJ	08104	2600 MT. EPHRAIN DR.	(609)757-5183
POD	ST. CROIX	VI	00820	4200 UNITED SHOP. PLAZA	(809)778-5380
POD	ST. THOMAS	VI	00802	VETERANS DR.	(809)774-8530

RO = REGIONAL OFFICE   DO = DISTRICT OFFICE   BO = BRANCH OFFICE   POD = POST OF DUTY

NORTH CAROLINA

TYPE	CITY	STATE	ZIP CODE	ADDRESS	PHONE NUMBER
RO	ATLANTA	GA	30367	1375 PEACHTREE ST., NE	(404)347-2797
DO	ATLANTA	GA	30309	1720 PEACHTREE RD., NW	(404)347-4749
DO	BIRMINGHAM	AL	35203-2398	2121 8TH AVE. N.	(205)731-1344
DO	CHARLOTTE	NC	28202	200 N. COLLEGE ST.	(704)344-6563
DO	COLUMBIA	SC	29201	1835 ASSEMBLY ST.	(803)765-5376
DO	JACKSON	MS	39201	101 W. CAPITOL ST.	(601)965-5325
DO	JACKSONVILLE	FL	32256-7504	7825 BAYMEADOWS WAY	(904)443-1900
DO	LOUISVILLE	KY	40202	600 DR. M.L. KING JR PL	(502)582-5976

DO	CORAL GABLES	FL	33146-2911	1320 S. DIXIE HGWY.	(305)536-5521
DO	NASHVILLE	TN	37228-1500	50 VANTAGE WAY	(615)736-5881
BO	GULFPORT	MS	39501-7758	1 HANCOCK PLAZA	(601)863-4449
POD	STATESBORO	GA	30458	52 N. MAIN ST.	(912)489-8719
POD	TAMPA	FL	33602-3945	501 E. POLK ST.	(813)228-2594
POD	W. PALM BEACH	FL	33407-2044	5601 CORPORATE WAY	(407)689-3922

RO = REGIONAL OFFICE   DO = DISTRICT OFFICE   BO = BRANCH OFFICE   POD = POST OF DUTY

NORTH DAKOTA

TYPE	CITY	STATE	ZIP CODE	ADDRESS	PHONE NUMBER
RO	DENVER	CO	80202	999 18TH STREET	(303)294-7021
DO	CASPER	WY	82602	100 EAST B STREET	(307)261-5761
DO	DENVER	CO	80201	721 19TH STREET	(303)844-3984
DO	FARGO	ND	58108	657 2ND AVE NORTH	(701)239-5131
DO	HELENA	MT	59626	301 SOUTH PARK	(406)449-5381
DO	SALT LAKE CITY	UT	84138	125 SOUTH STATE ST.	(801)524-5800
DO	SIOUX FALLS	SD	57102	101 SOUTH MAIN AVENUE	(605)330-4231

RO = REGIONAL OFFICE   DO = DISTRICT OFFICE   BO = BRANCH OFFICE
POD = POST OF DUTY   DAO = DISASTER AREA OFFICE

OHIO

TYPE	CITY	STATE	ZIP CODE	ADDRESS	PHONE NUMBER
RO	CHICAGO	IL	60606-6611	300 S. RIVERSIDE PLAZA	(312)353-5000
DO	CHICAGO	IL	60661-1093	500 W. MADISON ST.	(312)353-4528
DO	CLEVELAND	OH	44199	1240 E. 9TH ST.	(216)522-4180
DO	COLUMBUS	OH	43215	85 MARCONI BLVD.	(614)469-6860
DO	DETROIT	MI	48226	477 MICHIGAN AVE.	(313)226-6075
DO	INDIANAPOLIS	IN	46204-1873	429 N. PENNSYLVANIA	(317)226-7272
DO	MADISON	WI	53703	212 E. WASHINGTON AVE.	(608)264-5261
DO	MINNEAPOLIS	MN	55403-1563	100 N. 6TH ST.	(612)370-2324
BO	CINCINNATTI	OH	45202	525 VINE ST.	(513)684-2814
BO	MILWAUKEE	WI	53203	310 W. WISCONSIN AVE	(414)297-3941
BO	MARQUETTE	MI	49885	300 S. FRONT ST.	(906)225-1108
BO	SPRINGFILED	IL	62704	511 W. CAPITOL ST.	(217)492-4416

RO = REGIONAL OFFICE   DO = DISTRICT OFFICE   BO = BRANCH OFFICE

OKLAHOMA

TYPE	CITY	STATE	ZIP CODE	ADDRESS	PHONE NUMBER
RO	DALLAS	TX	75235	8625 KING GEORGE DR	(214)767-7635
DO	ALBUQUERQUE	NM	87102	625 SILVER AVENUE, SW	(505)766-1870
DO	DALLAS	TX	75242	1100 COMMERCE STREET	(214)767-0600
DO	EL PASO	TX	79935	10737 GATEWAY WEST	(915)541-5676
DO	HOUSTON	TX	77054	2525 MURWORTH	(713)660-4401
DO	LITTLE ROCK	AR	72202	2120 RIVERFRONT DRIVE	(501)324-5278
DO	HARLINGEN	TX	78550	222 EAST VAN BUREN ST	(512)427-8533
DO	LUBBOCK	TX	79401	1611 TENTH STREET	(806)743-7462
DO	NEW ORLEANS	LA	70112	1661 CANAL STREET	(504)589-2744
DO	OKLAHOMA CITY	OK	73102	200 NORTH WEST 5TH ST	(405)231-4301

DO	SAN ANTONIO	TX	78216	7400 BLANCO ROAD	(512)229-4535
BO	CORPUS CHRISTI	TX	78476	606 NORTH CARANCAHUA	(512)888-3301
BO	FT. WORTH	TX	76102	819 TAYLOR STREET	(817)334-3777
POD	AUSTIN	TX	78701	300 EAST 8TH STREET	(512)482-5288
POD	MARSHALL	TX	75670	505 EAST TRAVIS	(903)935-5257
POD	SHREVEPORT	LA	71101	500 FANNIN STREET	(318)226-5196

RO=REGIONAL OFFICE   DO=DISTRICT OFFICE   BO=BRANCH OFFICE
POD=POST OF DUTY   DAO=DISASTER AREA OFFICE

OREGON

TYPE	CITY	STATE	ZIP CODE	ADDRESS	PHONE NUMBER
RO	SEATTLE	WA	98121	2615 4TH AVENUE	(206)553-5676
DO	ANCHORAGE	AK	99513	222 WEST 8TH AVENUE	(907)271-4022
DO	BOISE	ID	83702	1020 MAIN STREET	(208)334-1096
DO	PORTLAND	OR	97201	222 S.W. COLUMBIA	(503)326-5223
DO	SEATTLE	WA	98174	915 SECOND AVENUE	(206)553-1420
DO	SPOKANE	WA	99204	WEST 601 FIRST AVE	(509)353-2810

RO=REGIONAL OFFICE   DO=DISTRICT OFFICE   BO=BRANCH OFFICE
POD=POST OF DUTY   DAO=DISASTER AREA OFFICE

PENNSYLVANIA

TYPE	CITY	STATE	ZIP CODE	ADDRESS	PHONE NUMBER
RO	KING OF PRUSSIA	PA	19406	475 ALLENDALE RD.	(215)962-3700
DO	BALTIMORE	MD	21202	10 N. CALVERT ST.	(410)962-4392
DO	CLARKSBURG	WV	26301	168 W. MAIN ST.	(304)623-5631
DO	KING OF PRUSSIA	PA	19406	475 ALLENDALE RD.	(215)962-3804
DO	PITTSBURGH	PA	15222	960 PENN AVE.	(412)644-2780
DO	RICHMOND	VA	23240	400 N. 8TH ST.	(804)771-2400
DO	WASHINGTON	DC	20036	1111 18TH ST., N.W.	(202)634-1500
BO	CHARLESTON	WV	25301	550 EAGAN ST.	(304)347-5220
BO	HARRISBURG	PA	17101	100 CHESTNUT ST.	(717)782-3840
BO	WILKES-BARRE	PA	18702	20 N. PENNSYLVANIA AVE.	(717)826-6497
BO	WILMINGTON	DE	19801	920 N. KING ST.	(302)573-6295

RO=REGIONAL OFFICE   DO=DISTRICT OFFICE   BO=BRANCH OFFICE

RHODE ISLAND

TYPE	CITY	STATE	ZIP CODE	ADDRESS	PHONE NUMBER
RO	BOSTON	MA	02110	155 FEDERAL ST.	(617)451-2023
DO	BOSTON	MA	02222-1093	10 CAUSEWAY ST.	(617)565-5590
DO	AUGUSTA	ME	04330	40 WESTERN AVE.	(207)622-8378
DO	CONCORD	NH	03302-1257	143 N. MAIN ST.	(603)225-1400
DO	HARTFORD	CT	06106	330 MAIN ST.	(203)240-4700
DO	MONTPELIER	VT	05602	87 STATE ST.	(802)828-4422
DO	PROVIDENCE	RI	02903	380 WESTMINISTER MALL	(401)528-4561
BO	SPRINGFIELD	MA	01103	1550 MAIN ST.	(413)785-0268

RO=REGIONAL OFFICE   DO=DISTRICT OFFICE   BO=BRANCH OFFICE

SOUTH CAROLINA

TYPE	CITY	STATE	ZIP CODE	ADDRESS	PHONE NUMBER
RO	ATLANTA	GA	30367	1375 PEACHTREE ST., NE	(404)347-2797
DO	ATLANTA	GA	30309	1720 PEACHTREE RD., NW	(404)347-4749
DO	BIRMINGHAM	AL	35203-2398	2121 8TH AVE. N.	(205)731-1344
DO	CHARLOTTE	NC	28202	200 N. COLLEGE ST.	(704)344-6563
DO	COLUMBIA	SC	29201	1835 ASSEMBLY ST.	(803)765-5376
DO	JACKSON	MS	39201	101 W. CAPITOL ST.	(601)965-5325
DO	JACKSONVILLE	FL	32256-7504	7825 BAYMEADOWS WAY	(904)443-1900
DO	LOUISVILLE	KY	40202	600 DR. M.L. KING JR PL	(502)582-5976
DO	CORAL GABLES	FL	33146-2911	1320 S. DIXIE HGWY.	(305)536-5521
DO	NASHVILLE	TN	37228-1500	50 VANTAGE WAY	(615)736-5881
BO	GULFPORT	MS	39501-7758	1 HANCOCK PLAZA	(601)863-4449
POD	STATESBORO	GA	30458	52 N. MAIN ST.	(912)489-8719
POD	TAMPA	FL	33602-3945	501 E. POLK ST.	(813)228-2594
POD	W. PALM BEACH	FL	33407-2044	5601 CORPORATE WAY	(407)689-3922

RO = REGIONAL OFFICE   DO = DISTRICT OFFICE   BO = BRANCH OFFICE   POD = POST OF DUTY

SOUTH DAKOTA

TYPE	CITY	STATE	ZIP CODE	ADDRESS	PHONE NUMBER
RO	DENVER	CO	80202	999 18TH STREET	(303)294-7021
DO	CASPER	WY	82602	100 EAST B STREET	(307)261-5761
DO	DENVER	CO	80201	721 19TH STREET	(303)844-3984
DO	FARGO	ND	58108	657 2ND AVE NORTH	(701)239-5131
DO	HELENA	MT	59626	301 SOUTH PARK	(406)449-5381
DO	SALT LAKE CITY	UT	84138	125 SOUTH STATE ST.	(801)524-5800
DO	SIOUX FALLS	SD	57102	101 SOUTH MAIN AVENUE	(605)330-4231

RO = REGIONAL OFFICE   DO = DISTRICT OFFICE   BO = BRANCH OFFICE
POD = POST OF DUTY   DAO = DISASTER AREA OFFICE

TENNESEE

TYPE	CITY	STATE	ZIP CODE	ADDRESS	PHONE NUMBER
RO	ATLANTA	GA	30367	1375 PEACHTREE ST., NE	(404)347-2797
DO	ATLANTA	GA	30309	1720 PEACHTREE RD., NW	(404)347-4749
DO	BIRMINGHAM	AL	35203-2398	2121 8TH AVE. N.	(205)731-1344
DO	CHARLOTTE	NC	28202	200 N. COLLEGE ST.	(704)344-6563
DO	COLUMBIA	SC	29201	1835 ASSEMBLY ST.	(803)765-5376
DO	JACKSON	MS	39201	101 W. CAPITOL ST.	(601)965-5325
DO	JACKSONVILLE	FL	32256-7504	7825 BAYMEADOWS WAY	(904)443-1900
DO	LOUISVILLE	KY	40202	600 DR. M.L. KING JR PL	(502)582-5976
DO	CORAL GABLES	FL	33146-2911	1320 S. DIXIE HGWY.	(305)536-5521
DO	NASHVILLE	TN	37228-1500	50 VANTAGE WAY	(615)736-5881
BO	GULFPORT	MS	39501-7758	1 HANCOCK PLAZA	(601)863-4449
POD	STATESBORO	GA	30458	52 N. MAIN ST.	(912)489-8719
POD	TAMPA	FL	33602-3945	501 E. POLK ST.	(813)228-2594
POD	W. PALM BEACH	FL	33407-2044	5601 CORPORATE WAY	(407)689-3922

RO = REGIONAL OFFICE   DO = DISTRICT OFFICE   BO = BRANCH OFFICE   POD = POST OF DUTY

TEXAS

TYPE	CITY	STATE	ZIP CODE	ADDRESS	PHONE NUMBER
RO	DALLAS	TX	75235	8625 KING GEORGE DR	(214)767-7635
DO	ALBUQUERQUE	NM	87102	625 SILVER AVENUE, SW	(505)766-1870
DO	DALLAS	TX	75242	1100 COMMERCE STREET	(214)767-0600
DO	EL PASO	TX	79935	10737 GATEWAY WEST	(915)541-5676
DO	HOUSTON	TX	77054	2525 MURWORTH	(713)660-4401
DO	LITTLE ROCK	AR	72202	2120 RIVERFRONT DRIVE	(501)324-5278
DO	HARLINGEN	TX	78550	222 EAST VAN BUREN ST	(512)427-8533
DO	LUBBOCK	TX	79401	1611 TENTH STREET	(806)743-7462
DO	NEW ORLEANS	LA	70112	1661 CANAL STREET	(504)589-2744
DO	OKLAHOMA CITY	OK	73102	200 NORTH WEST 5TH ST	(405)231-4301
DO	SAN ANTONIO	TX	78216	7400 BLANCO ROAD	(512)229-4535
BO	CORPUS CHRISTI	TX	78476	606 NORTH CARANCAHUA	(512)888-3301
BO	FT. WORTH	TX	76102	819 TAYLOR STREET	(817)334-3777
POD	AUSTIN	TX	78701	300 EAST 8TH STREET	(512)482-5288
POD	MARSHALL	TX	75670	505 EAST TRAVIS	(903)935-5257
POD	SHREVEPORT	LA	71101	500 FANNIN STREET	(318)226-5196

RO = REGIONAL OFFICE   DO = DISTRICT OFFICE   BO = BRANCH OFFICE
POD = POST OF DUTY   DAO = DISASTER AREA OFFICE

UTAH

TYPE	CITY	STATE	ZIP CODE	ADDRESS	PHONE NUMBER
RO	DENVER	CO	80202	999 18TH STREET	(303)294-7021
DO	CASPER	WY	82602	100 EAST B STREET	(307)261-5761
DO	DENVER	CO	80201	721 19TH STREET	(303)844-3984
DO	FARGO	ND	58108	657 2ND AVE NORTH	(701)239-5131
DO	HELENA	MT	59626	301 SOUTH PARK	(406)449-5381
DO	SALT LAKE CITY	UT	84138	125 SOUTH STATE ST.	(801)524-5800
DO	SIOUX FALLS	SD	57102	101 SOUTH MAIN AVENUE	(605)330-4231

RO = REGIONAL OFFICE   DO = DISTRICT OFFICE   BO = BRANCH OFFICE
POD = POST OF DUTY   DAO = DISASTER AREA OFFICE

VERMONT

TYPE	CITY	STATE	ZIP CODE	ADDRESS	PHONE NUMBER
RO	BOSTON	MA	02110	155 FEDERAL ST.	(617)451-2023
DO	BOSTON	MA	02222-1093	10 CAUSEWAY ST.	(617)565-5590
DO	AUGUSTA	ME	04330	40 WESTERN AVE.	(207)622-8378
DO	CONCORD	NH	03302-1257	143 N. MAIN ST.	(603)225-1400
DO	HARTFORD	CT	06106	330 MAIN ST.	(203)240-4700
DO	MONTPELIER	VT	05602	87 STATE ST.	(802)828-4422
DO	PROVIDENCE	RI	02903	380 WESTMINISTER MALL	(401)528-4561
BO	SPRINGFIELD	MA	01103	1550 MAIN ST.	(413)785-0268

RO = REGIONAL OFFICE   DO = DISTRICT OFFICE   BO = BRANCH OFFICE

VIRGINIA

TYPE	CITY	STATE	ZIP CODE	ADDRESS	PHONE NUMBER
RO	KING OF PRUSSIA	PA	19406	475 ALLENDALE RD.	(215)962-3700
DO	BALTIMORE	MD	21202	10 N. CALVERT ST.	(410)962-4392
DO	CLARKSBURG	WV	26301	168 W. MAIN ST.	(304)623-5631
DO	KING OF PRUSSIA	PA	19406	475 ALLENDALE RD.	(215)962-3804
DO	PITTSBURGH	PA	15222	960 PENN AVE.	(412)644-2780
DO	RICHMOND	VA	23240	400 N. 8TH ST.	(804)771-2400
DO	WASHINGTON	DC	20036	1111 18TH ST., N.W.	(202)634-1500
BO	CHARLESTON	WV	25301	550 EAGAN ST.	(304)347-5220
BO	HARRISBURG	PA	17101	100 CHESTNUT ST.	(717)782-3840
BO	WILKES-BARRE	PA	18702	20 N. PENNSYLVANIA AVE.	(717)826-6497
BO	WILMINGTON	DE	19801	920 N. KING ST.	(302)573-6295

RO = REGIONAL OFFICE   DO = DISTRICT OFFICE   BO = BRANCH OFFICE

WASHINGTON

TYPE	CITY	STATE	ZIP CODE	ADDRESS	PHONE NUMBER
RO	SEATTLE	WA	98121	2615 4TH AVENUE	(206)553-5676
DO	ANCHORAGE	AK	99513	222 WEST 8TH AVENUE	(907)271-4022
DO	BOISE	ID	83702	1020 MAIN STREET	(208)334-1096
DO	PORTLAND	OR	97201	222 S.W. COLUMBIA	(503)326-5223
DO	SEATTLE	WA	98174	915 SECOND AVENUE	(206)220-6520
DO	SPOKANE	WA	99204	WEST 601 FIRST AVE	(509)353-2810

RO = REGIONAL OFFICE   DO = DISTRICT OFFICE   BO = BRANCH OFFICE
POD = POST OF DUTY   DAO = DISASTER AREA OFFICE

WEST VIRGINIA

TYPE	CITY	STATE	ZIP CODE	ADDRESS	PHONE NUMBER
RO	KING OF PRUSSIA	PA	19406	475 ALLENDALE RD.	(215)962-3700
DO	BALTIMORE	MD	21202	10 N. CALVERT ST.	(410)962-4392
DO	CLARKSBURG	WV	26301	168 W. MAIN ST.	(304)623-5631
DO	KING OF PRUSSIA	PA	19406	475 ALLENDALE RD.	(215)962-3804
DO	PITTSBURGH	PA	15222	960 PENN AVE.	(412)644-2780
DO	RICHMOND	VA	23240	400 N. 8TH ST.	(804)771-2400
DO	WASHINGTON	DC	20036	1111 18TH ST., N.W.	(202)634-1500
BO	CHARLESTON	WV	25301	550 EAGAN ST.	(304)347-5220
BO	HARRISBURG	PA	17101	100 CHESTNUT ST.	(717)782-3840
BO	WILKES-BARRE	PA	18702	20 N. PENNSYLVANIA AVE.	(717)826-6497
BO	WILMINGTON	DE	19801	920 N. KING ST.	(302)573-6295

RO = REGIONAL OFFICE   DO = DISTRICT OFFICE   BO = BRANCH OFFICE

WISCONSIN

TYPE	CITY	STATE	ZIP CODE	ADDRESS	PHONE NUMBER
RO	CHICAGO	IL	60606-6611	300 S. RIVERSIDE PLAZA	(312)353-5000
DO	CHICAGO	IL	60661-1093	500 W. MADISON ST.	(312)353-4528
DO	CLEVELAND	OH	44199	1240 E. 9TH ST.	(216)522-4180

DO	COLUMBUS	OH	43215	85 MARCONI BLVD.	(614)469-6860
DO	DETROIT	MI	48226	477 MICHIGAN AVE.	(313)226-6075
DO	INDIANAPOLIS	IN	46204-1873	429 N. PENNSYLVANIA	(317)226-7272
DO	MADISON	WI	53703	212 E. WASHINGTON AVE.	(608)264-5261
DO	MINNEAPOLIS	MN	55403-1563	100 N. 6TH ST.	(612)370-2324
BO	CINCINNATTI	OH	45202	525 VINE ST.	(513)684-2814
BO	MILWAUKEE	WI	53203	310 W. WISCONSIN AVE	(414)297-3941
BO	MARQUETTE	MI	49885	300 S. FRONT ST.	(906)225-1108
BO	SPRINGFIELD	IL	62704	511 W. CAPITOL ST.	(217)492-4416

RO = REGIONAL OFFICE   DO = DISTRICT OFFICE   BO = BRANCH OFFICE

WYOMING

TYPE	CITY	STATE	ZIP CODE	ADDRESS	PHONE NUMBER
RO	DENVER	CO	80202	999 18TH STREET	(303)294-7021
DO	CASPER	WY	82602	100 EAST B STREET	(307)261-5761
DO	DENVER	CO	80201	721 19TH STREET	(303)844-3984
DO	FARGO	ND	58108	657 2ND AVE NORTH	(701)239-5131
DO	HELENA	MT	59626	301 SOUTH PARK	(406)449-5381
DO	SALT LAKE CTY	UT	84138	125 SOUTH STATE ST.	(801)524-5800
DO	SIOUX FALLS	SD	57102	101 SOUTH MAIN AVENUE	(605)330-4231

RO = REGIONAL OFFICE   DO = DISTRICT OFFICE   BO = BRANCH OFFICE
POD = POST OF DUTY   DAO = DISASTER AREA OFFICE

GUAM

No Data Found

PUERTO RICO

TYPE	CITY	STATE	ZIP CODE	ADDRESS	PHONE NUMBER
RO	NEW YORK	NY	10278	26 FEDERAL PLAZA	(212)264-1450
DO	BUFFALO	NY	14202	111 WEST HURON ST.	(716)846-4301
DO	NEWARK	NJ	07102	60 PARK PLACE	(201)645-2434
DO	NEW YORK	NY	10278	26 FEDERAL PLAZA	(212)264-2454
DO	HATO REY	PR	00918	CARLOS CHARDON AVE.	(809)766-5572
DO	SYRACUSE	NY	13260	100 S. CLINTON ST.	(315)423-5383
BO	ELMIRA	NY	14901	333 EAST WATER ST.	(607)734-8130
BO	MELVILLE	NY	11747	35 PINELAWN RD.	(516)454-0750
BO	ROCHESTER	NY	14614	100 STATE ST.	(716)263-6700
POD	ALBANY	NY	12207	445 BROADWAY	(518)472-6300
POD	CAMDEN	NJ	08104	2600 MT. EPHRAIN DR.	(609)757-5183
POD	ST. CROIX	VI	00820	4200 UNITED SHOP. PLAZA	(809)778-5380
POD	ST. THOMAS	VI	00802	VETERANS DR.	(809)774-8530

RO = REGIONAL OFFICE   DO = DISTRICT OFFICE   BO = BRANCH OFFICE   POD = POST OF DUTY

TRUST TERRITORY OF THE PACIFIC ISLANDS

No Data Found

VIRGIN ISLANDS

TYPE	CITY	STATE	ZIP CODE	ADDRESS	PHONE NUMBER
RO	NEW YORK	NY	10278	26 FEDERAL PLAZA	(212)264-1450
DO	BUFFALO	NY	14202	111 WEST HURON ST.	(716)846-4301
DO	NEWARK	NJ	07102	60 PARK PLACE	(201)645-2434
DO	NEW YORK	NY	10278	26 FEDERAL PLAZA	(212)264-2454
DO	HATO REY	PR	00918	CARLOS CHARDON AVE.	(809)766-5572
DO	SYRACUSE	NY	13260	100 S. CLINTON ST.	(315)423-5383
BO	ELMIRA	NY	14901	333 EAST WATER ST.	(607)734-8130
BO	MELVILLE	NY	11747	35 PINELAWN RD.	(516)454-0750
BO	ROCHESTER	NY	14614	100 STATE ST.	(716)263-6700
POD	ALBANY	NY	12207	445 BROADWAY	(518)472-6300
POD	CAMDEN	NJ	08104	2600 MT. EPHRAIN DR.	(609)757-5183
POD	ST. CROIX	VI	00820	4200 UNITED SHOP. PLAZA	(809)778-5380
POD	ST. THOMAS	VI	00802	VETERANS DR.	(809)774-8530

RO = REGIONAL OFFICE   DO = DISTRICT OFFICE   BO = BRANCH OFFICE   POD = POST OF DUTY

AMERICAN SAMOA

No Data Found for this selection.

Index